The Poet as Analyst

JAMES R. LAWLER

The Poet as Analyst

ESSAYS ON PAUL VALÉRY

University of California Press

Berkeley   Los Angeles   London

1974

University of California Press
Berkeley and Los Angeles, California
University of California Press, Ltd.
London, England
Copyright © 1974 by The Regents of the University of California
ISBN: 0-520-02450-8
Library of Congress Catalog Card Number: 73-76114
Printed in the United States of America

Contents

Preface   vii

1. "Je vois le Christ . . ."   1
   "Sinistre"   32

2. "Existe! Sois enfin toi-même . . ."   36
   "Air de Sémiramis"   322

3. "L'Ange frais de l'œil nu . . ."   74
   "Profusion du soir, poème abandonné . . ."   326

4. "J'ai adoré cet homme . . ."   117
   "Valvins," "Psaume sur une voix"   330

5. "Les larmes: hélas! c'est bien moi . . ."   137
   La Jeune Parque, "La Pythie"   331

6. "Lucidité, phœnix de ce vertige . . ."   149
   The theme of "la belle endormie"   333

7. "O roi des ombres fait de flamme . . ."   166
   "Neige," "A l'aurore," "Heure"   340

8. "Je pense . . . , je sens . . ."   201
   "L'Oiseau cruel," "Chanson à part," "Le Philosophe et
   la 'Jeune Parque' "   342

9. "Il faut être un saint . . ,"   230
   "Le Sonnet d'Irène"   347

10. "Après tout, j'ai fait ce que j'ai pu . . ." 244
The last *Cahiers*

Epilogue: Two Confrontations 282

Appendix 321

Index 349

Preface

THE ESSAYS in this book were written over the last ten years during a time of considerable renewal in Valéry studies. They represent an attempt to describe the methods, and to explore the sensibility, of a poet and thinker whom I hold to be one of the most important in French literature. "M. Mallarmé a fait une expérience," he wrote in 1897 in an early article; and likewise we may say that his own work constitutes an experiment, the gist of which was to pursue a passion for analysis as far as he could take it. To find the measure of his mental operations, to purify language so as to achieve control, to seek the reduction of the mind to an ultimate clarity—these were the motives that drove him to compile the immense series of his *Cahiers*, which were published posthumously between 1957 and 1961; and a similar ambition informed the composition of his poems.

Having previously done a commentary on *Charmes*, I have approached Valéry on this occasion by way of lesser known works that have attracted little or no critical scrutiny. The *Cahiers* record his tireless search to enunciate a wholly personal point of view, and in one chapter I have examined eight of them in order to bring out their main concerns. But, with respect to the poems, I have also been able to make use of the poet's manuscripts which show the processes of formal definition and thematic development as they gradually evolved. The aim is not, of course, to demonstrate that the poems are better than the initial drafts, but rather to see the movement that led, beyond a great variety of verbal and rhythmic possibilities, to those versions that bear

Valéry's signature and stand as his definitive expression. "Devant le papier l'artiste *se fait*," Mallarmé wrote. In the beginning is a theme, a phrase, a cadence, an idea; but it must find substance and shape, and, being brought to maturity, speak with the particular voice which the poet recognizes as the one he has sought.

We shall find, then, that the need to summon consciousness to the task of isolating intellectual motifs and discovering their appropriate language is a fundamental characteristic. Indeed, Valéry may well be denoted as the poet of analysis, for in analysis lies the spur, and the method, and his inexhaustible delight. Yet, at the same time, the completed work makes a striking portrait of the man he was. However much he sought escape from his sensibility through a deluge of reason, the words he left, couched in classical style, are no less a self-revelation than if he had chosen art as an avenue of confession. By indirections he speaks to us, I believe, with the heart.

I have followed by and large a chronological progression in the choice of texts. This principle could not be observed with strictness since Valéry returns again and again to certain poems, totally refashioning their language, so that "Sinistre," "Sémiramis," and "Profusion du soir," for instance, are as much poems of his forties and fifties as they are of his twenties; in other sections I have allowed myself, when probing a theme, to range backwards and forwards over the entire span of the poet's work. But "Sinistre" seems to me a useful point of departure, which allows us to gauge *ab initio* the nervous intensity, the alliance of anguish and energy that Valéry himself indicated as the basis of his personality. Thus, apropos of a photograph of himself, he wrote:

> Que si j'étais placé devant cette effigie,
> Inconnu de moi-même, ignorant de mes traits,
> A tant de plis affreux d'angoisse et d'énergie
> Je lirais mes tourments et me reconnaîtrais.[1]

Written in decasyllabic quatrains, maintaining a high-pitched intensity, "Sinistre" enacts an intellectual drama by means of the imagery of a shipwreck associated with the figure of Christ. One can give due weight to the influence of Poe, Baudelaire, Mallarmé, and Rimbaud, yet still not explain away the energy and the anguish that have so immediately personal an accent.

"Air de Sémiramis," on the other hand, takes us into a widely divergent atmosphere. Valéry here adopted a legend that had been popular with many artists before him—although the crystallizing factor would seem to have been a Degas painting. Yet he transformed it into a shrill expression of intellectual pride which, answering the fantastic shipwreck, constructs a domain of its own. This is, as it were, his *cogito,* like a cry that fills the void.

His long and complex "Profusion du soir" is without doubt one of the major poems. It has been little appreciated; or rather, we might say, it has been seen primarily as the forerunner of other and greater works. I have considered it separately, finding in it a religious text with Christian echoes that is the patient unraveling of the poet's link with an external force. The eye and its object, this limpid Angel and the corresponding angel of sunset, meet and exchange values. Nothing exists, neither past nor future, beyond the present composition of bountiful grace and the self's gratitude. Certainly, death is felt as is the sorrow of coming loss; but what is uppermost at this privileged moment within an extraordinary theater of the mind is the language of reconciliation.

For such a poet, whose intellectual demands were so rigorous and whose sensibility was so dangerously exposed, the meeting with Stéphane Mallarmé became a capital event.

---

1 "Au-dessous d'un portrait," *Mélange, Œuvres,* 2 vols. ed. Jean Hytier (Paris: Gallimard, Pléiade, 1957–1960), I, 302. An earlier unpublished version is entitled "Au bas de ma photographie" and contains a variant last line: "*J'ajusterais mon âme* et me reconnaîtrais."

If he found in him a gracious manner that was unique, he came to learn that this elegance was founded on a moral and spiritual crisis of devastating nature which induced a complete reappraisal of the notion of poetry. Valéry's remarks are diverse as he speaks now from affection, now from admiration. We realize that, already in 1897, he had carried to great lengths his attempt to "make a brain," that is to say, to translate into his own language the mental processes behind Mallarmé's poems; his article, however, remained unpublished, and was abandoned after Mallarmé died. Yet it served to determine his own attitude and, in particular, to dictate his refusal of the title of poet; for how could he be compared to Mallarmé, who had lived and thought and written with poetry alone as his goal, whereas he felt himself to be as much—no, more—of an analyst as he was a poet?

Turning more particularly to the role of the sensibility, I have concentrated in the fifth essay on the motif of tears which recurs in several poems. We find that the phrase "larmes de l'esprit," used in one manuscript to describe his grief on Mallarmé's death, leads forward, over nearly twenty years, to the poignant correspondence of mind and world in *La Jeune Parque;* it also expresses the harmony distilled from the hiddenmost sources of feeling in "La Pythie," appearing as the symbolic voice of poetry, ritual and exultant: "Honneur des Hommes, Saint Langage."

Nevertheless, as Valéry remarked, "si nous pouvons quelquefois parvenir à nos antipodes, nous ne pouvons guère ensuite qu'en revenir." [2] In the sixth essay I have looked at a theme that, although long traditional in European lyricism, is handled in an original way. Throughout his career, from his twentieth year to well into his maturity, Valéry chose to depict "la belle endormie." His treatments, varying greatly one from the other, reveal, when we see them together, the enduring desire to comprehend a form in

2 "Fragments des mémoires d'un poème," *Œuvres,* I, 1488.

deeply sensuous terms; yet this form remains as inexhaustible as the mind itself. The seven versions thus lead us back to a prose poem that sees thought in the image of a woman who ceaselessly moves between simultaneity and ultimate fire, the whole and the one, voluptuousness and power.

The next study likewise examines a central preoccupation in Valéry's work. As he wrote on one occasion: "Le Soleil est l'objet le plus dieu du monde, et le culte héliaque, le plus raisonnable possible," and he expressed in various ways its ever-changing, therefore divine, character which imposes a pattern on the universe, a paradoxical conjuncture of light and shade. I have looked at three short poems—two dedicated to dawn, the third to sunset—showing the wide gamut of tones and language, of feeling and abstraction, of measure and frenzy, into which the mind translates a complex relationship with the god that Valéry's Serpent names its "roi des ombres fait de flamme."

Towards the end of his life, he underwent yet one more so-called "puberty" when he produced a number of poems, as well as *La Cantate du Narcisse* and *Mon Faust*. The period has not been closely studied, and I have, therefore, taken three poems which date from these years. The urgency, the pathos, the artistic control are immediately apparent; but the treatments allow us to recall the twin poles of irony and incantation, detached statement and magical spell, which match the constant and complementary moods of reason and mysticism, thought and feeling.

Given over to the idea of "saintliness," the ninth chapter takes as its pivot a late poem which he signed with the fanciful name, Monsieur de Saint-Ambroyse. This disguise is typical of the many masks he assumed, which were his "way of making himself other than he [was]." In a factitiously baroque sonnet, he declares the omnipotence of his love, asserting in the face of all evidence to the contrary that Irene has eyes for him alone. Although the note is forced and the tone playful, his poem is symptomatic of a determination to control the world, to be master of events, to reach once and for all an elusive end.

Parallel to the poetry, we can also consult the *Cahiers* for the last six years of his life. These late notebooks are little more than a quarter of the total mass of twenty-nine volumes, or some twenty-six thousand pages. Concluding half a century of meditation, they are of particular interest in that they allow us to see, as he himself saw, the consistency of his "exercice matinal." We discover the final perspectives of his research, and glean pertinent remarks on poets and poetry; but, above all, we are sensitive to the magnificent legacy of his *Cahiers* in which we can watch his obstinate endeavor to construct, by dint of uncounted time, an ideal palace of thought.

Finally, the epilogue turns to the criticisms of two foreign observers, T. S. Eliot and E. M. Cioran, who have each sought to articulate Valéry's achievement. Over a period of nearly forty years, Eliot provided a series of remarks that show his keen appreciation of his contemporary. Generous in his praise of the poems, excited by the other's criticism and theory, impressed by his conversation, he showed himself to be especially anxious to envisage Valéry as a culminating point in a tradition, beyond which, no doubt, French poetry would have to look elsewhere for a new beginning. One can naturally find that there are gaps in Eliot's several commentaries: he does not often go deeply enough; nor does he mention for instance that Dada and Surrealism did not wait on Valéry's death, but were in fact already violently reacting against him shortly after his major poems appeared. And he might well have pointed to the role that aspects of Valéry's thought and work have played over recent years in literary criticism and formalist experiments in the novel, so that one may speak of a fresh interest in him among younger writers and critics. Yet Eliot had the virtue of directing the attention of an English-speaking audience to what he called the "perennial fascination" of this work, looking at it with the practiced eye of a poet who, after his own fashion, had similarly sought the right language for his time.

Cioran, on the other hand, has drawn up a niggardly balance sheet that salvages little more than the occasional moralist of a finished Europe and a finite civilization. He undoubtedly owes Valéry at least as much as he does any other writer, but in looking at the thinker, the theoretician, and the poet, he fails to convey the intrinsic vitality of a typical Valéry page, the excitement of its texture, the mental activity it implies. Nor is he sensitive to the human drama which is inscribed in each one of the writings and which this book seeks to indicate: anguish and energy, pride and reconciliation, sensuousness and affection, dark recesses of tears and Apollonian aspirations, divided sensibility and "saintliness." There can be no easy definition of an author in whom will and affectivity were both intense and frequently at odds. Yet his work, however much it eschewed personal statement, is eloquent of the man ("j'eus beau me nier à la suite et me contredire, la succession s'est faite, l'addition s'est réalisée").[3] It seems to me to offer the noble, if pathetic, text of an abiding restlessness that was forever unable to accept any absolute other than its own endless quest for transcendence.

It is a pleasure for me to express my deep gratitude to the late Madame Paul Valéry who, over many years, on my short visits from Australia, allowed me to consult the poet's manuscripts and received me with rare kindness, and to Madame Agathe Rouart-Valéry and Monsieur Claude Valéry for their warm understanding. I also wish to thank Madame Jean Voilier for her ever-generous help and encouragement.

I am especially grateful to the Australian Research Grants Committee for its financial support, and to the Universities

[3] *Cahiers*, 29 vols. (Paris: Centre National de la Recherche Scientifique, 1957–1961), IV, 181.

of Western Australia and California at Los Angeles in which
the present book was written.

"Je vois le Christ . . ." is a revised version of "The Shipwreck of Paul Valéry," *Essays in French Literature,* November 1966; "Existe! Sois enfin toi-même . . ." appeared in the
Australian Journal of French Studies, May–August 1971; the
third essay "L'Ange frais de l'œil nu . . ." was originally
published in *Essays in French Literature,* November 1970;
"O roi des ombres fait de flamme . . ." incorporates the
material of "Light in Valéry," *Australian Journal of French
Studies,* July–September 1969; "Lucidité, phœnix de ce
vertige . . ." appeared first in *Modern Language Notes,*
June 1972; "J'ai adoré cet homme . . ." is a revised and
expanded version of "Saint Mallarmé," *Yale French Studies,*
June 1970; "Les larmes: hélas! c'est bien moi . . ." was published in *Books Abroad,* October 1971; "Je pense . . . je
sens . . ." appeared as "Valéry's Later Poetry," *Australian
Journal of French Studies,* October–December 1967; "Après
tout, j'ai fait ce que j'ai pu . . ." is an English version of the
essay "Huit Cahiers de Paul Valéry," *Revue d'histoire
littéraire de la France,* January–March 1963; "Il faut être un
saint . . ." is a revised and expanded version of the study
"Paul Valéry et Saint Ambroise," *Cahiers de l'Association
internationale des Etudes françaises,* March 1965; while the
epilogue rehandles "T. S. Eliot et Paul Valéry," *Mercure de
France,* January 1961, and "Paul Valéry and His Idols: A
Centennial View," *Meanjin,* Spring 1971. I am much obliged
to the editors of the above mentioned journals for their
courtesy in allowing me to reprint this material.

The poems of Valéry are reproduced by kind permission
of the copyright holders, © Editions Gallimard, Paris. For
ease of reference the main texts are quoted at length in the
appendix.

University of California   J. R. L.
Los Angeles

1: "Je vois le Christ . . ."

THREE YEARS before his death, the last edition of the poetic works to appear during Valéry's lifetime introduced a set of twelve new poems under the title *Pièces diverses*. Although they were far from constituting the full body of his unpublished verse to that date, these "quelques brefs poèmes de divers âges et de formes assez différentes" are plainly what he held to be of durable worth. The forms are varied and do not duplicate those of previous sequences; nor do they offer pleasing prosodic symmetries as do the nine heptasyllabic *dizains* at either end of *Charmes*. We can be sure moreover that they are, as Valéry states, of sundry vintage; the manuscripts confirm our first impression that certain compositions date from the First World War or still earlier, while others are the writings of a man approaching his seventies. Thus, no unifying subject may be said to produce an aesthetic design of its own. Yet, despite these reservations, the choice is without doubt a contribution of major importance insofar as it discloses an enlarged gamut of Valéry's art. In the following pages I wish to discuss a ballad from *Pièces diverses* which is, I believe, the uniquely moving expression of a drama of the mind.

The second poem of his final collection, "Sinistre" fathoms in energetic diction and form the mental crisis of the poet's twenty-first year by which to all appearances his time of idols was overcome. If he had taken much for

granted in the way of language and sentiment and thought
—"les notions qui m'embarbouillaient l'esprit"[1]—he now
felt the need to remould his thinking under the sign of a
supreme Demon of analysis. This was his legendary Genoa
night of October 1892 with its physical and emotional thun-
derbolts, a moment that orientated his efforts once and for
all as imperiously as a mystical insight. He knew he must
henceforth be on constant guard; he understood that he
must scourge in order to survive. We discover then a current
of violence, a destructive passion whose presence comes to
the fore and to which he gave the name *caligulisme.* "Je
fus ou suis l'idée de ce moment qui foudroie tous les autres
possibles ou connus."[2] In like manner "Sinistre" conveys an
anguished lucidity that forcefully rejects familiar comfort.

Intense, urgent in its movement, it is a poem unparalleled
in Valéry with respect to the full development of this theme.
One may note that its tone is not without echo in a few
poems of *Charmes* such as the "Ebauche d'un Serpent," the
obsecration of "La Pythie," the eighteenth stanza of "Le
Cimetière marin" ("Maigre immortalité noire et dorée, /
Consolatrice affreusement laurée . . ."), and certain lines of
"Le Rameur." But the most interesting parallel I can suggest
is a fragment from the first notebook of *Charmes* in which
the theme of revolt finds a symbolic framework in the figure
of Job:

> Las de râcler en vain l'abominable ulcère
> Vers les cieux irritants (insultés) j'ai lancé mon tesson
> Et je dresse au soleil dont je fais un frisson
> Toute ma nudité qu'un lange immonde enserre.
> Le goût m'a saisi de ce mal nécessaire
> Mon cœur a trop chanté la menteuse chanson
> Et les psaumes . . . . qui sont
> Le vil honneur de l'immense adversaire

---

[1] Letter to Gide, 10 November 1894, *Correspondance André Gide-Paul
Valéry,* ed. Robert Mallet (Paris: Gallimard, 1955), 218.
[2] *Cahiers,* XXVII, 822.

Peut-être soulagé par ce vrai mouvement
Tous mes maux affranchis d'une âme qui se ment
La pourpre épouvantable la lèpre candide
Vont-ils s'évanouir devant la vérité
Fais que j'exhale enfin formidable et sordide
Le blasphème très pur qui exprime la vérité.[3]

If the poet was patently dissatisfied with this fragment, deleting the last few words and commenting, "Rien ne va plus: Buona sera," it nevertheless shows a not dissimilar attempt to compose a poem that possesses Biblical echoes. The stridency of the voice recalls the finale of "Sinistre," while, however halting the meter, the last two lines indicate the aggressive stance that is the rebel's surest defense against his adversary and former lord. Revolt is the recourse of him who would undo a spell and conquer his freedom. Do we not find in the same notebook a remark that may serve as the keynote of such declamatory writing? "Pour conjurer le sort—gâter, casser, perdre quelque chose." Time, circumstances, bric-à-brac, beliefs must be broken—as we shall read in "Sinistre"—like an instrument.

An important detail regarding the poem's genesis is its date of composition, which can hardly be gauged from internal evidence. We might be ready to assume, from the foregoing remarks, that since we find in it the reflection of Valéry's moment of critical decision, it was also probably composed at the same time. I believe that it was originally conceived and drafted in late 1892 or shortly thereafter, as Valéry was at pains to affirm on the occasion of its first

---

[3] A previously unpublished fragment. I have given a description of this notebook, which contains drafts of several poems of *Charmes*, in my book *Lecture de Valéry: une étude de "Charmes"* (Paris: Presses Universitaires de France, 1963), 10–13. It belongs to Madame Jean Voilier who graciously allowed me to consult it. Throughout this book I shall not describe the technical aspects of the manuscripts, since my principal aim is to provide succinctly their sense and substance. It is to be hoped that a photographic reproduction of the various drafts will be undertaken in the not too distant future, as was done for the *Cahiers*.

publication in 1939.[4] On the other hand, we have his statement to J. P. Monod in which he declared that the poem was
written in 1909; yet here he might well have been referring
to a particular version that more fully elaborated an initial
draft.[5] In any case, as I have been able to ascertain, it was
actively revised and rewritten in 1917, being one of the
manuscripts bearing the precise mention "4–5 October 17," [6]
and came to figure alongside "Le Cimetière marin" in an
early plan of *Charmes*. The ten poems named are arranged
in the following order: "Aurore," "L'Insinuant," "La
Pythie," "Les Grenades," "Heure" (later included in *Pièces
diverses*), "Mare nostrum" (the original title of "Le Cimetière marin"), "Sinistre," "Caresse" (also included in *Pièces
diverses*), "Palme," "Ode secrète." Did this period coincide
with any particular event in Valéry's life so that "Sinistre"
emerged as a personal affirmation in the midst of renewed
pressure? One thing is sure: it would seem to be no mere
coincidence that the Genoa crisis likewise took place on the
night of the 4th to 5th October 1892 ("Nuit effroyable—
passée sur mon lit—orage partout—ma chambre éblouissante
par chaque éclair—Et tout mon sort se jouait dans ma tête.
Je suis entre moi et moi . . .").[7] Moreover, it is worth em-

---

[4] "Le désordre qui 'règne' (comme on dit) dans *Mélange* s'étend à la
chronologie. Telle chose a été écrite il y a près de cinquante ans. Telle
autre est d'avant-hier: entre ce bref poème 'Sinistre' et la *Cantate du
Narcisse*, presque un demi-siècle s'est écoulé. Cette quantité de temps ne
signifie rien en matière de l'esprit . . ." ("Avis au lecteur," *Mélange*,
Œuvres, I, 285).

[5] See Jacques Duchesne-Guillemin: *Etudes pour un Paul Valéry*
(Neuchâtel: Editions de la Baconnière, 1964), 222.

[6] A description of this draft is given below.

[7] "Introduction biographique" by Agathe Rouart-Valéry, Paul Valéry:
Œuvres, I, 20. A fuller version of this text is to be found in a photographic reproduction included in J. P. Monod's essay: *Regard sur Paul
Valéry* (Lausanne, Editions des Terreaux, 1946), opposite p. 40, in
which we read, beside a drawing of ships in port and an elegant light-
house ("Il est comme le mât du grand port"), the following lines: "Nuit
infinie. *Critique*. Peut-être l'effet de cette tension de l'air et de l'esprit.
Et ces crevaisons violentes redoublées du ciel, ces illuminations brusques

phasizing that for Valéry to have dated his manuscript with such care was quite contrary to his usual practice. Here, I suggest, the desire was perhaps foremost in his thoughts to commemorate, twenty-five years later to the day, a time of decision.

The language of "Sinistre" thus contains the dramatized construction of an experience which quite naturally, in its frame of metaphors, calls on his long acquaintance with the sea and ships, acquired during his childhood at Sète. So natural in fact must the analogy of the shipwreck have seemed to him that he used it on other occasions to evoke the fatal limits of consciousness in sleep or death.[8] Yet, in saying this, we must hasten also to recall that the poem takes its place in a distinct poetic tradition born in the nineteenth century, that of the spiritual voyage with its tribulations, its mortal dangers. Byron, Coleridge, and Gerard Manley Hopkins would have to be named;[9] so would Vigny, Gautier, Nerval, and, of course, Baudelaire, whose "Le Voyage" is

---

saccadées entre les murs de chaux nue. Je me sens AUTRE ce matin. Mais—se sentir Autre—cela ne peut durer—soit que l'on redevienne et que le premier l'emporte; soit que le nouvel homme absorbe et annule. . . ."

[8] Compare "Comme le grand navire s'enfonce et sombre lentement gardant ses ressources, ses machines, ses lumières, ses instruments (. . .), Ainsi dans la nuit et dans le dessous de soi-même l'esprit descend au sommeil avec tous ses appareils et ses possibles." ("Final," *Œuvres*, I, 354). Likewise, in "Colloque dans un être" we read: "N'est-ce pas une merveille supérieure que de penser que l'on possède en soi de quoi disparaître à soi-même,—cependant que toutes les choses, comme prises, quelles qu'elles soient, dans un seul et même filet qui les traîne insensiblement vers l'ombre,—les personnes, les pensées, les désirs, les valeurs et les biens et les maux, et mon corps et les dieux, se retirent, se dissolvent, s'anéantissent, s'obscurcissent ensemble? . . . Rien n'a eu lieu. Tout s'efface à la fois. Est-ce beau? Quand le navire sombre, le ciel s'évanouit et la mer s'évapore . . ." (ibid., 365-366).

[9] I am, of course, thinking in particular of *The Wreck of the Deutschland*. It is interesting to note the pleasure Valéry found in reading Hopkins, and Charles Williams and Robert Bridges on Hopkins, when he discovered the Oxford University Press edition of the works during a visit to London in 1934 (*Cahiers*, XVII, 666).

close to "Sinistre" by its accent of suffering and desperate
heroism.[10] Another important link is the Stéphane Mallarmé of the early poems written at Tournon and Avignon,
with his impassioned emphasis in "Brise marine":

> Et, peut-être, les mâts, invitant les orages
> Sont-ils de ceux qu'un vent penche sur les naufrages
> Perdus, sans mâts, sans mâts ni fertiles îlots . . .
> Mais, ô mon cœur, entends le chant des matelots!

This was a poetry of spiritual torment that could not fail to
move Valéry, especially when he realized the extent of
Mallarmé's later conquest, the agony that was absorbed into
philosophical calm and gracious companionship by the *ter-
rorism of politeness*, as Jean-Paul Sartre has called it.[11]
Mallarmé was a "révolté," Valéry later told Gide in a few
perspicacious lines, "qui a donné finalement à sa révolte tant
de disproportion et de profondeur, une révolte si pénétrante,
si moléculaire qu'elle a fini par le sourire universel que nous
lui connûmes." [12] One cannot fail to compare the characteristic courtesy Valéry brought to public duties and to a
lionizing audience, saying at the end of his life, "Ci-gît moi,
tué par les autres." [13] Yet he kept his rebellious fiber for
correspondence with a few intimate friends, and for occasional pages like "Sinistre."

I have mentioned the main line of descent in the light of
which, I think, the poem under discussion is to be envisaged.
But two central names for Valéry, Edgar Allan Poe and
Rimbaud, remain to be evoked. The former is implicitly

---

[10] A stimulating essay on the use of sea imagery in nineteenth century literature has been written by W. H. Auden: *The Enchaféd Flood*
(London: Faber and Faber, 1951).

[11] Preface to *Poésies* of Stéphane Mallarmé (Paris: Gallimard, Poésie,
1966), 5.

[12] Letter to Gide, July 1914, *Correspondance André Gide-Paul Valéry*,
437.

[13] J. P. Monod: *Regard sur Paul Valéry*, 53.

designated in one of the manuscripts of "Sinistre," along-side the opening, by the words "Gordon Pym." There is assuredly a direct relationship to be traced with Poe's famous narrative of the voyage of the whaler "Grampus" and the sufferings endured by Pym as he lies in the hold, beset by fear of starvation, death by thirst, suffocation, and premature burial; then the terrible storm that shakes the vessel after the mutiny and the vision of the ghost ship with its figures suggestive of a crucifixion; finally, the mysterious conclusion depicting a great white being. Is this an adventure story, or an allegory, a fable of the spiritual life, as one might construe from the last few pages? It matters little to us here what was Poe's true intention, but it is clear that the account fired Valéry's imagination, as did so much in Poe, and that he came naturally to transpose some of its elements into the substance of his own expression. He would write "le Poème du Navire" [14] and use in some measure Poe's iconography, which had already proved fascinating for the previous generation of French poets. In studying "Sinistre," I shall have occasion to refer to a number of quite eloquent parallels.

Furthermore, we must call attention to the author of the "Bateau ivre" who swept Valéry off his feet when first he read the poem in 1891. He wrote to Pierre Louÿs on the 14th of February of that year: "Je suis encore dans la saoulerie prodigieuse des vers de Rimbaud récemment lus. Que dites-

---

[14] The project of writing "Navis, Poème du navire" is mentioned in the first notebook of *Charmes* alongside a draft of "César" (*Album de vers anciens*) with the epigraph "Imperatoria brevitas." It shows an important elaboration of the theme: "Navis—Poème du navire mais un navire senti tel. Système de bois et étais—de *Tensions*—de forces intérieures. Le tout livré à l'aventure cosmique de la mer. Hasards et lois. Porteur de vie—Système entièrement dû à la volonté. Conflit direct de volontés et de risques,—de savoir et de pouvoirs.—Comment l'inerte monté par hommes se comporte devant l'inerte monstrueux.—L'onde forte balance la nef comme une fronde le caillou.—Le *vent*—Masse de l'air en mouvement." (Previously unpublished.)

vous du 'Bateau ivre'! . . ." [15] and again in August, addressing himself this time to Gide: "Je suis ivre de la beauté des
choses de la mer et je m'efforce d'en saisir l'âme *aventureuse*
et *triomphale*. . . . Relisez l'admirable 'Bateau ivre' pour
comprendre. Cette poésie est étonnante, véridique et un peu
folle—comme la boussole." [16] The epithets used by Valéry
might equally well be applied to his poem that celebrates a
soul-rending crisis. We may observe that many subsequent
comments on the *Illuminations* and the *Saison en enfer* can
be adduced from his various writings (thus, contrary to
Claudel, he preferred the *Illuminations*); but a curiously
harsh critical appraisal of the "Bateau ivre" seventeen years
after he first read it, in 1908, should not be overlooked.
While reciting the poem to Degas, his admiration suddenly
crumbled, and he described his feeling to Gide: "Figure-toi,
mon vieux—qu'à mesure que je débitais mon 'Bateau,' je
trouvais cela de plus en plus nigaud. . . . Et pas moi,—le
bateau! Je n'avais pas revu ni remâché ces vers depuis des
ans et des ans. Le voilà qui reparaît à l'entrée du port de
l'esprit et je le trouve . . . inutile." [17] Although I have no
evidence from his correspondence or private notes that he
ever revised his opinion, I believe that "Sinistre" constitutes
in a sense a tacit tribute to the "Bateau ivre" in that it develops a pattern of references, and even verbal details, that
arise from an intimate knowledge of Rimbaud's composition. His protagonist is an "ivrogne étrange" who undergoes
the fury of the waters (Valéry: "écroulement des trombes,"
Rimbaud: "écroulement des eaux," "les trombes / Et les
ressacs"), his boat is washed clean of the smell of wine and
life (Valéry: "Lave l'odeur de la vie et du vin"; Rimbaud:
"L'eau verte . . . des taches de vins bleus et des vomissures / Me lava . . ."), while he too has his moments of

[15] Quoted by Octave Nadal: "Paul Valéry et l'événement de 1892,"
Mercure de France, April 1955, 623.
[16] *Correspondance André Gide-Paul Valéry*, 116.
[17] Ibid., 417.

vision (Valéry: "Je vois . . . Je vois . . ."; Rimbaud: "J'ai vu . . . J'ai vu . . . etc."). And it is not only such minor points of contact, but above all the force and intensity of Valéry's poem as a whole, its mystical excitement, that makes the reader propose a comparison with the "Bateau ivre." [18] Yet it will be seen that "Sinistre" is certainly not imitative in any simple way, for whereas Rimbaud sings in the first part of his poem of the multiple richness of the physical sensibility, Valéry attains in confronting the ocean an elemental asceticism. He joins a celebrated line of Romantic poets and Poe and Rimbaud; but we shall see that he turns their poetry of adventure to an individual end.

The reader of *La Jeune Parque* and *Charmes* cannot fail to be especially surprised by the reference to Christ in the last stanza. Nowhere else is Valéry's language more directly Christian than it is here: "Je vois le Christ amarré sur la vergue! . . ." To confirm the religious implications of the poem we may observe that Valéry at one stage intended to include a highly significant epigraph from the Vulgate[19] and considered three tentative quotations: "Amarum est nos

---

[18] For an incisive contrast between Rimbaud's procedure and Valéry's own, one could not do better than refer to this passage from the fifteenth notebook: "Tandis que tels poètes (Rimbaud, etc.) ont plutôt visé à donner l'impression d'un *état extraordinaire* (vision—résonance réciproque des choses—exploration désespérée des sens, et de l'expression) d'autres, et moi, avons cherché à donner l'idée d'un 'monde' ou système de choses bien plus séparé du monde commun—mais fait de ses éléments les mêmes—les liaisons seules étant choisies—et aussi les définitions. Ceci par définitions beaucoup plus serrées. Mais en refusant à ce point, on refuse du très puissant." It seems to me clear that "Sinistre" is a case which develops the visionary style that was normally couched by him in a wholly different manner.

[19] Valéry frequently chose Latin epigraphs for his poems, not all of which he maintained in the published versions. One may mention the line from Prudentius' *Apotheosis* (1,979), which he considered using for "La Pythie" but later abandoned: "Obmutesce, furor, linguam canis improba, morde"; and the quotation from the Vulgate: "Qui legitime certaverit" (2 Tim. 6) which features on a manuscript of "Ebauche d'un Serpent."

. . ." (the last words are illegible); "Non amatur qui navem
. ∴ ." (again the end of the line is illegible); and "Erat navis
in medio mari." The last of these, which had already appeared on a previous draft, comes from the Gospel according
to St. Mark:

And when even was come, the ship was in the midst of the sea
(*erat navis in medio mari*), and he alone on the land.
   And he saw them toiling in rowing, for the wind was contrary
unto them; and about the fourth watch of the night he cometh
unto them, walking upon the sea, and would have passed by them.
   But when they saw him walking upon the sea, they supposed it
had been a spirit, and cried out:
   For they all saw him and were troubled. And immediately he
talked with them, and saith unto them: Be of good cheer: it is I:
be not afraid.
   And he went up unto them in the ship; and the wind ceased:
and they were sore amazed in themselves beyond measure, and
wondered.

(MARK VII, v. 47–51)

Plainly the epigraph establishes an atmosphere that is
dominated by the presence of Christ. The five words of the
Vulgate chosen by Valéry highlight the ship's struggle in the
storm as it advances alone without miraculous help. We
may therefore infer that the poet intended at one stage to
make an overt reference to the fear and awe of Christ's
disciples, which he found no doubt in some way comparable
to his own agitation.[20] As for the two other fragments, they
are more difficult to discuss because of the illegibility of the
handwriting, but it would not appear unlikely that the first
represents a borrowing from the Book of Jeremiah in which
we read: "marum et amarum est reliquisse te Dominum
Deum tuum" ("It is [an evil thing and] bitter, that thou hast
forsaken the Lord thy God . . .") (Jeremiah II, v. 19). It is,
of course, possible that Valéry had another text in mind, but
none in the Vulgate appears to offer so close a parallel.

---

[20] In *Cahiers*, VI, 701, written in August 1917, we find once again the
quotation, "Erat navis in medio mari." It is placed suggestively along-

The third quotation is even more vague and I must confess that, having failed to read the final verb, I am not able to propose a precise origin. If one might suggest, in a purely hypothetical way, a reading such as "non amatur qui navem [gubernat]" ("the ship's captain is unloved"), I am the first to admit that such an emendation can hardly carry much weight. Nevertheless, it is possible for us to conclude that, just as in several other poems, Valéry toyed with the idea of an epigraph which would provide his composition with a particular tone and motif, although the words he chose did not necessarily preside over the poem's genesis: indeed, we can be sure that they were added at a later stage, when much of "Sinistre" had already been completed; yet, they quite patently indicate that in writing his poem his concern turned on religious associations.

I have alluded to the unpublished manuscripts that contain material of considerable interest such as the date of composition and the epigraphs just mentioned. I wish now to refer in detail to the first draft, or rather the page of jottings which preceded the original version and which we shall call MS A. To convey its disarray, I have spaced the words so as to suggest the original disposition. As clearly as any other document, I believe, it illustrates the manner in which imagination and analysis were intimately wedded in Valéry's art of poetry. No logical order is followed as language is sought; images proposed; antitheses outlined; and the notion

---

side two other quotations which may be said to reflect aspects of the same emotional complex expressed in "Sinistre." The first is taken from Eunapius's *Lives of the Philosophers* and recalls how Porphyry was affected by the teaching of Plotinus: "He conceived a hatred of his own body and of being human" (the words are indeed typical of the "angelic" Valéry). The second is a verse from Jeremiah XXX (Valéry incorrectly writes XXXI), verse 22: "Creavit Dominus novum super terram: femina circumdedit virum" ("for the Lord hath created a new thing in the earth, a woman shall compass a man"). The verse is interpreted as being a promise of the coming of Christ.

of a unifying center, or group of movements, established. We observe that the presence of death is fundamental from the start as the hull is interpreted as a corpse and the sea as living death.

coque—corps aveuglément tiré (a)
décline—cercle décrit par un point (b)
roidir—mollir (c)
route (d)
   navire (e)
   compas (f)   un peu ivre (g)
   habitacle (h)   la nage (i)
à tâtons contre la coque (j)
   cogne, jase (k)
   nausée (l)
   nord (m)
un grand coup d'ombre contre

                            épaule (n)
yeux mouillés
odeur (o)

                          groupe de mts (p)
                          astres
                          vaisseau efforts
                          mer
mer aux bras déployés
se ploie et se drape
   et se déploie
qui déplie un tombeau (q)
Mer—mort
      vie
mort vivante (r)
connu et reconnu (s)
   nu
De tout son poids qui se travaille (redresse) en trombes
Elle se joue à nu des astres seuls (t)
   Quelle heure (onde) tonne (cogne) aux membres de la
   coque

Ce grand coup d'ombre où craque notre sort
Quelle grande tombe horrible
(Quel ossement misérable) s'entrechoque
Dans la mâture un mouvement (un vacarme) de mort (u)
La mer élève et rabaisse ses tombes
Tout (Vomit) autour du grand marin épouvanté (v)

(a) The initial word will find its way into the first line of "Sinistre." The poet defines it in terms that apply the image of the hull to a self that is the plaything of the elements; it thus opens directly onto the allegorical contrast between dependence and self-reliant lucidity that underlies the poem. This boat, inert yet human, makes me think of a few isolated, previously unpublished lines from a series of notes on poetry in which Valéry proposes a method of description: "Si tu veux décrire un objet—fais par exemple un bateau, fais comme si c'était un corps à la fois vivant, *sentant* et *inerte*.—Mets ton corps à la place de l'objet et ressens, par exemple, la traction—épaule du navire mû."

(b) One notes the ambiguity of the word which was perhaps partly evoked by alliteration: at one and the same time it conveys a visual image such as the angle of the mast bending under the tempest, and the deviation of behavior from an established norm; it is a curvature that is measured with reference to its point of origin. Valéry does not include this verb in "Sinistre," but makes a somewhat comparable use of "dérive" (st. 5).

(c) Antithesis is especially appropriate in a poem destined to suggest the surge of the ocean. These words were not incorporated into "Sinistre," where we find instead "élève" and "recreuse," "creuse" and "comble."

(d) Again the word is not retained. In the final version Valéry will not mention the steadfast maintenance of a certain course and goal, but rather the unredeemed isolation of the sailor ("égaré sur la mer").

(e) Valéry's vessel, unlike Rimbaud's boat ("bateau"), is a

large craft with its own dignity and weight: the only word he uses to describe it is "navire" (sts. 3, 7).

(f) If no mention is made in the final version of a compass, we shall observe the word "calcule," which signifies the total lucidity that provokes the shipwreck of the sailor's past. It is not easy to surmise how the image would have been developed but we find an interesting parallel in these lines from Valéry's preface to *Rhumbs* which compare thought to the needle of a compass: "Comme l'aiguille du compas demeure assez constante, tandis que la route varie, ainsi peut-on regarder les caprices ou bien les applications successives de notre pensée, les variations de notre attention, les incidents de la vie mentale, les divertissements de notre mémoire, la diversité de nos désirs, de nos émotions et de nos impulsions—comme des écarts définis par contraste avec je ne sais quelle constance dans l'intention profonde et essentielle de l'esprit—sorte de présence à soi-même qui l'oppose à chacun de ses instants." (A further echo for us, linking physical and spiritual movement, is Vigny's magnificent image of the pair of compasses: "La pensée est semblable au compas qui perce le point sur lequel il tourne, quoique sa seconde branche décrive un cercle éloigné. L'homme succombe dans son travail et est percé par le compas; mais la ligne que l'autre branche a décrite reste gravée à jamais pour le bien des races futures.") [21]

(g) Reminiscent of Rimbaud, the notion will be included in "Sinistre" with the word "ivrogne" (st. 3).

(h) "Habitacle" is a marine term that signifies the binnacle; in Biblical or poetic language, it also signifies a dwelling place (thus Valéry will write in "L'Homme et la coquille": "Voilà, nous apprend-on, comme se constitue l'habitacle et le mouvant refuge de cet étrange animal, qu'un muscle vêt, qu'il revêt d'une coque"). Such verbal am-

---

[21] Alfred de Vigny, "Le Journal d'un poète," *Œuvres complètes*, ed F. Baldensberger, 2 vols (Paris: Gallimard, Pléiade, 1948), II, 901.

bivalence no doubt appealed to him in planning "Sinistre," but the word was not retained in later versions.

(i) Swimming, in Valéry's eyes, was the "purest" of sports and he wrote several descriptions of it, including that most succinct and muscular decasyllable of "Le Cimetière marin": "Courons à l'onde en rejaillir vivant." The buffeting of the boat, the efforts of the swimmer ("L'abîme et moi formons une machine") offer suggestive parallels of vital struggle

(j) With these words we notice the emerging images of the first line of the final version. "Coque" is repeated, but instead of the previous emphasis on blind obedience to fate ("corps aveuglément tiré"), Valéry depicts the unsure approach of an external force that imparts the heavy blows of destiny.

(k) The linking of these two verbs is surprising, and in a sense antithetical: "cogne" evokes the sound of a fearsome force, while "jaser" refers to a vain, frivolous chattering (one's poetic memory connects it with Verlaine's *Fêtes galantes:* "Et la mandoline jase / Parmi les frissons de brise"). The contrast was not retained in the writing of the poem.

(l) This word, which will be introduced in the third stanza, conveys wildness of movement and the poet's rejection of his ship. At the same time, it calls up associations with the "vomissures" of "Bateau ivre."

(m) Attracted by "compas" and "habitacle," "nord" designates the presence of a fixed direction in the midst of the storm. But it is "l'Est" which will be mentioned (st. 5) as the cardinal point to which the elements sweep all things in their fury.

(n) Here we see the first really striking verbal discovery ("coup d'ombre"), prolonging the alliteration of "cogne" and "coque" through an image of mysterious menace and death. The allusion to "épaule," presumably the nameless shoulder of the shadows pounding on the hull, will not be retained. We may think of Poe's similar description: "I was suddenly aware of a concussion resembling nothing I had ever before experienced, and which impressed me with a vague conception, if indeed I then thought of anything, that the whole foundations of the solid globe were suddenly rent asunder, and that the day of universal dissolution was at hand." [22]

(o) The image of tear-filled eyes is associated with the fury of the sea and, perhaps, regret for what has been lost. It is, however, revulsion that will be emphasized in the poem, the narrator experiencing "l'odeur de la vie et du vin" as an impurity to be cleansed away.

(p) One of the most interesting of all these notes shows Valéry establishing the interrelationship of a set of three *movements:* stars, vessel, and sea. At the center of the metaphorical pattern is this dynamic correspondence, a huge impetus that commands the universe of the sensibility. It will be carried over into the poem, obviously with regard to the vessel and the sea, but also the "astres," in headlong flight following the rotation of the planet and the passage of time which, from the beginning, presides over the plot. It is noteworthy that a somewhat similar passage occurs in Poe: "Shortly after this period I fell into a state of partial insensibility, during which the most pleasing images floated in my imagination; such as green trees, waving meadows of ripe grain, processions of dancing girls, troops of cavalry, and other fantasies. I now remember that, in all which passed before my mind's eye, *motion* was a predominant idea. Thus, I never fancied any stationary object, such as a house, a mountain, or anything of that kind; but windmills, ships, large birds, balloons, people on horseback, carriages driving furiously, and similar moving objects, presented themselves in endless succession." [23]

(q) These three remarks are an attempt to expand the allegorical implications of the heaving sea that is first en-

22 *The Works of Edgar Allan Poe,* 6 vols (New York: Charles Scribner's Sons, 1914), 5, 258
23 Ibid., 129.

visaged in an attitude of welcome, with arms open like wings
outstretched; then, as the endless repetition of a mass that
shuts and opens like "la mer, la mer toujours recommencée"
of "Le Cimetière marin"; and finally, when the development
reaches its climax, as a fatal entrance to death ("qui déplie
un tombeau"). This notion will find its way into "Sinistre"
in the third stanza where the infinite repetitiousness of the
waves is linked with the notion of the grave:

> La mer élève et recreuse des tombes,
> La même eau creuse et comble le ravin.

(r) The paradoxical union of life and death in the image
of the sea, of powerful activity and the somber presence of a
mortal thrust, will be fundamental in "Sinistre" as in "Le
Cimetière marin." In both poems it is a fertile source of
poetic tension.

(s) This would seem to be a further evocation of the sea,
known in its constant renewal, recognized in its constant
sameness. At the same time the rhyme produces the new
idea of nakedness which is further expressed in the two
decasyllables that follow and will also be introduced into the
poem (st. 2: "Sur l'avant nu, l'écroulement des trombes").

(t) The two lines found here capture the meter of
"Sinistre" and the energetic movement of the sea. The mas-
sive waves leap magnificently upwards in a naked game of
love with their only suitors, the stars . . . Valéry's decasyllables convey a strong sense of agitation and strain but,
although the key rhyme of "trombes" will be kept, they
will make way for the remarkable concision of the phrase
"l'écroulement des trombes."

(u) The first stanza to be composed incorporates many of
the details already noted, but introduces the exclamatory
tone ("Quelle . . .", "Quelle . . .") which will be effective
in establishing the urgency of the action. One may point to
the relative thinness of a few phrases in comparison with
later versions: "grande tombe horrible," "ossement misé-

rable." "Dans la mâture" will be replaced by "dans nos agrès" (echoed in st. 5 by "gréée"), reinforcing to considerable advantage the phonetic pattern.

(v) The last imperfect decasyllable of this fragment contains the image of the self as a terrified captain. For the third time the use of the adjective "grand" illustrates Valéry's desire to compose a tableau of impressive dimensions despite the speed of the meter; as for the "marin" he will be replaced by the hero of sts. 3 and 4, whose ambitions symbolize a universal intelligence.

Here then are the first gropings towards the language and form Valéry was to make his own. The second sheet (MS B), to which I would like to draw attention, carries the composition much further in that it drafts out the poem's beginning, middle, and end, and introduces in particular the reference to Christ. The original title given is "Chant du Naufrage" which, because it was perhaps felt to be over-specific, is replaced on this same manuscript by the more general heading "Le Sinistre." (In a subsequent version, the definite article was obliterated: the meaning now combines the sense of disaster, such as that of a shipwreck, and a grim foreboding.) Next to the title we read, as I have previously observed, the important allusion meant for the poet's eyes alone: "Gordon Pym."

> Quelle heure cogne aux membres de la coque
> Ce grand coup d'ombre où craque notre sort
> Quelle puissance effroyable (infinie) (impalpable) (a)
> 　　　　　　　　　　　　　　　　entrechoque
> Dans la mâture un ossement de mort
>
> La mer abaisse (élève) et rabaisse des tombes
> Sur notre avant (avant nu) déjà (l'écroulement) de lourdes
> 　　　　　　　　　　(d'éblouissantes) tombes (b)
> Lavent l'odeur de la vie et du vin
> La mer (houle) élève et rabaisse des tombes
>
> Homme hideux à qui le corps chavire (c)
> Perdu (ivre) glacé . . .

Tant la nausée attachée au navire
Brise dans l'âme un dieu (effort) qui veut crier (d)

Tu lis écrit sur des souvenirs épars
Tu vois le Christ sur la maîtresse vergue

Mort comme toi ses pouvoirs et ses liens (e)
　　　　　　　　　　ses regards sur les tiens (f)
Dans l'œil sanglant tu liras cet exergue

(a) The words of the first stanza are practically those of the final version, but the poet still hesitates with regard to the choice of an adjective to describe the power of the storm. We note the variant "infinie" which would have given too patently, one supposes, a religious resonance.

(b) "Lourdes" might well have been expected as a description of the tomblike waves, but "éblouissantes" surprises by the element of light it brings into the poem; it will be deleted. We should observe that it finds its way into the description of the sea in "Le Cimetière marin": "Sur mes yeux clos, secrets éblouissants . . ."

(c) Although the final reading "en qui le cœur chavire" is not far from this, it is much more effective.

(d) "Brise dans l'âme un dieu qui veut crier," as Valéry originally wrote, is surely a most revealing line. The poet's subject is properly the "death of God," felt to the limits of an anguished sensibility.

(e) One may meditate on the process of creation involved here: was it the word "écrit" which by its sound called up the image of Christ? We cannot rule out the possibility. The first line will serve as the background of st. 6, despite its present banality, whereas the next line opens up the climactic terror of the poet's spiritual vision.

(f) Here the direct relationship between Christ and the self is made explicit, as will not be the case in the final version. The image of the dying Christ who stares with fascinating glance denotes the poet's loss of faith and the painful submergence of the past.

By the end of MS B, as we have seen, Valéry was well on the way to completing his poem. We are fortunately in the position of being able to follow the way the poem further developed through three other drafts that have come down to us. MS C, first entitled "Le Sinistre," but later modified by the deletion of the definite article, bears the date "4–5 octobre 17" and the epigraph "Erat navis in medio mari"; it comprises versions of sts. 1, 2, 5, 4, 6, 7, arranged in that order, with the beginnings of st. 3 on the verso after one abortive attempt ("Adieu, grandeur du jour, lucidité . . ."). MS Ci offers a revision of st. 3, but does not represent a notable progress. Finally MS D brings us very close to the published version and sets the stanzas in their definitive order, although it contains several persistent difficulties of expression that had still to be resolved; it reproduces the epigraph of MS C and adds to it the two others we discussed above. I shall resume briefly the variants:

Stanza 1: We find prolonged hesitation over lines 3 ("Quelle présence . . .", "Quelle puissance . . .", "Quel présage . . .") (MS C) and line 4 ("Dans la mâture, un ossement de mort . . ." (C, D), "aux ossements . . .") (C). Two question marks in MS D at the end of lines 2 and 4 introduce an analytical tone that will finally be preferred to an exclamatory one.

Stanza 2: We note with special interest highly significant variants in MS C and D, just as the image of the "dieu qui veut crier" in the previous draft seemed to us to be striking evidence of Valéry's religious concern: line 2: "Ivre de soif, et impuissant à prier" (C); "Ivre de soif, impuissant à prier" (D); "Ivrogne étrange, et mort entre deux morts" (D), which evokes the image of a crucifixion; also "entre deux démons," and "entre deux mers" which would have prepared the rhyme "un affre d'enfer" (D); "A quoi pensez-vous? Je ne sais penser" (D); line 3: "Tant la nausée attachée au navire" (C, D); line 4: "Arrache l'âme au pouvoir de crier" (C); "Arrache à l'âme un besoin de crier" (D).

Stanza 4: The first draft of this stanza is to be found at the bottom of MS C. It begins with three lines, later abandoned, that have the tone of a lyrical confession:

> Adieu, grandeur du jour, lucidité
> Que je possède entre mille forces
> Et choisis entre mes avenirs sans nombre

But this tender declaration is placed alongside a fragment that will be the direct forerunner of the proud "Excelsior" pose of the final version. (Incidentally we may recall that Valéry was acquainted with Hardy's verse and later translated one of his poems):

> Je suis connaissant le moment
> Où dans un phénomène minuscule
> L'univers casse comme un instrument

The scientific metaphor, suggested, one supposes, by the words "compas" and "habitacle" in MS A, is further elaborated on a separate sheet (MS Ci) :

> Je me fais l'effet de l'aiguille minuscule
> Où par un phénomène minuscule
> L'esprit (l'heure) s'arrête et se rompt l'instrument
>   (et le monde se casse comme un instrument)

Finally MS D puts the quatrain in its definitive position, line 1 now echoing the first line of st. 3. There remain variants for line 2 ("Je suis cerveau, capable du moment"; "Moi le cerveau trop clair . . .") and line 4 ("L'univers casse, comme un instrument / avec son instrument"; "De l'univers va casser l'instrument").

Stanza 5: In MS C this stanza is found in third place, before "Homme hideux. . . ." The variants are not numerous: interestingly enough, line 1 originally read: "Maudit soit-il l'homme qui t'a gréé," but "l'homme" is quickly crossed out and replaced by the strong term of abuse "le porc"; line 3, "dans les fonds noirs" instead of "dans tes fonds noirs"; and line 4, "bat ce bois mort en dérive vers l'Est." In MS D the last line still shows some hesitation and we note: "Bat

au bois mort qui dérive dans l'Est"; "Danse et connaît en
dérive vers l'Est."

Stanza 6: MS C reads: line 1 "L'abîme entier n'est plus
qu'une machine"; line 2: "univers" is proposed as an alternative to "souvenirs"; line 3: alongside the definitive version,
the variants: "Je te vois, Rose, et tes tasses de Chine"
("Rose" seems most likely, as far as one can make out, to be
a literary name); line 4 "La femme grasse et la rougeur (le
seuil d'or) des bars." In MS D, although the other three lines
have their definitive form, the language of line 4 has still
not reached its final directness: "La femme grasse et la
rougeur (au seuil rouge) des bars."

Stanza 7: We have already seen the appearance of this
image in MS B. MS C reads: line 1: "Je vois le Christ sur la
maîtresse vergue"; line 2: "Il danse à mort, nos crachats sont
les siens!" line 3: "Dans l'œil sanglant (et dans cet œil) je
crois lire en exergue," "m'éclaire cet exergue," "ne vois-tu
cet exergue," "me fait lire cet exergue"; line 4: "Un grand
navire a sombré corps et biens." In MS D the wording brings
us much closer to the final version but several variants remain: "Je vois le Christ attaché (amarré) sur la vergue";
line 2: "nos crachats sont les siens (as in MS C); line 3: "Son
œil sanglant (Mais l'œil sanglant) m'éclaire cet exergue";
line 4: "Un grand navire a sombré (péri) corps et biens!"

The décasyllabic meter adopted is the same as that for "Le
Cimetière marin," concerning which one recalls Valéry's
brief comment when he attempted to reconstruct his state of
mind and intentions in the most personal poem of *Charmes:*
"je me fis quelques réflexions sur ce type fort peu employé
dans la poésie moderne; il me semblait pauvre et monotone.
Il était peu de chose auprès de l'alexandrin, que trois ou
quatre générations de grands artistes ont prodigieusement
élaboré." [24] Yet, as we know, he took up the challenge of

---

[24] "Au sujet du Cimetière marin," *Œuvres,* I, 1503.

this verse form: in the case of "Le Cimetière marin" he conceived a six-line stanza rhyming aabccb in which the pattern of couplet and enclosed quatrain arrests the movement and conveys a deliberate process of meditation, of "moments" of thought. In "Sinistre," on the other hand, emphasis is placed on action as it unfolds, on the drama that has its culmination in the final stanza; it is therefore the ballad form (abab) with its rapidity and constant progress of alternating feminine and masculine rhymes, that is most appropriate. The rhythm of the decasyllable, like the rhyme-scheme adopted, is quite different from that of "Le Cimetière marin": whereas the caesural pause varies widely in the latter poem (4/6, 6/4, 12/2/6, 1/3/6, 1/1/2/6, 2/2/2/2/2, 8/2, 2/8 . . .), "Sinistre" maintains a regular 4/6 break with three minor exceptions.[25] This is the persistent summons to attention, the pulse already present in image and sound in the first words, to which the whole sensibility will respond:

> Quelle heure cogne aux membres de la coque

The terror of an hour of reckoning is reinforced by an asymmetrical rhythm as well as harsh alliteration. Throughout the poem the same measure, and a similar predominance of plosives, will form a sound pattern that is restless but vigorously controlled.

> Quelle heure cogne aux membres de la coque
> Ce grand coup d'ombre où craque notre sort?

[25] Lines 3, 15, 22. Compare Paul Claudel: "un rythme essentiellement français, celui de la *Chanson de Roland* et de Villon, le décamètre avec la césure sur le 4e pied, et ces six syllabes à la suite qui développent la position une fois affirmée. Rien de plus mâle et de plus souple, c'est la liberté dans la régularité et le pair avec l'impair. Quel dommage que notre poésie ait abandonné, pour le laisser à la complainte populaire, un mètre si avantageux" ("Francis Jammes," *Œuvres en prose*, ed. Jacques Petit and Charles Galperine [Paris: Gallimard, Pléiade, 1965], 564).

Quelle puissance impalpable entre-choque
Dans nos agrès des ossements de mort? [26]

Below and above, in the ship's bowels and in its rigging,
the present moment is fraught with danger. The noise of
the storm suggests a time of crisis in which the self is subject
to a power undefined. As to the general significance of such a
threat, there can assuredly be no doubt: it is a baleful
portent already rattling naked bones. A whole world, a
destiny is being demolished in some terrible upheaval; the
second line declares this with extraordinary energy, while
harsh alliteration throughout the quatrain beats the alarm.
And yet, despite his apprehension, the speaker does not surrender to a menace so keenly felt. Instead of crying out in
fear, he begins his tale of mystery and imagination with
two questions that demonstrate his desire to unravel a meaning. He will be master in his own household ("Je veux être
maître chez moi," Valéry wrote to Gide in November 1894)
by looking at the object of his fear face to face.

We may recall that the second line, as noted above, offers
the first recognizable decasyllable among the original jottings
for "Sinistre," and that around it the poem was made. It
wonderfully suggests the notion of a violent conjuncture.

Sur l'avant nu, l'écroulement des trombes
Lave l'odeur de la vie et du vin:
La mer élève et recreuse des tombes.
La même eau creuse et comble le ravin.

For the ship foundering in the storm all is not lost, as the
mind can now perceive. The waters bring with them a
cleansing that washes away the contingencies of events, sensations, thought. Here the self realizes it is reduced to its
own essence, its soul laid bare in front of the boiling chal-

---

[26] *Œuvres*, I, 301. "Sinistre" was originally published in *Mélange*
(Gallimard, 1939); it also appeared in a war front journal entitled *La
Tranche de culasse* (April 2, 1940) where it was subtitled "vers de
jeunesse": line 2 reads "Ce grand coup sombre . . ."; line 13: "Homme
pourtant . . ."; and the last line is not written in capitals.

lenge of the sea. What it must clearly envisage, and name in
its own way, is the sense of an ultimate limit which will
brook no half-measures. The rhythmic rise and fall of the
waves, time that passes monotonously ("élève et creuse,"
"creuse et comble") tells him over and over again of the fate
against which he must weigh his treasures and his identity,
for the one irrefutable yardstick is death. In this regard, I
cannot help thinking of a passage from a letter Valéry
addressed to André Gide: "Mon cher," he writes, "je vis
depuis longtemps dans la morale de la mort. Cette limite
si éclatante procure à ma pensée le mouvement et la vie. Je
crois que peu d'hommes depuis les fanatiques ont pris cette
base charmante, enivrante et libérale. Tout ce que j'ai bien
voulu, je l'ai voulu en fixant le mot: Fin." [27] In the second
stanza of "Sinistre," we are presented with the vital tension
of this experience as the ship struggles against tremendous
odds and, going to the end of its endurance, realizes an
austere purity. A little-known passage from one of Valéry's
prose-poems may serve as an additional commentary, its
theme and immediacy being closely parallel to those of the
lines we are examining:

> Entends indéfiniment, écoute
> Le chant de l'attente et le choc du temps,
> Le bercement constant du compte,
> L'identité, la quantité,
> Et la voix d'ombre vaine et forte,
> La voix massive de la mer
> Se redire: je gagne et perds,
> Je perds et gagne . . .
> Oh! jeter un temps hors du temps! [28]

[27] Letter to Gide, 10 November 1894, *Correspondance André Gide-
Paul Valéry*, p. 217. Compare "Dès qu'on a été sûr de mourir et tout à
fait—de ne plus continuer à se sentir ailleurs, ni de revenir sous une
autre forme, ni d'errer vaguement comme un gaz pensant, bien des
choses ont été altérées" (*Cahiers*, I, 443).

[28] "Comme au bord de la mer," *Morceaux choisis* (Paris: Gallimard,
1930), 56–57.

As in "Sinistre," a monotonous beating of the waves, a voice
that emerges from the shadows like the voice of fate, an insistent meter are the inescapable conditions in the face of
which the poet must found a durableness of his own making.

> Homme hideux, en qui le cœur chavire,
> Ivrogne étrange égaré sur la mer
> Dont la nausée attachée au navire
> Arrache à l'âme un désir de l'enfer,

By its construction the third stanza prepares us for the
complementary panel of the diptych that comes with the
next quatrain. The focus has changed from the ship to the
self as the speaker grows conscious of his central role in the
fight. It is not only his ship that is capsizing, but his heart;
fearsome, isolated, drunken, he resembles the plaything of
the storm. Yet if the progression has so far been towards
some grim and inevitable meeting with death, the attitude is
suddenly one of complete revolt. By remaining on the ship
with its past contamination and the nausea it induces, the
poet would never be free. Instead, he proclaims his strangeness: his desire has turned to hell itself, the most provocative
of ambitions. Rendered naked by the knowledge of death, his
soul discovers its only escape in absolute, "Satanic" refusal.

> Homme total, je tremble et je calcule,
> Cerveau trop clair, capable du moment
> Où, dans un phénomène minuscule,
> Le temps se brise ainsi qu'un instrument . . .

The proud rebel declares his self-reliance. He is captain
of his fate ("total," "capable"), sensibility and intellect working together in such a way that they not only comprehend
but consume the world in the fire of scrutiny ("cerveau trop
pur"). Even death, or time, which seemed all-menacing in
the first two stanzas, is now reduced to the status of a fragile
thing. For the "César de soi-même," [29] what he most fears
becomes the object with which he builds, a tool that can be

---

[29] *Cahiers*, I, 274.

mastered and used. Most significantly, it can also be destroyed since the Luciferian mind enjoys a mental acuteness that brings the supreme illusion that it can break time like a watch in some gesture of deific conjuration.[30] "Et ainsi," Valéry writes in his twenty-fourth notebook,[31] "Et ainsi je serais sans être et je ne serais pas sans ne pas être—et la mort n'étant qu'un effet du monde naturel, comme la vie, toutes deux inséparables de lui, il arriverait que le décomposant et le résolvant de la sorte, et la vie avec lui, la mort s'évanouirait avec elle et avec lui."

> Maudit soit-il le porc qui t'a gréée,
> Arche pourrie en qui grouille le lest!
> Dans tes fonds noirs, toute chose créée
> Bat ton bois mort en dérive vers l'Est . . .

Now it is no longer the outside struggle with the sea that preoccupies the speaker (st. 1-2), nor his own stand (st. 3-4), but the world of the ship. The third section begins with a change of tone as lucidity breeds a curse on both master and cargo: the words of the poet's imprecation surprise us by a familiarity and a brutal emphasis that are rare if not unique in Valéry ("porc," "pourrie," "grouille"). Here is the scorn of him who wishes wholly to reject the thing he once held dear, who condemns because he has prized. The use of "porc" to refer to the rigger—god or man one cannot say—who made the ship ready to sail is particularly violent, while the second line couples the image of the ark and the idea of rottenness, an inert mass of ballast and swarming agitation.[32] What is this useless burden that is buffeted against the ship's sides, against lifeless wood, if not experi-

---

[30] Compare: "Striking a light, I looked at the watch; but it was run down, and there were, consequently, no means of determining how long I had slept" (*The Works of Edgar Allan Poe*, 5, 34).

[31] *Cahiers*, XXIV, 3.

[32] Compare: "The ballast now shifted in a mass to leeward (the stowage had been knocking about perfectly at random for some time) and for a few moments we thought nothing could save us from capsizing" (*The Works of Edgar Allan Poe*, 5, 122).

ence itself ("toute chose créée"), the vast and varied matter
of the speaker's memory? A world is enclosed in this ship
that helplessly drifts before the storm and follows the wheel-
ing of earth and time.

> L'abîme et moi formons une machine
> Qui jongle avec des souvenirs épars:
> Je vois ma mère et mes tasses de Chine,
> La putain grasse au seuil fauve des bars;

Once more the poet uses imagery that underlines the
mechanical nature of the action ("machine") but plays down
its drama ("jongle"). His curses have become a seeming detachment that is pleased to recall affective scenes of the past
without yielding to their power. As a token of such sport he
mentions details of his childhood and adolescence: his
mother, porcelain cups, a prostitute—childhood, precious
and brittle memories, casual eroticism. Nowhere else in
Valéry's poetry does one find references of a similar trivial
and particularized kind, making us think of a Baudelairian
tradition rather than one of Mallarmé or Rimbaud, echoing
the stream-of-consciousness poetry of the Symbolist and post-
Symbolist period with its "realistic" vocabulary ("putain
grasse," "bars") in contrast to the exalted timbre that is characteristically Valéryan. Nevertheless, despite the tone, we
have no difficulty in detecting in this stanza more than a trace
of sentiment, albeit disciplined, which will find its full expression in the next lines, for no polarity could be more
fundamental in Valéry than that of extreme rigorousness
and extreme sensitivity: "Volonté d'épuiser, de passer à la
limite," he writes of himself, "il est étrange que cette fureur
glacée d'extermination, d'exécution par la rigueur soit liée
étroitement en moi avec le sentiment douloureux du cœur
serré, de la tendresse à un point infiniment tendre." [33]

[33] *Cahiers*, XII, 352.

Je vois le Christ amarré sur la vergue! . . .
Il danse à mort, sombrant avec les siens,
Son œil sanglant m'éclaire cet exergue:
UN GRAND NAVIRE A PERI CORPS ET BIENS! . . .

The subdued enumeration of the previous quatrain is suddenly replaced by an image that fills out a sort of mystical
vision. The poem takes on new depth and seriousness in an
ultimate hallucination by which we leave the atmosphere
of Baudelaire for the visionary world of the Gospel, of
Rimbaud, of Poe.[34] There is, however, no marvelous illumination, but the known figure of the Christ bound to his
mast, performing a mad dance of death. Thus it is, we
realize, that the poem reaches its climax and its true center,
the poet having taken up and expressed the experience of a
loss of faith, and the drowning of personal "idols." The ac-

[34] One is reminded especially of Pym's hallucinations: "No person
was seen upon her decks until she arrived within about a quarter of
a mile of us. We then saw three seamen, whom by their dress we took
to be Hollanders. Two of these were lying on some old sails near the
forecastle, and the third, who appeared to be looking at us with great
curiosity, was leaning over the starboard bow near the bowsprit. This
last was a stout and tall man, with a very dark skin. He seemed by his
manner to be encouraging us to have patience, nodding to us in a
cheerful although rather odd way, and smiling constantly, so as to
display a set of the most brilliantly white teeth. As his vessel drew
nearer, we saw a red flannel cap, which he had on, fall from his head
into the water; but of this he took little or no notice, continuing his
odd smiles and gesticulations. I relate these things and circumstances
minutely, and I relate them, it must be understood, precisely as they
'appeared' to us (. . .). Shall I ever forget the triple horror of that
spectacle? Twenty-five or thirty human bodies, among whom were
several females, lay scattered about between the counter and the galley
in the last and most loathsome state of putrefaction. We plainly saw
that not a soul lived in that fated vessel! Yet we could not help
shouting to the dead for help? Yes, long and loudly did we beg, in the
agony of the moment, that those silent and disgusting images would
stay for us, would not abandon us to become like them, would receive
us among their goodly company! We were raving with horror and
despair—thoroughly mad through the anguish of our grievous disap-
pointment" (*The Works of Edgar Allan Poe*, 5, 140).

tion is over; yet, although the event has been objectified, the final episode is not narrated with the imposed firmness of st. 6. The poet's voice is strident, his scene suffused with blood.[35] The pride of the prelusive climax in st. 4 is answered by this contained agony that is the ransom of victory and allows us to gauge the torment of a sensibility that has chosen to live by the intellect alone and deny consolations great and small. Unveiling a vibrant identity that struggles in the face of death, the poet's spiritual drama makes him witness the grievous destruction of a cherished self.

Valéry's allegorical ballad treats one of the most original themes of his poetic work: a tragic event of the intellectual sensibility. Excitement and apprehension, pride and anguish are here not provoked by any external incident but by consciousness itself that goes to the limits of its powers and wrestles with its secret angel. As his scheme of reference for these emotions, Valéry adopts the metaphor of the shipwreck, and its Biblical, Romantic, and Symbolist lineage, which admirably serves to contain an action unfolding in the present as if even now the disaster were taking place. The pace is rapid; meter, alliteration, and sudden changes of tone give to the diction, as we have had occasion to see, a startling alertness; while the language combines diverse modes of discourse—abstract, traditional, concrete, trivial—in a way that pregnantly suggests the agitation of the mind. Instead of creating a poetic universe that adopts ordinary language but places it in a wholly new, or "pure," framework of metaphors, meanings, and symmetries, "Sinistre" creates an extraordinary state, a vision that stirs the intellect

35 "And 'blood,' too, that word of all words—so rife at all times with mystery, and suffering, and terror—how trebly full of import did it now appear; how chilly and heavily (disjointed, as it thus was, from any foregoing words to qualify or render it distinct) did its vague syllables fall, amid the deep gloom of my prison, into the innermost recesses of my soul!" Ibid., 53.

and the senses, its style diverging from that by which Valéry
is characteristically recognizable and furnishing on one level
his most dramatic exercise in visionary poetics.

We are struck by the feeling of precipitate haste that
dominates the poem but in fact, despite the ballad form, the
development is far from linear. Following the basic model of
the quatrain, "Sinistre" is constructed in four distinct parts:
firstly (sts 1–2), the coming of death is heard in the fatal
sound of waters washing away all that is foreign; then (sts.
3–4) the self declares its own identity, tragically going to the
logical end of its desires like some Lucifer, heroically maintaining the rights of the intellect; the poet now curses the
ship on which he is borne (st. 5), since it is nothing but a
rotten hulk ("arche pourrie"), a dead form ("bois mort")
that drifts and has no will of its own: having already suc-
cumbed, its movement is passive in contrast to the attitudes
of the sea and the self, and it can be looked on from a distance, as the exclamation "maudit" breaks its former spell;
finally (sts. 6–7) the ship is described anew in personal terms:
it offers the meeting place of past and present, sea and self,
the poet's experience and his lucidity. Although its "dead"
appearance has already been described, the last lines also
show the death of its crew, who constitute the precious yet
disparate images around which the poet's years have centered. Thus there is in the form a variation of focus that
brings us forward to a supreme climax while maintaining in
each part the idea of death like an obsession, or some terribly
intimate enemy.

We may conclude that "Sinistre" composes a time of
tumultuous decision far removed from the atmosphere of
Charmes. The self praises the self-sufficient intellect, but it
does not fail to recall memories to which a charge of
affectivity is attached and which induce by their passing the
anguish we noted throughout. In Valéry's controlled language a whole complex of abstract thought and emotion is
stated, a deeply significant pattern shaped. We are moved

by the intensity of the verbal action, the insistency of the
meter, so that the drama makes us respond to the experience
he describes in general terms in one of his essays. "Je crois,"
he writes in his "Discours sur Emile Verhaeren":

> qu'il est bien peu de poètes qui ne subissent entre la vingtième et
> la trentième année une crise essentielle où se joue le destin de
> leurs dons. Une crise, c'est-à-dire un jugement par les forces en
> présence,—une confrontation toujours tragique des ambitions, des
> pouvoirs, des idéaux, des souvenirs et des pressentiments,—en un
> mot, un combat de tous les éléments de contradiction, de tous les
> thèmes antagonistes qu'une vie déjà assez longue et assez éprouvée
> pour les avoir réunis, propose à leur âme déchirée, et dont elle
> impose le conflit à l'organisme en détresse.[36]

Yet, in saying this, we must underline once more that
"Sinistre" loses none of its power, but on the contrary grows
in significance, when we consider that it expresses, as no
other page in Valéry's work, the hidden processes of his own
"event" of 1892. I cannot help recalling a brief fragment
from one of the earliest of his notebooks in which he points
to the experience that engendered his most personal ambition: "pour avoir frôlé, une fois, bêtement, les abîmes de
l'esprit." [37] The ocean of the mind, in its frightening depths,
is precisely what we discover in Valéry's poem; and the one
way of being its master, as these few words imply, was to
adopt a stance brutally opposed to the "silliness" that had
taken him to the brink of suicide. He would give pride of
place to the intellect, exchange heterogeneous idols for the
sole cult of analysis: "Il n'est pas de labeur dont je ne me
sente capable pour prouver à moi-même que je suis cependant l'unique et je tends à créer mon empire inviolable
par tous moyens." [38] Critics have attempted, after studying
his correspondence with Fourment, Gide, and others and
making use of the *Cahiers,* to determine the various factors
of this crisis, above all his undeclared passion for Mme. de
R., and the effect on him of the works of Mallarmé and

---

36 *Œuvres*, I, 759.   37 *Cahiers*, II, 517.   38 Ibid., III, 562.

Rimbaud, poetry that made him question the nature and use
of his talents.[39] But I think I have given sufficient evidence
to show that "Sinistre" casts additional light on his moment
of decision, demonstrating by its very existence that Valéry
had not easily wiped out the traces of the past in order to
accomplish the wholly decisive break he had sought. This
we might have realized from the number of times he returned in his *Cahiers* to the "event" and tried to scrutinize
it, but his approach, it seems to me, is nowhere as charged
with personal meaning as it is in "Sinistre."

The most striking aspect of the emotional force of the
poem is undoubtedly the Christian undercurrent that is apparent in the original epigraph, in the metaphors, in certain
expressions, and, of course, in the vision of the last stanza. It
would be inappropriate to resume schematically what we
know of Valéry's religious position (on this matter, much
has still to be said); yet if he sought from 1892 to deny all
vague words and concepts, Christianity was one of the idols
of his youth he most wished to flee: "Tout infinitisme m'est
ennemi." [40] On the whole, the echoes of Christian symbolism
in his work cannot be deemed sympathetic in tone. One recalls, for example, the "colombe prédestinée" ironically
named by that master dialectician the Serpent,[41] and the

---

[39] Notably Octave Nadal in his article, "Paul Valéry et l'événement
de 1892," and in the introduction to his edition of *Paul Valéry-Gustave
Fourment: Correspondance* (Paris: Gallimard, 1957), 15 ff.

[40] Letter to Reverend Gillet, 30 January 1927, *Lettres à Quelques-uns*
(Paris: Gallimard, 1952), 163.

[41]   Arbre, grand Arbre, Ombre des Cieux,
        Irrésistible Arbre des arbres,
        Qui dans les faiblesses des marbres,
        Poursuis des sucs délicieux,
        Toi qui pousses tels labyrinthes
        Par qui les ténèbres étreintes
        S'iront perdre dans le saphir
        De l'éternelle matinée,
        Douce perte, arome ou zéphir
        Ou colombe prédestinée . . . (st. 28).

traditional imagery of the shepherd and his sheep in "Le
Cimetière marin" by which the speaker points up his own
directly opposite attitude.[42] On the other hand, reference
must assuredly be made to passages in which, as if despite
himself, Valéry mentions Christ, the least expected of them,
and the most remarkable, occurring on the last page of the
last notebook: "Le mot Amour ne s'est trouvé associé an
nom de Dieu que depuis le Christ." [43] Here again, however,
it would be hazardous to interpret such words as any reversal
of the attitude he adopted more than half a century before.

Nevertheless, he well knew that the period before he fixed
his dream of an essential self was to a certain extent inseparable from Christianity, not purely as a faith but as a
vital metaphor, an imaginative nexus. At the age of twenty,
eighteen months before the "event," he wrote to Mallarmé:
"De nos jours, l'antique foi s'est dispersée entre des savants
et des artistes. L'on croit à son art comme à un éternel
crucifié, on l'exalte, on le renie, et, dans les heures pâles et
sanglantes, l'on cherche une bonne parole, un geste lumi-
neux vers le futur, et c'est ce que j'ai osé venir vous
demander, cher Maître." [44] Christianity provides in these

42   Chienne splendide, écarte l'idolâtre!
          Quand solitaire au sourire de pâtre,
          Je pais longtemps, moutons mystérieux,
          Le blanc troupeau de mes tranquilles tombes,
          Eloignes-en les prudentes colombes,
          Les songes vains, les anges curieux! (st. 11).

43 *Cahiers*, XXIX, 911.

44 Letter to Stéphane Mallarmé, 18 April 1891, *Lettres à Quelques-
uns*, p. 47. We cannot fail to be struck in another way by the un-
answered query of the analyst in the midst of the research that is contained in the notebooks: "que si penser à tout ceci, ce fût penser à
Dieu . . ." (*Cahiers*, XI, 192). One of the most curious documents we
have on this subject, apart from "Sinistre," is the account of a pil-
grimage in which Valéry participated: ". . . Ce fin fond d'église où se
passe quelque chose de non clair. Mystère, niaiserie; rien ou miracle.
Je sens un *autre* m'envahir. On me revêt d'un frisson primitif. Il y a un
souffle sur ma chair, hérissant la séparation du froid et du chaud. Est-ce
la Grâce, l'Esprit, l'intime Etranger?" The question is finally resolved,

lines, as in other passages one might cite, a language that keeps its power of suggestion even when the tenor of the image is secular, since for the adolescent Valéry the universe possessed a center and point of attraction beyond himself. But when in 1892 his focus became internal and he wilfully denied the idols of his youth, he was led to conceive his transformation in terms of a narrative of fearsome impact and tragic choice; and if "Sinistre" provides an incisive portrayal of this self-violation, it also unbares the presence that still bound him, by the emotions it stirred if by nothing else, to a buried past.

---

however, not by a Pauline conversion, but by analysis: "Tout ce qui est affectif est obtus, pensai-je. Affectif est tout ce qui nous atteint par des voies simples, au moyen d'organes qui n'ont les finesses ni les multiples *coordonnées* des organes spéciaux des sens" (*Œuvres*, II, 670–671).

2: "Existe! Sois enfin toi-même . . ."

WE HAVE SEEN the shipwreck of heart and soul, and an initial cleavage. Yet, as laboriously as Mallarmé, Valéry remade his shattered world, determined that he would be the sport of the gods no longer since he knew the rules and henceforth could assert an ironic detachment. The works he now undertook were envisaged in a new way: he began his *Cahiers,* composed *Monsieur Teste* and the *Introduction à la méthode de Léonard de Vinci,* and conceived and wrote (although on occasion left unfinished) several poems. A few of these writings I take to be among his very finest; and, in particular, I believe that none of his better known and celebrated poems has quite the brilliance of "Air de Sémiramis." Others are more subtle or complex or suggestive of the total play of the sensibility, but they do not equal the splendid energy of this voice which unravels its song of pride and affirms the dictatorship of the mind, the dream of an all-embracing control. We follow the rhythms of a dynamic emergence from night that coincides with the realization of the self as the pivot of the world. Having responded to the call of dawn, Sémiramis becomes at the end of her monologue a center of light akin to the sun in respect of which time, people, emotions, and things are but the instruments of her will.

Originally published in the journal *Les Ecrits nouveaux* of July 1920 under the title "Sémiramis (Fragment d'un très ancien poème)," it was included the same year in the *Album*

36

de vers anciens but also in the first (1922) and second (1926) editions of *Charmes*. This very fluctuation is significant of the place it occupies astride the early and mature forms of Valéry's art. It seems natural that it should appear in a group of pieces that contains "César," "Orphée," "Naissance de Vénus," the sonnets of legendary power and enchantment and triumphant awakening: at the end of the *Album* it subsumes their themes in a major composition. On the other hand, it likewise corresponds to the initial threads of *Charmes* which treat of day's first light, architecture, creation and self-creation. In this sense it serves as an admirable example of the continuity of Valéry's work, in the same way as the actual writing bridges his productions of the 1890s and his return to poetic pursuits after 1912.

One is tempted to see it as a kind of exercise in Parnassian style. "Sémiramis" not only recalls the plastic richness of Rimbaud, but also possesses the immediacy of an "illumination" narrated in the first person singular. The affinity is perhaps closer still with regard to the musical ambitions of both poets: surely one of the most striking things about the "Bateau ivre" and Rimbaud's other great poems is the control of sound and tone which, above and beyond individual images, carries the motif; in parallel fashion Valéry seeks before all things to give us an "air," the melody of a soul, his heroine's "psalm," to which end he employs a wide range of means. Thus the name "Sémiramis" itself, used twice in the text, marks two peaks of the emotional development—in st. 9 ("Monte, ô Sémiramis . . .") where the tone reaches a summit of pride, and in st. 26, with the last exultant line of the poem. It becomes in fact a kind of key signature as it is suggested in anagrammatic manner throughout the text, "Sémiramis" being echoed in "Existe! Sois enfin toi-même . . . ," "ces gémissements de marbres et de câbles," "m'évanouisse"—a series of words and expressions that take up and relate seductive power and beauty and alien harshness to a central sonority.

The same care for musical resonance is apparent in the
frequency of exclamation marks, of which there are no less
than forty-three in the space of twenty-six stanzas. They
correspond to the predominance of independent clauses,
short rhythmic groups, and the unusual number of imperatives whereby the poem achieves great intensity of
auditory and emotional impact ("aux cimes de la voix," as
Valéry observes). Other features have a similar effect of reinforcing the phonetic substance such as the interaction of
closed and open o, which is found throughout and gives a
vitality of its own to the poem, thus:

> C'est une vaste PEAU FAUVE que mon royAUME!
> J'ai tué le lion qui PORtait cette PEAU;
> Mais enCOR le fumet du féROCE fanTOME
> FLOTTE chargé de MORT, et garde mon trouPEAU!

On other occasions it is the open o that dominates, emphasizing with especial force the phonetic and semantic
resonance of the word "or":

> . . . "Existe! . . . Sois enfin toi-même! dit l'AURORE,
> O grande âme, il est temps que tu FORmes un CORPS!
> Hâte-toi de choisir un jour digne d'éCLORE,
> Parmi tant d'autres feux, tes imMORtels tréSORS!

These, then, are some of the particular means—we shall
observe many more in our reading—whereby Valéry creates
a bold tone and formal pattern that are the counterparts of
his heroic theme.

He informs us that he chose this subject because of his
recollection of an early painting by Degas or, more ac-
curately, of an appraisal he read by the well-known critic
Louis Dimier of Degas's 1861 canvas entitled "Sémiramis
construisant une ville." The canvas, one of a series completed between 1860 and 1865 which includes "Jeunes filles
spartiates provoquant les garçons," "Alexandre et le Bucé-
phale," "La Fille de Jephté," and "Les Malheurs de la ville
d'Orléans," hangs today in the Jeu de Paume. It shows the
queen in white robe standing on a high balcony of Babylon.

Surrounded by ten of her followers, all but two of whom
are dark-clad women, she gazes to the left upon the towers
of her young city. Behind her an attendant is holding a magnificent horse, one of the first to appear in Degas's work.
Sémiramis alone, with her right forefinger pointing to
Babylon, and the horse that is the token of her power, are
not distracted but directly confront her domain.[1] The
stylized treatment has undoubted strength, even if it is
worlds away from the Degas we know best. (Valéry was to
put the change that later occurred in the painter's work in
terms that recall his own crisis of 1892: "Le problème de
Degas, c'est-à-dire le parti qu'il dut prendre à l'âge des
décisions d'un artiste, en présence des tendances du jour, des

[1] For this painting Degas did several studies and sketches of which
Valéry probably knew more than one. Paul A. Lemoisne, in his monu-
mental *Degas et son œuvre* (Paris: P. Brame et C. M. de Hauke, 1946, 4
volumes) reproduces five different versions (vol. 2, pp. 44 45), and includes an interesting note on the sketches (vol. 1, p. 43): "Pour cette
toile de Sémiramis, il existe aussi plusieurs esquisses, deux avec d'assez
sensibles variantes: fond d'arbres et d'échafaudages au lieu de la perspective du fleuve, femme montant en char derrière les suivantes (un peu
surprenante avec sa longue robe, mais dont il reste une admirable étude
de nu), groupe de voiles à gauche sur le fleuve; la suivante en noir
n'existe pas; à côté de la fillette agenouillée, un échassier, etc . . . La
troisième esquisse, au pastel, est à peu près semblable au tableau;
enfin une délicieuse toile montre un large fleuve pris de la berge de
façon à peu près semblable. Degas avait-il eu l'idée de continuer le
tableau à droite? Toujours est-il qu'il existe un beau dessin d'un aurige
féminin qui semble bien se rattacher à ce sujet. Et ce qu'il faut voir
pour bien comprendre Degas, surtout à cette époque, ce sont tous ses
magnifiques dessins préparatoires exécutés avec une science et une
conscience qu'anime déjà son besoin de vie et de réalité, ces études de
draperies dont certaines rappellent des dessins de Léonard. Le Louvre,
seul, en possède toute une série: il faut les feuilleter pour saisir sur
quelle base solide s'appuiera plus tard la fantaisie novatrice de Degas.
Nous retrouvons même dans ses carnets, à plusieurs reprises, et dans un
lavis, une première idée très différente de ce tableau. Le cortège,
Sémiramis, et ses suivantes, accompagnées de femmes dans des chars,
descend vers la droite sur les murs de Babylone, au fond, divers monu-
ments, au premier plan des ouvriers et des buissons; mais, évidemment,
l'artiste n'en aima pas l'arrangement et l'abandonna pour la vue d'en
haut plus neuve et mieux dans ses goûts déjà."

écoles et des styles rivaux, il le résolut en adoptant les
formules simplificatrices du 'réalisme'. Il abandonna 'Sémiramis' et les fabrications du genre noble pour s'attacher à
regarder ce qui se voit.") [2] We are struck by the fact that the
painting, which had so obviously been admired by Valéry,
is more muted and academic than the poem. Degas's
Sémiramis is regally gracious, but she lacks the solitary
shrillness that Valéry conveys. The poet has isolated his
figure, dramatized her stance, and, where Degas depicted
first and foremost a womanly presence, he has spelt out a
tension between feminine and masculine qualities and the
explicit sublimation of tenderness.

Apart from this transposition of one art into another—
"ut pictura poesis"—it is possible to find patent literary
parallels. Thus Jean Hytier has surmised that Valéry was
echoing one of Voltaire's plays, *Sémiramis,* published in
1748, which recounts the queen's incestuous love for her son
Arzace and her final death at his hands.[3] Voltaire's heroine,
however, is not a symbol of power but of guilty passion, and
is made to serve as a reminder of divine retribution ("Par
ce terrible exemple, apprenez tous du moins / Que les crimes
secrets ont les dieux pour témoins"). At no time do we have
the portrait of cruel authority and virile power, but rather
a conscience-stricken Racinian figure. I would rather draw
attention to another handling of the myth which Valéry
certainly knew and which may, I believe, have been much
more directly influential than Voltaire: I refer to the first
sonnet in the sequence of *Les Princesses* which Théodore de
Banville composed in 1874 in order to evoke "le souvenir de
ces femmes toujours entrevues dans la splendeur de l'écarlate
et sous les feux des escarboucles," "miroir des cieux riants,

---

2 "Degas Danse Dessin," *Œuvres,* II, 1202.
3 Jean Hytier underlines the use of the term "roi" whereby Voltaire,
before Valéry, describes Sémiramis's virility ("Formules valéryennes,"
The Romanic Review XLII, no. 3 [October 1956], 185–187; later collected in *Questions de littérature* [Geneva: Droz, 1967], 147–148).

trésor des âges." [4] The rhyme-scheme is regular, the expression full of Parnassian flourish in this short piece devoted to the mythical Assyrian queen:

> Sémiramis, qui règne et dont la gloire éclate,
> Mène après elle, ainsi que le ferait un Dieu,
> Les rois vaincus, on voit dans une mer de feu,
> Les astres resplendir sur sa robe écarlate.
>
> Attentive à la voix du fleuve qui la flatte,
> Elle écoute gémir et chanter le flot bleu,
> En traversant le pont triomphal que par jeu
> Sa main dominatrice a jeté sur l'Euphrate.
>
> Or, tandis qu'elle passe, humiliant le jour,
> Un soldat bactrien murmure, fou d'amour:
> Je voudrais la tenir entre mes bras, dussé-je,
>
> Après, être mangé tout vivant par des chiens!
> Alors Sémiramis, la colombe de neige,
> Tourne vers lui son front céleste et lui dit: Viens! [5]

Much more than the heroines of Voltaire or Crébillon or Lefranc de Pompignan or Péladan or Rossini or even Victor Hugo, who perhaps inspired in some degree both Degas and Banville ("Gloire à Sémiramis la fatale! . . . / La lumière se fit spectre dans l'Orient, / Et fut Sémiramis . . ."),[6] Banville suggests the image of grandiose dominion and violence, love and cruelty, which Valéry would develop at length in his dramatic monologue. Yet the sonnet also lacks what one might perhaps call the solar assertiveness, the fantasy of omnipotence that characterizes the later "Sémiramis," the provocative effect of the conjoined arrow and rose, "enchanteresse" and "roi," as Valéry's heroine flees to the symbolic tower of her imaginings.

---

4 Théodore de Banville, *Œuvres* (Paris: Lemerre, 1890), 216–217.
5 Ibid., 219–220.
6 "Les Jardins de Babylone," *La Légende des siècles*. This rapprochement has been made by Francis Scarfe, *The Art of Paul Valéry* (London: Heinemann, 1954), 157, and later, Charles G. Whiting, *Valéry jeune poète* (Paris: Presses Universitaires de France, 1960), 147.

Banville was then quite possibly a conscious memory,
Degas an explicit one (indeed, one of the manuscripts bears
a profile portrait in ink of the canvas as remembered by the
poet: Sémiramis is looking to the left, as in the painting; she
wears a long dress and Assyrian crown; her left arm is raised
with two fingers outstretched to designate the city; yet, unlike the queen of the painting who has her right arm by her
side, Valéry's Sémiramis holds a dagger pointed in front of
her). Nevertheless, the poem was built on these elements in
a wholly personal way, and charged with a gravity that owes
its origin to something deeper than romantic exoticism, for
it channels the desires and secret fancies of the man who also
created a Caesar of his own ("César, calme César, le pied sur
toutes choses"), and dreamt of an ideal Leonardo and a like
Stratonice—monsters all, strange Hippogryphs of his my-
thology of the intellect. Enthusiasm and pride and power
are here linked with scorn, naivety with the refusal of
naivety. Like Leonardo, Sémiramis is the mistress of the possible: she builds a city, organizes a space in the way
Eupalinos will do; yet these are merely tokens of her self-
construction, her triumph over the contingent. Consciousness and knowledge fuse in an ecstatic frenzy with the
energies of the body to form a kind of pure energy. Thus
the queen forcefully interprets the bidding she hears:
"Existe! . . . Sois enfin toi-même . . . !" Her *cogito* is a
sense of infinite competence by which man becomes the
architect of himself and the world, and is more than man:
"Ma première amour fut l'architecture," writes Valéry, "et
celle des vaisseaux comme celle des édifices terrestres (. . .).
Je ne sais pas encore exprimer au juste ce que j'aimais dans
les constructions. Il me semble que j'y trouvais confusément
l'idée de nobles actes, de machines—de mouvements sur-
humains et entrés dans le réel. Les matériaux ont été en
mouvement jusqu'à une certaine position où ils se sont
gênés. Rien ne me touche plus que la maîtrise et l'arbitraire
et jusqu'à l'abus du pouvoir, quand cette liberté s'impose à

ce qui n'est pas libre, le pénètre et se mesure avec les lois." [7]
In "Air de Sémiramis," we have a poem that expresses
Valéryan consciousness as a sublime will transforming the
inert body and demonstrating supremacy by its spoils.

There can be no doubt that the text was elaborated after
the writing of *La Jeune Parque* and alongside the pieces
which came to figure in *Charmes*, so that Valéry could well
hold it in 1922 to be an integral part of that collection.
He insisted, however, that it had in fact been conceived
long before, at the turn of the century, at the time he began
and left unfinished the original version of "Profusion du
soir." Did this first attempt result from his reading of a
review by Dimier of the Goupil album of 1898, which reproduced in facsimile Degas's pencil and pastel studies for
Sémiramis now in the Cabinet des dessins of the Louvre?
This I have been unable to ascertain, although it may
appear feasible. (I find my surmise confirmed in some degree by a hitherto unpublished letter to Mallarmé dated 24
June 1898 in which he writes: "J'ai vu aussi l'album miracu-
leux des 20 Degas qui est à faire damner tous ceux qui n'ont
pas un millier de francs tout naturel dans leurs doigts"; and
he continues: "Mais ce crayon incorruptible . . . on sent
qu'il irait partout où il voudrait; chaque nouveau regard
avance sur l'antérieur et au fond d'une danseuse,—on voit
une main extraordinaire et on est vu par un œil plein
d'autorité") In any case the initial draft, written in ink on
lined paper, gives every indication of dating from this
period. Already it bears the definitive title, to be changed
only on the occasion of the first publication; it makes a
precise reference to the article that spurred the writing;
above all, it presents in an individual way the mixture of
prose and verse, analysis and metaphor, which led directly
to the formulation of an exuberant language:[8]

---

7 *Cahiers*, VI, 917.
8 Previously unpublished.

Songé à ceci à cause
art [icle] de Dimier
s[ur] Degas et contre
ce tableau.

Air de Sémiramis

De ces ponts suspendus, de ces ponts de roses (a)
                                                   Le balcon
                        riches
Je jette de vastes regards (b). Transparence de
l'air et de ma pensée—choses qui se conviennent
les unes aux autres (c)
Ces fourmis sont à moi. Mon orgueil les dispose.
   Ce chien aboie.
                                    compte les choses
                        Ces villes sont des choses (d).

Toutes choses Ces abîmes sont peuplés comme l'Océan (e)
petites
image de la   de ces puissantes perspectives
puissance (f) Toute cette puissance, ces *perspectives* me
                        montent à la tête

Je respire de si haut, ces capiteuses altitudes et
   distances
Le volume entier de ce monde. Ivresse de la
   grandeur.
                        La vue à la *puissance* de l'idée
                                    et du vin (h)

Vision—   Je m'évanouis dans mes pensées
âme qui
fait respirer   —âme de cet empire (i)
largement   Tout mon empire est à mes narines comme une
   évaporation infiniment pénétrante, qui fait
   ouvrir les poumons comme des *ailes*
   intérieures.
Je respire mon pouvoir. . . . Ma domination
   m'élève au ciel (j).

Tous ces métiers, on entend geindre le câble
et cogner le marteau. L'eau souffre
les machines et jaillit aux *interstices*—
tuyaux bâtisse (k)
Le chant lui-même est un pas piétinant

Crescendo   Et au plus haut de ma puissance, de ma
vision, comme l'oiseau sur le cèdre
—je chante!
Je ne puis plus parler.   Aboi du chien. (l)
Montée de l'orgueil, de l'excitation, du
dépassement de soi—aux cimes de la voix. (m)
Strophes bâties—4 x 8? 4 x 7? 10 x 7? (n)
C'est l'âme de tel jour que Sémiramis (o).

Many observations suggest themselves, but I should like to
note the following points:

(a) The draft begins with a rhythmic balance, a lyrical
repetition, an expectant form: at the same time the words
express the sense of height that will characterize the whole
poem. A view is proposed from a lofty point which requires
of all things a relation of dependence.

(b) Sémiramis is embarking on a hymn of vision; but,
unlike the self of "Profusion du soir," she will not cease to
be lord and creator of all she sees, her grandeur being un-
tainted by the vagaries of twilight.

(c) The sensibility and the world are of equal lucidity, of
like rigor. This is Sémiramis's happiness; she feels herself to
be as absolute as nature: "A l'image des dieux la grande âme
est injuste / Tant elle s'appareille à la nécessité."

(d) Here we find the first phrase that will be introduced
into the final version of the poem. In st. 10 we read: "Ces
fourmis sont à moi! Ces villes sont mes choses. . . ." It is
noteworthy that Valéry falls into a twelve syllable meter
with two equal hemistiches, although he had not yet finally
decided, as we shall see below, the prosodic form he was to
adopt.

(e) This is the first sign of the sea imagery which will

occur in st. 10 ("Ose l'abîme") and elsewhere in the poem
(st. 4: "Et comme du nageur, dans le plein de la mer"; st. 15:
"une ville analogue à la mer"; st. 26: "O mouvements marins
des amants confondus").

(f) The note is significant with respect to a whole sequence
of images in the final text: thus Sémiramis will refer to "Ce
calme éloignement d'événements secrets," "le bouillonnement des actes indistincts," and speak of her "ruches."

(g) The poet underlines the self-intoxication that will prevail in his monologue: "O de quelle grandeur, elle tient sa
grandeur . . ." (st. 14).

(h) A vertigo of pride is translated in terms of the body:
it is air inhaled deeply, a heady wine. Sémiramis's glance and
her ambition are as one in the excited fervor with which she
absorbs the world.

(i) These words will be taken up in the imperative mood
in the second last line of the poem: "Que je m'évanouisse
en mes vastes pensées. . . ." The self has become center and
circumference, spirit and substance of what it sees.

(j) Here again the prose analysis leads directly to the final
version in which we find: "mon cœur soulevé d'ailes intérieures" (st. 14) and the olfactory imagery of the lines that
follow ("Poitrine, gouffre d'ombre aux narines de chair, /
Aspire cet encens . . .").

(k) The auditory images will give rise to a fine passage
that sings of the stones as they move according to the desires
of the Orphic imagination ("ces gémissements de marbres et
de câbles"). The role of water will not, however, be mentioned.

(l) The theme dissolves into the evocation of the quality
of the voice: pure lyricism takes charge as Sémiramis chants
with animal intensity; she is both bird and dog, speaking
from the depths of instinct, beyond the frontiers of reason.
The barking, here mentioned for the second time, recalls
the impassioned suffering of "La Pythie" ("ces mots écu-
mants," ". . . le désordre / D'une bouche qui veut se

mordre"), yet it is linked to the piercing sweetness of the bird—the instinctive cry often heard in Valéry of the "cruel" bird—innocent, spontaneous, irrefutable.

(m) The tone corresponds to a climax of vaulting emotion that leads from pride and excitement to transcendence of the self, Sémiramis having become one with the world of her dream as in the last quatrain of the poem.

(n) We may be surprised by the metrical patterns Valéry considered using. The first two schemes of octosyllabic or heptasyllabic quatrains seem frail, although he was later to employ the latter form to effect in the eleven stanzas of "Poésie." The third scheme is found in Hugo; Valéry turned to it first in the nineties and, later, at the time of *Charmes* for two of his finest odes, "Aurore" and "Palme." Yet the alexandrines he finally chose are much more appropriate to the mass and energy of his theme.

(o) The words sum up the generality of this figure who incarnates a moment of desire, a sensation of universal power —"la vie même en tant que désir, ou sensation d'une puissance en elle qui lui fait croire qu'elle est capable de plus de connaissance et d'actions que toute existence particulière n'en peut obtenir." [9] We note that the word *âme* occurs twice in this text, describing Sémiramis as "âme de cet empire" and "âme de tel jour," and no less than four times in the final version of the poem.

It is rare for us to possess a draft of this kind for one of Valéry's major poems. The way in which the lyrical motifs and rhythms were discovered in the course of the meditation is clear: the poet expresses a spiritual state by means of a series of concrete images that suggest the accord of body and mind, physiology (eyes, head, breath, lungs, voice) and psychology (pride, power, intoxication, domination, vision, transcendence). It is evident that with no more than a few words of the final version actually written, he already had in

---

[9] *Cahiers,* XXII, 819.

hand the matrix of his poem, the sense of this moment of intellectual fervor. No local or exotic detail is present, so that the intensity indicates a universal protagonist—male or female, ancient or modern—who gives vent to his egoism. Yet by introducing the legend of Sémiramis, the voice will bear with it as it were the proof of its own efficacy; it will also allow the energetic and paradoxical fusion of feminine qualities and virility.

Without attempting to exhaust the details of the many versions that followed, I would like to mention three important drafts in the first notebook of *Charmes*.[10] One of these shows a drawing of the queen holding her dagger raised, which I mentioned earlier. It is accompanied by the words "Psaume: Sémiramis," which indicate the ritual nature of this song of praise ("Les Psaumes," writes Valéry, "participent de l'hymne et de l'élégie, combinaison qui accomplit une alliance remarquable des sentiments collectifs lyriquement exprimés avec ceux qui procèdent du plus intime de la personne et de sa foi").[11] The title is followed by the first version of st. 13 preceded by the words "j'invoque . . ." which gives the timbre of a voice that posits a world according to its own whims:

> O repas de puissance, intelligible orgie
> O parvis vaporeux de toits et de forêts!
> Tentes des serviteurs de ma seule énergie
> Où leurs amours me font des hommes

Whereas the first two lines have all but reached their final form, the last two will be wholly changed. In the meantime, Valéry placed beneath "hommes" the syllable *rets* in his search for the rhyme with "forêts." Alongside these four lines, a bracket, with the letter "B", signifies no doubt that the quatrain, when completed, was to be incorporated into

10 I have described this unpublished notebook in general terms in *Lecture de Valéry*, 10–13.

11 "Cantiques spirituels," *Œuvres*, I, 449.

the second part of Sémiramis's invocation. Finally, beneath it, we observe an isolated line ("C'est une vaste peau fauve que mon royaume") that would later become the opening line of st. 11.

We cannot but be struck by the fact that this draft, which dates from 1917, is in fact written on the same pages as are stylistically divergent poems like "Les Pas" and "La Pythie" and "Le Rameur"; yet as far as the actual composition is concerned, the quasi-Parnassian queen is as much a product of the time of *Charmes* as they are. The same notebook contains another development that was not retained, although certain lines were, one may think, worthy of surviving:

> Ouvre à Sémiramis de gloire consumée
> Car je suis l'œil la main la (présence) puissance et le
> > [poste
> Qui me disputerait cet immense regard
> Si pur qu'il changerait le monde en holocauste
> Si clair qu'il fait dans l'ombre hésiter le Hasard . . .
> Les amants la nuit m'ont . . . assaillie et connue
> Qui n'ont jamais revu la lumière du jour.
> A peine. . . .
> Que d'une voix nouvelle arrachée à l'amour
> Je tirais du silence un tumulte d'eunuques
> Et je précipitais les mâles chez les morts
> J'accomplissais la nuit dans leurs (stupides) puissantes nuques
> D'étalons accablés par les dons de mon corps.

The first lines have a strength that might well have reinforced the proud grandiloquence of the opening, but the second half, with its brutal attitude to love, was due to find an even more striking expression in st. 22 to st. 24.

In the same 1917 notebook, a third passage is of great interest. It is couched in the abstract terms of an analytical poet considering his project, defining his means:

> Sém. Place de chaque chose dans l'ouïe
> > Ordre auditif ou espace

Espaces—aud[itif]—visuel—intellect[uel]
   dépassement de la vue par l'idée
Idéalisation de repères
Choses emboîtées
   L'ordre (comme s'il existait)
Sujet proprement poétique
   Elle ferme les yeux
   Elle se retrouve seule, femme, être
Musicalité rhétorique. N[ombre] d'images

Valéry is clearly trying to sharpen the focus of the musical qualities of his poem, to connect them with the use of visual imagery and ideas. The three "spaces"—hearing, sight, intellect—must become as it were, dovetailed, interlocked: an order is postulated in which things are both concrete and symbolic (and at the same time part of a greater harmony). The world of this monologue is a vision as elemental as a dream. In his richly metaphorical language Valéry will seek a rhetoric that aims to be the very music of Sémiramis ("Toute âme est une mélodie qu'il s'agit de renouer," Mallarmé wrote; and Valéry, on "La Pythie": "Logique de la Pythie. Chemin de l'idée. Employer le corps à *former* les idées. Ce corps instrument de musique, de netteté").[12]

Another series of jottings, written about the same time, offers an attempt to translate the language of the sun as it calls on the queen to rise from sleep. It ends with a revised version, here typewritten, of the quatrain we observed in the first notebook of *Charmes*, but now close to its definitive form:

Il te faut reconstruire un corps digne de toi
Conquis-toi d'abord
Que ton rein s'irrite et se construise un corps
      se dresse

                                    de soi
Rêve, il te faut construire un corps digne de toi

12 Paul Valéry, in the first notebook of *Charmes*, commenting on "La Pythie." (Compare *Lecture de Valéry*, 134.)

    Quitte-moi ce visage qui veut dormir encore
            que la lumière soit
    O rêves Il est temps de leur donner un corps
              vous
    Il est temps de partir, brise tes songes, sors
    Relève ce regard qui veut dormir encore
    O rêve
    Altitude demande
    Et de la capiteuse étendue enivrée
    Altitude demande une immense unité
           attend l'astre
    Altitude à l'aurore attend l'astre
          tenir
    Ose / apprendre / des morts l'art délicat de vivre
    Regard. Nous avons le silence et les pleurs.
    Repas de ma puissance, intelligible orgie,
    Quel parvis vaporeux de toits et de forêts
    Place   fatale
    Tremble aux pieds de la pure et splendide vigie
    Un champ mystérieux de vie et de secrets.
          chancelant
    Un voile remué d'événements secrets.

The second person mode of address in the first lines constitutes the first draft of the sun's familiar command, as
found in the second section of the final text, to throw off
sleep and compose the body in full awareness. The phrases,
mostly alexandrines, show the late stage of the draft, and the
dynamic form Valéry sought: "Il te faut . . . ," "Conquis-
toi . . . ," "Que ton rein . . . ," "Quitte-moi . . . ," "Il est
temps . . ." (which will be maintained: "O grande âme, il
est temps que tu formes un corps"). We also note the attempt
at a playful formula which would give the ring of a proverb
("Altitude demande . . ."), the self having become synon-
ymous with height. Another two alexandrines sound a note
of nostalgia and languorousness, a moment of regret which
did not survive this manuscript. Finally, the quatrain that
was to become st. 13 is rehandled in terms that create a sense
of mystery ("mystérieux," "secrets," "voile"), suggested more

abstractly in the final version by two four-syllable nouns
("Ce calme éloignement d'événements secrets").

Several other versions attempt to bring the poem to its
final state, including a draft with the droll subtitle, "Reine
of the Apes," which intermingles French and English in
Stendhalian manner in order to render the self-congratula-
tion of Valéry's heroine in the presence of her people. Yet,
when the poem appeared for the first time, an important
motif—the sexual one contained in st. 22, 23, and 24 of the
poem as we now know it—was still missing. The three new
stanzas were added in 1926 when the poem appeared in both
the *Album* and *Charmes,* at the same time as "Anne,"
written similarly in alexandrine quatrains with alternate
rhymes. Indeed, parts of one long development in manuscript form which served the growth of "Anne" could equally
well have been introduced into the "Air." However, the
guidelines of the structure already laid down prescribed, as
we shall see, a section of no more than three stanzas. Thus,
Valéry came to complete a poem conceived no doubt before 1900—"pendant une ère d'ivresse de ma volonté et
parmi d'étranges excès de conscience de soi" [13]—which he
took up with all the artistic refinement that typifies his
maturity. Here at last was a chance to develop, as he had
only vaguely realized at the time, the emblem of an exultant
and all-embracing ambition.

The first words voice the rebirth of mind, body, world.
Sémiramis speaks of her meeting with dawn from the view-
point of a consciousness detailing the initial movements of
thought and eye and external phenomena:

> Dès l'aube, chers Rayons, mon front songe à vous ceindre!
> A peine il se redresse, il voit d'un œil qui dort
> Sur le marbre absolu, le temps pâle se peindre,
> L'heure sur moi descendre et croître jusqu'à l'or . . . [14]

[13] "Monsieur Teste," *Œuvres,* II, 11.
[14] *Œuvres,* I, 91.

She treats the sun as her object, claims it as a legitimate tribute which enables her to delimit the clear marble of reality, the visible domain of her future deeds. The gradation of morning colors is briefly suggested—"le temps pâle," "l'heure," "l'or"—but there is no patient attention to minute changes such as we find in "Aurore." On the contrary, all things are presented urgently in these two periods, the first introduced by "Dès l'aube," the second emphasizing a similar immediacy by the use of "A peine," nervous rhythms, an insistent sound. The will encounters an external force: its upward thrust ("se redresse") is answered ("descendre"), its aspiration rewarded ("croître jusqu'à l'or").

> . . . «Existe! . . . Sois enfin toi-même! dit l'Aurore,
> O grande âme, il est temps que tu formes un corps!
> Hâte-toi de choisir un jour digne d'éclore,
> Parmi tant d'autres feux, tes immortels trésors!

The response is felt in terms of an imperative summons. Employing an intimate mode of address, four exclamation marks, repeated commands, a varied metrical pattern, this quatrain presents the figure of self-creation. It asserts an irreducible energy which, before all else, is the source of identity. Here the four rhymes are homophones and echo one of the rhymes of the first stanza like an essential accord, an echoing reveille. At the right and proper time of her choosing Sémiramis will come to wholeness after the fashion of a sculpture of which she herself is sculptor, or a fruit, a flower, a diamond ("parmi tant d'autres feux"). But her elation is founded firstly in pride: the discovery of life is at one and the same time the rejection of death ("grande âme," "tes immortels trésors"), an overweening affirmation of transcendence.

> Déjà, contre la nuit lutte l'âpre trompette!
> Une lèvre vivante attaque l'air glacé;
> L'or pur, de tour en tour, éclate et se répète,
> Rappelant tout l'espace aux splendeurs du passé!

Not yet the self, but surrounding objects are active, participating in a vital struggle. The animistic language evokes the resonant trumpet in military terms as well as those of the synesthesia of sight and sound. Three periods, four main verbs, repeat the message, mime the energy with which Sémiramis apprehends the new yet ever familiar world around her. The first word itself recalls the first word of the poem, underlining the immediate event, boldly anticipating the future; it introduces a vigorous grammatical inversion, a dominant series of plosives, the rhythmic élan produced by the frequent recurrence of mute e in the first two lines. Nevertheless, the scene is not interpreted in sensible images only, for the second half of the stanza contains a moral tone that endows the present with the ideal virtues of the past.

> Remonte aux vrais regards! Tire-toi de tes ombres
> Et comme du nageur, dans le plein de la mer,
> Le talon tout-puissant l'expulse des eaux sombres,
> Toi, frappe au fond de l'être! Interpelle ta chair,

Once again, as in st. 2, the summons is addressed to the will, but is now reinforced by the "object lesson"—*leçon de choses*—that was provided in the previous lines. The imperatives offer a forceful representation of awakening: "remonte," "tire-toi," "frappe," "interpelle." It is the conflict between height and depth, light and darkness, truth and shadow—an affirmation and a simultaneous refusal for which Valéry finds the magnificently appropriate metaphor of the swimmer returning from the bottom of the sea. The fricatives and plosives are the audible vehicle of the image of the heel, which has been isolated with a painter's, or rather cinematographer's sharp eye. Yet this small point is big with consequences, omnipotent with respect to its surroundings. Several other images of swimming occur in Valéry's work ("le jeu le plus pur," "le jeu comparable à l'amour," l'action où tout mon corps se fait tout signes et tout forces"),[15] but none

---

[15] "Inspirations méditerranéennes," *Œuvres*, I, 1090.

is more dramatic than these words that depict the act by
which the self asserts conscious control over its body.

> Traverse sans retard ses invincibles trames,
> Epuise l'infini de l'effort impuissant,
> Et débarrasse-toi d'un désordre de drames
> Qu'engendrent sur ton lit les monstres de ton sang!

Now, instead of the single simile of the ocean, the imperatives call up three separate fields of reference: a web
to be crossed, a well to be exhausted, a drama to be brought
to an end. The force of opposition is emphasized by the use
of "invincibles," "l'infini de l'effort impuissant," until in the
last two lines the struggle becomes much more concrete with
the depiction of a spectacle whose action corresponds fatally
to the secret fancies of the blood. Through lethargy and
dreams, then, an essential point of awareness will emerge
as in childbirth—which is no doubt the image latent in all
three metaphors. Moreover, the phonetic pattern reflects
this tension by the constant interplay of nasal sounds and
the sharpness of the vowel i.

> J'accours de l'Orient suffire à ton caprice!
> Et je te viens offrir mes plus purs aliments;
> Que d'espace et de vent ta flamme se nourrisse!
> Viens te joindre à l'éclat de mes pressentiments!»

Dawn's last words achieve great urgency from the opening
verb "j'accours" and the twice repeated "viens" which is
used in the first and second persons, both as description and
command. On the one hand, an offering is made—dawn has
come for Sémiramis alone, to satisfy her every whim; on the
other, we hear a final invitation addressed to her as she still
hesitates to open her soul to space, to become the flame that
will match the splendor of day. Thus will her marriage be
realized with the sun; the structure of the quatrain echoes
the balance of complementary elements, while the expression
"te joindre" underlines it. (This same verb, taken up again
at the end of the poem, will fulfil an important role within

the formal organization). All is movement towards a supreme
instant which lines 2 and 3 translate onto the plane of primitive orality by way of the images of food.

> —Je réponds! . . . Je surgis de ma profonde absence!
> Mon cœur m'arrache aux morts que frôlait mon sommeil,
> Et vers mon but, grand aigle éclatant de puissance,
> Il m'emporte! . . . Je vole au-devant du soleil!

Four sentences, an irregular rhythm, the thrice repeated
"Je" compose a sudden and unswerving response. The self
is at the center of things, in full command, wholly turned
towards its goal: it knows without any chance of error where
it must go. As the stanza works to a climax Sémiramis re-
enacts the flight of Icarus—but she will experience no fall.
The images are based on a contrast between height and
depth, which in turn embraces the notions of presence and
absence, life and death. In lines 2 and 3 the harshness of the
language admirably conveys the tension between these poles
("Mon cœur m'arrache aux morts," "grand aigle éclatant de
puissance"); but the complete resolution is stated boldly in
the first lines, then reaffirmed in the last.

> Je ne prends qu'une rose et fuis. . . . La belle flèche
> Au flanc! . . . Ma tête enfante une foule de pas. . . .
> Ils courent vers ma tour favorite, où la fraîche
> Altitude m'appelle, et je lui tends les bras!

As in the previous stanza, the syntax follows an envelope
pattern (first person, third person, first person again), which
counterpoints and gives vibrancy to the scheme of alternate
rhymes. The word "vers" is repeated also ("vers mon but,"
"vers ma tour favorite"). However, Sémiramis no longer sees
herself as another Icarus but as a mistress fleeing to the embrace of her lover, answering his call. The run-on lines,
the ellipses, the sound—the fricatives in particular—underline her expectancy; at the same time the images denote a
close attention to the body, a sensuous vision of the self in
its physiological reality, caught headlong so to speak in its

anticipation of sexual union. Sémiramis is girt with her sword, but armed above all with the self-awareness that permits her to act and to watch herself act.

> Monte, ô Sémiramis, maîtresse d'une spire
> Qui d'un cœur sans amour s'élance au seul honneur!
> Ton œil impérial a soif du grand empire
> A qui ton sceptre dur fait sentir le bonheur . . .

Now she addresses herself as if she were some divinity, calling on her magical name in the first sentence, exalting her own attributes in the second. The stanza brings to a climax the images of lofty aspiration and control, which are here expressed in the guise of passionate energy ("s'élance"), vital thirst ("soif du grand empire"). Yet the lines stand in paradoxical relationship to the previous ones for, after the images of erotic desire, they insist that Sémiramis is loveless, that her heart which burst forth like an eagle seeks honor alone, that her appetency aims to achieve harsh dominion over an empire, severity being the only happiness she admits; hence the nervous tension, the urgency of this expression of desire, and the transcendence of desire, which the sound pattern so tightly welds.

> Ose l'abîme! . . . Passe un dernier pont de roses!
> Je t'approche, péril! Orgueil plus irrité!
> Ces fourmis sont à moi! Ces villes sont mes choses,
> Ces chemins sont les traits de mon autorité!

A new section of the poem begins with these lines in which Sémiramis turns her attention from herself to the external world. Her consequent excitement is suggested by six exclamations, but also by the focal presence of danger in the first two lines. The opening sentence sets the atmosphere of mortal challenge, which the irregular caesura after the fifth syllable points up. The words are impressive (indeed, they were to move Claudel so much when he read them that he considered they should be isolated, without any perfunctory alexandrine measure to be filled out; *"Ose l'abîme:* Après

cela, il n'y a plus que le blanc qui est possible").[16] Yet
Valéry does continue—with three more exclamations of
varied syntax which develop the same notion beyond re-
straining sentiment to a further summit of pride. The language is generalized, hence typical of a peak of intimate
emotion, but resolves itself in the second half of the stanza
into a precise objectivity that expresses the disdain bred by
absolute power: Sémiramis treats men as ants, cities as things,
roads as arrows. The transition from internal grandeur has
been effected, the menace overcome, by a vanity more vast
that can dissect the world from a superhuman distance.

> C'est une vaste peau fauve que mon royaume!
> J'ai tué le lion qui portait cette peau;
> Mais encor le fumet du féroce fantôme
> Flotte chargé de mort, et garde mon troupeau!

The long closed o sound is continued from st. 10 with still
greater force. The idea of danger is also pursued, but it is
no more a threat to which Sémiramis is subjected: rather is
it the threat she herself causes to weigh fiercely on her
people. One metaphor serves as the vehicle for this surprising reversal of attitudes, which is presented with considerable complexity. If the lion's skin is the visual appearance of the empire in early daylight, it also carries suggestions of savage energy and death which are captured in
the remaining lines. Sémiramis uses the past tense for the
first time (it will recur in st. 23) for a personal confession by
which she recalls the way she attained her solitary power.
Is she thinking of the king she slew—or, instead, of her
nation's soul? In any case, narrative detail is caught up in
the same figurative language that sustains the whole
quatrain so that there is no loss of immediacy. Now the
image becomes olfactory, denoting cruel death, yet para-

16 Letter to Paul Valéry, quoted in my article "A Symbolist Dialogue," *Essays in French Literature*, no. 4 (November 1967), 88; later
included in my book *The Language of French Symbolism* (Princeton
University Press, 1969), 123.

doxically imposing protection. Thus menace and safeguard, murder and pastoral peace, are subsumed, united, by the possessiveness of Sémiramis, mistress supreme of "mon royaume" and "mon troupeau."

> Enfin, j'offre au soleil le secret de mes charmes!
> Jamais il n'a doré de seuil si gracieux!
> De ma fragilité je goûte les alarmes
> Entre le double appel de la terre et des cieux.

A further reversal of attitudes occurs, although this quatrain again revolves around the idea of danger that was introduced in sts. 10 and 11. Sémiramis sings of her self-love, the beauty she cherishes above all, and at the same time she makes sacrifice of it to the sun. Such equivocalness is the very law of her being: for if she recognizes no master but the light above, to which she yields her pride as to a true and worthy lover, the words "fragilité," "alarmes," "entre le double appel," in the second half of the stanza, underline the affection with which she clings to the world. The threat is, however, no longer from any precipitous cliff of the imagination ("abîme," "péril"); nor is it placed outside her, in the external scene ("le fumet du féroce fantôme"); it resides in her very sensibility, and she accepts it without reservations, savoring the dual appeal in whose dangers she finds her rare delight. At this point, she reaches a new summit of self-affirmation: this antipole of power, this frailty, is the self extended to the limits of its strength.

> Repas de ma puissance, intelligible orgie,
> Quel parvis vaporeux de toits et de forêts
> Place aux pieds de la pure et divine vigie,
> Ce calme éloignement d'événements secrets!

Stanza 13, which lies at the mathematical center of the poem, brings a new motif and tone. Introduced by two appositions that establish the note of incantation, a single period gives expression to the heady alliance of sensuousness and the intellect. Sémiramis thinks no more of the secret she bears within her; on the contrary, she delights in the distance that separates her from the anecdotal and purely intimate part of her being. The inversion is a daring one by which the appositions of the opening are balanced by the subject of the verb, the symmetrical last line, which reads like a chiasmus ("ce calme" is echoed by "secrets," "éloignement" by "événements") achieving here, as on two earlier occasions, an envelope structure that strains against the pattern of the rhymes. Thus Sémiramis calls on the imagery of food, nature, religion, and architecture, as well as on an abstract vocabulary, to paint a classical equilibrium, a hieratic scene in which she receives a tribute fit for spirit and body, such as the one she herself previously offered to the light of day.

> L'âme enfin sur ce faîte a trouvé ses demeures!
> O de quelle grandeur, elle tient sa grandeur
> Quand mon cœur soulevé d'ailes intérieures
> Ouvre au ciel en moi-même une autre profondeur!

The moment of delight is developed with the self now oblivious of the world, aware only of its own potential, rejoicing in this time of expansiveness. Two exclamations make up the measure, which is given remarkable force by the pattern of internal echoes: "demeures," "grandeur" (twice), "cœur," "intérieures," "profondeur"; "quelle," "elle," "ailes," "ciel"; and "trouvé," "soulevé," "ouvre." Sémiramis gives us as it were a physical sense of the soul: intoxicated by sound and words, she chooses them first and foremost to express her vaulting pride ("O de quelle grandeur, elle tient sa grandeur"). But this soul corresponds to a conscious breathing, a diastole like the flight of a soaring bird ("mon cœur soulevé d'ailes intérieures") recalling the summit ("faîte") of the first line—which finds a complementary systole, or abyss waiting to be filled. Below and above, Sémiramis discovers then an ideal space, which the first words evoke with pleasure and a static satisfaction, and which the other lines suggest by the sensation of a far-flung

freedom to be explored. We remember a not dissimilar incantation of the soul in the eighth stanza of "Le Cimetière
marin" ("O pour moi seul, à moi seul, en moi-même / . . .
J'attends l'écho de ma grandeur interne"), but there the poet
was touched with anguish at the bitter taste of emptiness,
whereas Sémiramis exults in the feeling of an infinite domain of action.

> Anxieuse d'azur, de gloire consumée,
> Poitrine, gouffre d'ombre aux narines de chair,
> Aspire cet encens d'âmes et de fumée
> Qui monte d'une ville analogue à la mer!

The same movement of expansion which we found in st.
14 now grows, but the terms have become concrete, sensuous.
A command urges the self—no longer a soul but a breast
("poitrine")—to absorb to the limit of its strength, to breathe
deeply of the sacrifice that is made to its glory. A wonderful
parallel is established between self and scene: on the one
hand, Sémiramis is a waiting ocean, a "gouffre d'ombre aux
narines de chair," while Babylon is similarly "une ville
analogue à la mer"; in like manner, she who is both
"anxieuse d'azur" and "de gloire consumée," is offered a
world that marries the concrete and the abstract—"cet
encens d'âme et de fumée"—by way of a sufficient and necessary response. Sémiramis "aspires," the incense "rises" to
her, the self and the world are caught up in a single attitude
of desire which seeks to capture sweet-smelling fame, a goal
both intangible and seductive.

> Soleil, soleil, regarde en toi rire mes ruches!
> L'intense et sans repos Babylone bruit,
> Toute rumeurs de chars, clairons, chaînes de cruches
> Et plaintes de la pierre au mortel qui construit.

Turning away from the self, Sémiramis ushers in a new
section of her song which is devoted to architecture. With
Dionysian joy she calls on the sun to watch this fruitful
activity, like that of so many hives, as the city is constructed

to her dictates. We find, however, a mixture of sense impressions, the visual image at first proposed by the word "ruches" being transformed into a sequence of auditory ones. Conveyed at first abstractly by two heavy epithets that precede the noun, the whole complex disorder suggests itself in the diverse noises of building. Valéry makes considerable use of alliteration to imitate the action (r, hard c, ch), to compose both the idea and its accompanying agitation. But two opposite yet complementary points of view are contained in these lines: building is laughter ("rire") in the light of the sun, but laughter that is born out of suffering ("plaintes de la pierre") as the architect triumphs over the resistance of matter. Like the visual and auditory images, these two emotions combine to express the vital tension of artistic creation.

> Qu'ils flattent mon désir de temples implacables,
> Les sons aigus de scie et les cris des ciseaux,
> Et ces gémissements de marbres et de câbles
> Qui peuplent l'air vivant de structure et d'oiseaux!

A similar contrast between suffering and beauty is drawn in these lines that describe the process of construction. Stridency is written into the sound pattern (hard c, s, and especially the insistent vowel i), yet for Sémiramis, this is a subject of rejoicing. She finds the answer to her need of absolute law in these buildings that allow no compromise with the adventitious; hence, the paradox of delight in that which is "implacable," of life and song and ornament emerging from cries and moans. The first line proposes an impersonal ideal, the last emphasizes birth, and multiple movement, and the plurivalent imagery of the birds of stone wrought by men's hands and their fruitful labor. In one shrill period Sémiramis can thus utter her self-centered satisfaction, her contentment to preside over the making of a stylized, essential "nature."

> Je vois mon temple neuf naître parmi les mondes,
> Et mon vœu prendre place au séjour des destins;

> Il semble de soi-même au ciel monter par ondes
> Sous le bouillonnement des actes indistincts.

The motif of construction ends with these lines that present a complex attitude. The first half continues the image of birth which was introduced in the previous stanza, although the emphasis is now placed on architectural solidity which the artist contemplates as it were from afar. But Valéry also shows the coincidence of conception and creation as the two parallel lines dependent on the verb "je vois" affirm the same event in two different ways—concretely ("mon temple neuf"), then abstractly ("mon vœu"). The work of art is a new object that imposes itself on time and space ("parmi les mondes"), yet is of a substance as absolute as an idea ("au séjour des destins"). Nevertheless, having asserted this stability, Sémiramis then transforms the scene into one of vigorous activity: instead of the assured calm of the verb "prendre place," we find "monter par ondes" and "sous le bouillonnement des actes indistincts," words that call on the imagery of movement, height, depth, of birth from water not unlike the swimmer's, of vague submarine energy that comes to fruition.

> Peuple stupide, à qui ma puissance m'enchaîne,
> Hélas! mon orgueil même a besoin de tes bras!
> Et que ferait mon cœur s'il n'aimait cette haine
> Dont l'innombrable tête est si douce à mes pas?

By her invocation to her people, which is followed by a rhetorical question addressed to the self, Sémiramis brings about another refocusing of the poem. She who was so vain acknowledges her limits, bends to the salutary rule of irony: "Hélas!" However powerful she may be, she is linked to the mob she despises; however proud, she needs their efforts. Such is the glance of lucidity she casts on her own pretensions, clearly recognizing the let and hindrance to her freedom. The second half of the stanza repeats the same notion, although in different terms: her link with men is no longer so much an ironical relationship as a paradoxical necessity:

now she walks free and unfettered, and thrives on the savage scorn she feels for the silly monster underfoot. Love and hatred are thus coexistent within her, the one feeding on the other; and the sound pattern translates the fervor of this tension by insistent assonance, serving to convey an eloquent charge of emotion ("enchaîne," "même," "ferait," "n'aimait cette haine," "tête").

> Plate, elle me murmure une musique telle
> Que le calme de l'onde en fait de sa fureur,
> Quand elle se rapaise aux pieds d'une mortelle
> Mais qu'elle se réserve un retour de terreur.

In a single period without exclamation marks or invocations, the new quatrain continues the motif of the people, as well as its association with hatred as developed in st. 20. But the emotion that was in Sémiramis is here transposed, having become a trait of the crowd. A reference already familiar to us is again introduced with the simile of the sea in its rise and fall, which is also suggested mimetically by the total rhythm of the sentence and—one might perhaps say—the buoyancy of open and mute e. Calm reigns then ("plate," "calme," "se rapaise"), yet no easy peace, for it is a fury halted, a fragile resolution.

> En vain j'entends monter contre ma face auguste
> Ce murmure de crainte et de férocité:
> A l'image des dieux la grande âme est injuste
> Tant elle s'appareille à la nécessité!

The objective description yields to a further expression of pride by which Sémiramis reasserts her identity, relates yet again all things to the self. She postulates a world hostile to her alone, whose noise is not one of fertile construction but of opposition and fear. The hatred she felt for her people (st. 19), that she then heard as part of the external scene (st. 20), is now directed towards her. But she is in a commanding position as her renewed recourse to the word "monter" shows; she can conjure away her enemies by the

words "en vain," as well as by the image of her imperial
mask ("ma face auguste"). The second half of the stanza
exorcises this danger still more cogently, the auditory image
being replaced by an abstract vocabulary: this is the universal language of destiny, a sternness with which Sémiramis
identifies herself, for she is "la grande âme" (with none of
the self-irony the phrase possesses in "Le Cimetière marin"),
"la nécessité." In this way the quatrain has a classical balance
of proposition and counter-proposition, thrust and parry, its
clarity of definition being reinforced by the dentals and
closed e, and especially evident in the rhymes "férocité" and
"nécessité" which control the pattern.

> Des douceurs de l'amour quoique parfois touchée,
> Pourtant nulle tendresse et nuls renoncements
> Ne me laissent captive et victime couchée
> Dans les puissants liens du sommeil des amants!

At a point where abstraction seemed to rule, Sémiramis
fixes her attention on love instead of fate. She begins this
new section of the poem comprising three stanzas with a personal confession that affirms both her sensibility and her self-
control. The semantic structure follows an envelope pattern
once again, the first and last lines corresponding to each
other in the same way as lines 2 and 3 (the parallel is emphasized by the balance of "nulle tendresse et nuls renoncements" and "captive et victime couchée"). The emotional
tension springs from the contrast between love and refusal
to surrender, sweetness and sobriety; but the language which
expresses it is hardly more concrete than that of st. 21. Conscious detachment holds passion at bay, the soft ou of
"douceur," "amour," "touchée," "pourtant," "couchée" giving only a trace of sensuousness.

> Baisers, baves d'amour, basses béatitudes,
> O mouvements marins des amants confondus,
> Mon cœur m'a conseillé de telles solitudes,
> Et j'ai placé si haut mes jardins suspendus

The alliteration of the first line is purposely gauche to suggest Sémiramis's disdain, in a manner not unlike that of the Serpent's apostrophe to men: "O bêtes blanches et béates." This love which she rejects is heavy, at the furthest remove from her own ideal; the angelic imagination is ill at ease in the world, and Sémiramis could say with Valéry: "L'amour consiste à être bêtes ensemble." The second line, however, is of a different ink: it possesses a beauty of sound and image that conveys sensuous delight, and could well find an appropriate place in a hymn to celebrate love; yet here it forms part of the single phonetic substance of the quatrain (reinforced by four rhymes that are closely linked), and of the semantic contrast with the last two lines, in which the sea is replaced by hanging gardens, entwined lovers by loneliness, physical detail by the counsels of the heart. The notion of height ("j'ai placé si haut") again accompanies pride, inviolable rigor.

> Que mes suprêmes fleurs n'attendent que la foudre
> Et qu'en dépit des pleurs des amants les plus beaux,
> A mes roses, la main qui touche tombe en poudre:
> Mes plus doux souvenirs bâtissent des tombeaux!

The voice continues at a high pitch, the run-on stanza bringing to a conclusion the motif of love. In keeping with this climax, Valéry has recourse to three superlatives ("suprêmes," "plus beaux," "plus doux") which correspond to the extravagant ruthlessness of Sémiramis. In the same way flowers will be answered by a thunderbolt, weeping beauty by dust, sweetness by the grave. Thus a series of images associates love with death, yet in different ways—and it is this which gives the quatrain its intensity. On the one hand, death is the desired consummation of the soul whose exigencies are absolute: Sémiramis accepts a transcendent marriage with fate like that of Mallarmé's St. John the Baptist; on the other, it is the vengeance she herself exacts from lesser mortals who have dared to approach her, for the self-conscious artist refuses to be subject to contingency. Once

more the sound is wrought with great force as words from
previous stanzas are redeployed, the sinuous presence of a
vowel exploited ("foudre," "touche," "poudre," "doux,"
"souvenirs"), additional resonance obtained by caesural
rhymes ("fleurs," "pleurs"). The last line is particularly
effective with its lapidary formulation that shows Sémiramis
again as architect even when she is most bent on destruction.

> Qu'ils sont doux à mon cœur les temples qu'il enfante
> Quand tiré lentement du songe de mes seins,
> Je vois un monument de masse triomphante
> Joindre dans mes regards l'ombre de mes desseins!

By the repetition of the epithet "doux" we are aware of a
felt continuity, but there has been a change of focus in
this first of the last two stanzas of the finale. Sémiramis resumes her delight by way of a single strong exclamation: yet
she sings of no epidermic pleasure, but of the self-content-
ment that has been from the beginning her secret goal
('L'objet de l'esprit est d'être content devant soi-même'),[17]
and which she now sees accomplished in knowledge and
power united, dream and monument. An idea has been
rendered visible by the will of the artist, materialized by dint
of lucid precision. The four lines are constructed with a view
to giving us the wonder of this new birth which recalls the
births evoked in st. 2, 5, and 18, the forward movement that
has led to the congruency of shadow and substance. The
repetition of a number of key-words ("doux," "cœur,"
"temples," "enfante," "tiré," "songe," "ombre") also serves
to concentrate the past monologue, to which the verb
"joindre," echoed from st. 6, gives triumphant direction
and sense.

> Battez, cymbales d'or, mamelles cadencées,
> Et roses palpitant sur ma pure paroi!
> Que je m'évanouisse en mes vastes pensées,
> Sage Sémiramis, enchanteresse et roi!

---

17 Valéry adds: "Cela ne dure guère" (*Mélange, Œuvres,* I, 341).

The finale comes to a stirring close, not on the note of
proud satisfaction we found in st. 25, but on two commands
addressed to the self. It is a renewed exhortation to vitality,
which echoes the sun's imperatives in the second section of
the poem but now proceeds without intermediary from
consciousness to sensibility. The first two lines contain a rich
gamut of sense impressions—auditory, visual, olfactory—
which suggest the clash and rhythm of Sémiramis. She
creates music on the instrument that is her body, recalling
the trumpet and bugles of dawn; at the same time she is
beauty pulsing with life, redolent of ideal flowers. For this
splendid imagery, the repeated open a sound and the interplay of voiced and voiceless plosives provide the phonetic
gesture of an urgent bidding. Nevertheless, the last period is
quite different in kind: the command, couched in abstract
terms, gives expression to a desirable absorption, the ambition of the ego to disappear into its thought, to be reduced
to its essence. This is the highest reach of the poem and the
ultimate moment of an existential quest that would identify
itself with intellectual power, wisdom, seductiveness. Placed
at the end of the poem, the words "enchanteresse" and "roi"
assume, then, a climactic force, positing a hermaphroditic
principle that, provocatively phrased, is the true point of
convergence of the poem's lines of force.

Fourteen years after the original publication of his poem,
Valéry took up the theme once again in a "mélodrame" in
three acts and two interludes which was presented at the
Paris Opera. It put emphasis on the exotic aspects of the
legend, which was played out on stage under the eye of the
goddess Dirceto, and included four astrologers who intoned
the names of barbarous gods. A scene of love, and Sémiramis's refusal to submit, were the nexus of the action which
ended on the heroine's metamorphosis into a dove—the
divine idea of the self that crowns her ambitions. "J'ai voulu
être si grande," she says, "que les hommes plus tard ne

pussent croire que j'aie véritablement existé. . . ." [18] In rhythmic prose that leaves considerable freedom to Arthur Honegger's score, Valéry projects his figures visually and acoustically, offering us less an independent text as such than a decisive linear movement. The libretto shows us without any possible doubt Valéry's enduring interest in the legend; yet for his most striking treatment of it, it is necessary to return to the full-throated contralto of the original poem which speaks to us with such authority and strength. Here, as I have sought to suggest, are some of the most memorable lines in all his work; here is a harsh lyricism that proceeds unwaveringly; here also is a concentrated intensity of tone. Much more brilliantly than in his play, Valéry creates the religious chant, or "psalm," of an anti-Teste, who must needs assert effective power.

We saw that the poem has many predecessors in the arts, and that it drew in particular on Degas. But if it is a tableau of precise intellectual control, it is also a notable demonstration of the theme by way of its form. The metrical pattern, the phonetic texture, the language—all are handled with admirable skill. Moreover, the total structure reveals itself to be finely accomplished, despite the fact that on first acquaintance the reader may tend to hear little more than the single note of petulant excitement. Thus, a critic has observed the "same jerkiness and inadequacy of preparation that obliged us to classify 'Narcisse parle', as we must, with the 'Air', as immature ;[19] and other readers have likewise been sensitive to an apparent imbalance in the weighting of the parts as indicated by the breaks: the first quatrain is followed by a group of six others, then by a further nineteen. Abruptness is held in check, however, by the systems of propositions and counter-propositions within each stanza which function in parallel fashion to those of "Le Cime-

18 "Sémiramis," *Œuvres*, I, 195.
19 Francis Scarfe, *The Art of Paul Valéry*, 158.

tière marin" as they enter into tension with the rest of the
poem, creating separate moments of stress and resolution of
stress. The controlled alliance of concrete and abstract vocabulary, the contrast and complementarity of images,
sounds, syntax that became evident to us, emphasize the
distance of this language from the domain of ordinary discourse. Yet the organization of the whole is clearly distinct
from that of "Le Cimetière marin," for instance; and this
form, at the other extreme from the deliberate logical and
metaphorical teasing of a set of data, goes a long way towards explaining the originality and success of "Sémiramis."

The parallel I think of is less with Valéry's other major
poetry so much as with that of Rimbaud, as I mentioned
before, or with Rimbaud's great disciple Paul Claudel who
wrote: "Mes pensées ne se suivent pas logiquement, elles se
provoquent harmonieusement." [20] We tend to place Claudel
and Valéry poles apart, but it is evident that they have much
in common, not least with regard to their sensitivity to
music. In "Sémiramis" Valéry has worked with a musical
analogy in mind, suggesting to us a crescendo by the three
main typographical divisions, but writing into these same
parts a subtle modulation. It appears to me that there are
nine sections of the poem which lead graciously from opening to close: (1) the opening statement of the theme, the
initial self-awareness of mind and body, already contains the
curve of aspiration and response (st. 1); then (2) comes the
call of the sun which heralds the future awakening, illustrates the summons with the many faces of external nature
—light, sound, space, wind—stirs the depths of being (sts.
2–6); now (3) we find a series of images of height—material
and emotional, tower and pride (sts. 7–9)—which are followed by those of diverse dangers (4): the stern confrontation of the soul with the outside world, the threat exercised

20 Paul Claudel, "Cahier VI," September 1919, *Journal*, ed. François
Varillon and Jacques Petit, 2 vols (Paris: Gallimard, Pléiade, 1968), I,
453.

by Sémiramis over her empire, but also the delicate equilibrium within Sémiramis between pride and tenderness—"De ma fragilité je goûte les alarmes" (sts. 10–12). At the beginning of the second half of the poem a feast of the intellect is presented in three stages (5): the world as burnt offering, the inner space of Sémiramis's own expansiveness ("O de quelle grandeur, elle tient sa grandeur"), the seductive perfumes of inner satisfaction and outward aspiration ("Anxieuse d'azur, de gloire consumée") (sts. 13 15); the queen exults in the art of construction (6) which she considers with respect to the sun ("Soleil, soleil, regarde en toi . . .") and to the self ("Qu'ils flattent mon désir . . ."), seeing her city both as a personal conception and act ("Je vois mon temple neuf naître . . .") and an impersonal achievement which evolves as it were independently ("Il semble de soi-même au ciel monter par ondes" (sts. 16–18); the following section presents the mass of people to which Sémiramis is of necessity bound ("à qui ma puissance m'enchaîne") in terms full of her scorn (7), but also envisages the equal scorn the mob has for her, like a mounting tide, as well as the scorn with which she herself meets this wave of hostility (sts. 19–21); the contrary emotion of love is now described (8), although passive surrender is rejected in favor of solitary pride and murderous determination (sts. 22–24); while the last two stanzas (9) provide a recapitulation of the whole poem (sts. 25–26) as the artist proclaims the self's triumph in the complementary attitudes of concrete affirmation and abstract absorption. In this way Valéry is able to underline the nondiscursive character of a monologue that proceeds by motifs, or figures, in the manner of a musical composition, the speaker exercising her control according to a strict ternary rhythm in six of the nine parts. Mistress of her language as she is of herself, Sémiramis reduces the world to an imposed pattern of song.

In the final instance, however, this poem, with its economy and elegance, is anything but impassive, for it moves us uniquely and most deeply by the personal drama it contains. It offers a tableau of intellectual ruthlessness which brings to mind Valéry's Leonardo in the full flush of his power. In conveying the idea of "universality" the poet adduces some of his most cherished images—light, architecture, music, body—and all the ambition of his twenties, together with the poetic force he achieved two decades later when writing *La Jeune Parque.* The voice translates his exhilaration, just as the linguistic texture shows the complexity of tensions that speak of a vital conflict, at the end of which the self chooses its own extinction and is consumed in the fire it creates.

To burn and be burnt, to annex all so that all may be surrendered: for Sémiramis the goal is a focal point of consciousness, her idea of the world, which would take unto itself her whole personality. And this "folly" is indeed Valéry's own. As he writes in one of the most extraordinary pages of his notebooks to which I feel compelled to turn again and again as to an essential formulation: "J'aurais voulu te vouer à former le cristal de chaque chose, ma Tête, et que tu divises le désordre que présente l'espace et que développe le temps, pour en tirer les puretés qui te fassent ton monde propre, de manière que ta lumière dans cette structure réfringente revienne et se ferme sur elle-même dans l'instant, substituant à l'espace l'ordre et au temps une éternité." [21] Likewise, in "L'Ange," which he published a few short months before his death: "Et il s'interrogeait dans l'univers de sa substance spirituelle merveilleusement pure, où toutes les idées vivaient également distantes entre elles et lui-même, et dans une telle perfection de leur harmonie et promptitude de leurs correspondances, qu'on eût dit qu'il eût pu s'évanouir, et le système, étincelant comme un diadème, de leur nécessité simultanée subsister par soi seul

---

[21] *Cahiers,* XXIV, 3.

dans sa sublime plénitude." [22] The ultimate purity dissolves life and death, its crystalline order as intrinsically necessary as a diamond.

Valéry sought such a system which, he dreamed, would be more rigorous still than the stellar space of Mallarmé, with none of the vestiges of a tragic struggle against chaos and old night that subsist in the Mallarméan chimera and garland of stars. "Air de Sémiramis" seems to me to propose a hyperbolic myth of the intellect, of the *cogito* brought to an ideal summit where the female and the male unite and where the instant of power yields to the divine, which is its own pure limit. "La plus grande gloire n'est-elle point celle des Dieux qui se sont faits inconcevables?" [23] While "Profusion du soir" and *La Jeune Parque* temper their élan with an elegiac mood and sense of measure, Sémiramis, by her very nature—and it was also a central aspect of Valéry's passion—follows only her inmost pride.

22 "L'Ange," *Œuvres*, I, 206.
23 "Sémiramis," *Œuvres*, I, 195.

3: "L'Ange frais de l'œil nu . . ."

IN THE 1942 edition of *Poésies* one of the most moving pieces is dedicated to Paul Claudel. This was clearly a consequence of the praise Claudel had given the poem when he read it for the first time in 1941: "Je ne connaissais pas le fragment de poème sur le soleil couchant que je trouve dans l'*Album de vers anciens*," he wrote to his friend. "Il est admirable." [1] Valéry responded by way of this personal tribute to his great Catholic contemporary on the publication of the revised edition of his work the following year. That he should have been peculiarly sensitive to such a comment need not surprise us, for although "Profusion du soir" is one of his more ambitious compositions, it hardly drew the attention of his readers when it was included in the second edition of the *Album de vers anciens* in 1926. But Valéry had unquestionably put into it a great part of his intellectual aspirations between his adolescence and the early 1920s. Indeed, it was to serve him as the expression of an end-limit of one aspect of his experience, which he referred to and discussed with friends like J. P. Monod and Lucienne Julien Cain in the last decade of his life. Moreover, in *Mon Faust*, written in 1940, he makes what is for us a significant allusion to the poem when his hero speaks to Lust at sunset: "mon corps ne sait pas encore, et mon

[1] Letter of 5 September 1942 (see my article "A Symbolist Dialogue," *Essays in French Literature*, Number Four, November 1967, 83).

esprit ne me dit rien. Seule, chante cette heure, la profusion du soir." [2] By inserting the title into Faust's musing he calls up associations of the setting sun with plenitude of grace which had been developed abstractly in "Profusion du soir" but which, in the case of Faust, form a prelude to the erotic.

Yet despite Valéry's apparent affection for it the poem has to this day received little notice. Two critics alone would seem to have given it the careful reading it deserves by attempting to explore its subtleties at requisite length. The first was Charles G. Whiting in an essay published in the United States in 1962, who argued that "Profusion du soir" is an early treatment of the themes of "Le Cimetière marin"; that it fails as a poem because it is excessively vague and lacks unity; and that its principal virtue must lie in the fact that it is a humble harbinger of a later triumph. " 'Profusion du soir' is hardly a masterpiece," Mr. Whiting concludes. "And yet a knowledge of this poem with its many announcements of the great poem to come adds another dimension to 'Le Cimetière marin', that of time and maturation." [3] The unfortunate thing about his hypothesis is that the main part of "Profusion du soir" was composed some years after the completion of "Le Cimetière marin." For this error Valéry himself is largely responsible: it was he who included the piece among the "vers anciens" alongside "Air de Sémiramis" and described it in a prefatory note of the 1926 edition as "un poème assez long, jadis abandonné." Now, if it is true that it was begun about 1898 and left unfinished, it was reworked and, to all intents and purposes, composed for the first time in the years subsequent to the major poetic works of his maturity. A note made by J. P. Monod after a conversation with Valéry relates the facts of the matter: "Profusion du soir—Poème (sonnet) fait au Mini-

2 *Œuvres*, II, 320.

3 " 'Profusion du soir' and 'Le Cimetière marin'," *PMLA* LXXVII, no. 1 (1962), 139.

stère de la Guerre. Repris—arrêté—repris—Puis retravaillé
APRES CHARMES soit vers 1922 pour corser l'Album de
vers anciens (dixit P. V. 9.5.36)." [4] Thus, to judge it as a first
step incompletely achieved towards "Le Cimetière marin"
is incorrect; instead, one would have to maintain that it
represents an endeavor to accomplish something in a very
different mode, to which the poet brought the wealth of
his artistic ability as it had been exercised by the writing
of *La Jeune Parque* and *Charmes*. Mr. Whiting's initial
assumption with respect to the chronology of "Profusion du
soir" mars, I believe, his analysis, so that the central criticism of vagueness which he attaches to the poem seems to be
based more on erroneous dating than on a defect he sharply
distinguishes in the text.[5]

The other article to which I should like to refer is by
Giancarlo Fasano and appeared in the fourth volume of
Saggi e ricerche di letteratura francese under the title,
" 'Profusion du soir': Genesi di alcune strutture poetiche." [6]
Here the prime interest of the critic is again historical, the
poem being in his eyes "il primo documento di un'intenzione
creativa destinata a realizzarsi soltanto assai più tardi, nella
Jeune Parque." [7] It is curious to note the parallel attitudes
of these two scholars, whose studies appeared so soon after
one another, and who chose the poem for what it promised
and left unsaid rather than for its intrinsic worth, in the
belief that it had been put aside at the beginning of Valéry's
so-called "silence." This does not, however, prevent Signor
Fasano from proposing a careful gloss in which he makes
perceptive remarks on the ideological development and relates it to comparable passages in Valéry's theoretical writ-

4 *Paul Valéry: Pré-Teste* (Catalogue edited by François Chapon,
Bibliothèque littéraire Jacques Doucet, 1966), 42.

5 Mr. Whiting's earlier book, *Valéry jeune poète*, contains a criticism
of "Profusion du soir" (pp. 119–129).

6 *Saggi e ricerche di letteratura francese*, vol. 4 (1963), 279–321.

7 Ibid., 289.

ings. One must observe that his concern is not strictly speaking with "poetic structures," as his title states, but with abstract ones, so that he constantly tends to reduce images to patterns, to analyze thought to the exclusion of the scene (thus: "il tramonto non è occasione di pensiero, ma oggetto restituito dal pensiero 'exempli gratia', termine soltanto virtuale di relazione, spazio postulato perchè le figure di una geometria che non si vuole più euclidea possano iscriversi, et che contiene perciò tutte e soltanto le proprietà necessarie perché le operazioni progettate possano compiervisi").[8] If such an approach is doubtless useful in that it shows the depth of Valéry's commitment as a thinker, it unfortunately allows scant attention to be paid to the artistic grasp, the mastery of diction and structure that are, I believe, found here in individual terms.

I shall state plainly at the outset that "Profusion du soir" does not seem to me to be an immature and ill formulated poem but that, on the contrary, it presupposes the formidable poetic skill of Valéry's most productive years; that its imagery and structure, far from being vague, show astonishing precision; in sum, that it captures a unique cycle of thought, the gradual transmutation of an attitude in a sequence of clearly enunciated steps. A similar remark might, of course, be made of *La Jeune Parque* or "Le Cimetière marin." Where "Profusion du soir" differs is in the nature of the theme and in the language and form, unidentifiable with those of any other of Valéry's poems. We have in fact a *contemplatio* in the literal sense of a solemn meditation on a sacred space, the confrontation of the eye with nature at its most bounteous, in which the self drinks deeply of transcendence. The poet gazes at the setting sun, invokes, describes, unfolds his images of desire and knowledge, identification and detachment, that are held between the corresponding notions of "nativity" in the opening son-

8 Ibid., 298.

net and "maternity" in the last line. He becomes aware of
his role as a magical composer of language, although at last
things must fall apart, and death prepares to engulf him.
But it is then that the poem ends with the sacrifice of the
self, this gift which reproduces and renews the grace that
has been at the origin of song. The whole process of contemplation is thus worked out from beginning to end—not
in the loose way in which the genre was interpreted by
Lamartine and Hugo ("Les mémoires d'une âme . . ."
"toutes les impressions, tous les souvenirs, toutes les réalités,
tous les fantômes vagues, riants ou funèbres que peut con-
tenir une conscience, revenus et rappelés rayon à rayon,
soupir à soupir, dans la même nuée sombre"),[9] but as the
construction of a mind tracing out the rhythms of light and
darkness, sunset and stars, the eternal return of birth and
death.

For this pattern and its religious dimensions, Valéry found
an image that seems to me to designate with marvelous
brevity the presiding notion: "L'Ange frais de l'œil
nu. . . ." Such is the glance of contemplation brought to a
degree of intensity worthy of its subject, which gathers much
of its power from Christian suggestions. Yet we may also
observe that the word "Ange" is found in the poet's *Cahiers*
in a special sense, as a self wholly divorced from the contingent; thus, in the twelfth notebook one comes upon the
following lines: "J'appelle Ange un point de vue des points
de vue. Il possède, cet observateur, une science que nous
n'avons pas et dont nous pouvons nous douter." [10] As in
the notebooks, so in the poem, the Angel signifies an ideal
capacity to marry sensation and intellect, sight and insight.
The two epithets "frais" and "nu" translate the sensuous
precision with which Valéry envisages it: a freshness that
can gauge the force of the sun, a nudity that has the rigor

9 Victor Hugo: "Préface," *Les Contemplations* (Paris: Garnier, 1962),
1.
   10 *Cahiers*, XII, 888.

of a sword. For the glance is not passive but active, penetrating all things, going to the heart of opaque reality. I
know of no better comment to place alongside "Profusion"
than a few lines from the fourth notebook that describe
the fervor of Valéry's own will to perceive. They move us
so much the more for being written in retrospect, with the
regret implicit in the poet's use of the imperfect tense: "Te
rappelles-tu le temps où tu étais ange? Ange sans Christ, je
me souviens. C'était une affaire de regard et de volonté,
l'idée de tout traverser avec mes yeux. Je n'aimais que le
feu. Je croyais que rien à la fin ne résisterait à mon regard
et désir de regard—ou plutôt je croyais que quelqu'un
pourrait être ainsi et que moi j'avais l'idée nette et absolue
de celui-là." [11] The vaulting ambition of transcendence,
purity of method, passionate commitment—these qualities
are resumed in Valéry's brief phrase, just as they characterize the language of his poem.

In this respect we could not be further from the atmosphere of *La Jeune Parque* and *Charmes,* or, for that matter,
the other poems of the *Album de vers anciens.* The goal is
to compose a visionary poem, austere, general in its elements, which rejects at every moment the temptation to
yield to description, or narrative, or precise myth. The
reader is refused the pleasure of that form of self-implica-
tion and self-definition pursued by the Parque, or the per-
sona of "Le Cimetière marin." On the contrary, "Profusion" sustains a constant elevation of language, obliges
the reader to think and feel within these general terms,
compels him to recreate intellectual and sensible processes
by the powers of the imagination. In fact, I take it to be
perhaps the most uncompromising of Valéry's poetic works,
which shows him breaking new ground after the composition of his other great pieces. That he did not continue in
this path is our loss, but he clearly recognized the singu-

11 *Ibid.,* IV, 705.

larity of what he had accomplished as one may deduce from
a statement he made to Lucienne Julien Cain concerning
"Profusion": "De cette œuvre, Valéry a dit qu'elle était
'entièrement symboliste', entendant par là, suivant une des
rares définitions qu'il ait données de ce mot, que, plutôt
que d'imposer en elle un 'état d'âme', elle incitait le lecteur
à 'créer' le sien, quel qu'il fût." [12] I take it that his poem
does indeed correspond to these principles and that, in so
doing, it finds its model much more in Rimbaud than Mallarmé—the Rimbaud I think of being the controlled rhet-
orician of the *Illuminations* who places himself in front
of and above us, inventing the language of his dream. In
like manner Valéry's semantic field is both general and restricted in scope: sky, sun and sea, fire, night, the gods;
certain parts of the body ("œil," "bouche," "cœur," "peau,"
"bras," "doigt," "sein," "rein"); and the acts that translate
the structure of a contemplative self as it rediscovers basic
attitudes and emotions: evoking, worshipping, drinking,
playing, building, scorning, fearing, giving. It is by this
simple pattern that a vision as vital as sensation itself is
created.

Nevertheless, as I have observed, there is no attempt to
construct a fabulous continuity. Within the limits of his
small vocabulary Valéry handles words like a musician, ring-
ing changes by his use of repetitions that suggest modulations of the same substance. Thus "ange" is both the crystalline purity of the glance ("L'Ange frais de l'œil nu . . .")
and the sunset ("Un ange nage"); "ivre" describes the self
("ivre des feux d'un triomphe passif") and the flag flapping
in the evening air ("Ivre de brise un sylphe aux couleurs de
drapeau"); "nuit" conjures up night's coming ("La nuit
presse!") but also death ("Grands yeux qui redoutez la véritable nuit!"). Yet these are isolated examples; the poem is
in reality made up of a whole network of such echoes: "or"
is found four times, and the allied "doré" twice; "œil" four

12 *Trois Essais sur Paul Valéry* (Paris: Gallimard, 1958), 36.

times, "yeux" once, "regard" three times, "voir" twice,
"voici" twice; "soir" four times; "cieux" three times;
"espace" three times; "rose" three times; "boire" three
times; "charme" twice,"charmait" once; while a very considerable number of other nouns occur twice ("adieu," "air,"
"bras," "désir," "femme," "feux," "horizon," "joie," "ombre," "port," "sein," "soleil," "sommeil," "vapeur," "vin") as
well as a series of key adjectives: "abandonné" (and "abandonne"), "adorable" (and "adore"), "ardent," "beau," "brûlant" (and "brûle"), "grand" (and "grandeur"), "haut" (and
"hauteur"), "lointain" (and "loin"), "lourd" and "pesant,"
"mystérieux" (and "mystère"), "puissant" ("puissance,"
"puissamment"), "pur." Such repetitions musicalize the
poem, compose a scheme of sound and sense which serves to
distance it from the domain of referential language. However, they take on peculiar efficacy in "Profusion" because
of the syntax Valéry adopted and consistently maintained
which resembles the grammatical framework of no other of
his poems. This may at first appear rather bizarre, but it
shows the mark of a creative will that must seek the appropriate language for each type of experience. ("And every
attempt is a wholly new start, / And a different kind of failure," Valéry might have written with Eliot.)[13] The features
are patently clear: firstly, although one does hear on two
occasions the tones of reasoned discourse ("Mon œil, quoiqu'il s'attache au sort souple des ondes . . ." "Pourtant je
place aux cieux les ébats d'un esprit . . ."), the language
is above all exclamatory, and this despite the use of abstract
terms (thus, "Regard!", "O Conseil!", "Station solennelle!",
"O sagesse . . . !"). Secondly, Valéry employs the repetition
of parallel constructions so as to dramatize attitudes, to express with concentrated intensity the development of a mind
in time and space (thus, "Là, m'appelle la mer! . . . Là, se
penche l'illustre / Vénus Vertigineuse . . . ," "Car voici le
signal, voici l'or des adieux," "Adieu, Adieu!", "Hâtez-vous,

13 *Four Quartets* (Faber and Faber, 1944), 21.

hâtez-vous!", "Fermez-vous! Fermez-vous!"; or the preposition "dans" in the sonnet; or the refrain in the second last
section). Thirdly, we note the frequent recourse to apposition in a way that is unique in Valéry's work; thus, in the
opening section:

> Haute nativité d'étoile élucidée,
> Un diamant . . .

again

> . . . un délice tranquille,
> Horizon des sommeils, stupeur des cœurs pieux,
> Persuasive approche, insidieux reptile,
> Et rose que respire un mortel immobile . . .

again, with similar force:

> Lourds frontons du sommeil toujours inachevés,
> Rideaux bizarrement d'un rubis relevés,
> Pour le mauvais regard d'une sombre planète,
> Les temps sont accomplis . . .

finally:

> Fermez-vous! Fermez-vous! Fenêtres offensées!
> Grands yeux qui redoutez la véritable nuit!

This syntactical device corresponds to the other traits we
have observed: the poet conveys a sense of fullness, exults
in the substance he perceives with the eye of his imagination. He also shows with admirable brevity the different
levels on which the scene is interpreted—natural and intellectual, objective and subjective, mythical and particular—
linking disparate levels of vision. An additional technique,
closely allied to the others, is that of cumulative coordina-
tion as encountered throughout the poem. It achieves a
transition between elements that would ordinarily be isolated; thus:

> Les temps sont accomplis, les désirs se sont tus,
> Et dans la bouche d'or, bâillements combattus,
> S'écartèlent les mots que charmait le poète . . .

again:

> Hâtez-vous, hâtez-vous! . . . La nuit presse! . . . Tantale
> Va périr! Et la joie éphémère des cieux!

again:

> Et toi, de ces hauteurs d'astres ensemencées . . .

The poet brings about a constant refocusing of images as one detail elliptically succeeds the next, bridges the hiatus, points up the abundance of images that the mind describes at each moment of thought.

Yet grammar and vocabulary cannot be divorced from the prosodic form which serves them. The lines are regular alexandrines, but Valéry handles them with consummate suppleness, composing his poem of twelve sections with individual rhyme schemes of their own. Of the full range of rhymes, only one is found in more than one part: I refer to the combination "pieux-cieux" in the second section, which is echoed in sections 3, 10, and 12, and thereby becomes a unifying factor within the sound pattern. The parts vary in length from the smallest of four lines to the longest of eighteen, though in all but two cases the schemes are based on either two or three rhymes. This is most strikingly so in the sonnet which employs three rhymes only (abab-abab-ccb bcb) and the third section ("Sur tes ardents autels . . .") comprising nine lines, likewise built on three rhymes (fe-ffggh-gh). But on two occasions, diversity wins out, so that the twelve lines of the seventh section contain five rhymes, while the last eighteen lines have no less than eight. Statistics of this sort are hardly revealing in themselves, but they indicate the care for rhythmic and tonal change that is written into "Profusion," commanding at times the appearance of a preeminently melodic moment of balanced expectancy, at others calling on our sense of fatal progression as time asserts its sway. I shall return later to the plan as a whole to examine the way the parts, despite their formal divergences, constitute a kind of structural necessity as they

enter into relationship with the initial sonnet. For the moment I shall merely underline the art with which the sound
pattern has been organized, and suggest that its composition, as the drafts reveal, was one of Valéry's prime concerns
in making the poem as we know it.

It is no doubt futile to seek the precise point of origin of
"Profusion." Valéry told Lucienne Julien Cain that it was
inspired by a Mediterranean sky, and perhaps a particular
one that he remembered from Sète, or Montpellier, or
Genoa.[14] I should like to mention another possibility that
seems to be plausible: in a notebook of 1898 I find a passage
dated "Nuit du 10 oct. 98" which describes at some length
the setting sun (here not specifically a Mediterranean one,
I think, for Valéry did not go south that month): "Et maintenant, tu pars. Déjà voici la fonte de la ville entière qui se
défait dans l'eau et voici travailler (s'émouvoir) et rouler les
unes sur les autres les grandes images colorées de la terre
(la fumée des champs, des plaines emportées), les contours
des terres, et des sables, les morceaux verdâtres, voici enfin
sur le dernier fil de la mer pendre la dernière montagne
comme une grosse goutte bleuissante et qui tombe dans une
vague dressée." [15] There is here, in little, the same care to
depict time's construction and demolition, its greatness and
decline, its color and mass, that will characterize the poem;
and if some skyscapes of a similar nature are to be found
elsewhere in Valéry's writings, none seems so manifestly
to recall the movement and imagery of "Profusion du soir."
Nor can we fail to compare the date of the passage with the
like date Valéry gave Monod for the poem's genesis.

Another possible source, this time undated but no doubt
from the middle or late 1890s, consists of an interesting set
of manuscripts contained in the Valeryanum of the Biblio-

14 *Trois Essais sur Paul Valéry*, 36: "Au départ, un ciel du Midi l'a
inspirée. . . ."
15 *Cahiers*, I, 505.

thèque Jacques Doucet. It relates to a prose poem beginning with the words: "L'Enfant moribond brûlant déjà à
la fenêtre . . . ," which echoes in clearly recognizable terms
"Les Fenêtres" of Mallarmé.[16] With great power it introduces the themes of sunset, fire and death, and a corresponding figuration of the writer's sensibility. Lost in beauty—
"nudité de fièvre à la fièvre du couchant"—the child would
seek to be at one with this visible yet transcendental substance, so voluptuous for the mind that invents its own
pleasures: "Plus haut que la chair—ma chair se tord et
agonise—Dans vos bras je veux me consumer. . . ." The
scene presents the imaginative projection onto the evening
sky of Mallarmé's poem of angelism, beyond the "triste
hôpital," just as in his own later "Profusion." Even more
significant for us is an accompanying page that shows him
striving to develop the motif in a verse form, to use alexandrines in stanzas of uneven length having internal unity of
sound but which, by their discontinuity, would suggest
"l'abîme de silence." This coincides in a general way with
the prosodic structure of "Profusion." One may think of it
also in connection with the pace Valéry describes: "Prélude
andante, le reste en scherzo." Yet certain other notations
point still more surely to the poem as we know it. The central expression of Valéry's aim may be said to be summed
up in the phrase at the bottom of the sheet: "Appétition
des sens supérieurs," which is further explained by the sensuousness and spirituality ("sensualité exaspérée spiritual-
ité latente et reine") that come together in a "spasme."
Hence the need for a special vocabulary ("mots abstraits et
abstraction élémentaire"), for words that suggest the essential mystery ("Notation de l'innommable: éclair, or, azur
etc. . . ."); hence no doubt three capital points of reference:
Siegfried, Pascal, Poe's *Eureka.* Valéry is thus dreaming of
an ecstasy, a mystical communion, the reduction of all things

---

[16] Reproduced in *Paul Valéry: Pré-Teste,* 19.

to their essence. In the margin he underlines the word
"BRULER" and gives what he takes to be the controlling
thought of his variation: "Idée mère—mirage dans la mort,
de l'union pure." Now, clearly, neither the prose-poem nor
this poem-to-be was brought to fulfilment, but I would submit that the drafts stand as a stage on the path that led to
"Profusion." The comments were indeed to bear fruit, although the notion of a description followed by a monologue ("Faut-il qu'il parle? Oui"), on the same lines as "Les
Fenêtres," was rejected in favor of a simple monologue in
which the exalted state of the speaker and his changing
moods would be created rather than affirmed.

Yet there is one of Valéry's literary works that precedes
both these texts—that precedes even the "crisis of Genoa"
—and seems to me, more than either, the true spiritual
ancestor of the poem. I am thinking of "Purs drames,"
which appeared in the review *Les Entretiens politiques et
littéraires* of March 1892, when Valéry had not yet left
Montpellier.[17] In many respects it occupies a place apart
from the rest of his writing; if it has never stirred his critics,
he nevertheless thought of it as marking a significant step
in his own growth and noted its role carefully in one of the
chronological tables of his intellectual life that he consigned
to his *Cahiers*. For these pure dramas are those of the poet's
creative glance which distinguishes—by means of "la lueur
lustrale d'un œil pur"—the Platonic design: "Ancienne
vanité que de ranimer le spectacle angélique et maintenant
maudit où ces nudités se jouaient de *vivre*." The natural
scene becomes Edenic, ideal if tenuous, brilliant with the
force of the eye's "vertu d'enfance"; it is the locus of the
transformations which he achieves, not as an external observer but an "Angel" in the midst of his essential images.
The last paragraph provides the illustration of a gratuitous

---

[17] The text is included in *Paul Valéry: Œuvres*, I, 1597–1598.

geometry of the emotions that recalls the sunset of "Profusion":

Aime donc le Drame pur d'une ligne ou l'espace de couleur céleste ou vitale. Elle n'existe qu'en mouvement beau. Elle est la plus sûre de toutes les choses, l'ornement de toutes les vies. Devine! Elle éternise les siècles du sourire, elle se penche ensuite avec mélancolie, se noue, se concentre en spire—ou songe; file, et se laisse enfuir dans la joie d'une direction supérieure, se recourbe, habitude ou souvenir, puis rencontre au delà de tous les astres, une Autre que d'inconnus destins distraient vers le même Occident, et ne terminera plus de fleurir, de disparaître dans la merveille du feu,—éprise, diverse, monotone,—mince et noire.

Similarly, the poem will place in the sky "les ébats d'un esprit," using objects to depict an abstract meaning, producing a theater of the mind. In this sense "Purs drames," however far it is from the skyscape of 1898 described in the *Cahiers*, or the projected poem on mental appetency of a like date, or, still more, the completed "Profusion," directly adumbrates the will to see, and to see according to what one conceives ("abstraction motrice, bien plus que philosophique"),[18] which he later developed with such opulence.

These links are no doubt real, if necessarily in some degree speculative: we are on surer ground when it comes to the actual process of composition. For this we can go back to a single sheet of paper with the letterhead of the War Ministry and the incomplete date "189 . . ." (Valéry entered the service of the Ministry in May 1897) which bears the original draft on one side, while the development on the verso leads directly to the first lines of the poem as we know them. The initial jottings have a balladlike rhythm closer to that of "Heure," Valéry's short divertimento on the

---

[18] *Correspondance André Gide-Paul Valéry,* 489: " 'Le Cimetière marin' serait donc le type de ma 'poésie' vraie et surtout les parties plus abstraites de ce poème. C'est une espèce de 'lyrisme' (*mi capisco*) net et abstrait mais d'une abstraction motrice, bien plus que philosophique."

theme of the setting sun which is contemporaneous with the poems of *Charmes,* than to "Profusion du soir."

<pre>
               glace
          Péris, flamme charmante, ombre de favorite
Aile   Flamme qui me cachais la page non écrite
Ame   Toi qui danses nue entre mes yeux et moi
          Tout ce qui danse nu
          et qui sembles attendre
                    inattendue
          L'idée se roule, se carbonise, se consume.[19]
</pre>

The poet invokes the loved form that is near death, consents to the fate to which it is subjected. Across the soft lilt of a farewell, the sensuous image grows, becomes a naked dance, a silent expectancy in the alien world. The mind is absorbed by what it sees, held by the mistress before whom it has fallen silent ("la page non écrite"). Yet she is not some external object, but intimately present ("entre mes yeux et moi"), as close as the senses and the self. Although the tender tone reminds us of "Heure," we already find the first signs of the ambiguity at the heart of the later "Profusion," the coincidence of natural scene and inner drama. This bond between the sensuous and the abstract is most tellingly portrayed in the last line in which the idea becomes a self-consuming substance in the likeness of a flame. Thus Valéry had found the true beginnings of his poem; and although accent and rhythm were to change completely, he held the key, I take it, to the strange dual language of "Profusion."

On the verso of the same sheet, apparently written at the same time, the images and diction slowly take shape before giving rise to a striking improvisation.

<pre>
Péris, flamme charmante ombre de favorite
Rideau flottant sur la ténèbre
Adieu. Toi qui cachais la nuit
          qui me cachais la page non écrite
</pre>

[19] Previously unpublished.

                    toi qui dansais entre mes yeux et moi
                          mourant dans la hauteur
                                aigle
        Regard, je bois le jour et l'ombre et je caresse
        L'horizon ou l'oiseau qui varie à l'extrême
        Hauteur
        Le palais fabuleux de l'extrême hauteur
        Douce lumière, air tendre, brise habile.
        Ω terre brume air tendre herbe où la brise habile
        Et si le doux travail d'une étoile germant
                                naissant
        Perce ton front de fleur d'un premier diamant
              la pulpe d'or
            grotte intérieure   idée
                                              toi
        Appelle-toi—appelle au fond de l'ombre, moi
              moi
        Nue—pour d'un cœur pur battant avec émoi
                        chair   et toute la nuit seule
        Heurte toute la nuit et (interrompue)
        . . . pour que ton cœur battant avec émoi
        Pur heurte la nuit jusqu'à mon cœur tranquille
        Les cheveux assoupis sur ta face candide.[20]

The opening lines, a reprise of the others, show the technique of multiple images that compose a series of levels of
meaning—flame, shadow, curtain, ardor, dance, death—although the phrasing is far from definitive and will not be
taken up in later drafts. However, the passage that follows
already contains unmistakable traits of the language and
tone of the first quatrain of "Profusion." It begins with the
unusual construction "Regard, je . . ." as if the self, limited
to a glance, knew and felt nothing but what the eye told it.
Similarly to be retained and developed is the duality of "je
bois" and "je caresse" as well as the image of the bird
("aigle," "oiseau"), here explicit, later to be veiled. We are
struck also by the original reading of line 4, not as "le grain
mystérieux . . . ," but "le palais fabuleux . . . ," which

20 Previously unpublished.

combines the notion of thought's temple with the mythical language that expresses it. In the next two lines Valéry returns to the simple description of sunlight and breeze, gentle and supple movement, before evoking the appearance of a star, both diamond and idea; it is a dramatic event in the arena of thought, in the way the next words, by the equivalence of "grotte intérieure" and "idée," expressly designate; it will give rise to the admirable second tercet of the sonnet where the same images recur ("Haute nativité d'étoile élucidée / Un diamant . . ."). The version ends, with a discontinuity characteristic of the draft, on an urgent summons to the sky to effect the imagined encounter between two hearts—the poet's calm one and the pulsing emotion he reads in the sunset. He is ready to welcome the closest contact possible with the object that fills his glance, to note, to accept, to be moved by its light, to detail its features with the same loving care as he would those of a mistress. It is evident that the natural phenomenon has already assumed something of the immediacy of a mystical vision.

Yet if this is Valéry's theme, no question ever arises, as we study the two sets of drafts that have reached us, of an easy discovery of form and language, of the impulsive capture of an illumination. They include a very considerable number of separate versions and a host of individual variants which are ample proof of the exceptional amount of work that was devoted to the composition. One might, of course, observe that the same is true of "Le Cimetière marin," or "La Pythie," or "Ebauche d'un serpent." What distinguishes the writing of "Profusion du soir," however, is, firstly, the length of time it took to complete—some quarter of a century, during which Valéry evolved greatly as a poet —and secondly, the striking changes in prosody and structure that were to be essayed before the adoption of the final version. It may well be that we lack some of the intermediate steps, but the extant manuscripts provide their own eloquent record of the act of creation.

An incidental, yet perhaps insuperable, difficulty is to ascertain the approximate date of writing. With respect to the two drafts already examined this is reasonably easy because of the letterhead and Valéry's own statement concerning the poem's origin. But the great number of other versions bear no such distinguishing marks. One detail is nevertheless significant: right from the first draft we shall now examine, almost all are typewritten, no doubt on the old "Oliver" that served for copying *La Jeune Parque* and some of the correspondence from 1908 onwards. Furthermore, a quatrain of "Pour votre Hêtre 'Suprême'" is sketched out on the verso of a manuscript: "Tu l'as automne consumé / Dans un ciel froidement suave / Ce grand bois (mélèze) (platane) toujours allumé (accoutumé) / De qui mon regard fut esclave." [21] Such features allow us to pinpoint at least some of the writing as having quite probably been done in 1917, between July, when the composition of Valéry's short elegy was begun at Cuverville, and November of that year. Thus, I would conclude that "Profusion du soir" seems to have been taken up during the time of composition of *Charmes,* when much of the expression and the pattern of the whole were brought into focus, but that the full complexity of theme, form, and language was not worked out until some years later, or, as the poet himself put it, "après *Charmes.*"

I should like to refer first of all to two typed drafts that give us a conception of the formal research Valéry was to pursue with such patience in connection with the poem. Both bear the title "Ciel" and are almost identical in thought and imagery, although the second version shows the evidence of extensive revision. The really distinctive factor is the prosodic scheme, still far from the sonnet on which the final version opens. Instead, we find a sequence of three

[21] Previously unpublished. I have examined the genesis of this poem and its relation to the subsequent "Au Platane," in *Lecture de Valéry,* 42–45.

quatrains whose alternate rhymes are identical (abab-cbcb-
dbdb):

> Du soleil retenant la puissante paresse
> La lumière en ruine accable son auteur.
> Regard! Je bois le jour et l'ombre, et je caresse
> Le grain mystérieux de l'extrême hauteur.
>
> Les travaux du couchant dans la sphère vidée
> Connaissent sans oiseaux leur entière grandeur,
> Laissant dans le champ pur battre toute l'idée
> Ivre d'ample silence et de libre pudeur.
>
> Une volute lente et longue d'une lieue
> Roulant les lourds appas de sa blanche torpeur
> Où se joue une joie, une soif d'être bleue
> Tire le noir navire épuisé de vapeur.[22]

It is noteworthy that only two of these lines (1.2 and 3) were
wholly rejected, whereas eight were incorporated without
change into the definitive version, and two (1.1 and 3) underwent slight modifications. But the text as it stands gives
no idea of the force and breadth to come. Valéry was to
transform this balladlike note that flows freely on its
rhythms and rhymes while yet maintaining one dominant
element of stability by the use of identical rhymes in each
stanza. The next, no doubt contemporaneous, version shows
a purely prosodic experiment: Valéry recopied the same
poem, keeping the same title and almost the exact wording,
but created a very different atmosphere by altering the
rhymes.

---

[22] Previously unpublished. After line 8 we note two variant lines:

> Aux merveilles du vide ils suspendent l'ardeur
>   (traînent leur splendeur)
> La merveille du vide altère sa pudeur

On the verso:

> Moi qui jette étonné l'ombre d'un personnage
> Je me sens qui me trempe au ciel transcendant
>   au bonheur transcendant
>   au sein du souverain
> Et de la nuit la pourpre et la hauteur.

Du soleil retenant la puissante paresse
Regard! Je bois le jour et l'ombre et je caresse
Le grain mystérieux de l'extrême hauteur.
La lumière en ruine accable son auteur;
Les travaux du couchant dans la sphère vidée,
Laissant dans le champ pur battre toute l'idée
Connaissent sans oiseaux leur entière grandeur.
L'ange vierge de l'œil nage dans la splendeur.
Une volute lourde et longue d'une lieue
Où se joue une joie, une soif d'être bleue
Et de perdre dans l'air le poids de sa torpeur
Traîne le noir navire épuisé de vapeur.[23]

The recomposition is of a modest kind, but its effect is wholly distinctive. The repetition of the same rhymes in alternate couplets conveys a clearly defined insistence, a formal gravity, at the expense of the previous fluidity.

Of these two versions, the poet doubtless felt that the second offered more promise since in the next version, which remained untitled, he adopted the same lines for his opening but, as he did so, added new sensuousness of imagery and tone.

Du soleil retenant la puissante paresse
Regard! Je bois le jour et l'ombre et je caresse
Le grain mystérieux de l'extrême hauteur.
La lumière en ruine écrase son auteur
Les travaux du couchant dans la sphère vidée
Laissant dans le champ pur battre toute l'idée
Connaissent sans oiseaux leur entière grandeur.
Aux merveilles du vide ils épuisent leur splendeur.
La masse d'un Olympe au silence s'exile.

23 Previously unpublished. Variants: line 2: "le jour et l'ombre (le vin céleste)"; line 4: "accable (écrase)"; line 8: "L'ange vierge (le seul ange, L'ange frais / humide), nage (vire, vogue, règne, est seul), dans la splendeur (vit de la profondeur)"; line 9: "longue (lente)"; line 10: Où se joue une joie, une soif (Roulant les charmes lourds de sa soif)"; line 11: "Et de perdre dans l'air le poids (Déliant dans l'azur) (Dénouant le sort), le poids (l'âme / l'arbre / la neige), de sa torpeur (sa neigeuse torpeur)." Isolated line: "Je bois le suc du jour mûr caressé (du jour l'essence)." On the verso: "l'éblouissante chûte (sic) et noble enchanteresse."

Elle m'accorde ici les ennuis d'un vainqueur
Une apparition des trônes de mon cœur.
Je sais. Tu rêves d'être un principe tranquille
Lentement descendu dans un homme immobile
Dont l'œil doré mûrit le soir ambitieux
Et regarde que brûle un passé précieux.
Tu adores mourir et faire l'admirable
L'image illuminer d'un moment vénérable
Une divinité s'accoude. Un ange nage.
Moi, je jette étonné l'ombre d'un personnage
La distance dorée et la belle fortune.[24]

The tone is that of a soliloquy which presents the measure
of a situation on the even pace of its rhyming couplets.
Although the emotion is of an exalted kind, the form constantly checks lyricism so that the description takes on the
plain necessity of a confrontation with fate. Valéry introduces allusions to Olympus, a divinity, an angel—the gods
who will be called on to give depth and resonance to the
poem, but here they are kept within the strict bounds prescribed by dramatic economy.

Of a wholly different nature, the next version turns to
terza rima in order to develop the same images along new
lines. The result is a striking poem in its own right:

Du soleil soutenant la puissante paresse,
L'ange frais de l'œil nu plonge dans son auteur;
Regard! Je bois le jour et l'ombre et je caresse

Le grain mystérieux de l'extrême hauteur.
Les travaux du couchant dans la sphère vidée
Comme change d'un mort la face avec lenteur

24 Previously unpublished. Variants: line 2: "le jour et l'ombre (le
fond des feux)"; line 6: "toute l'idée (la seule idée)"; line 7: below this
line these words have been inserted: "Et l'ange frais de l'œil . . .":
line 8: "épuisent (pendent)"; line 9: "au silence (impalpable)"; line 12:
below this line another has been deleted: "Un seul regard épuisé
en un songe inutile"; line 14: "le soir (un mal)"; line 15: a line has
been inserted above these words: "Sur le détail lointain d'un nuage /
moment / rien mémorable"; line 17: "moment (songe)," "vénérable" has
been crossed out and replaced by "mémorable"; line 19: "je (qui)"; line
20: "et la belle (entr'ouvrir . . .)."

Laissant dans le champ pur battre toute l'idée
Connaissent sans oiseaux leur entière grandeur.
Seule, doute là-haut la pointe élucidée

D'un diamant qui germe et perce la splendeur.
Une robuste neige du silence s'exile
Dont la lumière en ruine atteignait la pudeur.

Je sais: tu rêves d'être un principe tranquille
O force des sommeils et des songes pieux
Lentement descendu dans un homme immobile

Dont l'œil doré mûrit son mal ambitieux
Sur tel détail de feu son regard favorable
S'abandonne à brûler le passé précieux.

Tu adores mourir et faire l'adorable
Sombre soleil qui sais au théâtre pensif
Bâtir d'une vapeur un moment mémorable.

Aux yeux démesurés allume le récif
De ces enchantements regonflei sa rancune
Et le noir spectateur d'un triomphe passif

Il voit sur une écume expirer sa fortune.[25]

---

[25] Previously unpublished. Variants: line 11: "robuste (copieuse),"
"s'exile (s'effile)"; line 14: "O force (Aliment)," "songes" is replaced by
"trônes"; line 16: "doré (perdu)," "son mal (un monstre, mythe, pacte,
rire, fruit, germe, terme)"; line 17: "tel (un)," "de feu (ardent)"; line
18: "S'abandonne (Se consume) (Et se fige)"; line 19: "Tu adores
(Adore-t-il)," "et faire (se pleure) (éternellement)"; line 20: "soleil" is replaced by "seigneur," sais (peux) (viens)"; line 23: "sa (ta); line 24:
"d'un triomphe (étrangement)"; line 25: "il voit (où dort)," "d'or" is
written above "écume." At the bottom of the draft we note a few
isolated jottings:

Agir le germe pur qui perce la splendeur
Triomphe en se mourant (tristement) du spectateur passif
Fais de . . .
De cet illuminé
La muette machine.

On the verso Valéry essays a number of rhymes: "poêle, moelle; limite,
imite, mythe, stalagmite; sel, archipel, bel, tel, autel, appel, quel, réel,
babel; éternel, solennel, mortel, universel, naturel"; and beneath:

Valéry had made accomplished use of the *terza rima* in the
early piece, "La Suave Agonie" of 1891 and, most notably,
in his beautiful "La Fileuse," similarly published for the
first time in 1891 and later to become the introductory
poem of the *Album de vers anciens.* The form, as he handled it, has not Dante's lapidary precision, but rather a delicate sinuousness. In the case of "La Fileuse," for instance,
where the tercets are—all save the last—end-stopped, a continuity prevails in the midst of resignation and surrender:

> Mais la dormeuse file une laine isolée;
> Mystérieusement l'ombre frêle se tresse
> Au fil de ses doigts longs et qui dorment, filée.
>
> Le songe se dévide avec une paresse
> Angélique, et sans cesse au doux fuseau crédule,
> La chevelure ondule au gré de la caresse. . . .[26]

On the other hand, in the draft of "Profusion," the tercets
coincide only twice with the syntactical break, so that the
reader is conscious of a pattern that weaves across the natural pauses, only hinting at the "abîme de silence" which it
rejects. One can criticize the present state of certain lines of
this version: besides, the poet himself proposed several variants; but it can hardly be denied that it has lyrical subtlety
and coherence. Yet Valéry was not satisfied and would seek
to write a poem that would be both more vast and more
complex. He went a long way towards achieving this with
the next version, which is characterized in the first place by
prosodic diversity in a way we have not yet seen in the
drafts.

The title offers an interesting detail that is worth a moment's reflexion. Valéry writes "Fantaisie du soir," which
places new emphasis on variety and richness of the imagina-

Rose calme profonde ombre sage de vasque
ô pâle retraite
ô pâle favorite aurore vagabonde
[26] *Œuvres,* I, 75.

tion, and leads on to the wide canvas that will be employed.
But we note that an alternative is also suggested: "Breuvage
du soir." At first sight this may well seem a pleasantry on
Valéry's part: the notion was, however, transposed in a later
draft entitled "Infusion du soir" and even treated in a mock-
serious vein in a letter-poem that is included in the dossier
of drafts for "Profusion": "L'ennui revêt sa distance dorée /
Le ciel est un café prodigieux ce soir mon cher / Roberto,
(tabacs) avec divin et danses / de nuages. Dieu lui-même
y. . . ." [27] It seizes on an image we have seen three times
already ("Je bois le jour . . ."), producing in this version
"ce vin bu," "flacon," "liqueur des soirs pieux," "aliment
des sommeils," conveying yet more fully the poet's appetency, the fervor with which he drinks the spiritual nourishment that is offered to him by night. In fact, the whole draft
brings this sensuous aspect tellingly into relief.

> La lumière en ruine accable son auteur.
> Du soleil soutenant la puissante paresse
> Regard! Je bois le suc céleste et je caresse
> Le grain mystérieux de l'extrême hauteur.
> Les travaux du couchant dans la sphère vidée
> Laissant dans le champ pur battre toute l'idée
> Connaissent sans oiseaux leur entière grandeur.
> Et l'ange frais de l'œil sent dans la profondeur
> Douce nativité germant élucidée
> Agir un diamant qui perce la splendeur.
> Une robuste neige du silence s'exile.
> Je sais. Tu rêves d'être un principe tranquille
> Aliment des sommeils, liqueur des soirs pieux
> Lentement descendu dans un homme immobile
> Dont l'œil doré mûrit un monstre ambitieux
> Sur un détail ardent, son mal trop favorable
> Brûle complaisamment le passé précieux.
> Il adore mourir et faire l'adorable
> Sombre seigneur qui vient au théâtre pensif
> Bâtir d'une vapeur un moment désirable.
> Et le noir spectateur d'un triomphe passif

[27] Previously unpublished.

De cet illuminé fais suspendre la rancune
Aux yeux démesurés resplendir le récif
Où doit sur l'or d'écume expirer la fortune.[28]

The lines are marked by an original handling of the rhyme scheme that demonstrates constant playfulness. Nine rhymes are found in the space of twenty-four lines, and these are placed with unusual diversity (abba / ccb / bcb / d / dede / ge / ghg / hihi) so that, instead of the controlled pattern we saw before, the poem establishes new frontiers of rhythmic ease and musicality. The same is true of the images which develop the technique of apposition more fully than before, and point to the characteristic verbal combinations of the completed poem. The most striking feature of the draft, however, is the way it shows Valéry moving towards the subtle interchange of first, second, and third person modes of address. The self is the purity of a glance ("regard," "l'ange frais de l'œil") but also what it contemplates ("un principe tranquille"); it is the distant observer ("sombre seigneur," "noir spectateur"), but also an active participant

---

[28] Previously unpublished. Alternative title: "Breuvage du soir," variant of line 1: "L'ange frais de l'œil nu plonge dans son auteur"; line 3: "le suc céleste (le fruit, l'image immense)"; line 8: "sent (sait) (devine avec pudeur)"; line 9: "Douce nativité (Nativité tacite)," "germant (à peine)"; line 11: "du silence (olympienne)," "s'exile (exile) / La charge de tonnerre et de seins copieux / Le tonnerre nourri dans ses corps copieux / nourri aux seins copieux)"; line 13: "liqueur (pression, poison, stupeur)"; line 14: "descendu (pénétré)," "un homme (le / ce monstre, corps)"; line 15: "doré (riche)," "un monstre ambitieux (un mythe délicieux)"; line 16: "un (tel)," "de feu (ardent)," "mal (art, vice)"; line 17: "complaisamment (sans le boire, au lieu de boire, loin qu'il le boive)"; line 19: "qui vient (soleil qui fais)"; line 20: "Bâtir d'une vapeur (il bâtit de vapeur)," "moment (siècle)"; line 21: "Et le noir spectateur (Noir spectateur qu'il boive)"; line 22: "suspendre la rancune à l'heure opportune) (de braise)." Beneath these typewritten lines with their many added variants we find four lines written in ink:

Ce vin bu, l'homme (l'être) bâille et brise le flacon
A une merveille du vide il garde une (avec) rancune
Mais le charme qui file une soie flotte (retient) sur le (au) balcon
Une confusion de femme et de flocon

("je bois . . . ," "je caresse"), the worshipper who at the same time is a self-conscious actor ("il adore mourir et faire l'adorable"). Thus, Valéry makes explicit some of the observer's complex sensibility as it is engaged in the act of seeing.

The final unpublished draft which I shall briefly examine is longer than any previous version, but makes up only a third of the poem as it was to appear. From the point of view of the poetic form, it marks a similarly radical step to the last draft in that the first section is conceived as an irregular sonnet based on three rhymes (little will henceforth be changed in its wording); while it also adopts the use of verse paragraphs that recall *La Jeune Parque* and "Narcisse" in everything but the variations that are rung on the rhyme schemes. Valéry had broken from the classical alexandrine with its Racinian, Hugolian, and Mallarméan heritage to forge harmonies supple yet sustained, allowing the composition of a lyrical monologue that conveys the gradations of time as it yields to emotion or arrests it, combining a hymn of praise with a song of self-awareness.

> Du soleil soutenant la puissante paresse
> Quand le jour en ruine accable son auteur
> Regard! Je bois le suc céleste et je caresse
> Le grain mystérieux de l'extrême hauteur.
> Je porte au sein brûlant ma lucide tendresse
> Et m'empare des feux de l'antique inventeur,
>
> Mais le dieu par degrés qui se désintéresse
> Dans la pourpre de l'air s'altère avec lenteur.
> Puisse dans le champ pur battre toute l'idée!
> Les travaux du couchant dans la sphère vidée
> Connaissent sans oiseau leur entière grandeur.
> L'ange frais de l'œil nu perçoit dans sa pudeur
> Haute nativité tacite élucidée
> Un diamant agir qui perce la splendeur.
>
> Je sais. Tu rêves d'être un principe tranquille
> Horizon des sommeils, stupeur des soirs pieux
> Persuasive approche, insidieux reptile,

Et rose que respire un mortel immobile
Dont l'œil doré mûrit un monstre ambitieux.
Sur un détail de feu son regard favorable
Brûle sans le connaître un passé précieux.

Tu adores mourir et feindre l'adorable,
Tu bâtis de vapeur le palais mémorable
Et l'esclave ébloui d'un triomphe passif
Habite au sombre éther la stupeur du beau récif
Aux yeux démesurés menaçant la fortune,
Tandis que dénoué du théâtre pensif
Un léger masque errant glisse la mince lune . . .

Ce vin bu, l'homme bâille, et brise le flacon!
Aux merveilles du vide, il garde une rancune,
Mais le charme du soir fume sur le balcon
Une confusion de femme et de flocon,

Telle divinité s'accoude. Un ange nage.
Moi, qui jette étonné l'ombre d'un personnage
Toutefois délié dans le plein souverain,
Je me sens qui me trempe et nu qui me dédaigne.
Tout le corps de mon choix dans mes regards se baigne,
Vivant au sein futur le souvenir marin.[29]

No longer an elegy, "Regard du soir," as this version is called, has an amplitude and deliberate calm that announce the suggestiveness of "Profusion." The blanks that divide the parts (further emphasized in the definitive version by typographical markers) are the means by which silence is evoked, pauses created, which in turn give their rhythm to

[29] Previously unpublished. Variants: line 15: "Je sais (O soir)"; line 23: "le palais (une arche) (mon palais)"; line 26: "Menaçant (menace)," line 33: "Telle divinité s'accoude (Vénus même / là-haut s'accoude au bord)," "Un ange (L'âme)"; line 35: "délie (je suis pur)," "plein (soir)"; line 36: "qui me trempe (libre aussi)," "nu (beau)." Beneath these typewritten lines we find some isolated jottings:

Il rétablit l'espace à chaque tour de rein
Tandis que le front lourd pèserait sur ma joue
Mon dauphin
Il s'épargne un destin par
Une maternité muette de pensées

the whole. (We think of Mallarmé's ideal work of art:
"Tout devient suspens, disposition fragmentaire avec alter-
nance et vis-à-vis, concourant au rythme total, lequel serait
le poème tu, aux blancs; seulement traduit, en une manière,
par chaque pendentif.") [30] It permits great flexibility of point
of view. Much had still to be done, including the solution
of the problem as to how the monologue was to be ended;
but if the first part was well near its final form, the draft
also shows an isolated line ("Une maternité muette de
pensées") which sprang from this moment of writing and
was to constitute the surprising yet natural conclusion of
the poem.

Another aspect was to be introduced which would give
legendary resonance to the act of contemplation. This is
foreshadowed in one of the numerous drafts that followed;
we read:

> Sisyphe—Danaïde—Tantale—Ixion
> Je n'enfante jamais que mon léger démon
> Salamandre[31]

The first allusions denote the poet's pathetic attempts to
overcome an insuperable reality (Sisyphe, Danaïde, Tantale), to embrace the tenuous substance he extolls (Ixion).
Of the four myths mentioned, only the third was retained:
"Hâtez-vous, hâtez-vous! . . . La nuit presse! . . . Tantale / Va périr!" which appears in the last section. The alexandrine, with its many suggestions, and the reference to the

---

[30] Stéphane Mallarmé: *Œuvres complètes,* ed. Henri Mondor et
G. Jean-Aubry (Paris: Gallimard, Pléiade, 1945), 367.

[31] Previously unpublished. Another elliptic fragment is in typewritten
form:

> Avec la bouche amère et le masque rieur
> Une mer où se fond le corps inférieur
> Crâne dans l'écume Boisson
> Ce dieu terriblement mortel quasi debout
> Vêtu de froid, d'Océan
> Mouillés, agenouillés

salamander that lives in the flame like the eye in what it beholds, were discarded. Yet the jotting makes us conscious of the search for a gamut of images that produced "la Fortune," "l'illustre Vénus Vertigineuse," "l'Olympe," "Tantale," and one direct echo of the Æneid to be incorporated in the last section, thereby emphasizing the elevation of diction, the classical tone and temper.

The title leads us to the center of the poem. It suggests on the one hand nature's plenty ("vin céleste," "grain," "épandre," "flacon," "confusion," "éternel verseau," "semant," "nuages trop pleins," "seins copieux," "fécondé"), on the other, "l'insatiable port" where the poet receives the bounty that, with his last gesture, he offers back to the gods. This sense is carried over into the subtitle "poème abandonné," whereby we are reminded not only of the long unfinished state of "Profusion" but also of the many echoes of the action of giving throughout the poem, which culminate in the poet's final oblation, carried out with devout "abandon" of utilitarian goals, of the work he has composed.

Unfolding a long period of twenty-six syllables, building up our suspense with a brilliant inversion, the first words resume the poet's pride. His contemplation ("Regard!") masterfully spans the sun whose grandeur invests his language: metaphor, capital letter, alliteration, interior rhymes.

> Du Soleil soutenant la puissante paresse
> Qui plane et s'abandonne à l'œil contemplateur,
> Regard! . . . Je bois le vin céleste, et je caresse
> Le grain mystérieux de l'extrême hauteur.[32]

The latent image is that of surrender to some cosmic game of love, of a bird that hangs on the wing before yielding to a superior force. Yet the relationship between the glance and its divinity is quickly transposed to a different level:

---

[32] *Œuvres*, I, 86. The poem was first published in 1926 in the volume *Quelques Vers anciens* and included in the second edition of *Album de vers anciens* which appeared the same year.

whereas the duality has been expressed in nonimmediate terms, with the objectivity that is implied by the exclamation and the words "l'œil contemplateur," the next lines emphasize the personal energies involved ("Je bois . . . je caresse"). The poet brings a complex commitment of the self: he savors his abstract goal like a wine, while cherishing in the seed the imagined nourishment to be. Thus, the last two lines provide sensuous particularity; they also show the divided mood of the self that is centered on the point of a glance; both given over to present excitement and already rejoicing in the future, it exhausts and at the same time creates its delight.

> Je porte au sein brûlant ma lucide tendresse,
> Je joue avec les feux de l'antique inventeur;
> Mais le dieu par degrés qui se désintéresse
> Dans la pourpre de l'air s'altère avec lenteur.

Like the first quatrain, these lines form a diptych of complementary elements. In the beginning we find the total homage of emotion and intellect, the conscious participation in love and mythical game. It is a dual response to the passionate warmth of the sun, to the age-old creativity by which it forever lights the world afresh. Yet thought, as it turns on the pivotal "mais," measures the inexorable inroads of time ("par degrés," "avec lenteur"). The god's former surrender has become indifference, his fires royal purple. In the same way the two reflexive verbs describe a self-centered transformation that is the retreat from past commitment, the ruin of a supreme instant. The answer to the tribute of senses and mind is, then, this rejection for which the accompanying sound makes a bitter austereness.

> Laissant dans le champ pur battre toute l'idée,
> Les travaux du couchant dans la sphère vidée
> Connaissent sans oiseaux leur entière grandeur.

Now a new moment is described in which the god has wholly disappeared. There is emptiness ("le champ pur,"

"la sphère vidée") which only an absolute purity can inhabit; but Valéry uses a conventional phrase to designate
the forces of movement and construction ("les travaux du
couchant"), for the sunset has no precise contour. Birdlike,
the toils enjoy an extension of their wings, a complete freedom, without need of a tangible bird for their soaring flight.
Corresponding to "l'extrême hauteur" of the first quatrain,
their "entière grandeur" is achieved by the exhaustion of
details, the negation of individual presences so that a dominant consciousness ("l'idée") and its objective fulfilment
("connaissent") can be written beyond formal limits.

> L'Ange frais de l'œil nu pressent dans sa pudeur,
> Haute nativité d'étoile élucidée,
> Un diamant agir qui berce la splendeur . . .

Similarly abstract in formulation, the last lines bring the
sonnet to its climax. The focus of description changes from
the spectacle to the interrelationship between scene and self.
The beholder's glance, however, is no longer a "regard,"
an "œil contemplateur," but "l'Ange frais de l'œil nu," its
modesty having become ideal to match the pure object of
vision. For this new coming stretches to an exalted conception that echoes Christian symbols. Born of intellectual clarity ("élucidée"), it is both star and diamond, consequence
and principle, an infant but also a mother who controls the
whole of brightness.

> O soir, tu viens épandre un délice tranquille,
> Horizon des sommeils, stupeur des cœurs pieux,
> Persuasive approche, insidieux reptile,
> Et rose que respire un mortel immobile
> Dont l'œil doré s'engage aux promesses des cieux.

The sonnet has ended, tone and mode of address change,
as the poet sings an apostrophe to the many-faced god of
evening. It comprises the same substance as the sonnet, but
developed in more tender and discursive terms. Here is his
"profusion"—grace that brings calm and delight and builds,

by way of two rhymes, to a climax of seductiveness. The appositions do not so much attract attention to themselves as to the progression they enunciate: by one abstract term after another a glissando of moments leads, from the frontiers of sleep that reduce the world to a single ambit, to unquestioning torpor; to the wiles of persuasion and subversion; and, finally, to a perfume that binds the poet, with all the urgency of his mortal self, to the future he reads in the sky. Although the language eschews concrete precision, it conveys the cumulative charm to which intellect and sensibility surrender. The bounty is presented in a sentence of five lines, the sensuous qualities of which are reinforced by the striking dicreses of "persu-asive" and "insidi-eux." (We are reminded of the like success of this technique elsewhere in Valéry, for example the words "Délici-eux linceuls, mon désordre ti-ède" which the Parque murmurs to herself.)

> Sur tes ardents autels son regard favorable
> Brûle, l'âme distraite, un passé précieux.

The transition from scene to spectator is achieved in this couplet that combines a rhyme from the next section with another from the old. The poet continues to describe himself in objective terms while maintaining the familiar second person singular to address the evening. He is both committed to the drama and wilfully abstracted from it—close to the source of delight, yet in constant surveillance of his reactions. Now, however, his relationship to the object of worship has again changed: he is no passive being who submits to time's beauty but an active glance attuned to the sacrificial ceremony of nature, which yields its treasure of past experience to consuming fire. Nor is this holocaust associated with anguish, for the soul is wholly intent on the prospect its meditation has introduced, and former preciousness is immolated without regret.

> Il adore dans l'or qui se rend adorable
> Bâtir d'une vapeur un temple mémorable,

> Suspendre au sombre éther son risque et son récif,
> Et vole, ivre des feux d'un triomphe passif,
> Sur l'abîme aux ponts d'or rejoindre la Fortune;
> —Tandis qu'aux bords lointains du Théâtre pensif,
> Sous un masque léger glisse la mince lune . . .

The active self takes full charge and flies in imagination to victory over the submissive fires of evening ("ivre des feux d'un triomphe passif"). This is the exultation of the sensibility which worships, not so much a divinity, as its own divine powers of creation. The poet is borne forward by the continuity of phrasing and sound ("adore," "or," "adorable," "mémorable," "or," "Fortune," "bords") to construct a temple that is the marvelous image of his yearning. Yet in his intoxication (still couched in language which distances the drama by use of the third person) the sense of danger and death is not lost ("risque," "récif," "abîme aux ponts d'or"); in fact it lends greater price to his quest as he becomes some Icarus who dares all to achieve all ("Et vole, ivre des feux . . ."). The name of his goal ("la Fortune") itself shows the hazards involved, but he will be identified with chance, and as it were insuperable because having become part of the spring of things. Classical concepts enrich the contemplation, which allows him at the end of this section to introduce the rising moon as no more than a masked actress in the spectacle of thought.

> . . . Ce vin bu, l'homme bâille, et brise le flacon.
> Aux merveilles du vide il garde une rancune;
> Mais le charme du soir fume sur le balcon
> Une confusion de femme et de flocon . . .

The moment of excitement is over: three words, an absolute construction, sum up the previous development that echoes the third line of the poem ("Je bois le vin céleste . . ."). Symbolically the poet breaks the spell in a gesture of boredom, resentful of further submission, rejecting the attention he lavished on emptiness. He has been the lucid master who gave himself over to clear meditation, but now he is resentful of the vain projects he nurtured. Yet the moon brings a new sensuousness by way of insistent alliteration, assonance, almost identical words at the rhyme, softly outlined images: woman, vapor, perfume, the downiness of silk or wool or snow—"ces produits infinis que peut former la sensibilité et le meilleur exemple de ce que l'on peut appeler ou méditer de ce qui s'entend par 'charme.' " [33] Instead of returning to things mundane by the poet's sudden realization that an act of the mind has been accomplished and that his joy has grown sour, he continues to explore a scene whose treasure he knows to be unexhausted.

> —O Conseil! . . . Station solennelle! . . . Balance
> D'un doigt doré pesant les motifs du silence!
> O sagesse sensible entre les dieux ardents!
> —De l'espace trop beau, préserve-moi, balustre!
> Là, m'appelle la mer! . . . Là, se penche l'illustre
> Vénus Vertigineuse avec ses bras fondants!

The new moment is one of expansiveness as mind and senses delicately weigh the depths of silence. (We know that the derivation of "penser" from "peser" gave Valéry a suggestive metaphor to which he often referred, as here in line 2.) The exultant mood is presented by way of a graded series of exclamations which detail the wisdom the poet savors; but his words, as well as the run on line and halting rhythm, insinuate the threatened nature of his pause. In the second half of the passage the drama comes to a peak in the urgent imperative, the insistent repetition of "Là . . . !", above all in the wonderful last line with its huge voluptuousness. The poet strains at the bannister of time, expresses the tension between wisdom and the love to which he is imperiously drawn across space and sea. With admirable cogency the expression "Vénus Vertigineuse," acting as a counterpoise to the excited acceptance of the first three lines, conveys the mythical chasm of desire.

[33] *Cahiers,* XXIV, 346.

> Mon œil, quoiqu'il s'attache au sort souple des ondes,
> Et boive comme en songe à l'éternel verseau,
> Garde une chambre fixe et capable des mondes;
> Et ma cupidité des surprises profondes
> Voit à peine au travers du transparent berceau
> Cette femme d'écume et d'algue et d'or que roule
> Sur le sable et le sel la meule de la houle.

Now the tone is wholly different as the poet once more distances his drama. He retreats from vertigo into poised self-awareness in order to affirm a balanced duality. The eye of contemplation is a double instrument that can drink deep of the waters of inspiration while yet maintaining its own control; and this same interrelationship between dreaming and alertness, absorption and detachment, comes into play in the presence of Venus who, for all her rich attributes of sand, salt and foam (evoked for us in a brilliant chiasmus), cannot conceal her origins that are forever new. Thus we have the rediscovery of the ambivalence of mother and infant, the tender encounter of beginning and end, that already appeared in the last tercet of the sonnet.

> Pourtant je place aux cieux les ébats d'un esprit;
> Je vois dans leurs vapeurs des terres inconnues,
> Des déesses de fleurs feindre d'être des nues,
> Des puissances d'orage errer à demi nues,
> Et sur les roches d'air du soir qui s'assombrit,
> Telle divinité s'accoude. Un ange nage.
> Il restaure l'espace à chaque tour de rein.
> Moi, qui jette ici-bas l'ombre d'un personnage,
> Toutefois délié dans le plein souverain,
> Je me sens qui me trempe, et pur qui me dédaigne!
> Vivant au sein futur le souvenir marin,
> Tout le corps de mon choix dans mes regards se baigne!

Nevertheless, despite the balanced control of the visual sensibility as expressed in the preceding lines, the poet declares that he is a creator rather than a spectator for he directs the solemn performance of his desires which he projects onto the scene. Here the intellect is fashioning a vast mystery from the base matter of mist and cloud, treating a secret as complex as love. In the first seven lines, the enjoyment of so many fantasies is enumerated—these gods of fragile beauty and storm, of supple gesture and movement, who move larger than life in some grand frame. The self lyrically imagines ideal forces of freedom that frolic against a darkening sky, an angel to reflect the Angel of his glance. Then the poet's sensuous pride swells to take him to the heart of what he contemplates: godlike, he becomes the cynosure of his own glance and marries future and past in an instant of rapture, in lines that are among Valéry's finest with respect to their harmonious fluency.

> Une crête écumeuse, énorme et colorée,
> Barre, puissamment pure, et plisse le parvis.
> Roule jusqu'à mon cœur la distance dorée,
> Vague! . . . Croulants soleils aux horizons ravis,
> Tu n'iras pas plus loin que la ligne ignorée
> Qui divise les dieux des ombres où je vis.

The mood again changes in accord with the changing scene. The first two lines mark the transition as the revered space on which a monument of thought has been built ("parvis" recalls the literal significance of the phrase "l'œil contemplateur" in line 2) is touched by a crest of colored light that brings potential destruction. But the poet allays the idea of ruin by evoking the wave's purity and calling on it to allow him to touch golden light. He commands its intervention, then confidently affirms, as if he were some demiurge, that it shall not grow beyond the limits he prescribes for it. The exorcism is thus dually couched: the new element of modification must either bring the gods nearer according to the poet's whim, or be held immobile. Balanced against one another, the two propositions are his urgent attempt to weave a verbal spell. However, his accent is plaintive, and the last words refer to the shadows that already encompass him.

Une volute lente et longue d'une lieue
Semant les charmes lourds de sa blanche torpeur
Où se joue une joie, une soif d'être bleue,
Tire le noir navire épuisé de vapeur . . .

As in the previous section, the poet turns to the outward
scene to detail a point of change. Now the single sentence,
with its long descriptive phrase, its heavy vowels and alliteration, creates the notion of languorousness. It is the image
of longing, a tender moment reluctant to fade. One last link
binds joy and nostalgia: the whiteness of a whorl of cloud
that has not lost all trace of the past day would seem to
draw the black boat of which the onlooker for the first time
is conscious. Thus, if all the playfulness of the mind has
not been lost, its charm is at present distended as it strives
to prevail over lethargy.

Mais pesants et neigeux les monts du crépuscule,
Les nuages trop pleins et leurs seins copieux,
Toute la majesté de l'Olympe recule,
Car voici le signal, voici l'or des adieux,
Et l'espace a humé la barque minuscule . . .

The movement of regret is translated by the pattern of
rhymes, the gentle rhythm, the images of separation. The
appositions in the first three lines show the sensibility
divided between object and metaphor: these clouds with
their full-bosomed shapes are not just clouds but mountains;
above all they are resumed as the majesty of Olympus. The
pantheon of mythical forms, the grace of so much inspiration, yields to reality but is not yet overcome; in a similar
way, the "navire" is a toy "barque" that has been lost from
sight; but although it takes the eye to a particular point of
familiar detail, the forces of time and space that engulf it
still retain for the imagination a magical power.

Lourds frontons du sommeil toujours inachevés,
Rideaux bizarrement d'un rubis relevés
Pour le mauvais regard d'une sombre planète,
Les temps sont accomplis, les désirs se sont tus,

> Et dans la bouche d'or, bâillements combattus,
> S'écartèlent les mots que charmait le poète . . .
> Les temps sont accomplis, les désirs se sont tus.

At last, with the lyrical affection that is heard in his refrain, the spectator bids farewell to the sky, to the ideas that
have accompanied beauty and its decline—and to the verbal
texture he has woven to celebrate it. He has become conscious of himself as poet, naming himself, and the act of
composition he has carried out, with the objective awareness signified by his use of the third person. On the one
hand, time has come to its final transfiguration; on the other,
his magic guidance of words in respect of the scene is drawing to an end. He can realize the tenuousness of the relationship at this point when the moment has run its course in
the image of his desires. However, the correspondence of
scene and mind has not yet wholly dissolved as the appositions that qualify "les temps" and "les désirs" indicate. They
denote architectural form and mass, clouds heavy with the
force of sleep but still not having found their ultimate
shape; they are also the curtains of evening adorned with
a ruby to seduce the glance that would violate their secrets.
We observe that these traits have their close counterpart in
the "bâillements combattus" of the poet's words, his "bouche
d'or," the verb "charmait." And yet, in another way, the
twin movements of night and words are exactly opposite
since the former constitute and compose their last avatar,
whereas the latter are undergoing a dire dispersion ("s'écartèlent").

> Adieu, Adieu! . . . Vers vous, ô mes belles images,
> Mes bras tendent toujours l'insatiable port!
> Venez, effarouchés, hérissant vos plumages,
> Voiliers aventureux que talonne la mort!
> Hâtez-vous, hâtez-vous! . . . La nuit presse! . . . Tantale
> Va périr! Et la joie éphémère des cieux!
> Une rose naguère aux ténèbres fatale,
> Une toute dernière rose occidentale
> Pâlit affreusement sur le soir spacieux . . .

> Je ne vois plus frémir au mât du belvédère
> Ivre de brise un sylphe aux couleurs de drapeau,
> Et ce grand port n'est plus qu'un noir débarcadère,
> Couru du vent glacé que sent venir ma peau!
>
> Fermez-vous! Fermez-vous! Fenêtres offensées!
> Grands yeux qui redoutez la véritable nuit!
> Et toi, de ces hauteurs d'astres ensemencées,
> Accepte, fécondé de mystère et d'ennui,
> Une maternité muette de pensées . . .

Divided into four sections, with distinct functions that show a marked evolution of mood from passionate yearning to unstinting gift, the longest section brings the poem to a close. In the first lines, exclamations and repetitions translate the desire to capture one last glimpse of beauty in its death agony. The Virgilian pathos of line 2 is placed alongside the image of frail boats pursued by fearsome night that recalls, in the word "plumages," the metaphor of the bird's flight from the start of the poem. Yet it is not only beauty that is about to die but also the heroic image of the poet himself who is ever unassuaged, this Tantalus who would drink the whole of delight. The word "affreusement," the imagery, the idea of fate that commands time as it does the rose, bring the poem to a climax of wildness.

The four lines that follow have an almost naive tone as the poet details the disappearance of the elements of light and color. He no longer looks to the broad expanse of sky but to the tower and port that are close at hand, yet even they have changed: the lively sprite of air, the flag, strains no more to absorb the breeze or to surrender completely to its power, but has been engulfed by darkness; the great port has been reduced to the dimension of a somber landing stage that is buffeted by cold night and death—death that the poet feels to be meant for him. It is a contraction of the scene, a homecoming of the most austere kind.

This powerful spell must be broken: the moment when everything was contemplation of light has yielded to dark-

ness, ephemeral joy to fear. The four exclamations express
an urgent compulsion to escape death, to return to the
closed world and comfort of the self. Once more Valéry
makes use of an apposition which places the vehicle, a conventional metaphor, beside the tenor, and thereby shows the
abstract nature of a drama that has no recourse to sensuous
imagery to convey its meaning. The words "offensées" and
"redoutez," however, give us twin aspects of the poet's emotion: on the one hand, the vigorous violation of the sensibility by the thought of death, on the other, an immediate
awareness, through the fear provoked in him, of life's preciousness.

Nevertheless, the poem does not end thus but on the gift
of the self to a night alive with stars. The words exorcise
the pervasive thought of death by way of the notions of
birth and fertility: all is renewed; a world has been engendered from the long exploration of mystery—this call to
exhaust an inexhaustible beauty—and ennui—the gracious
inactivity that was at the furthest remove from practical
goals. The poet completes the creative cycle by yielding up
to night his spiritual elegy which is both thought's end and
another beginning. In the same way he recaptures the paradoxical duality of mother and child, maternity and nativity,
reconciled past and future, which the original sonnet introduced.

We have, then, followed a monologue of the self as it explores the relationship between nature and the sensibility,
sensation and thought. Avoiding narrative or description, it
traces out a quest that calls on the basic attitudes of desire
and fear, thirst and delight; but the drama is mental, not
physical, and the appetency that of the glance. Valéry gives
us a religious poem—the song of man's link with a transcendental force that he posits in the visible universe—
which concludes with the coming of night and the recognition of an idea of the world, a language like a field of stars,

or grain, in which all is potential and as it were forewritten.
The search is justified by its end, the long discourse, with
its many variations of mood, turns to discover itself as the
very poem of contemplation. Thus we may say that "Profusion du soir" is in an exact way, as I suggested earlier,
the realization of the creative process that Valéry defined
memorably in one of his notebooks: "Quel poème admirable que la contemplation se nourrissant d'elle-même. Répétition sans accoutumance, répétition qui excite le désir et
provoque la conscience au lieu de s'en défaire peu à peu.
Ce qui ne fait penser à nulle autre chose; et puis au lieu de
s'éclairer par la pensée,—l'éclaire, cela est beau, et par sa
seule présence." [34]

The theme, as well as the vocabulary and syntax, are
unique in his work for their sustained elevation. We have
also noticed the unusual form, with its twelve clearly separated parts that translate instants of thought as the poet
comes to apprehend and interpret day's decline. The tone
changes; the rhyme schemes do also, as the alexandrines
bend to an abstract pattern. Yet we may ask whether the
sequence follows no more than a temporal line or whether,
on the contrary, some architectural principle is presiding.
This I believe to be the case. Indeed, the first section seems
to me not only to set the scene and introduce the drama,
but to offer the dominant theme that already contains the
rest, as in certain symphonies. One recalls the choice of
musical structures Mallarmé counseled poets to adopt, for
example in the following statement from "Le Mystère dans
les lettres": "On peut (. . .) commencer d'un éclat triom-
phal trop brusque pour durer; invitant que se groupe, en
retard, libérée par l'écho, la surprise." [35] In Valéry's poem
too, I would submit, we have a similar interplay between
an initial brilliance that is strongly characterized, then taken

34 *Cahiers*, V, 524.
35 Stéphane Mallarmé, *Œuvres complètes*, 384.

up by the rest of the poem on a less concentrated level, the
whole structure moving between the twin poles of "nativité"
and "maternité" that signify bounty.

The sonnet is the only one of its kind in Valéry's work.
By its form it suggests a tension between movement (the
alternate rhymes recall the rhythms of a ballad) and constancy, time and suspense. Yet, once the voice reaches the
height of passionate lucidity in the second tercet, it breaks
off to invoke the delights of evening and retrace at leisure,
through the eleven remaining sections, the exchange between desire and knowledge that typifies incisive attention.
The mode of address alternates as in the sonnet between
first and third persons before the poet conjures up anew
his ideal, now in the immediate terms of the second person
singular, through an act of personal renunciation.

Such a composition, it is clear, does not allow of "vagueness" but demands extreme precision within its given compass. In place of the flesh and-blood protagonist we come to
recognize in *La Jeune Parque* or "Le Cimetière marin," we
find here a single point of view maintained from beginning
to end under the Valéryan discipline of perfection and
purity and power, that would identify the world with the
reach of a glance: "Et pendant une éternité, il ne cessa de
connaître et de ne pas comprendre." [36] Yet must we finally
see "Profusion du soir" in the terms in which Claudel, however much an admirer of Valéry's art, came to judge his
achievement: "cet effort vain, et d'avance découragé, à se
dégager de soi-même?" [37] I do not think so; for, despite
nightfall, the Angel-without-Christ no longer desperately
seeks to cling to a lost image. On the contrary, he postulates
the existence of another self—mysterious, born of a long
moment's time without event—to which his tribute of abundance is due. Although this conclusion is tenuous, emerging

36 "L'Ange," *Œuvres*, I, 206.
37 Paul Claudel: "Huitième Cahier" (1937–1942), *Journal* II, 410.

with some ambiguity in the face of death, it is nonetheless
real, and echoes nature's gift, so that knowledge and self-
knowledge reach the state of reconciliation—more, gratitude
—that is likewise implicit in the last words of the Parque.
Using to the full the severe framework of its language, the
piece unravels then, it seems to me, a thread as essential as
that of Valéry's other great poems, which it transposes,
without past or future, onto the plane of the eye's pure
presence.

4: "J'ai adoré cet homme . . ."

IN THE preceding pages I have frequently had occasion to refer to Stéphane Mallarmé, to suggest points of comparison, to indicate affinities. Over the past fifty years many critics have, of course, emphasized Valéry's indebtedness to his master, although few have been as scathing as Paul Léautaud in his feline review of *La Jeune Parque:* "C'est une belle chose, la fidélité . . . C'est une force souvent. C'est peut-être aussi, en littérature, la plus désastreuse des faiblesses." [1] Other balance-sheets have come from readers who found at times the sensitive words of a Maurice Blanchot; but more than enough were bluffly dogmatic in a way that failed to bring Mallarmé's influence into perspective. I am however convinced that a study of this relationship can take us fairly to the heart of Valéry, for it was a familiar mystery to which he felt impelled to turn again and again. "Certains jours, pour moi, je fête la Saint Mallarmé, souvenirs, ambition ancienne, admiration et amour, tristesse, dépit, grandeurs," he noted in 1902;[2] and so it was until his death. In the following essay I should like to detail the material we have at our disposal for such an inquiry—some of it quite recently brought to light, a small portion still unpublished—but all, I think, worthy of further consideration.

1 *Mercure de France,* August 1, 1917, p. 494.
2 *Cahiers,* II, 880.

A rich source with which to begin is the *Ecrits divers sur
Stéphane Mallarmé* published in 1950. Rather rashly as it
now appears, the nameless editor claimed in his introductory gloss: "Le présent ouvrage contient tous les écrits de
Paul Valéry sur Stéphane Mallarmé." It comprises ten essays and lectures which had all appeared between 1920 and
1944 and are here arranged with a few signal deviations
in the order of composition. We may regret that a stricter
editorial policy was not adopted; even more, that Valéry
himself did not collect them and make the single exhaustive
work which he had planned as early as 1897 ("mon machin
sur Mallarmé," as he told Gide), but later despaired of
writing ("l'étude rigoureuse qu'il eût aimé de faire et qu'il
ne fera jamais"), then finally took up once again in the last
years of his life.[3] Yet in its less than perfect form it is one
of the most moving tributes any great poet has paid another. Few writings have done more for our understanding
of certain aspects of Mallarmé's aesthetics—the concept of
meaning variable according to the reader's point of view,
of art as exercise, preciousness, sterility, obscurity. Valéry
defines Mallarmé's accomplishment in memorable terms:
"L'extrême pureté de la foi en matière de poésie," "cette
précision, cette constance et cette assurance héroïque";
Mallarmé, he says, was "le personnage de l'art savant et le
suprême état de l'ambition littéraire la plus relevée," *"le
virtuose de cette discipline de pureté."* Alongside such
praise, glimpses are given of the man he was, at the other
extreme from the grandiose ambitions he held for poetry
itself: "cet audacieux, cet homme si simple, si doux, si
naturellement noble et charmant." The total effect is to
compose a portrait that impresses us by the refinement
of Valéry's prose and the admiration he so generously states.
But he also insists on the "influence" Mallarmé had on him
and suggests its almost epiphanous nature. Thus he writes:

[3] *Correspondance André Gide-Paul Valéry,* 437.

"J'ai adoré cet homme extraordinaire . . ."; "j'éprouvai la progression foudroyante d'une conquête spirituelle décisive"; again: "Son œuvre me fut dès le premier regard, et pour toujours un sujet de merveille." Here we have indeed the mainspring of the book which gives it an intense beauty of its own, for nothing could be further from description or objective scrutiny than the deep personal involvement that speaks to us from every page.

The same note is heard variously in the seven letters that are included in a loosely chronological order in the volume. The most touching of all are the two sent to Gide and to Jules Valéry just after Mallarmé's death in which the details of the little funeral are given together with Valéry's huge sense of loss. But even more extraordinary perhaps are the two letters written to Albert Thibaudet in 1912 in which he strives to bring out in the clearest possible way his personal debt, which he takes to be above all a moral one ("Il a servi, sert encore de conscience à quelques-uns. Les uns l'ont *bonne,* et les autres *mauvaise*").

To this small number of letters chosen from the mass of Valéry's correspondence many other items deserve to be added. We might refer to a number of important remarks to André Gide which came to light in 1955 when the full volume of their correspondence was published; in particular, I think of Valéry's comments, two years after writing to Thibaudet, on reading the manuscripts of Mallarmé's early poems like "Parce que de la viande était à point rôtie . . ." which were not published until 1945 in the *Œuvres complètes.* We need to refer also to the sheaf of letters written between 1890 and 1898 to Mallarmé himself which should occupy a place in any future edition of the *Ecrits divers.* Some of them have already been published, such as the first two with their awkward style which he sent from Montpellier in 1890 and 1891 ("Un jeune homme perdu au fond de la province . . . ose se présenter à vous . . ."; "Pour une seconde fois, je viens solliciter de

vous un conseil . . ."),[4] and the last, dated 3 July 1898, an-
nouncing that he will come to Valvins to see his friend
(whom he addressed as "Cher Monsieur," and no longer
"Cher Maître," from December 1896). A fourth letter written on 15 January 1894 in Montpellier is contained in *Lettres à Quelques-uns;* it gives some idea of Valéry's preoccupation with mental functioning when he speaks of a general theory of Tools (". . . comprendre dans une même
figure—tout ce qui, en toute chose, est le Moyen . . . une
théorie de l'*Instrument*"), which Monod tells us Valéry
remembered clearly in the last years of his life, stating on
the 25th June 1939 that it was "very important." The only
other letter of some length, sketched out in note form but
not sent to Mallarmé, was reproduced by Monod in his
Regard sur Valéry.[5] Here Valéry laments his newfound post
in the War Ministry with all the drudgery it entails, and
observes in characteristic manner: "Je ne connais pas de
supplice plus pur que l'impossibilité imposée de penser."

Yet one of the constant notes of the whole correspondence is the image of Valvins as some kind of idyllic escape
—from Paris, the War Ministry, his own taedium vitae:
"Valvins m'attire"; "Le fantastique de Valvins s'accroît
démesurément dans mon esprit,—au moindre remous d'air
suppliant les fenêtres du bureau" (2 June 1897); and he
continues: "Je me rappelle que dans le noir bout du chemin
jusqu'à la gare,—par un résumé curieux,—toutes les impressions du moment, ciel complet, être avec vous, et la

---

4 The original draft of the first letter to Mallarmé has recently been
published by Lloyd J. Austin, together with an earlier version which
was never sent ("Les premiers rapports entre Valéry et Mallarmé,"
Entretiens sur Paul Valéry, Paris: Presses Universitaires de France,
1972). Valéry, writing under the full impact of this early encounter,
says: "Quelques bribes de Votre Œuvre par hasard découverte en des
recueils m'ont assoiffé irrémédiablement"; again: "Je compare avec
amour ces prodigieux vers à d'inestimables liqueurs qui, tombant perle
à perle sur une langue experte éveillent d'infinies jouissances."

5 Pp. 29–30.

barre du lendemain,—se mouraient, autour d'une subite et unique envie de travail infini, là tout de suite, imprévoyante, comme fait d'ailleurs la réflexion elle-même." Again: "Valvins! cependant. Et ce n'est pas un coin de terre que j'appelle ainsi. C'est la tête fraîche, le corps disparu ou délicieux, le travail véritable, improductif, foudroyant— enfin la rencontre que je serais sûr de faire, au coin du bois, de vous" (24 April 1898). There is then poetic justice in the fact that the volume of *Ecrits divers* concludes with the poem "Valvins," written in 1897 as one of a series presented to Mallarmé by his young friends and later included in slightly revised form in the *Album de vers anciens*. If at first sight the interest it presents is not great, it well repays a closer reading.

The original manuscript, to be found in the Valerynum of the Bibliothèque Sainte-Geneviève, comprises a single unlined sheet of paper with writing on both sides. As in the case of the account of his first meeting with Mallarmé, it is not so much the words that hold our attention first of all as two drawings: the first of a naked woman standing upright, the other, on the reverse side of the sheet, of a skiff like Mallarmé's own. It is the nude which provides the key to the initial tone of the sonnet, for the first lines are a sensuous evocation:

> Si tu marches comme un cheval
> Si tu viens, si ton corps se plie ou si tu es
> Toi que le jour trempe
>   qui (te) trempe à toutes attitudes

The poet seeks to capture an image of lithe energy, flowing movement, a plasticity bathed in light. The only Mallarméan trait one might mention is the repeated use of the words "Si tu . . . ," also adopted in the final version, which recall Mallarmé's expressed desire to write a poem called simply "Si tu . . . ," as Claudel recorded in his "Notes sur Mallarmé." Valéry may then have had recourse to this

syntactic form as a secret tribute, although the language
found in these lines is quite untypical of his master.

Now the concrete nature of the vision is emphasized in
a passage that follows the marginal observation "Peau
pleine":

> C'est toi qui toujours pleine et complète, Clara
> Te trempes vite dans toutes les attitudes
> Si ton corps se ploie ou tel un cheval courra
> Si tu viens danser ou dormir changer mes habitudes
> Le cheval en venant qui se déforme et brille
> Et qui sue au soleil, retentit et se fond

This opulent skin—woman, water, horse—will suddenly
change in the next line as the contours sharpen to offer the
image of a fluid skiff, sunlight, the Seine at Valvins—"Une
Seine de jours et d'osiers tresse / Et mélange ta voile au
meilleur de l'été." Here was a beginning, which would be
refined to the final state as it is contained in the *Album:*

> Si tu veux dénouer la forêt qui t'aère
> Heureuse, tu te fonds aux feuilles, si tu es
> Dans la fluide yole à jamais littéraire,
> Traînant quelques soleils ardemment situés
>
> Aux blancheurs de son flanc que la Seine caresse
> Emue, ou pressentant l'après-midi chanté,
> Selon que le grand bois trempe une longue tresse
> Et mélange ta voile au meilleur de l'été.
>
> Mais toujours près de toi que le silence livre
> Aux cris multipliés de tout le brut azur,
> L'ombre de quelque page éparse d'aucun livre
>
> Tremble, reflet de voile vagabonde sur
> La poudreuse peau de la rivière verte
> Parmi le long regard de la Seine entr'ouverte[6]

It is evident that when Valéry came to elaborate his
poem he made a point of using a language peculiarly associated with Mallarmé: Valvins, the Seine, the skiff, the

---

6 Paul Valéry, *Œuvres*, 85.

page, the book, whiteness, hair, silence, the afternoon that
the Faun has sung—"l'après-midi chanté." In the same way
"Aux cris multipliés de tout le brut azur" makes us think
of the early poem "L'Azur" ("En vain! L'Azur triomphe,
et je l'entends qui chante / Dans les cloches . . . ," or "le
cri de l'étendue" of "L'Action restreinte"); "L'ombre de
quelque page éparse d'aucun livre" recalls several parallel
passages that have the unmistakable savor of Mallarmé;
while the comparison of sail and page entails a like image
in "Salut" ("Le blanc souci de notre toile"). The syntax
bears a similar imprint with its two long periods, its precious "selon que" and "parmi," and the pivotal "mais"
which, as in sonnets of Mallarmé ("Mais proche la croisée
au nord vacante . . . ," "Mais chez qui du rêve se
dore . . . ," "Mais langoureusement longe . . .") is less ad-
versative than the sign of a changed modulation. As for
the general meaning of the poem two basic ideas of the
Mallarméan aesthetic provide the framework for octave and
sestet: the poet is he who explains the world, joyfully vio-
lates its mystery, "unknots the forest"; at the same time he
tames chaos and old night and obsessive solitude by cap-
turing an image of beauty, the pure potentiality of expression of a blank page like the white sail that contains
all movement. This is the high calling of literature: "l'ex-
plication orphique de la Terre qui est le seul devoir du
poète et le jeu littéraire par excellence." [7]

And yet, despite its theme and isolated traits of diction
and form, the sonnet is Valéry's own, possessing a sensuousness and plasticity that are unmistakable. It does not move
like a dancer on points, but with a full breadth of summer
warmth, the commitment of mind and senses, the greenness
of forest and river, a confident gravity of tone. Mallarmé's
letter of thanks on receiving the poem pointed to a quality
he knew to be wholly distinct from his own: "Tant de vous

[7] Stéphane Mallarmé, *Œuvres complètes*, 378.

ce sonnet, Valéry, ému et riche abstraitement." The terms
have perhaps never been bettered as a definition of Valéry.

In addition to the manuscript of "Valvins" to which we
have referred, the Valeryanum also contains three other
documents of some importance. One deserves our special
scrutiny since it records Valéry's first meeting with Mallarmé on 10 October 1891 when he made a brief visit to
Paris from Montpellier. The text was reproduced by Monod
in his small book *Regard sur Valéry* in 1947, and later in
the Pléiade, but it contains minor errors of transcription
and one regrettable omission: thus, in the sentence, "Cet
homme devient savant sans une hésitation—puis épique
. . . " (Monod), a parenthesis eloquent of Valéry's self-
assurance is missing after "hésitation": "j'aime à voir que
j'ai pesé déjà—*hier*—tout ce qu'il dit." Yet, besides the
precocious tone, the manuscript shows the great pains
Valéry took to get everything down in minute detail, not
only his report of the themes of the conversation, his keen
observation of Mallarmé's gestures and of the attitudes of
Madame Mallarmé and Geneviève, but also in two precise
drawings: on one side of the unlined sheet he depicts Mallarmé holding his pipe in his left hand and making a point
with his right. Two paintings are behind him, while nearby
are a sofa, an armchair, a table with a lamp hanging low
over it, a cup, a tobacco-box and matches. The very metic-
ulousness is the best token of the young poet's desire to
absorb and evaluate all. A second manuscript dates no
doubt from the same period. Written in pencil on two
sides of an unlined sheet of paper bearing the heading
"chez Mallarmé mardi" it begins: "Quillard puis Thorel
très vagues" (Pierre Quillard, poet and playwright and long
an habitué of the "mardis," and the critic Jean Thorel).
Then Mallarmé speaks at length of Villiers who had died
two years before ("Il avait, sa vie durant, la foi du curé de
campagne unie à l'hégélianisme") and Rimbaud, at that
time unknown to Mallarmé and his guests, dying in the

Hôpital de la Conception in Marseilles ("il est colon en Algérie dit-on après avoir vendu des bœufs en l'Inde [sic]. Me faisant l'effet d'une blanchisseuse aux mains pleines d'engelures"). Once again Valéry takes care to note the articulations of Mallarmé's talk which is principally anecdotal but includes critical insights into Villier's work. A third important document collected by Monod was written some fifty years later. The handwriting is Monod's and is an attempt by him, as late as November 1942, to glean what he could about a relationship which he took to be essential ("J'insiste sur le point que P. V. qui ne respecte pas grand'chose respecte S.M.—et je cherche à forcer là-dessus ses retranchements. Cela me paraît un domaine ultime de la sensibilité. Peut-être."). This is not the place to reproduce the whole document which is formulated with the same devotion and self-effacement that Monod brought to every dealing with his friend. He seeks precision about the Mallarmé poems Valéry knew before he came to Paris and the date of his conversations with Mallarmé about Poe's *Eureka* (in 1891, at the beginning of their friendship, and in the winter of 1893, Valéry answers: "quelle soirée pour moi, centrale comme la strette d'une fugue," he told Thibaudet in 1912). Valéry underlines once again that Mallarmé was for him the poet he needed most desperately to devour; that he loved him "comme le tigre aime la gazelle." "J'attachais un grand prix à *une partie* de l'esprit de S.M.—pas à tout, mais je reconnais le pouvoir où qu'il soit. Il y avait là un système, une organisation." Monod took pains to bring their talk around to the vital reservations he had to make about Mallarmé: what was the subject he wanted to broach with him and which he thought of as the "centre invisible, nerveux et caché"? He affirms that Valéry could not but find the "sacerdotal" aspect irritating in Mallarmé and summed up the concern he felt in the presence of the proclaimed mystery of "beauty" by this question: "Comment, professionnellement parlant, arri-

vait-il à admettre à ses propres yeux sa propre obscurité."
Could a defensible aesthetics, let alone philosophy, be
based on such apparent nebulousness? And yet Valéry is
ready to admit in his next conversation with Monod that
Mallarmé's influence on him was far from being restricted to
the realm of poetics: "Souvent je me posais la question:
que penserait S.M.? Il avait compris l'importance de la
forme, d'où son mépris des philosophes qui n'ont pas de
forme."

These notes were made by Monod less than three short
years before Valéry's death. To enlarge on them illuminat-
ingly we now possess the *Cahiers* with their record of half-a-
century's meditation. I have counted one hundred and
eighty-one separate passages relating to Mallarmé, some
cursory, others substantial; nevertheless their sum total is
less significant than their comparative frequency: thus, if we
divide the notebooks into eight approximately equal periods,
we find that the seven periods from 1894 to 1938 have each
between ten and fourteen references, with the exception
of one peak of twenty between 1919 and 1925 at the time
when Valéry was preparing the articles entitled "Le Coup
de dés," "Stéphane Mallarmé" and "Dernière visite à Mallarmé" collected in *Ecrits divers,* whereas no less than
eighty-one references occur between 1938 and 1944, which
are largely attributable to his new resolve to write a work
he had long deferred—un "Lui et Moi"—which would form
part of his memoirs.

But the full importance of these and other remarks from
the last notebooks can only be appreciated when they are
considered in relation to the observations written in the
forty-five years that go before. Thus his final praise for *Un
Coup de dés* may revealingly be placed alongside references
that are much less alive to its virtues in the first notebook,
or of a different tenor. Similarly it is of value to note the
different formulations of Mallarmé's metaphysics: the ninth
notebook speaks rather prettily of "une sorte de goût de

marivaudage avec l'Absolu," while the twenty-fifth, written
some fifteen years later, shows more concern with nuances:
"une 'mystique,' " Valéry writes, "à demi sincère, à demi
politique, etc., mais inutile, sinon inévitable—vu dates." A
parallel development can be seen on other topics discussed
in the notebooks such as obscurity, metaphors, musical
"motifs," which confirms our impression that Valéry succeeded in his last years in heightening his perception of
Mallarmé's originality, which he still strove—compulsively
one might say—to define. I shall return to the notations
contained in the final eight notebooks in a later chapter.

Yet another testimony is a "poem-in-the-rough," or free
verse composition, sketched out in 1912 when Valéry was
to all appearances far from poetry. It is untitled, but bears
the marginal annotation "SM" in the fourth *Cahier*.[8] Not
until 1927 was it published: in that year a revised version
appeared in the section "Littérature" of *Autres Rhumbs*,
later to be included in *Tel Quel II*; but neither of these
publications refers to Mallarmé, since the poem has become simply a "Psaume sur une voix." It is, then, somewhat of a surprise, if we consult *The Virginia Quarterly
Review* for Winter 1939, to find the same piece given with
its title in an expanded form: "Psaume sur une voix: à
propos de Stéphane Mallarmé." Is it an oversight that all
French editions carry the short title? Or does this reflect
Valéry's singular discreetness with respect to his French
readers? In any case the poem can be said to take on for
us a fresh emotional dimension when we know that it com-
memorates, some fourteen years after Mallarmé's death, the
cult of admiration he had for his gracious host in the rue
de Rome and Valvins.

A demi voix,
D'une voix douce et faible disant de grandes choses;
D'importantes, d'étonnantes, de profondes et justes choses,

8 *Cahiers*, IV, 684.

D'une voix douce et faible.
La menace du tonnerre, la présence d'absolus
Dans une voix de rouge-gorge,
Dans le détail fin d'une flûte, et la délicatesse du son pur.
Tout le soleil suggéré
Au moyen d'un demi-sourire.
(O demi voix),
Et d'une sorte de murmure
En français infiniment pur.
Qui n'eût saisi les mots, qui l'eût ouï à quelque distance,
Aurait cru qu'il disait des riens.
Et c'étaient des riens pour l'oreille
Rassurée.
Mais ce contraste et cette musique,
Cette voix ridant l'air à peine,
Cette puissance chuchotée,
Ces perspectives, ces découvertes,
Ces abîmes et ces manœuvres devinés,

Ce sourire congédiant l'univers! . . .

Je songe aussi pour finir
Au bruit de soie seul et discret
D'un feu qui se consume en créant toute la chambre,
Et qui se parle,
Ou qui me parle
Presque pour soi.

The final version as shown above differs in minor points
only from the original draft. It is a "document," a "créa-
tion tout individuelle" as Valéry put it in *The Virginia
Quarterly Review,* expressing a movement of praise to
which he could apply the term "psalm" as he did to the
much more fully elaborated "Air de Sémiramis." Yet it has
a moving quality of keenly felt perception, and a corresponding rhetorical coherence. It describes allusively Mallarmé's manner of speaking which, as we know from the
recollections of his friends and as the *Divagations* help us
to imagine, was one of his most winning talents. Yet Valéry
does not explain or justify, but instead prefers present par-

ticiples to principal verbs so as to produce a kind of instan-
taneous impression. In the wake of Kahn and the *vers
libristes,* harmony is achieved by assonance, repetition, and
by the thematic development in three parts which describes
a variation on the antithesis of smallness and greatness. In
the first section apparent slightness contains depth as
thunder is juxtaposed to the robin-redbreast and the flute.
Valéry's imagery embraces both nature and art, just as the
delicate charm of Mallarmé calls the world into question
("La signification du *monde,*" as the first draft reads). The
second section begins with smallness and moves to a climax
of audacity when the poet dismisses the world: "Ce sourire
congédiant l'univers!" In using the familiar and the cosmic
the vocabulary is contrastive, its dramatic effects reinforced
by the syntactical diversity of short statements followed by
elliptical exclamations. The last lines offer the contrast of
a further smallness which the lyrical self introduces as a
final term to its musing. "Voix" is echoed in "soie" and
"pour soi": the interior scene of rustling silk, fire, gentle
murmur is as it were the objective correlative of the remembered voice. It also conjures up the atmosphere of
Mallarmé's last sonnets, those spells uttered by the "reclus
du cabinet des Signes" as Claudel called him,[9] whose function was to create the dazzling console table that stands in
its right and necessary place despite tragic death. It would
be possible to draw verbal parallels from Mallarmé's work
which would indicate the appropriateness of the chosen
metaphors; but it is sufficient for our purpose to emphasize
the fervent dignity of the tribute, and the importance it
gives to the virtues of modesty and daring that Mallarmé
paradoxically conjoined.

It may well be that more documents concerning this relationship will come to light as the poet's manuscripts are
further examined, although it is hard to think they could

9 Paul Claudel, "La Catastrophe d'Igitur," *Œuvres en prose,* 511.

change substantially the record we possess. One other field
of inquiry which will undoubtedly prove to be fruitful is
the poetry itself—less the numerous *quatorzains* and diver-
timenti and homages (whose very genre and vocabulary
point to a close reading of the *Vers de circonstance*), less
poems like "Narcisse parle" (in which *Hérodiade* and
L'Après-midi d'un Faune are clearly inscribed), than his
great poems like *La Jeune Parque*. We remember Gide finding that the Mallarméan traits of style in the *Parque*
detracted from his pleasure ("pas encore assez détaché de Mallarmé," he wrote);[10] yet these are by no means characteristic of the poem as a whole. I should wish to maintain on
the other hand that Valéry consciously exploits Mallarmé
in certain parts, in the same way as he calls to witness elsewhere in the poem other major voices of French lyricism
in his effort to make an opera from their several strands.
In that sense, for instance, the passage beginning "Tout-
puissants étrangers, inévitables astres . . ." can be considered, in form and theme, to be a masterly pastiche of *Hérodiade,* developing in truly personal vein the apprehension
of a wound inflicted on the purity of consciousness. Such
is Valéry's fidelity to Mallarmé, who established for him
an idea of Poetry—"pater poeticus in aeternum," to adapt
the words of the discourse on Goethe—that seemed to epit-
omize an ultimate elegance of language and life. As such,
he became a hidden source of strength, and not the weak-
ness Léautaud and others have urged. Having placed the
end of his search in a perfected self, Valéry never forgot
the superb irritant of a self wholly devoted to the idea of
Beauty.

After laying aside the preceding pages, I recently had the
privilege of consulting a dossier that had been found by
Madame Rouart-Valéry as she was preparing to send her

---

[10] André Gide, *Journal,* 2 vols. (Paris: Gallimard, 1939–48), I, 843.

father's papers to the Bibliothèque Nationale. It contains
unpublished manuscripts from different periods which I
shall not attempt to describe in extenso but which are all
related to aspects of the poet's relationship with Mallarmé.
There is, for example, a letter to Geneviève Mallarmé following a visit to Valvins: although it is undated and without its envelope, it can be placed in the first days of October 1898, less than a month after the poet's death. On
that occasion Valéry read Mallarmé's hastily scribbled re-
quest to burn his papers; he also saw for the first time two
fragments of *Hérodiade:* "Le Cantique de Saint Jean" and
a sequence of alexandrines. He told Gide that he was later
unable to recall any of the lines he had read ("Impression
bizarre et pénible—au retour dans le train—de voir qu'aucun vers de ces fragments ne m'était resté").[11] To Geneviève
he expressed the same feelings in these terms:

> Les papiers que vous avez permis que je tienne un instant, je les
> vois encore, et pourtant, dès le retour, j'ai éprouvé cette chose
> étrange—que pas un seul vers, ni un mot ni rien ne m'en était
> resté; comme si la volonté de votre père s'accomplissait d'elle-
> même dans ma mémoire.

More than courtesy dictates his words; they describe a reduction to the essential of quasi-mystical nature, calling to
mind the extraordinary words by which Valéry commemo-
rated Mallarmé's death: "J'ai de ton pur esprit bu le feu
le plus beau."

Other important manuscripts comprise the drafts of the
two letters sent to Albert Thibaudet in 1912. I have already
mentioned their published version in *Ecrits divers,* but the
notes written before and around them show the considerable amount of thought that preceded the definitive expression. Valéry was intent to take the measure of Mallarmé's
originality at a time when, almost imperceptibly—yet
doubtless to some degree moved by his fresh reading of

---

11 *Correspondance André Gide-Paul Valéry,* 335.

Mallarmé's work—he was turning back to the art of poetry. On this occasion he summed up the lesson he drew from, or read into, Mallarmé in these words: "La pensée exprime la parole." This was the paradoxical reorientation of values introduced by *Hérodiade* and developed throughout the rest of the poems and essays. " 'Le mot, le langage—d'abord'. (Chef-d'œuvre de la Musique est—la Musique elle-même." Valéry emphasizes the generality with which Mallarmé approached the problem of poetic composition, and conceived it as being, in its purest state, forever allegorical of itself. He put the same idea in many ways in subsequent essays on Mallarmé, but never perhaps more pithily. On the same page he goes on to state what he takes to be the exceptional historical importance of this changed point of view, in words the like of which we do not find elsewhere: "Tout un retournement, une inversion 'historique' en général accomplie par des générations en un ou deux siècles ici, en un temps d'homme—Comme si—une révolution des équinoxes achevée en une année."

   In his contact with Mallarmé, the young Valéry came to recognize more acutely than ever before his own identity. He made the discovery, he says, of "l'ultimum violent, ce derrière quoi il ne peut plus y avoir conscience": a focus of thought, a vital separateness, an ultimate violence, an *ego ipsissimus,* lay for him at the heart of this most ardent of encounters. He became capable of measuring his "différence pure." Realizing then that he had of necessity to slough off poetry as an end in itself, he concentrated on mental functioning as his real concern: "Alors me suis-je mis à développer cela seul qui m'intéressait dans la genèse du poème." Mallarmé was the divine poison that induced the necessary reaction: "tant aimé épié"; "aimé, haï, cherché en moi pour trouver autre chose." This same thought will be put in many forms but nowhere more strikingly than in one notation pencilled on a small sheet of paper and collected with the pages we have been examining. It bears on

the recto the indication "Paris le 9 novembre 1906," together with some mathematical calculations. "Avoir connu
Mallarmé," he writes, "c'est l'honneur de mon hasard—de
l'avoir combattu, Jacob de cet ange, c'est l'honneur de ma
loi." By the struggle of the soul a lucky chance was transformed into a rule of life, for Jacob had wrestled with his
angel and been fortified; and Valéry registers the gravity of
the fight by way of the resonance of a Biblical allusion.

Yet doubtless the most important manuscripts contained
in the dossier are the drafts of an essay composed about 1897
in which, just before his "Méthodes" written for the *Mercure
de France* and devoted to Huysmans and Bréal, and as a
sequel to his study of Leonardo, Valéry attempted his first
intensive analysis of Mallarmé's significance. He began in
terms that denote with great vigor the impact of his first
reading: "Il y a quelques années, je connus voluptueusement l'œuvre de M. Mallarmé. Elle me saisit comme un acte
plus énergique que l'ordinaire attentat par l'écriture; ensuite, elle me garda pour d'autres motifs." Knowledge and
sensuous desire are linked in this meeting with a work
whose secret had to be deciphered. Valéry's style has considerable force as he pursues his meditation. Typical of the
language is the following extract with its alliance of abstraction and imagination: "Par-dessus tout, brillait une
volonté. J'appelai, sous ce nom quelconque, les sensations
que me donnait la marche d'un langage qui évitait à chaque
instant mes prévisions; qui s'interdisait de prendre des habi-
tudes, qui rompait régulièrement les groupes endormis, en-
durcis des idées implicites; qui rendait infructueuse l'expérience d'un liseur rapide." One cannot but regret that
this essay, written with such an admirable pen, did not appear while Mallarmé was still alive. It manages to say in
a brief compass what others would later discover, and what
the older Valéry would hardly ever state as pungently. Thus,
"Pour la première fois, le travail purement littéraire avait
été précédé d'une série d'opérations, dont les plus profondes

étaient de nature psychologique, et les plus importantes de nature abstraite." Although we cannot help feeling that the author brushes aside rather cavalierly the metaphysical and magical aspects of Mallarmé's thought, making him in the likeness of the poet he himself would become, the accent is put in salutary fashion on rigorous principles of method, and not on the apparent coynesses that either intrigued or irritated the casual critics of the day. He follows a personal precept that is set down explicitly in English as an epigraph for one draft of this essay: *"Make a brain."* Again, *"M. Mallarmé est un homme qui a fait une expérience. Son œuvre a un caractère historique frappant: pour la première fois depuis qu'il y a littérature on a usé de la littérature comme d'une chose abstraite, maniable en elle-même, indépendamment presque des choses signifiées, au moins dans une approximation."* This statement is highly important, I believe, in that it underlines the formalist approach to language which Mallarmé demonstrated in *Les Mots anglais* and carried to a degree of great refinement in his poetry. Of course, we can agree that Valéry had wilfully cast aside the philosophical infrastructure on which Mallarmé's practice was based; but his was an observation that needed to be made about poems in which pattern has such a primordial role.

I shall quote one last comment from the same essay in which Valéry's formalist reading is made as clear as possible without entering into concrete illustration: "Il s'est résolu à n'employer aucune des formes connues. Il a construit des types symétriques dans la langue, il a d'autre part conduit par l'antique instinct poétique posé en principe que les combinaisons de n'importe quel mot étaient possibles." The image Valéry offers us in this page is one which he would not put so baldly again. It turns our eyes to Mallarmé's constant experimentation with syntax ("génie syntaxier," as Claudel called him); it pinpoints the dance of imagery with its propositions and counterpropositions, its concerted use of symmetry (which Mallarmé referred to as "un deux à deux qui ronge et use les objets au nom d'une centrale pureté");[12] it alludes to the permutations of certain key words, renewed by each individual verbal sequence in which they are found. All of this is precisely true of Mallarmé; but, isolated as it is by Valéry from the conception of the Book and its finalism, the observations assume a schematic clarity of method which is foreign to the general tone of Mallarmé's own writings. When, then, Valéry writes concerning Mallarmé in the same essay: "Toute la littérature est contenue dans la courbe des mots," he seems to wish to point towards his own future poetry rather than to echo Mallarmé.

And yet the whole conclusion to which my reading of Valéry's work leads me is that, on the path of his poetic practice, Valéry found his anxious sensibility to be the central flame that replaced Mallarmé's quest for poetry. In "Sinistre" or "Sémiramis" or "Profusion du soir" or any of his major poems we are aware of an unmistakable tone, an original sense of language and structure, in sum an "art personnel"—the voice of a man. The rigor is there, ever alert, which his reading of Mallarmé had heightened; but he alone suffuses it with the particular drama we know and recognize. It is, then, perhaps appropriate that we should terminate our inspection of the Mallarmé dossier by referring, not to the mathematical schemes he underlines in this essay, but to some occasional verse no doubt written a decade later, but placed alongside the 1897 manuscripts. It is in the form of an undeveloped lyrical movement which recalls Valéry's affection for Mallarmé in the way of "Valvins" and "Psaume sur une voix"; but here the imagery—mirror, water, leaves, tomb—and the relaxed pattern of alternate rhymes are not just a verbal pattern, nor merely

12 "Tout le mystère est là: établir les identités secrètes par un deux à deux qui ronge et use les objets au nom d'une centrale pureté" (Stéphane Mallarmé, *Propos sur la poésie*, Monaco: Editions du Rocher, 1946, 174).

an emblem of gentleness and depth, but the felt language
of a poet who remained throughout his life intimately sensitive to the example of a master and friend:

> Celui auquel je pense était doux et profond
> Plus que l'eau du miroir dont il célèbre encore
> Dans ma mémoire l'ombre et les charmes qui sont
> Comme des feuilles—sur sa tombe que j'adore.

5: "Les larmes: hélas! c'est bien moi..."

ONE OF THE FINEST of Valéry's prose-poems is unfortunately absent from the Pléiade edition, as from his *Poems in the Rough* of the Bollingen works in English. It needs to be sought out under the title "Comme le temps est calme . . ." in a miscellany of verse and prose published in 1930. Yet I find myself going back to this piece, less than two pages in length, in which the poet treats his favorite motif of awakening. At the end of night, having come to meet space like a swimmer, he stands on the threshold of possible acts. His soul is both a sleeping woman and an angel of light, in turn meditative, melancholy, and as exultant as the bird that soars to a naked peak already flesh-colored and gold. In the silence he feels the duality within the self of the boy who admired a like scene and the man he now is; he discovers "un enfant aux cheveux gris" who once responded with the same tears, at the same hour: "Ma jeunesse jadis a langui et senti la montée des larmes, vers la même heure, et sous le même enchantement de la lune évanouissante." [1] Deeper than reason, these tears are the watcher's mysterious answer to the mystery without, bodying forth the enigma, offering a solution for the mind's dryness. They remind us that the arch-analyst Monsieur Teste possessed an extreme sensibility and that, because of

[1] "Comme le temps est calme . . . ," *Morceaux choisis* (Paris: Gallimard, 1930), 52.

it, he sought intellectual rigor so much the more. But he never was to rid himself of what he called the abysses of the mind. "Les larmes: hélas! c'est bien moi," he observed, "il n'y a pas moyen d'en douter." [2] Such is the ground-note of his life and work.

Valery's manuscripts may be numbered among the fullest records we have of the genesis of a series of major works and show his many modes of approach—by way of rhymes, isolated words, musical patterns, prose observations. An aspect of this writing that has not received attention is the way a lyrical development may well begin with a wholly intimate motif and later expunge every trace of particular reference. I recall for instance a draft which is of special interest. The handwriting and the official War Ministry paper with the incomplete heading "Paris le . . . 189 . . ." suggest that it predates the great poems of his maturity by some twenty years, and this is confirmed by the presence on the recto of a draft of "Valvins," the tributary sonnet Valéry sent to Mallarmé in 1897. It is, however, the verso that strikes us for it bears several lines evidently composed on the occasion of Mallarmé's death, concerning which the poet told his brother Jules: "cet événement (. . .) est un des plus grands chagrins de ma vie et une perte irréparable pour moi." [3] Beneath the words "Stéphane Mallarmé mélodieusement" (alternatively "mystérieusement"), we read the following lines:

> Et si la terre trouble hume ta chair chétive
> J'ai de ton pur (noble) esprit bu le feu le plus beau
>   je serai la tombe
>   de ton ombre pensive
> L'ombre de ne savoir si tu cherches encore
> Mon âme de ton âme est le vivant tombeau
> Ombrage quelquefois de ton ombre pensive

---

[2] *Cahiers*, I, 876: "Le rire: je suis toi et pourtant je ne suis pas toi. Les larmes: hélas! c'est bien moi, il n'y a pas moyen d'en douter."
[3] *Ecrits divers sur Stéphane Mallarmé* (Paris: Gallimard, 1950), 157.

Grief, and a sense of communion and continuity, give these isolated alexandrines a resonance that an elaborate homage might not have. They show the extraordinary filial duty Valéry believed he had contracted to Mallarmé. Yet there is more: alongside the fourth line some words have been jotted down, without place in the syntactical movement, but significant of the sentiment that guides the whole passage: "senti monter larmes de l'esprit." Welling up from an unknown source, the "tears of the mind" are his lament, the fitful language of a song to be.

This threnody after the manner of Mallarmé's commemorative poems for Poe, Baudelaire and others was not realized as a separate piece, although it nourished, subterraneously as it were, the composition of *La Jeune Parque* itself since Valéry was to add to and consolidate his lines by a new variation on the same theme. Thus, on the same sheet, a sequence of alexandrines takes its keynote from the initial phrase and the notion of death:

> Terre mêlée à l'herbe et rose, porte-moi
> Porte doucement moi, ô trouble et bienheureuse
> Terre, porté l'être jusqu'à la fleur tremblant avec émoi
> jusqu'à la place où se sent l'émoi
> l'idée
> Terre mêlée à l'herbe et rose, porte-moi
> Porte doucement, ô trouble et bienheureuse
> Terre   et mon ombre
> Qui laisse quelque esprit errant
> te laisses penser

Instead of a direct address from Valéry to Mallarmé, we have a tender incantation to the earth. Who is speaking? Is it the dead poet himself? There were further attempts to extend the motif and image, but the passage came to occupy long afterwards a place in the structure of the Parque's monologue as she is gradually led to feel the stresses of frail mortality:

> Où va-t-il, sans répondre à sa propre ignorance,
> Ce corps dans la nuit noire étonné de sa foi?

> Terre trouble . . . mêlée à l'algue, porte-moi,
> Porte doucement moi . . .

Again, with more poignancy still:

> Hélas! de mes pieds nus qui trouvera la trace
> Cessera-t-il longtemps de ne songer qu'à soi?
> Terre trouble, et mêlée à l'algue, porte-moi!

Valéry's intimate pain attains a legendary language; the "tears of the mind" which he shed for Mallarmé become those of the Parque and all men.

The moods of the two episodes to which I have referred —a morning ecstasy, a sorrowful loss—are opposite, but each is enunciated by the sensibility in a similar way. This points up an ambiguity within ourselves which Valéry was to explore in his notebooks. "Et il y a des larmes de joie et des rires empoisonnés parce que rien n'est simple," he observes.[4] He speculates that in primitive times laughter and tears may well have been alternative outlets for human emotion, that only gradually did they achieve separate functions even though they may still present inherent contradictions. "On trouve des hommes dont les mêmes émotions qui font la plupart pleurer, se traduisent par un rire."[5] Yet if tears can arise from pain or pleasure, they possess certain common characteristics. In the first place they are a subject of astonishment for the mind which cannot conceive how they were formed and extracted from the self. "Une larme qui vient de ton sang au moment de ta peine et qui coule sur ton visage, ignorante du prix payé, étonne l'esprit qui ne peut concevoir la cause et la génération de cette transformation."[6] We answer an unbearable event by an inner extinction of thought, and thereby reassert a balance. Our bodies find in weeping a compensation which permits them to continue to function normally:

---

4 *Mauvaises Pensées et autres, Œuvres,* II, 85.
5 Ibid., 897.
6 *Mélange, Œuvres,* I, 332.

"Avoir des machines pour la joie, pour la tristesse, des organes de l'impuissance à soutenir une pensée, que c'est étrange! Appareils compensateurs, évacuateurs d'une énergie laquelle correspond elle-même à des images indigestes, —insoutenables, inachevables." [7] Tears establish a kind of tabula rasa and a new beginning. Whatever their source, they perform a vital operation which brings with it the pleasure of our own transmutation. As usual, it is the complexity of the process that captivates Valéry. "Ce plaisir de faire fonctionner artificiellement telles glandes et amener tous les mouvements annexes et connexes qui les décrochent, qui justifient, achèvent le fonctionnement." [8] In the way of physical love or procreation, this elimination is the model of a complete "cycle" which, after his seminal reading of W. R. Hamilton (see p. 253), Valéry likened to the cycles of thermodynamics.

It is nonetheless possible to ascribe to tears diverse values. Some are easily come by, while others are far more precious. There are those that are born of common feelings and others that emanate from no banal drama. A temple can be the stuff tears are made of: not affecting our lives in any direct manner, but moving us by its very harmony. At such a time our effusion is beyond price, "d'une espèce divine"; "elle t'apprend que tu es sensible à des objets entièrement indifférents et inutiles à ta personne, à ton histoire, à tes intérêts, à toutes les affaires et circonstances qui te circonscrivent en tant que mortel." [9]

---

[7] *Analecta, Œuvres,* II, 710.

[8] Ibid., 709. In a few isolated lines among the pages of the first notebook of *Charmes,* Valéry begins a surprising development which indicates the complex emotions contained in a tear—anger, laughter, nostalgia, violence, love:

> Comme *l'enfant furieuse*—en pleurs
> A travers une larme aux riantes couleurs
> Croit voir l'oiseau qu'elle eût de ses mains
> Voluptueusement étranglé

[9] *Mélange, Œuvres,* I, 339.

Yet if an artifact can give rise to tears, it can also emerge, like tears, from the limbo of language by a strange crystallisation, an organic development that involves body and mind. Valéry links artistic creation and weeping, but without sentimentality. He who appeared frequently to his contemporaries to be a mere technician of verse, the hollow Strigelius in Jules Romains's *Les Hommes de bonne volonté*, compared the production of poetry to the most secret and personal and least controlled of processes. Thus he remarks in his twentieth notebook: "Et comme viennent les larmes aux yeux de l'ému, ainsi les paroles divines et *plus qu'exactes* du poète. Comme viennent les larmes d'un point de vue plus *profond* que toute liberté et que toute maîtrise des actions, ainsi viennent ces discours, langage qui n'obéit pas à la pensée dégagée, et qui se précipite avant. . . ." [10] The poet waits on his "fate," these words that he reads when he has written them as the precise revelation of a law he had not thought he knew, but recognizes as his own. He has brought into existence rather than invented, elicited rather than imposed. "Deducere carmen" is the epigraph Valéry chose for *Charmes* in order to state a program of creative effort whose constant allegiance is to an internal necessity. Like morning sweetness or the sorrowful regret for a lost master and friend, the poem he dreams of finds a path beyond the schemes of abstract thought which it tempers and renews.

In the light of these considerations it is instructive to return to the poetry to gauge the role of tears. One discovers, as the comments in his notebooks and manuscripts imply, that the image cannot be delimited in any simple way for it is both basic and plurivalent. From his earliest writings, long before he came to Paris, the occurrence of tears was a characteristic trait, if at first it echoed Romantic dolorism more clearly than it implied a personal vision;

10 *Cahiers*, XX, 678.

thus, in "La Mort du juste" dated 30th May 1884, a scene of domestic pathos was plainly derived from Hugo and Hugo's epigones: "C'était autour du lit du vieux père expirant. / Tous à genoux pleuraient . . ." As he entered on his Symbolist period, it was however used with growing subtlety in order to serve patently aesthetic ends. A sonnet published when he was not yet twenty, "Vierge incertaine," shows the delicate correspondence between a weeping statue and a fountain, with tears of love answering tears of loneliness. In the same manner "La Messe angélique" intermingles stars, tears, love, sadness: "Astres! grands yeux d'amants gonflés de larmes d'or!" But it was not until 1892 that nocturnal mystery on the one hand and personal regret on the other received the further dimension of art. As "Purs drames" was to put it in March of that year: "Il n'y a que les lignes simples pour faire pleurer le pur artiste, sans remords." Valéry was ready to write his "Narcisse" of 1892: alongside poems later included in the *Album de vers anciens* in which tears function as transcendent beauty ("Et là-haut, dans la lumière immense, / Nous nous sommes trouvés en pleurant") or as a point of ideal nostalgia like Helen's remembrance of Troy ("Je pleurais. Ils chantaient leurs triomphes obscurs . . ."), we encounter an identification with poetry in the elegiac lament of Narcissus. The offering he makes is that of tears ("Je viens au pur silence offrir mes larmes vaines"), which become the very substance of art by a magic transformation:

> Et toi, verse à la lune, humble flûte isolée,
> Une diversité de nos larmes d'argent.

In "Fragments du Narcisse," written some quarter of a century later, tears likewise occupy a central place: they signify the speaker's tragic longing as well as the sadness of nature ("l'arbre pleure," "le feuillage épars (. . .) pleure de toutes parts"), the anguish of love ("Ils se sentent des pleurs défendre leurs ténèbres"), the fragile pleasures of self-love

("Qu'ils sont doux les périls que nous pourrions choisir! /
(. . .) La même nuit en pleurs confondre nos yeux clos").
Yet, more than any particular trait, they convey the color
and tone, the sense of fatal transiency that informs the
poem.

Other works of Valéry's maturity take up the same nexus
of metaphors. Tears are nature's sorrow at the frustration
of thwarted love such as that which afflicts the trees in "Au
Platane":

> Ils vivent séparés, ils pleurent confondus
>   Dans une seule absence,
> Et leurs membres d'argent sont vainement fendus
>   A leur douce naissance.

Similarly, in "Le Cimetière marin," all the pathos of the
dead is evoked in a few words: "La larve file où se formaient
des pleurs." On the other hand, "La Dormeuse" contains
the unsoundable depths of a beauty whose source is hidden
like tears, and still more secret:

> Souffle, songes, silence, invincible accalmie,
>   Tu triomphes, ô paix plus puissante qu'un pleur . . .

Nevertheless, however varied these uses and admirable the
language, it is without doubt in *La Jeune Parque* and "La
Pythie," two of his greatest poems which are in a real sense
complementary, that the image has its most complex and
exciting treatment.

The young woman who wakes in the night and comes
to pursue her monologue "sur l'écueil mordu par la merveille" discovers the elegy of the world. As she speaks the
moist wind, the sea, the stars accompany her voice and pro-
long its plaint; but within the Parque herself we are aware
of another counterpoint, that of mind and body. Accompanying ideas, memories, resolutions, reasonings there is
an inner music, the basso continuo of the sensibility which
is the Parque's true center, her nonhistorical and nonanec-
dotal self. Although she appears to be caught up in an in-

tellectual dilemma her poem is, as Valéry noted, "une physiologie et une mélodie," or "un cours de physiologie," as he told Frédéric Lefèvre with not a little humor. He meant that a process of transformation has been articulated, an ordered cycle of the sensibility which serves as a basis for the Parque's thought, since it binds her consciousness to the body "comme une anémone de mer à son galet." [11] Now, in this drama, tears play a vital part from beginning to end, and indeed the initial moment of the poem is that wherein the Parque hears the weeping of a stranger who is her sister-self:

> Qui pleure là, sinon le vent simple, à cette heure
> Seule avec diamants extrêmes? . . . Mais qui pleure,
> Si proche de moi-même au moment de pleurer?

Written as it were in the margins of his early sonnet on Helen of Troy, these words recall the Mallarméan image of a wound inflicted on beauty; but here suffering does not signify, as it does in Mallarmé, a violation of mystery by the supreme artist who "explains" it, but the violation of a sensibility by the mind. This is the fatal confrontation like that of Narcissus with his reflection, or the Angel of Valéry's last published prose-poem with a tearful Man in the pool of his musing; it is the discovery of a pathetic division which the poem will seek to resolve. The passage of tears, followed step by step, establishes at the end a fresh beginning, for, if the Parque is known to the depths of her being, her sensibility finally remains in essence virginal: she is a "mère vierge toujours," her nature ever renewed:

> Tout va donc accomplir son acte solennel
> De toujours reparaître incomparable et chaste.

In the Parque, then, tears give sense and direction to the drama that is played out; they are the destiny within us,

---

[11] *Œuvres*, I, 865–866.

dominant like the crystalline stars ("Ces souverains éclats, ces invincibles armes"), connotative of our mortal nature:

> Très imminente larme, et seule à me répondre
> Larme qui fais trembler à mes regards humains
> Une variété de funèbres chemins . . .

Although the Parque is closed on herself in analysis, in sleep ("Les yeux dans les larmes"), she reaches the morning light of acceptance and self-recognition and exults in the sweetness of the sun that "bites" her like the serpent of consciousness in the first lines of her poem. At this point, tears appear in the form of spray that is flung from an ocean heaving with energy: "Un éblouissement d'étincelles glacées." This is the consummation of the kind of grace that Valéry described in a few lines of his manuscript under the title "Larme, Don": "Tu sais pour avoir voyagé dans l'arrière-pensée. A travers la roche mentale, l'ignorance, la masse. Chose au lieu d'idée, née de la même mère qu'une pensée. Chose qui se fait étrangère, équivalente, refus, divination."

How very far we are here from *La Cantate à trois voix*, Claudel's delicate composition on the theme of night and sadness and joyful discovery written a few years before *La Jeune Parque*, which yet presents many points of comparison, not the least of which is the image of tears: "Heure sereine! Tristesse et peine . . . Larmes vaines! tristesse et peine qui est vaine!" As in the opening section of Valéry's poem, so here: a modulation is built on the sound "heure" and its rhyme "pleure." The whole theme, however, will be the relationship of three women singing in the night— Laeta the Latin fiancée, Fausta the Polish wife, Beata the Egyptian widow—with the hour of emptiness, the apparent sadness of this moment of separation from the absent lover of each, who is Christ: they will learn, through the music they discover together, the true spiritual nature of happiness which requires immolation of the body. On the other

hand, if Valéry may well have been struck, when he put
pen to paper in 1913, by the dramatic efficacy of Claudel's
night-scene and the poignant insistence of one sound in the
first lines, his own poem follows the thread of a necessary
presence, a heaviness that resolves itself into lightness, a
secret gift that emerges and brings the rich treasure of life
in its train.

A parallel development is found in "La Pythie." At the
center of *Charmes* for which it serves as focal point, the
Pythoness's long hymn enacts the birth of poetry in an
astonishing tour de force, representing the animal torments
of a sensibility that has been invaded by "adulterous intelligence." The woman struggles in the mad throes of par-
turition; she protests, blasphemes, before recalling days of
sensuous happiness and calm; she turns to the future, ar-
gues with a monstrous god. But this conflict between being
and knowledge is resolved when she accepts the tear that
wells up from her body, an extract formed of her intimate
despair:

> Noirs témoins de tant de lumières
> Ne cherchez plus . . . Pleurez, mes yeux! . . .
> O pleurs dont les sources premières
> Sont trop profondes dans les cieux! . . .

And this tear becomes a stream, a voluptuous finger, a herd
of terrors—the fabulous metaphorical scheme of an irre-
sistible movement which the last lines of the poem convert
into the language of balance and judgement.

> Voici parler une Sagesse
> Et sonner cette auguste Voix
> Qui se connaît quand elle sonne
> N'être plus la voix de personne
> Tant que des ondes et des bois!

Conceived in pain, mysterious, the tear is apprehended at
last as the voice of poetry itself.[12]

[12] Compare this untitled poem of 1905 written in free verse which
expresses a like development from tears to speech (*Cahiers*, III, 772):

Thus, with moving amplitude, two major works show the force of the image we have pursued. A privileged note in Valéry, it indicates an all-too-human pathos which his Mediterranean sensibility knew well enough; or a magic charm exquisitely contained for him in the last hours of night; or, subsuming both associations, a diction that expresses the ideal self, the emotion as yet unnamed, an otherwise wordless meaning. "Quel sens cherche le mot dont le sens s'est perdu," we read in an unpublished draft of *La Jeune Parque*. Can we not then adopt tears as one emblem of this poet who survives in the words he found for his depths, in the lucid language that analyzes and names an intense theater of body and mind?

Larmes qui distillent, sourdent et tombent
Se séparant d'une masse cachée
Par une tension perceptible
Comme le trop-plein de l'impuissance
Equilibre de l'inavouable
Et de l'ineffable traversant
Malgré moi, malgré même
L'absence d'appareils pour lui
(Parler n'est-ce pas se mettre
En Equilibre?)

6: "Lucidité, phœnix de ce vertige . . ."

THROUGHOUT Valéry's work, one topic recurs with the regularity of a central theme. Eloquent of his constant endeavor to apprehend an elusive goal, "la belle endormie" is found time and again in the drawings that embellish his manuscripts, in his notebooks, his criticism, his poetry. She is the form given over to the beholder, a marvelously plastic Olympia in respect of whom he becomes both enchanted and enchanter. Yet we know that his act of contemplation is more than skin deep; that his glance seeks more than flesh; that here we must refer to the same *convoitise des secrets* he diagnosed in Degas, the same concern for intellectual and sensible possession he traced in Titian. "Joindre deux voluptés dans un acte sublime," he wrote, "où la possession de soi-même et de ses moyens, la possession de la Belle par tous les sens se fondent."[1] The woman is not asleep, but responsive to the probing eye and thought; nor is she merely a woman, but the means by which a mind will assuage its longings.

It can be no surprise that he was acutely sensitive to such a theme and that it provided ample matter for reflexion. His constant quest was to represent the quasi-physical structure of consciousness; and with an admirable feeling for

[1] Valéry is speaking of Titian ("Degas Danse Dessin," *Œuvres*, II, 1197). We may recall that Paul Claudel, in his dialogue "Le Poète et le Shamisen" of 1927, likened Valéry's work to "La belle dame du Prado."

149

line, an instinctive grasp of shape and mass, he took up his research like a voluptuary whose every moment is bound to a passion. To seize the wholeness of a complex thought, to contain a simultaneous vision of hazard and absorption, oblivion and pursuit, and the gamut of a myriad possibilities like the presence of a desirable form: this was the task of a lifetime. We may then justifiably give full weight to the comparison he used to designate his analysis: "J'aime la pensée véritable comme d'autres aiment le nu, qu'ils peindraient toute leur vie." [2] The poet surveys the sphere of consciousness, from its seeming tactility to its enigmatic center, as if it were some external thing whose treasure is inexhaustible.

And yet this form is not without its own abstract drama. The Mediterranean mixture of warmth and detachment can become a single brilliance; its gracious nebula of proposition and counter-proposition, its pulsing immobility, can collapse into a point of time—"ce moment qui foudroie tous les autres possibles ou connus." [3] Then language translates an ultimate moment like a crystal precipitated from a solution, or the self emerging from the multitude of its own thoughts. "Je ne suis plus qu'une de mes pensées / Devenue chose," says the Parque.[4] Night issues into dawn, and a hidden path and its end are uncovered where no path or end appeared to exist. The illumination affirms at the same time as it destroys, holds within itself the key that will be lost and sought again. Valéry thus experiences the seductive form—"le secret voluptueux de la forme sensible"—as both system and event, constellation and momentary fire; or, as he put it on one occasion, in words that posit the pattern of his self-awareness:

Lucidité, phœnix de ce vertige . . .[5]

2 *Cahiers,* IV, 881.   3 Ibid., XXVII, 822.
4 Previously unpublished.
5 Previously unpublished. Valéry uses the Latinate spelling of "phœnix" instead of the more usual "phénix."

The legendary phoenix occurs once in his work, in this decasyllable rejected from among the drafts of *La Jeune Parque,* but the sense is wholly typical: the bird of consumption and rebirth is the light of the intellect divested so to speak of its claim to reversibility, a clarity that crowns mental exercise, the self apprehended in an object of contemplation. In this instant a poignant song is heard: "Sur l'arbre de chair chante le minime oiseau spirituel." [6]

It was not always so. The earliest treatment of the theme turns on the progression of sleep as it triumphs over the body and mind in a largely external manner. "La Fileuse," for instance, at the beginning of the *Album de vers anciens,* suggests a gradual retreat from the world and, in poetic terms, the identification of form with sensuous surrender, "au gré de la caresse." The *terza rima* is used to convey continuity and a preciousness that echoes the first words in its last:

> Assise, la fileuse au bleu de la croisée . . .
> Au bleu de la croisée où tu filais la laine.

Valéry spoke in 1890 of his "PreRaphaelite" soul; likewise, in these lines written the following year, the mood is crepuscular and vaguely mystical as the woman is lulled by her "credulous spindle" and bathed in the "perfumes" of a rose-window. Sense impressions are mingled, a few words insistently repeated, and a series of verbs establishes the single scheme of sleep. In this way the spinner and her surroundings make a delicate composition of soft light and drowsiness and noncausal relationships. It is clear that this approach is par excellence painterly as it seldom was in the poems Valéry wrote before 1891. He may well have thought of the baroque poets, of Baudelaire and the very early Mallarmé in their handling of the same motif, although his own poem has no anguish, no search such as that which would "goûter le fard pleuré par tes paupières." Be-

sides, still other writers may have been more or less consciously recalled, as Leo Spitzer suggested in an essay on
"La Fileuse." [7] But the immediate source and provocation
was doubtless Courbet's "La Fileuse endormie" in the
Montpellier museum.[8] Valéry, of course, interpreted and
developed; he added the rose-window and hieratic note; he
even went so far as to transpose his spinner onto a legendary
plane in one early version that carries our thoughts forward
to *La Jeune Parque:*

Mais la Morte se croit la fileuse ancienne

Yet this image was later eliminated with the result that the
poem becomes, without myth or metaphysics, his masterly
response to Courbet's picture, and an accomplished example of *fin-de-siècle* revery. It clothes the first part of the
Album in the rhythms and imagined jewels of an adolescent dreamer—"Nous usions volontiers d'un vocabulaire
beaucoup incertain, toujours recherché" [9]—while serving at
the same time as a foil for later poems in which the treatment undergoes a radical change.

Already, we may say, the point of view inscribed in "La
Fileuse" is modified in "La Belle au bois dormant," later
to become the eighth poem of the *Album*. The original
version was written in the same year as "La Fileuse" and
similarly published in 1891. When we look back on it today with Valéry's other works in mind, we cannot but be
embarrassed by the artificiality of its atmosphere and its

---

[7] Leo Spitzer, "La genèse d'une poésie de Paul Valéry," *Renaissance,*
vols. 2–3, 311–321. The epigraph "Lilia . . . , neque nent" is a quotation from the Gospel according to St. Matthew (VI, v. 28): "Consider the
lilies of the field, how they grow; they toil not, neither do they spin."
Keats used the same epigraph for his "Ode on Indolence."

[8] This was shown by Jean Dubu in his article, "Valéry et Courbet:
origine de 'La Fileuse,'" published in the *Revue d'histoire littéraire de
la France,* no. 2 (April–June 1965), 239–243.

[9] "Sur les Narcisse," *Paul Valéry vivant* (Marseilles: Cahiers du Sud,
1946), 286.

overworked vaporousness. And yet it demonstrates, even more patently that "La Fileuse," the aura of magical possession with which the poet came to associate his theme. The development is not a temporal gradation but rather an immobile one that is held in the legendary distance of "un palais de roses pures." To this end the poet adopted the sonnet to which he later returned again and again so as to depict the sleeping woman and parallel motifs. If he was thereby following his masters of the second half of the nineteenth century, one needs to remember that the convention became for him the formal signature of his sensuousness. The four parts of "La Belle au bois dormant" show, then, an early attempt to encircle and comprehend a dream. Like "La Fileuse," it is more than an able stylistic exercise, although here the reference is musical, its delicacy modeled on Symbolist incantations. The nostalgia for an ideal control, and formal inventiveness, indicate a voluptuous eye that will grow more vigorous and demanding with the years.

Now it is precisely vigor and complexity that were introduced into "La Belle au bois dormant" (now called simply "Au bois dormant") when Valéry collected his early verse and republished it in 1920. Without altering the theme he revised the phrasing so that, as we read it in the *Album,* it has an appreciably different ring from its predecessor. Valéry had described the original version to Gide in November 1891 as silly— "un sonnet idiot," he said— and exclaimed: "Ah! si j'avais eu le temps de le lacérer." [10] When he took it up once more he made many changes: minor ones in the quatrains, the most significant of which is no doubt contained in lines 7 and 8. In contrast to the languid suavity of 1891 ("Ni s'enfuir la douceur pastorale des flûtes / Dont la rumeur antique emplit le bois dormant"), we now read:

10. *Correspondance André Gide-Paul Valéry,* p. 135.

> Ni, sur la forêt vague, un vent fondu de flûtes
> Déchirer la rumeur d'une phrase de cor.

The image of contained violence surely *lacerates* the som-
nolence and imposes new immediacy. In the tercets also,
numerous modifications deserve extensive comment, but in
general it is clear that Valéry has eliminated previous trite
abstractions ("nonchalante idylle," "sommeil tranquille,"
"rêves jolis," "éternel dormir") in favor of a brilliant development in which the pattern of positive statement followed
by negation balances that of the quatrains; but the language is suddenly more sensuous.

> Laisse, longue, l'écho rendormir la diane,
> O toujours plus égale à la molle liane
> Qui se balance et bat tes yeux ensevelis.
>
> Si proche de ta joue et si lente la rose
> Ne va pas dissiper ce délice de plis
> Secrètement sensible au rayon qui s'y pose.[11]

This is the mature Valéry whose verse may run the risk of
lushness, if hardly that of ethereality. The princess is pliant,
desirable, while the echoes in nature itself enunciate the
secrets of a woman's flesh. Another dimension has been
added that rounds out the theme and conveys its intensity.

The following year brought a wholly new treatment, this
time under the sway of the poet's fresh discovery of the
later Mallarmé. He told his friend J. P. Monod in 1942, in
response to a so-called "questionnaire," that before leaving
Montpellier he was already acquainted with a few of Mallarmé's greatest sonnets such as "Victorieusement fui le
suicide beau . . . ," "Quand l'ombre menaça de sa fatale
loi . . . ," "Toute gloire fume-t-il du soir . . . ," as well
as some others "dans des fascicules à 0.15 ou 0.20 achetés
dans des gares." [12] After composing his "Ballet," he no
doubt discarded it because of its highly derivative nature,

---

11 *Œuvres*, I, 79.
12 "Questionnaire P.V." in the Valeryanum of the Fonds Doucet.

but sent it to Gide in 1892 with the nine other pieces that
make up the collection he called "Ses Vers." It is, as Mallarmé had imagined that a good poem should be, "un
Ballet, représentable," expressing light and movement and
muted eroticism. Valéry does not describe the sleeping
woman but suggests her beauty obliquely in an aerial dance
of nothings—transparent insect, unspoken word, winged
minute, scattered flight of sparkles. He rejects concreteness
and wills his escape on these pleasurable images and
rhythms that exclude banality:

> Une nudité fraîche sous une paupière
> Balancée, amusée hors du chaos mondain[13]

Punctuation is suppressed; appositions suspend the resolution of the sense; two repeated prepositions "sur" and
"sous" discreetly govern the reciprocity of appearance and
concealment; while, not the least attractive element in the
disport of syntax, the final couplet points up preciousness
by an inversion and rare rhyme:

> Petit feu naturel d'un sidéral insecte
> Né sous le souffle d'or qui tes songes humecte.

(Valéry could not allow this rhyme to be lost and retained
it for his portrait of a modern and much more sensuous
Venus rising from the waves in "Baignée," later included
in the *Album*.) "Ballet" is then, it seems to me, a more
than able pastiche, and an important stage in the history
of the motif in Valéry. It sublimates voluptuousness, reduc-
ing it to refined imagery and sound, but this voluptuousness
that is distanced by poetic language will soon attain an
utterance less veiled.

A considerable change occurs when we turn to "Anne,"
which appeared for the first time in 1900 bearing the date
1893. It consisted of only six quatrains but grew in 1920
to nine, and finally thirteen in the second edition of the

---

13 *Œuvres*, I, 1592.

Album published in 1926. When we consult the folder that contains the various original drafts we find the cover decorated by Valéry with the drawing of a nude looking at herself in the mirror; and it is this plastic precision that strikes us in the first text entitled "Nox." Here the scene is not vague or legendary but realistic: "la dormeuse putain," as one early version puts it, is presented in a sequence of admirable details which depict curve and fold, shade and fullness. Anne, wholly given to the simplicity of sleep, has become the object of a glance that registers form and form alone in an extraordinarily mimetic language. The poet delights in poise, tension, gesture, which end on the piercing note of a bird as it renews the day. Only a trait or two indicate the abstract frame of reference written in the flesh: thus, the simile "comme un souvenir pressant ses propres chairs."

The final version, however, brought a significant amplification. Extending the poem to more than twice its original span, Valéry introduced two new points of view that enrich the poetic dimension considerably. Instead of the reposeful eye of the young poet, we have now the depiction of love as battle:

> . . . la vigueur et les gestes étranges
> Que pour tuer l'amour inventent les amants.

A series of provocative images of violence and shipwreck contrast, in Parnassian style, with the initial scene of physical surrender.

> L'amour t'aborde, armé des regards de la haine,
> Pour combattre dans l'ombre une hydre de baisers!

Then in st. 10 a further change of tone occurs as the poet addresses the woman directly in the moment before dawn. Her sleep is as death; her stillness a fatal posture ("vain marbre," "masque d'âme au sommeil à jamais immolée"). The last quatrain of the original text, following these three stanzas devoted to pathetic invocation, grows in strength as an image of resurrection beyond remorse—the bird—sings in the morning sun. These thirteen stanzas are thus handled in the final version with a resonance that has increased dramatically from the early text. "Anne" is no longer the relatively simple portrait of a woman asleep but has taken on the complexity of total experience.

We may say then that these four variations on a single theme, in "La Fileuse," "Au bois dormant," "Ballet," and "Anne," fix a scheme of relationships whose sum is a controlled delectation of the mind. "Intellectuel, Valéry? Quelle bêtise! C'est un voluptueux, et toute son œuvre est une attention voluptueuse." [14] Claudel's well-known words denote the wiles and whims and secret involvement of this poet of sensible form: over and again Lucifer will seduce Eve to become the artist of his fabling desire. Yet Valéry was to go much further in his exploration and renew his approach with incisiveness during the period of his mature work. Now the mind's vitality will be fired by the act of contemplation so that it no longer merely contains the object of its glance but, when it least suspects, is itself discovered in what it sees.

Perhaps the finest of these works is a sonnet which was listed at one time for inclusion in *Charmes* under the title of "La Nuit." It is especially noteworthy, when we approach it after the early treatments we have read, in that it shows none of Valéry's gifts for visual evocation, but rather strong reliance on the sense of touch. The woman is not glimpsed, but felt in the dark of the night; all is shaped to her body ("le tour dormant de ton flanc pur," "épaule pleine," "le fluide dessin"), to her warmth and breathing. The run-on lines, the insistent alliteration evoke this plasticity whose contours are fashioned in shadow. The poem seems to me a remarkable accomplishment which a study

[14] Paul Claudel: *Œuvres en prose*, 824.

of the original draft enables us to gauge all the better. We find that the first version is much simpler than the last since it entails no more than an enumeration of the woman's body in the way of the *vers anciens.* I refer in particular to the second quatrain, which is of considerable force:

> Brûle-là, et te tourne ô feu nu de mon soir
> Epaule où découlant selon la fraîche tresse
> Le temps parfumé roule et mêle une caresse
> Douce et nombreuse sur le délice tout noir.[15]

Valéry offers the intimate alliance of the tactile and olfactory which ends with the naming of the woman to whom the lines are addressed: she is Jeannie, that is, Madame Paul Valéry:

> Et toute une ténèbre écoutant le génie
> Tranquille de ton cœur
> Délicieusement renfermant ma Jeannie.

In characteristic manner he later excluded this personal note together with the Mallarméan preciousness of the rhyme. Instead, he embarked on an abstract analysis which served him in undertaking his revision. Beginning with an attempt to describe the attitude of the sleeping woman, he seized on the idea of her childlikeness: "Tout contact, chaleur, blottissement, enfant . . ." which led to the image implicit throughout the final version, and explicit in the last two lines: "Comme en germe—comme mon germe même—si j'étais / Et comme si j'étais en germe devant moi." This transition from the objective to the subjective, nowhere present in the early draft, brings about a complete transformation, for now the poet is not an observer, but a participant. A schematic representation gives an idea, if still an incomplete one, of the complexity that will be teased from the theme as Valéry laid the foundations for the four sections of his sonnet: "1. Toi-Exposition, 2. Moi-Lucide, 3. Chant, 4. Descente."

15 Previously unpublished.

After the balance of the first two parts, the plan indicates
a progression that leads the woman to turn toward her
lover and assume the innocence of sleep as from an instinctive affection: "Si proche et si lointaine / Toute / Réduite,
diminuée / à tâtons—instinctivement / Tu me cherches";
"Je sens tendre à moi tout l'instinct de ton ombre"; "Je me
sens te sourire au-dessus du vain jeu / De tes songes et du
sang"; "Tout le poids de ta chair tombe." Contemplation
becomes the awareness of change, the articulation of a distance that is also closeness, an absence that is also presence
—*"une présence d'absence,"* as Valéry wrote concerning
Manet's portrait of Berthe Morisot—as subtly desirable
as an ideal thought. The next version, and the definitive
one, express this in a paradoxical apostrophe:

> O toujours plus absente et toujours plus prochaine.

Yet whereas the form was held in the poet's consciousness,
he now sketches out a sequence of events that names a
necessity binding him to what he touches, but also to a
world beyond the reach of touch:

> Et ce bras qui m'enchaîne
> S'enchaîne à ton songe
> Au plus profond de ton songe et
> Ce songe s'enchaîne aux ombres.

This link with an intimate yet alien mystery is condensed
into line 9 of the final draft where it serves to introduce
an additional complexity, since the woman's very dreams
are grasped in terms of freshness and fluidity, and the marriage of rare light and warmth and breath. The last two
lines, like a Shakespearian couplet, provide the final discovery that takes the sonnet decisively out of the realm of
the *Album* into that of *Charmes*. The poet who was god
has become a child, given over to the breast of a mother;
he who was on a shore separate from humanity by his im-
perious stance is the most dependent and lost of men. And
yet this is not the end-limit of his descent into awareness.

The mother-child continuity is pursued to a point where the wheel comes full circle, and the sensibility that touched on the woman's dreams is itself encompassed, its inmost fancy known and absorbed. The form thus mirrors exactly the theme which turns on itself in a moment of self-revelation.

> Et ce bras mollement à tes songes m'enchaîne
> Dont je sens m'effleurer le fluide dessin
> De fraîcheur descendue au velours d'une haleine
>
> Jusqu'à la masse d'ambre et d'âme de ton sein
> Où perdu que je suis comme dans une mère
> Tu respires l'enfant de ma seule chimère.[16]

By the concentrated force of his attention the poet is transformed from the detached observer he was, fully confident in his powers; he is enclosed in his thought just as he encloses it. This movement is all the more striking in a poem that explores with such insistence the domain of touch until the last two lines formulate the drama of consciousness in an abstract analogy. Amid the intense play of the senses a self-irony is felt and known.

"Ma pensée est comme à tâtons dans elle-même." [17] That is the drama of "Ma nuit," this deeply personal sonnet of night which was never published during the poet's lifetime, but it also underpins the entire period of artistic rebirth culminating in *La Jeune Parque* and *Charmes*. Two poems in particular take up with admirable strength the theme of the sleeping beauty, not more movingly, I think, than "Ma nuit," if in terms of heightened sensuousness and painterly skill. "La Dormeuse" is of course close to "Anne," and still closer to "Ma nuit" by its scheme of self-recognition, but it has magnificent control of sunlight and shadow, image and sound, and the mental surprise that surpasses control and shows the sensibility as the creation of what it

---

[16] *Œuvres*, II, 1616.
[17] Letter to Jean Paulhan, 1922, quoted in the *Nouvelle Revue Française*, August 1971, p. 20.

sees. At first, there is only the questioning of an inert form whose youth and warmth and innocence suggest a holocaust in the name of tenderness. Drawn to the mask, the poet postulates a ritual vaporization that changes the woman into radiance and the air she breathes into a flower. Then the point of view is modified: instead of the vital thrust of the sensibility surging upwards from a secret center, the second quatrain proposes the weight of a liquid force that overcomes the body with a pathos beyond tears. In the first tercet all is surrender and yet absorption, like grace both given and received. Here, once again, the angle of vision has changed, together with the tone and mode of address. Yet this marriage of contemplation and speculation leads finally to the poem's most sensuously precise images whereby the circular attempt to embrace a form—"rotation autour d'un axe"—is suddenly arrested by the verb "veiller." The body is vigilant, and the eye that seemed to hold the woman captive is watched by what it sees. The fervent play of words and rhythms around a single form, and the poet's commitment as he seeks to encompass it, signify the mind itself.

> Oh! te saisir enfin! . . . Prendre ce calme torse
> Plus pur que d'une femme, et non formé de fruit.[18]

We are not, however, following the tragic soliloquy of Narcissus, for "La Dormeuse" constitutes a point of passionate attention which as it were precipitates the self—"par irritation insupportable qui a excité un *moi* no 2 à détacher de soi un *moi* premier—comme une meule trop centrifugée, ou *une masse nébuleuse en rotation*," as Valéry wrote concerning his own crisis of 1892.[19]

The same pattern is carried still further in the last poem of the group. "La Fausse Morte" appeared one year after "La Dormeuse" and makes a fitting conclusion to Valéry's

18 "Fragments du Narcisse," *Œuvres*, I, 129.
19 *Cahiers*, XVI, 45.

effort to exhaust a cycle of interpretation; indeed these
lines are in many ways at the opposite pole from "La
Fileuse," "Au bois dormant," "Ballet," and "Anne," and
complementary to "Ma nuit" and "La Dormeuse." The
poetic self is not content to observe but impelled to act;
and the woman, no longer inert, does violence to her beholder. The sexual drama, present in subdued fashion in
other poems, suddenly comes to the fore as this gentle love
song progresses on its balanced alexandrines and octosyllables. It recalls certain baroque poetry in its paradoxical
construction and imagery; but harmony and order prevail
by way of the rhythmic period which rediscovers its beginning in its end, and by the controlled resolutions of its
metaphorical structure. Shadow becomes illumination, lan-
guishment yields to energy, the dead woman is resurrected,
her lover experiences exuberant death. The motif thus discovers knowledge on its concave parabola of sound and
image: that which seemed to involve surrender to an invincible appeal brings its own intimate revelation. The
poem is, then, important as the final point in a series by
which the sensibility comes to know a form, recognizing its
versatility and attraction, its inertness and activity, and
thereby defining in the most concrete and personal manner
possible Valéry's conception of pure poetry. We recall the
famous passage from "Calepin d'un poète": "Si le poète
pouvait arriver à construire des œuvres où rien de ce qui
est de la prose n'apparaîtrait plus, des poèmes où la continuité musicale ne serait jamais interrompue, où les relations de signification seraient elles-mêmes perpétuellement
pareilles à des rapports harmoniques, *où la transmutation
des pensées les unes dans les autres paraîtrait plus importante que toute pensée,* où le jeu des figures contiendrait
la réalité du sujet, alors l'on pourrait parler de *poésie pure*
comme d'une chose existante." [20] Looked at in this light,

---

[20] *Œuvres*, I, 1463.

the seven poems we have examined—none of which by itself would be sufficient to make of Valéry a major poet—
compose a single play of figures, the varied texture of a
literary fugue. In the movement of a verbal sequence, he
creates for himself the lucid pattern of his commitment to
a particular theme:

> Flagelle-toi! . . . Parais l'impatient martyr
> Qui soi-même s'écorche,
> Et dispute à la flamme impuissante à partir
> Ses retours vers la torche! [21]

We have thus followed what I take to be a fundamental
motif written into poems conceived over a period of thirty
years, between 1891 and the time of *Charmes*. Nevertheless,
another text would need to be studied in detail; it stands
beside these poems and in a sense provides their fulcrum.
I refer to *Agathe ou la sainte du sommeil*, published in a
limited edition in 1956. It was begun in 1898 and taken up
on different occasions throughout the poet's life, most notably about 1912 and in the early twenties. Under a title he
preferred to all others which no doubt recalls Baudelaire,
Valéry sought to calculate a geometry of the mind that
would be achieved by a refusal to delimit any one thought
or image. "Retardons encore cette pensée, ne la laissons pas
parler, maintenons l'état de fusion, d'orientation intime.
Laissons-la seulement devenir la plus pure, prendre sa forme
la plus formelle." [22] By this spiritual exercise in decelera-
tion, the midnight of vision reduces consciousness to a space
of abstract notions, "système nul ou indifférent," which language translates by words like "vérité," "liberté," "pureté,"
"extrémité." But this rigorous detachment from any one
moment of thought brings the sentiment of power over all
moments. The text presents itself to us as a sequence that
is constantly resolved, in the plastic manner we found in

21 Ibid., 115.
22 *Cahiers*, III, 739.

the poems, into a texture whose equivocalness holds it at a remove from the self. "La destruction fut ma Béatrice": Valéry's perfect personage of night could well echo Mallarmé. And yet this woman who wakes in the darkness like her sister Parque holds within her consciousness a diamond point of desire, a brilliance of fire and beating heart— "cette palpitation." She knows a midday ("le midi admirable de ma présence") that answers the midnight of the beginning and can manifest itself in a stable moment ("une fixité splendide"). The mind now finds its inmost secret in this feminine form—"quelque créature extrêmement désirée de l'esprit"—who is not unlike the "moi projeté absolu" of Igitur. "Extérieure à tout chemin, inconnue à toute violence elle est gisant hors de toute figure et de toute ressemblance, en pleine certitude; comme un bloc est tranquille à une ligne de doigts." [23] This is the poem of consciousness as it is maintained in a state of control, but also the privileged form, the pearl, the figure that is called up by its very absence—"j'en découvre infiniment le manque"—and that must itself bear the name "Agathe."

So this passage unfolds a dialectic between two poles of thought. Oriented by the unusual frequency of its adverbs, it traces a kind of abstract mobility that is resumed in the end by the antithesis of two words: ". . . voluptueusement, la palpitation de l'espace multiple ne ravive plus qu'à peine ma chair; et . . . volontairement, je ne goûte plus d'idée isolée. . . ." *Voluptueusement, volontairement:* here is in sum the interplay of attitudes contained in the motif of the sleeping beauty which endows it with such vitality. These extremes may marry in a way that produces a controlled eroticism; they may also, from their opposition, give rise to an ironic self-awareness. At times, one might say, the self is master of what it surveys; at others, it experiences the wound of an intimate violation. "Je suis maître de

23 *Œuvres,* II, 1391.

former des images," writes Valéry. "Mais des images sont
maîtres de moi." [24] In this vital ambiguity of forms expressed with sensuous art in the theme we have examined,
but underlying his whole work, I admire what seems to me
a unique poetic activity as it conceives in order to lose
again, like a phoenix, its instant of knowledge.

[24] *Cahiers*, XXI, 356.

7: "O roi des ombres fait de flamme . . ."

FEW AUTHORS, I think, have been as preoccupied with the theme of light. We have only to consider his poetry or poetic prose alongside the contemporary works of Claudel and Apollinaire to recall its singular dedication to the cult of the sun. At times it translates an orgy of the senses such as we find in "Poésie brute" ("Au soleil sur mon lit après l'eau / Au soleil et au reflet énorme du soleil sur la mer, / Sous ma fenêtre / Et aux reflets et aux reflets des reflets / Du soleil et des soleils sur la mer . . ."),[1] at others it is characteristically associated with the cognitive process, with the mind reaching towards self-awareness as at the end of the Parque's struggle with familiar shadows or in the plaintive prayers of Narcisse. No doubt it would be highly revealing to isolate the theme with a view to a phenomenological study of its uses, and indeed an approach of this kind has been attempted by J. L. Faivre in a series of articles and, more recently still, by Jean Levaillant.[2] My present aim however is more modest: I wish to bring together "Neige," "A l'aurore," and "Heure," each collected in 1942 in *Pièces diverses*, which offer three moods, three moments of the sensi-

---

1 "Au soleil," *Œuvres*, I, 354.

2 J. L. Faivre, "Paul Valéry et le thème de la lumière," *Les Lettres romanes*, XX, no. 4; XXI, nos. 1, 4; XXII, nos. 1–2; Jean Levaillant, "Paul Valéry et la lumière," *Cahiers de l'Association internationale des Etudes françaises*, no. 22, May 1968.

bility that show Valéry's responsiveness to light, the acuteness of his glance, and the corresponding mastery of poetic expression which was his fruit of long desire. Wistfulness, doubt, serenity; objective description, the divided sensibility, a fragile harmony of world and intellect: the varied facets of the self are made known, no less plainly in these minor pieces than elsewhere, by way of a vital confrontation. We recall the Serpent's pleasure as he contemplates the spectacle, albeit an illusory one, of nature:

> Toujours le mensonge m'a plu
> Que tu répands sur l'absolu
> O roi des ombres fait de flamme!

Like several other poems Valéry published or sketched out among his notebooks, "Neige" takes for its theme the first light of morning. We know that in his notebooks it was also his favorite moment which he analyzed as the attentive eye saw it and discovered to be a regular stimulus for his meditations. "Il n'est pas pour moi de phénomène plus excitant que le réveil," he observed. "Je me rappelle des matins si purs, si premiers, si nus au sortir de la nuit, si jeunes et si frais que c'était à en pleurer de désespoir et d'amour." [3] But if dawn's coming was to constitute the décor of "Sémiramis," *La Jeune Parque* and "Aurore," it is much less ambitiously handled in the first short piece we are to examine. The tone is wholly personal, and the imagery taken from everyday life like a page in a diary in this intimate landscape comparable in manner to the numerous aquarelles Valéry painted in his *Cahiers*. Yet despite its apparent simplicity, it deserves more than a casual glance from the reader since it may well serve to typify, I believe, his artistic integrity.

Ten versions of the poem have come down to us, six of them in typed form, which reveal that even in his apparently slighter pieces the middle-aged author was vitally

[3] *Cahiers*, XII, 838.

concerned to achieve his highest ideals of expression. At one time we find "Neige" amongst a list of his major poems to be included in 1922 in the volume of *Charmes*. This would seem to indicate that he was well satisfied with its success, although the final version did not in fact appear until some twenty years later.

The original draft, or at least the earliest that seems to have survived, is written on an unlined sheet of paper that is now kept in the Valeryanum of the Bibliothèque Sainte-Geneviève. We see that the poet was experimenting with a scheme of rhymes which he was later to abandon:

> Quel silence, battu d'un morne bruit de bêche!
> Saisi jusques au creux de ma chère chaleur
> Je m'éveille, endormi par cette neige fraîche.
>
> Mes yeux trouvent un jour d'une dure pâleur
> Et la chair langoureuse (paresseuse) a peur de l'innocence.
> Oh! combien de flocons pendant ma douce absence
> Durent les sombres cieux perdre toute la nuit!
> Tandis que j'ignorais les ténèbres énormes
> Ce duvet descendu des hauteurs de l'ennui
>   (de leur muet ennui)
> A solennellement enseveli les formes.

Many of the details of the final version, including the contrast between violation and innocence, and seven of the fourteen rhyme words, are already present. Nevertheless, the ending still eluded Valéry as it would continue to do for a considerable time; the verbal shock of line 3 ("m'éveille," "endormi") would not be maintained; the mood introduced by "morne" in the first line as providing the emotional keynote of the poem would soon be replaced by a less direct and more suggestive epithet; while in the last lines the image of the solemn death of appearances was to be wholly renewed by the theme of enchantment.

These ten lines have been crossed out and are accompanied in the same manuscript by a second version which Valéry wrote immediately beneath:

Quel silence battu d'un morne bruit de bêche!
Je m'éveille endormi par cette neige fraîche
Qui me saisit la chair dans sa chère chaleur.
Mes yeux trouvent un jour d'une dure pâleur
Et saisie au profond de ma chère chaleur
L'âme . . . . a peur de l'innocence
Oh combien de flocons, pendant ma douce absence
                   (ô ma tiède absence)
Durent les sombres cieux perdre toute la nuit!
Ce duvet descendu des cimes de l'ennui
                   (sans bruit)
Tandis que j'ignorais les ténèbres énormes
A solennellement enseveli les formes.

If little has been changed in the expression, there are certainly a few modifications for the worse, as the poet was
quick to realize (for instance, the cloying alliteration of "la
chair dans sa chère chaleur"). The major progress, however,
is in the use of rhyming couplets which gives the poem its
tone of gentle monologue, of gradual discovery of the world
by means of precise, clearly measured touches. This technique was to remain constant through the succeeding versions.

The eight other drafts, to be found today among the
poet's papers, are wrapped in the 1930 edition of his essay
"De l'éminente dignité des arts du feu." They show an extraordinary care for composition as he took up again and
again the whole poem, altering isolated words or images,
modifying the phrasing. Thus for line 2 ("Je m'éveille, endormi par cette neige fraîche") he tried at various moments
a whole string of adjectives to improve on "endormi": "attendu," but also "ébahi," "étonné," "saisi," "engourdi,"
"émerveillé," "ébloui." In like manner he hesitated between "saisit" and "surprend," and "creux, "sein," and
"soin" in line 3, between "jour" and "ciel" in line 4; while
line 10 bears the signs of repeated revision: "Quelle molle
candeur (Et quelle immense paix) (Et quelle blanche paix)
(intimité / pureté) (Sous sa morne candeur) (D'une aveugle

candeur) (Du poids de sa candeur) (Tendre et lourde candeur) sourdement (lentement / mollement) augmentée (en-
fantée)." As for the last lines, which will be so masterly in
the final version, they were born of particular patience. We
have seen the first solution that was proposed; next, Valéry
attempted a somewhat similar approach:

> Tandis que je vivais à l'ombre de ma chair
> Je trouvais dans mon sang la rumeur de la mer

and its variant:

> De mon sang se formait la rumeur de la mer

again:

> Tandis que dans mon ombre (en mon sommeil)
>   ignoré de mon corps
> Je heurtais de l'âme . . .
> Je vivais loin de moi comme une fleur coupée

Yet, however suggestive these two images of blood as a
teeming ocean and the self as a cut flower, they were quickly
abandoned. As we examine subsequent manuscripts, we
come upon the outline of still further developments that
aim to bring the poem to a close, by means of this apostrophe:

> Je te salue, ô jour sans visage et sans voix
> Silence, Neige, pieuse Neige . . .
> Qui me fait . . . . muette chute

or by evoking mysterious origins:

> L'ombre rêvait d'un jour sans visage et sans voix
> Où les oiseaux perdus ne reconnaissent . . . . . toits

or the confusion of mind and senses:

> L'ouïe espère au loin (Le temps vide a perdu la surprise des pas)
> L'oiseau, même l'esprit (ni le regard) ne s'y retrouvent pas
> Tant s'est changé le monde en solitude sourde
> L'oiseau frémit et fuit le lourd recul
>   (. . . une hanche trop lourde)

These last lines are finely felt and offer scope for what
might have been an admirable sequence; instead, we find
Valéry taking up one image—the correspondence between a
lost bird and the bewitched glance—and leaving aside the
other details. Thus we read:

> Les regards, les oiseaux s'égarent sur les toits
> L'amour n'aperçoit plus . . .
> (frémit et fuit cette paix implacable)

again, in more amplified form:

> Les regards, les oiseaux s'égarent sur les toits
> Accablés du fardeau qui leur tombe des nues
> L'âme n'aperçoit que solitudes nues
> Qui la font s'étonner de vivre . . .

Valéry underlines the loneliness of both scene and spectator,
and the glance by which the self becomes conscious of its
presence as some alien thing. Yet once again he was not
satisfied and had to leave the problem of the conclusion unresolved for the time being. Was not *"Maturare!"* the oft
repeated exclamation of his Monsieur Teste? [4] Some twenty
years later, in 1939, "Neige" appeared in the collection of
prose and verse entitled *Mélange* where the image of the
lost glance was once again adopted ("regard perdu") but, as
we shall see, rendered wistful by the discovery in the midst of
whiteness of the concealed wealth of life and hope.

Consciousness is first stirred by an auditory impression
that sets the scene with wonderful particularity:

> Quel silence battu d'un simple bruit de bêche! . . . [5]

The exclamation concentrates for us the quality of stillness
and sound that, before anything, typifies a snow-clad morning. The silence is measured by the strokes of a spade with
which some early riser is clearing the path; and the isolated
alexandrine echoes in its rhythm and alliteration the

---

[4] *Monsieur Teste, Œuvres,* II, 18.
[5] *Œuvres,* I, 325.

wonder of a transformed atmosphere. Before thought and feeling, before self-consciousness, there is this sensation which translates a world discovered anew.

> Je m'éveille, attendu par cette neige fraîche
> Qui me saisit au creux de ma chère chaleur.

The poet now finds himself as it were, places his sensibility at the center of things, assumes awareness in relation to his surroundings. His sensations are tactile as the cold of fresh-fallen snow is described in terms of a body that has been impatiently waiting to seize upon his own. The harshness of this action ("me saisit au creux de ma chère chaleur") plays across the fullness of the sound. Warmth is suddenly confronted with cool, the senses with a radical violation.

> Mes yeux trouvent un jour d'une dure pâleur
> Et ma chair langoureuse a peur de l'innocence.

Visual sensation also enriches consciousness as, succinctly, the paradoxical union of harshness and pallor composes before the eyes of our imagination the peculiar hues of grey and white, the subdued glow of a morning when snow has fallen. The invading presence that we found in the previous lines with their erotic overtones yields before the glance which localizes it and strips it of lust. For it is the sensibility which now longs for bodily contact, its flesh heavy with desire ("ma chair langoureuse"); but voluptuousness is balanced by the restraint and awe imposed by the particular purity which a glance on the virgin snow has revealed. Thus these two lines modify, if not reverse, the scene as it was initially interpreted and bring vital equivocalness into the description.

> Oh! combien de flocons, pendant ma douce absence,
> Durent les sombres cieux perdre toute la nuit!

Turning away from sensation and sentiment, the poet speculates on the origin of the spectacle he has in front of him. He exclaims in wonderment at a transformation that

occurred whilst he was asleep and the sensibility was com-
fortably alone with itself and separate from the world ("ma
douce absence"), unaware that all appearances were being
changed. A miracle has been wrought: out of black night,
out of so many flakes, has come this mass of whiteness. The
past definite tense, by its unexpectedness and the weight it is
given at the beginning of the line (and, we may say, by its
echo of "dure" in line 4), emphasizes the completion of the
action, the fulfilment of renewal.

> Quel pur désert tombé des ténèbres sans bruit
> Vint effacer les traits de la terre enchantée
> Sous cette ample candeur sourdement augmentée
> Et la fondre en un lieu sans visage et sans voix . . .

The next seven lines constitute a single sentence which
contains a delicate modulation of the theme. At first the
mind continues its meditation on the coming of the snow
that has touched well-known landmarks and bewitched the
earth ("la terre enchantée"). The only movement is down-
wards ("tombé," "sous . . .") as a desert of purity, an ideal
and immaculate wasteland, imposes its sway. The notions of
innocence and whiteness are combined in the word "candeur" which conjures up the whole scene in the two
remarkable lines 10 and 11, so gravely sensuous in their
sound and imagery of absorption. The scene is bereft of
familiar detail and personality, and "sans bruit," "sourdement," "sans visage et sans voix" heighten the solitude
which will find its complementary balance in the last three
lines.

> Où le regard perdu relève quelques toits
> Qui cachent leur trésor de vie accoutumée
> A peine offrant le vœu d'une vague fumée.

For if a featureless landscape would seem to have banished
all life, and the eye is lost without familiar details, the poet
can nevertheless pick out the roofs which indicate, however frailly, the presence of homes and their dwellers. In-

stead of an enchanted desert he discovers a treasure of humble life that is still being pursued in secret. The sensuous imagery of the previous lines is answered by this modest visual image of the wisp of smoke rising from the hidden house, that provides the complementary upward movement to the "fall" of the previous lines.

"Neige" seems to me then a striking illustration of Valéry's control over the means and ends of his art. It is clearly unusual for him to propose a poem which treats one of the most frequently sung aspects of nature, and to do so without any attempt to allegorize as in "Au Platane" or "Les Grenades." Yet although he does not deviate from the principle of an exercise in description, he achieves a beautifully poised language that takes us far beyond the stable world of a Théophile Gautier, for instance. The complexity of his approach denotes the mature mind in its response to a privileged moment of experience.

We have already observed the patent evidence of poetry in the pattern of sound, which weaves these fourteen alexandrines into a line of discourse that confidently moves with a necessity of its own across five sentences, the last of which stretches out for seven verses as if to imitate a substance reduced at last to its essence, its final "vœu." But of course this is but the premise of the poem, not its central originality. From our reading of "Neige" we are aware that the form is a vehicle for depicting, not merely a series of impressions, but the process of awakening as it is registered by the whole sensibility. The song contains the gradual exploration of the world that involves hearing, touch, sight, affectivity, and speculation, and implicitly provides the representation of a lyrical and universal self totally engaged in the act of apprehending a scene that is known and yet suddenly strange. Just as in his other major compositions like *La Jeune Parque* and "Le Cimetière marin," but in a much smaller compass, Valéry shows the drama by which sensitivity and self-awareness meet and marry. Nor does he for one moment lose his grip on things, his direct relationship to external phenomena, which he perceives with clarity and rigor.

A further feature is clear: the structural method used by the poet consists of a sequence of semantic proposals and resolutions, a constant return to a point of equilibrium as one detail is contrasted with another and creates a sensuous substance that contains within itself a sequence of verbal tensions. We observed for instance in the last section that the wasteland has its complementary element in a precious fund of familiar life, shadows ("ténèbres") in whiteness ("candeur"), the descending movement ("tombé," "sous") in a rising one ("relève," "offrant le vœu d'une vague fumée"). In the same way the first part of the poem brings together silence and noise, cool and warmth, bodily desire and innocence, harshness and gentleness; while the snow has both a rapist's violence and the simple purity of nature. We realize that Valéry's language possesses a harmony he has won and not asserted, which gives his short elegy the subtlety of a statement alive with intellectual vigor.

A song takes up once again the interrelationship between the self and the first light of morning, but in quite different terms from "Neige." In "A l'aurore" dawn is a loving woman who brings an inestimable gift of charms and plentiful promise. Yet such beauty is not joy since the sensibility has suddenly grown aware of a fatal separation that divides it from the world. As poignantly as a Verlaine lament, the octosyllables express the pathos of solitude in measured coloring and tone: "La pensée triste, et voulue telle, ou crue voulue telle," as Verlaine put it.[6] The unpretentiousness of the form, the shifting rhythms, the delicacy of the language recall certain traits of the poet of *Les Poèmes*

---

[6] Paul Verlaine, *Œuvres poétiques complètes*, ed. Y. G. Le Dantec (Paris: Gallimard, Pléiade, 1959), 901.

saturniens or *Romances sans paroles;* and even the irregular
rhyme scheme of the first stanza makes us think of a similar
nostalgic insistence in Verlaine:

> Il pleure dans mon cœur
> Comme il pleut sur la ville.
> Quelle est cette langueur
> Qui pénètre mon cœur?

But Valéry's poem is none the less unmistakably his own,
above all by the sensuousness of the imagery and the manner
in which the intellect plies its theme from several points of
view—stating, pleading, doubting, questioning. The form
combines richness of sound, such as the exquisite use of
nasals and the continuity of *ou* throughout, with a rapid
meter that has neither time nor space for grandiloquence.

If we have no precise indication as to the date of composition it is reasonable to assume from the style, as well as
from the absence of any reference to it in the various manuscripts of the period 1912 to 1925, that it was written in the
middle 'thirties, about the time of the first draft of "L'Oiseau
cruel." The earliest document that has survived contains the
first quatrain typed in an almost definitive state:

> Ce matin, avant la chaleur,
> La tendresse de la couleur
> A peine éparse sur le monde
> Parfois étonne la douleur.

Immediately beneath this the final reading of line 4 is given
as a variant: "Etonne et blesse la douleur." Also on this
page we find in handwritten form the initial draft of the
second stanza, after a groping search for line 5: "O nuit, ma
nuit profonde / trop longue et trop profonde / qui fûtes
trop profonde / que j'ai toute soufferte. . . ." Then, below,
Valéry traces the profile of the quatrain, developing the
thought along lines we recognize, but conceiving it as a
question rather than the plea we shall later hear:

> O nuit qui fûtes si profonde
> M'allez-vous laisser éblouir
> Par une aurore rose et blonde
> O vais-je perdre mon malheur.

The three succeeding drafts (MSS B, C, and D), all type-written, provide evidence of the careful attention to detail which preceded the final version. I note the principal variants:

Stanza 1: the final reading of line 4 is still not settled and we find "Parfois étonne la douleur" (MS B), "Etonne (blesse) l'homme de douleur" (MS C).

Stanza 2: For lines 7 and 8 "Et cette fleur du jour (temps) offerte / Sur le front du temps (jour) gracieux" (MS B), "Et cette (leur) fleur immense (immense fleur) offerte."

Stanza 3: "Grande offrande d'ardentes roses / Mon cœur vous peut-il soutenir / Et voir rougissantes les choses (de roses) / Toutes nouvelles (La vie visible) (La vie heureuse) revenir?" (MS B); "Voir rougissantes sur les choses / Toutes promesses revenir (De leur ténèbre revenir)" (MS C).

Stanza 4: "Tant se fit (j'ai vu) de songes mélange / Sur (Dans) mes ténèbres sans sommeil / Qu'auprès des mensonges se range (Qu'à la fin parmi les mensonges) / L'étrange force (Je range les feux) du soleil" (MS B); "Tant (Mais) j'ai vu mélange de songes (se feindre tant de songes) / Dans (Sur) mes ténèbres sans sommeil . . " (MS B); "Tant il fit de songes mélange . . ." (MS D).

Stanza 5: For lines 18–20 there are a considerable number of readings contained in MS B: "Avec dégoût, avec désir (Comme un leurre ou comme un espoir) (comme un bien) / Cet or vierge sur une feuille (Ce jour très jeune sur la feuille) / Né parmi l'ombre d'où je viens (d'où tu viens) / Où l'espace (l'espoir) se laisse saisir."

Yet from the beginning, in both early versions and the final state, the lyrical impulse coincides with an elect moment of time that is the interval at the end of night and before the fullness of day.

> A l'aurore, avant la chaleur,
> La tendresse de la couleur
> A peine éparse sur le monde,
> Etonne et blesse la douleur.[7]

It is a world responding to the subtle touch of morning twilight, the grace of nature in the tender form of a woman. But to the sensibility that has endured a night-long vigil it comes as a surprise, and as a very wound inflicted on inner suffering. The distance between the world and the self, between beauty and brooding meditation, creates the tension the poem will attempt to resolve. What the self experiences, however fleeting the approach of light, has the force of a necessity that is echoed in the form. No language could be more universal, and the alliteration and assonance, the three rhymes (lines 1, 2, 4), in particular the interior rhyme of the key words "tendresse" and "blesse," reinforce our sense of fatal confrontation.

> O Nuit, que j'ai toute soufferte,
> Souffrez ce sourire des cieux
> Et cette immense fleur offerte
> Sur le front d'un jour gracieux.

The mode of address changes from statement to invocation as the voice suddenly rises in a personal summons to Night, which is the poet's own immediate past and present. The verb "souffrir" refers both to the weight of thought and to beauty, but on the second occasion it contains the additional sense of a plea for the acceptance of the proffered dawn. Thus the terms of the first quatrain are exactly answered by these lines which turn to the source of conflict in the new world that stands revealed. Already the poet has told us that light redoubles pain; but let pain give itself over to light, let it welcome the pleasure that advances decked with the morning sky.

[7] *Œuvres*, I, 159.

> Grande offrande de tant de roses,
> Le mal vous peut-il soutenir
> Et voir rougissantes les choses
> A leurs promesses revenir?

Nevertheless, despite the second stanza, the self cannot accept the injunction to embrace the dawn. Instead of surrendering wholly, it questions whether pain can suffer the bounteous grace that reddened with a virgin charm. A sensuous substance in its untouched promise is once more offered to the sensibility, just as each dawn uncovers the world afresh. The quatrain thus takes up the poles of suffering and beauty which were found in the first stanzas and, held by the same tension, it plaintively expresses the drama of internal time and time without.

> J'ai vu se feindre tant de songes
> Sur mes ténèbres sans sommeil
> Que je range entre les mensonges
> Même la force du soleil.

The fourth stanza answers the previous question with the voice of experience. The poet's sleepless night contained his intimate chimeras which he must needs liken to the image he now sees. Even though the sun has such evident strength, his personal memory tells him that it is merely another fiction or lie. Not only his memory, however, but the structure of the poem itself, for the sun has come upon night in exactly the same way as his intimate hopes and fears descended on his vigil ("sur le monde," "sur le front d'un jour gracieux," "sur mes ténèbres sans sommeil"), the language imposing its own cogent parallel.

> Et que je doute si j'accueille
> Par le dégoût, par le désir,
> Ce jour très jeune sur la feuille
> Dont l'or vierge se peut saisir.

Having noticed the pattern written into the previous lines that predetermines as it were the conflict between night

and day, we find it once more present in the final stanza
where it overshadows the image of leaves resplendent with
dawn ("Ce jour très jeune sur la feuille"). Beauty is at hand,
waiting to be plucked like fruit or maiden flesh, an untouched reserve that recalls the opening words ("aurore,"
"or"); but the poet has known this grace in another form,
and felt the illusions of waking dreams. The disabused intellect has already called it a lie, and now the emotions
hesitate between disgust and desire—conjuring up from
dawn a vision of promise and consummated hopes, but all
too well aware that hopes can be thwarted and that the self
may exchange its own certainty for a vain lure. The last
lines hesitate, then, between "dégoût" and "désir," like the
instant of dawn held precariously between past and future.

"A l'aurore" is the lyrical expression of a conflict in
which the poet finds himself refusing time, facility, virginal
nature. Although the theme is characteristic of Valéry, and
occurs both in his poems and notebooks, his song on this
occasion is unusual because of the immediacy of his tone
and the very lack of resolution of the line of discourse. No
final decision can be reached, no determination to turn
courageously against the evidence of light such as "L'Oiseau
cruel" offers. He remains torn between acceptance and
denial, unable to close his eyes to an inevitable beauty, yet
bound to the suffering he bears in his heart. The five stanzas
vary in register as the voice evokes the present, past and
future, states its tension, commands, questions, states it once
again, doubts. However, despite this diversity, the same poles
of the drama are woven and interwoven in such a way that
there is a striking concentration of imagery and idea. One
of the basic techniques of the poem is the phonetic insistence
which lends the structure a haunting musicality. We must
also mention the particular linguistic pattern fundamental
to the effect that has already been briefly observed. Used
four times, the preposition "sur" establishes the inescapable

connection between inner illusion and external phenomena;
it is the weight of destiny, the awareness of fiction. To this
depressing movement the three words "soufferte," "souffrir,"
and "soutenir" correspond by their emphasis on the heavy
burden of the soul. The details of vocabulary thus compose
for us, within the pure voice of a Verlaine song, the moving
portrait of a self that is too experienced to dream and too
sensitive to refuse to care. Here, we may say, is the muted cry
of the heart's bitter dilemma which *Le Solitaire,* written in
the last years of Valéry's life, conveys in less lyrical but
similarly pathetic terms:

> Le souci ne m'est point de quelque autre aventure,
> Moi qui sus l'ange vaincre et le démon trahir,
> J'en sais trop pour aimer, j'en sais trop pour haïr,
> Et je suis excédé d'être une créature.[8]

Yet if we associate dawn with his characteristic will to recompose the world, we cannot forget that sunset was for him
correspondingly propitious and announced tenderness, abundance, the achievement of a hardwon goal. "La fin du jour
est femme," he writes in *Mélange.*[9] He took it as his theme
in "Profusion du soir" and in his "La Ceinture" of the war
years, written in the form of an Elizabethan sonnet; while
at the end of his career it provides the sensuous backdrop
for the love-making of Faust and the Crystal Lady: "Ce
moment est d'un grand prix," Faust muses to the amorous
Lust: ". . . Il me possède comme ces accords de son qui
vont plus loin que la limite du désir de l'ouïe, et qui font
tout l'être se fondre, se rendre à je ne sais quelle naissance
de confusion bienheureuse de ses forces et de ses faiblesses.
Toute chose qui nous entoure chante. Le plus beau de ce
jour chante avant de mourir. . . ."[10] It is clear that, con-

---

8 "Le Solitaire," *Œuvres,* II, 402.
9 *Œuvres,* I, 303.
10 *Mon Faust, Œuvres,* II, 319.

ceived in these terms, no moment could be more suited
to reconcile the sensibility with its innate energies and stir
its song.

"Heure," as we shall find, offers a beautiful expression of
this threshold within the self. Among the first of Valéry's
poems to be listed for inclusion in *Charmes,* it was written
in 1917, although first published twenty-five years later in
Pièces diverses. The form chosen is close to the traditional
rondeau and, like the rondeau, contains a refrain and the
trembling immobility of only two rhymes. I consider it an
astonishing tour de force to have transformed so artificial
a pattern into an eminently moving poem. Above all, the
reader cannot but regret that Valéry did not more frequently turn to the use of *vers variés* since the modulations
of rhythm and the balance between alexandrines and the
feminine octosyllabic lilt are quite admirable. Yet this form
was not arrived at easily. The manuscripts show the poet ex-
ploring both musical potential and sense, and at first introducing proportionately more octosyllables than in the
final version. Indeed, the detailed study of the poem's genesis serves to illustrate in an instructive way the process
by which idea and image gradually came to be shaped; it
also offers a most striking example of poetic composition
by division, for "Heure" gave birth in the course of writing
to a second highly successful piece that was later included in
Charmes.

The earliest manuscript contains on one side a series of
jottings and isolated words:

Un silence si riche

robes   —   rentre   — baigne   — pèse
arche   concorde
huile
reconnaissance
abonde
facile

Le silence si riche et les vents asservis
Sur l'huile (merveilleuse) (vagabonde)

Underneath we note other lines in pencil which are illegible, as the poet groped for the expression and movement he was seeking. However, a beginning had been found, and on the back of the same page beneath the title *L'Heure* he endeavored to sustain this promise. The use of alexandrines and octosyllables is established; two rhymes are maintained throughout the whole; while the underlying theme, if not the metaphors to express it, is already clear. And yet, as we see, nothing could be less certain than these rhymes, less decisive than the language, for the poet was still far from the metaphors that would define the precise feeling of "Heure."

> Heure courante et pure au contour de carène!
> Si riche le silence et fine la carène
> (Que) Les charges de soleil (d'amour) (d'honneur)
> > de tes flancs assouvis
> > (cieux asservis)
> Et tous les biens que tu ravis
> A l'amertume riveraine,
> Sous la reconnaissance inclinent la carène
> De qui les cygnes sont suivis
> Sur l'huile merveilleuse ils polissent la (leur) traîne
> Tout s'écoule au contour d'une telle carène
> Le ventre lourd de l'arche aux soleils asservis

The movement is more a pursuit of music than of images and the word "carène," used four times, does not in fact occur in the final version, any more than the other metaphors of liquidity such as "l'huile merveilleuse" and "tout s'écoule." Valéry's language evokes the aftermath of some vast act of love ("tes flancs assouvis," "ventre lourd"), the rediscovery of calm, at the other extreme from the seductiveness and entrancing beauty of "Heure." We can see that not a single complete line or image of the final poem has yet been found, and only the swaying rhythm and the constant interplay of two rhymes lead directly to the next draft.

When we turn to MS B Valéry is well on the way to the poem as we know it, composing several lines in their defini-

tive form and sketching the pattern of one refrain. Nevertheless, we observe certain expressions that take off at a tangent
and either revert to elements of the previous draft, or introduce allusions to the scene in the manner of a description,
or refer in more abstract terms to a drama of the mind. Most
interesting of all no doubt is the emergence of a series of
alexandrines which develop the theme and images of "Intérieur" that was published twenty years before "Heure," in
Charmes.

> L'heure me vient sourire et se faire sirène
> Chanteras-tu longtemps rayon mon possesseur (a)
> Je tiens le mot, le dé, la sentence et la douceur (b)
> Je jouis de l'esprit (c)
> Voici l'heure le jour la source et la douceur (d)
> La chance inespérée (le hasard fabuleux) est aujourd'hui
>   une (infante/une heure) reine (e)

>   Heure courante et pure à la robe sereine
>   La narine naïve et la mine sereine (f)
>   Je ne redoute du
>   L'eau facile du jour
>   C'est après une pluie heureuse (g)
>   Danseras-tu longtemps sur le parvis
>   Chanteras-tu longtemps
>   Devant l'intelligence (l'intelligente et ténébreuse)
>   [reine (h)
>   Heure courante et noble au contour de carène
>   La puissance du calme me traîne
>   Tout s'écoule au contour d'une telle carène (i)
>   Une esclave aux regards chargés de douces chaînes
>   Passe entre mon esprit et sur les choses prochaines (j)
>   Ici respire et . . .
>   éclaire   prodigue ses doigts purs
>   Divisant mon regard (k)
>   Elle met une femme au milieu de ces murs
>   Toute chose la voit. Je ne vois que ses chaînes (l).

In this rather free improvisation several points are worthy
of note. The opening line has reached its definitive form and
many of the other images and expressions foreshadow the

future poem. But just as significant for us are the details
that show the poet striving towards his solution. Thus (a)
the second line denotes the light of the sunset as if it were a
violator possessing the voluptuous senses, and suggests considerably more action and force than we shall find in the
later version. At the same time an alternative rhyme scheme
is essayed but abandoned ("possesseur," "douceur"). The
third line (b) offers the first attempt to compose the en-
chanting verse of self containment and aesthetic pleasure
which will subsequently have a memorable expression:
"Voici l'HEURE, la soif, la source et la sirène." For the
moment, however, Valéry conceives it in terms of poetry and
of the future poem and, perhaps inescapably for us, as a
recollection of the Mallarméan dice that contain, so to
speak, the magic formula of the universe. The next hexa-
syllable (c) is banal in its phrasing but surely important in
that it places the scene under the sign of an internal drama
which consummates the alliance of the sensibility and the
intellect; it is the epitome of the poet-analyst. At his second
attempt to find a refrain (d), Valéry was close to his ultimate
success, but he had not yet decided on the rhyme scheme
which would entail the replacement of "douceur"; and
"source" had still to find its necessary contrast and justification in "soif." In line 6 (e), the unpredictability of the
miracle is emphasized, and its triumphant grace; the poet
will not keep the line despite the pertinence of the expression "hasard fabuleux," but the rhyme will remain (1.8:
"Ma solitude est reine"). The original opening we found in
MS A ("Heure courante et pure"), here reintroduced to
evoke the image of beauty in feminine traits, quickly peters
out (f). Now the allusion to the natural conditions (g) seems
flatly descriptive, an explanation of the phenomenon; once
again the poet will abruptly drop this movement. Instead
(h) he returns to a line he has written before (a) and finds a
new verb to suggest artistic seduction ("Danseras-tu . . .")
and another noun ("parvis") which refers to the solemn

mood of the temptress' ritual dance. We are reminded also that beauty is above all in the eyes of the beholder, and in the mind that gives it a language, by the octosyllable ("Devant l'intelligence reine") and the alternative alexandrine ("Devant l'intelligente et ténébreuse reine"). This second reading is noteworthy in calling attention for the only time in this draft to the idea of shadow and, by extension, death, which will play a central role in the final version. A further attempt is made (i) to start from the initial notion of fluidity ("carène," "traîne," "s'écoule") as it captivates and enthralls the observer and all things, which resolves itself into a new set of alexandrines that appear almost spontaneously and discover the characteristic images of "Intérieur" (j). Yet they have been long prepared by the hesitations and isolated details of the previous lines, and we may surmise that the image of the "esclave" has been secretly adumbrated by the words "cieux obscurs" and "soleils asservis" in MS A. Time is no longer a "possesseur," but a slave held within the light of the sky and the corresponding light of the intellect, who yet typifies by her graceful passing the essence of freedom and fancy.

If Valéry had not yet found the suggestive phrase "aux longs yeux" (which recalls for us the line from Baudelaire's "Chant d'automne": "J'aime de vos longs yeux la lumière verdâtre . . .") the striking agreement of the adjective "chargés" with "regards" is already present: the woman enjoys a gentle discipline of the eyes, a controlled vision, while her movements are unrestricted by cumbersome chains. The rhymes ("chaînes," "prochaines") are those of "Intérieur" and continue the sequence of "Heure," but the second line is conceived in wholly different terms and designates the composition of world, mind and image in a way that is undoubtedly too close to direct statement to satisfy Valéry. (k) Although the next jottings are not resolved into alexandrines they point to a marriage of sensuousness and purity by a hemistich that will be adopted without change in the final version. As for the phrase "divisant mon regard," Valéry refers back to the dual presence that was affirmed earlier: the poet has, almost by definition, a divided glance, which is paradoxically harmonized; he is both intelligence and pleasure, and seeks words for his delight. This "division" will be expressed in admirable fashion by the poem in which the woman "passe entre mes regards sans briser leur absence / Comme passe le verre au travers du soleil." (l) Here the poet composes two alexandrines, the first of which will be retained as the sudden recognition of gracious femininity, a form that is as humanly meaningful as an ideal woman in the intimate space of the poet's awareness. The second line does not at first sight square with the thought of the final version and will be abandoned, although it is repeated and echoed in two subsequent drafts. It indicates the contrast between two points of view; the world sees and accepts the woman in her wholeness, while the self gazes at the chains of discipline, the tender law of her movement which becomes for him a necessity: "Je suis libre, donc je m'enchaîne," Valéry wrote.

We realize then that this manuscript leads us a long way towards "Heure" as we know it, and that it provides evidence of further growth, and almost another dimension, by introducing a passage that will later constitute a separate piece. The next draft which is in typed form bears the title *L'Heure et la Femme* crossed out and replaced by *L'Heure*, together with the indication *Romance* designating the poetic mode. The "love lyric" now eschews completely the use of octosyllables:

L'heure me vient sourire et se faire sirène
Tout s'étonne de feux que jamais je ne vis. (a)
Danseras-tu longtemps, Rayon, sur le parvis
Sur la pourpre, devant l'intelligence reine? (b)
Voici l'heure, le jour (le mot), la source et la sirène! (c)
Heure courante (parfaite / nette / liquide) et pure (claire)
                      au contour de carène

Qui de l'âme polis (parfais) les secrets (tes charges)
                                        asservis (ravis) (d)
La puissance du calme inspire (invente / épouse) mes avis (e)
Je prononce sur moi (eux) / Sur eux j'ai prononcé la
                                        sentence sereine: (f)
Tout s'écoule au contour d'une telle carène. (g)
Une esclave aux longs yeux chargés de douces chaînes (h)
Respire et sur le jour prodigue ses doigts purs
Elle met une femme au milieu de ces murs
Passe entre mon esprit et les choses prochaines
Toute chose la voit. Je ne vois que ses chaînes. (i)

(a) The first and second lines are almost identical with
the definitive ones, but Valéry will prefer "s'éclairer" to
"s'étonner" and "jour" to "feux." It is true that this expression is more appropriate to describe a diamond, or a dia-
mond-like ocean ("Midi le juste y compose de feux / La mer
. . . ," we read in "Le Cimetière marin") than the broad
effulgence of the setting sun.

(b) The capital letter of "Rayon," the use of "parvis" and
"pourpre," denote a regal splendor. They remind us of the
magnificent description of sunset in "Fragments du Narcisse" in which "de tels souvenirs . . . empourprent sa
mort"; but the royal purple will be eliminated from
"Heure." As for the phrase "devant l'intelligence reine" it
takes up an expression we found in the previous draft and
emphasizes the appeal to the intellectual sensibility; it will
be left unsaid, but implicit, in later versions.

(c) The word "sirène" replaces "douceur" and brings us
almost to the final text. Nevertheless the complementarity of
"soif" and "source" has yet to be introduced. The variant
"mot" is significant, I think, in the same way as "sentence"
below; it echoes the nature of poetic creation itself as a
magical art of naming.

(d) The same image of fluidity we have already observed
leads into a line that is suggestive of the way in which the
external scene brings to full flower the formless thoughts and

impulses of the observer. But "les secrets" will become, more powerfully, "mes plus secrets démons."

(e) The interaction of scene and self is conveyed in three diversely suggestive terms: "inspire," an untypical verb in Valéry, suggests the romantic artist whose reason is guided by nature—and prepares the use of "respire" below, while "invente" is a much more provocative expression of the same idea; on the other hand, "épouse" opens up the theme of the marriage of imagination and intellect that will be present in the following lines. Yet none of these words was retained.

(f) The function of the poet as mediator, or high priest, of this union is articulated in a line later abandoned, in which language constitutes a kind of liturgy that expresses, and at the same time ritualizes, a supreme moment.

(g) It is worth underlining the importance in the genesis of the poem of this line and the rhyme "carène," which acted as catalysts although they are absent from the finished composition.

(h) The epithet "longs" has been found, but not "molles," which will surprise us more than the rather banal antithesis of "douces chaînes."

(i) This last sequence of alexandrines has developed considerably from the previous draft. It has little of the intimacy and tenderness we know in the final version but presents the contrast between sensuousness and abstract formulation that will be admirably combined in "Intérieur."

The next draft is also typed and bears the original title of the previous manuscript *L'Heure et la Femme*. It provides us with a substantial composition that introduces once more, as in the earliest versions, the use of octosyllables which complement the alexandrines and expand the musical, strictly non-expository, approach.

L'heure me vient sourire et se faire sirène
Tout s'étonne de feux que jamais je ne vis

Danseras-tu longtemps, Rayon, sur la parvis
   Devant la ténébreuse reine? (a)
Voici l'heure, le jour, la source et la sirène!

Mes plus âpres (rares) desseins pieusement servis
   Par cette chance souveraine (b)
S'échangent sans effort (à présent) contre l'air où je vis (c)
   Je suis la sentence sereine (d)
Je (L'or) danse devant l'arche aux transparents
                    (multiples) avis (e)
Heure courante et pure au contour de carène!
Les charges de soleil (bonheur) de tes flancs assouvis (f)
Le silence si riche (Si riche le silence) et les vents
                    (temps) asservis (g)
Par leur seule splendeur (douceur) font que l'arche se traîne (h)
   Et tous les biens que tu ravis
   A l'amertume riveraine (i)
Vers la reconnaissance inclinent la carène
   De qui les cygnes sont suivis (j)
Sur l'huile merveilleuse à polir la sirène (et fine la
            sirène (ils polissent la traîne) (k)
Tout s'écoule au contour d'une telle carène.

Une esclave aux longs yeux chargés de douces chaînes
De son geste léger prodigue les doigts purs
Passe entre mes regards comme parmi les chênes; (l)
Elle met une femme au milieu de ces murs
   Et touchant (Elle touche) aux choses prochaines
Toute chose la voit. Je ne vois que mes chaînes. (m)
Divise mon esprit où le vol indirect
De la grâce se mêle à l'étrange intellect. (n)

If by its richness of sound and sense this version is impressive, Valéry felt it was overlong and henceforth separated *L'Heure* from *La Femme* in his working. It is true that the poem was no more a song, and had begun to take on rather different dimensions; while the form itself seemed to require a break between the two sections, the rhyme schemes having grown distinct from each other. It is instructive to examine the details of this manuscript in order to observe the development of meaning and structure as they advance beyond what we already know:

(a) The expression is interesting in that it leaves ample room for suggestion; but this queen of shadows who contemplates the ballet of the sun will be redefined in less vague terms as "l'âme sombre et souveraine."

(b) The designs of the heart and mind in their native disorder ("âpres"), in their singularity ("rares"), are tended with solemn respect by a sovereign grace. The word "desseins" conveys a conscious prompting that Valéry will replace by "démons"—private sprites who are devilish by their unharnessed force as by their taunts.

(c) Communion between self and scene becomes an effortless exchange, the surrender of inner promptings for the fullness of a vital atmosphere. It is physical well-being, which will be replaced in the final version by the spiritual abundance of "une sagesse pure aux lucides avis."

(d) No longer does the poet merely pronounce the magic words as in the previous draft, for he has become an enchanted substance, a mysteriously "composed" self, a very poem. This idea will not recur in later drafts.

(e) The draft continues to emphasize the self's enchantment and its active participation in the spectacle: "Je danse. . . ." The observer moves freely and rhythmically at the heart of his delight. Yet Valéry also proposes the objective expression "L'or danse . . ." as a variant, indicating once again the essential duality of the sunset which is both vision and projection of the self. "Arche" is attracted by "carène," and carries with it the notions of calm and supernatural protection; but it receives an intellectual extension by the phrase "aux transparents (multiples) avis," the epithet *transparents* being, in particular, suggestive of light and associated with the lingering glow of the sky. The notion will be conveyed by the equally evocative "aux lucides avis" in the final version.

(f) The line echoes almost exactly a line of the first manuscript and its erotic associations; it will not be retained.

(g) "Asservis" occurs once again in this draft as in those

that precede it, here designating the docility of the forces of nature rather than the intimate forces of the self.

(h) The elements of nature, the ship that floats before the eyes of the spectator in the ocean of the sky, are transfixed as time lingers to savor the brilliance ("splendeur") and sweetness ("douceur") of a supreme moment.

(i) The antithesis is suggestive as it introduces the metaphor of some ideal violation, but it does not recur in later versions.

(j) The image of boat and tributary swans depicts the calm of some classical idyll. It will be incorporated into the following draft, but later discarded.

(k) Once again the image of lustrous liquidity occurs, having accompanied the genesis of the poem from the first draft, but later to be excluded.

(l) Valéry brings into his vision a reference to the oak, associated with religious rites in antiquity and Druidic times and with the Roman victor's crown, which offers a perfect rhyme for "chaînes." We think of a sacred wood traversed by the fleeting form of beauty.

(m) In a slight modification of the previous version the poet writes "Je ne vois que mes chaînes," not "ses chaînes." A new dimension is introduced which implies that, however universal the image in front of the observer's eyes—since it has become the cynosure and focus of all things—his glance seizes on the link that binds him irrevocably to the object of desire and which he possesses as it possesses him.

(n) The final lines of the draft describe the encounter between intellect and imagination, but show that neither the expression nor the thought had reached the admirable balance of "Intérieur," which ends in this way:

> Passe entre mes regards sans briser leur absence,
> Comme passe le verre au travers du soleil
> Et de la raison pure épargne l'appareil.

Instead of harmonious accord the word "divise" suggests, like the phrase "divisant mon regard" in the first manu-

script, that the act of looking brings to the point of clear
perception a radical separation of functions within the
mind, enabling us to see their distinction, to feel their necessity, to gauge their interaction ("se mêle"). The slave, the
hour are translated into the seductions ("vol indirect") of
grace, as if it were some divine bounty; while "indirect" prepares us for the dryness of the rhyme "intellect"—reason
that is alien ("étrange") to banal preoccupations just as it
is separate from the sensuous forms of the imagination, although ready to be nourished and refreshed by them. A
similar resolution will be essayed for these lines in the following manuscript until the rhymes "soleil"—"appareil"
allow Valéry to develop the complementarity of ideas without abrasiveness.

The final version we have been able to consult before the
definitive one places the two sections on different sides of
the manuscript, giving the title *L'Heure* to the former and
Intérieur to the latter. The changes are few, but significant
for us when we keep in mind the long process that has
brought us here:

> L'heure me vient sourire et se faire sirène;
> Tout s'éclaire d'un jour que jamais je ne vis.
> Danseras-tu longtemps, rayon, sur le parvis,
> Devant la ténébreuse reine?
> Voici l'heure, le jour (la soif), la source et la sirène!

> Mes plus secrets desseins picusement servis
>   Par une esclave souveraine,
> S'échangeront ce soir contre l'air où je vis:
> Je respire dans l'or des transparents avis,
>   Je suis la sentence sereine!

> Heure liquide et noble au contour de carène
> Si riche le silence et fine la sirène
> Que les charges d'orgueil de tes reins assouvis
>   Et tous les biens que tu ravis
>   A l'amertume riveraine,
> Vers la reconnaissance inclinent la carène
>   De qui les cygnes sont suivis

On the back of the same manuscript these lines are now
isolated from the rest of the poem:

> Une esclave aux grands yeux chargés de molles chaînes
> Change l'eau de mes fleurs, plonge aux glaces prochaines,
> Au lit mystérieux prodigue ses doigts purs;
> Elle met une femme au milieu de ces murs,
> Passe entre mes regards comme parmi les chênes.
> Toute chose la voit. Je ne vois que mes chaînes:
> L'imprévu régulier de ce trouble indirect
> Se donne et se refuse à l'étrange intellect.

We observe that Valéry has worked towards the self-suffi-
ciency of each poem, eliminating octosyllables in "Intérieur," finding the images that denote familiarity, while maintaining an ample pattern of all-embracing words and the
vers variés in "Heure." However, use is still not made of the
refrain we find in the final version; the transition from light
towards darkness and death has not been achieved; and the
transformation within the self—the funeral pyre of the past,
the lucid intensity of the present—has yet to bring to the
second section of "Heure" the deepening mood and self-
awareness that is to come. Thus one cannot fail to be struck,
in the final version as we know it, by the considerable in-
crease in musicality with respect to this draft and in the
sense of controlled charm. Within the limits imposed by the
rhymes, Valéry will avoid stilted vocabulary and rigid
rhythms and give us a carefully graduated development of
thought and sound, suppleness within order—an "imprévu
régulier," as this draft delicately indicates, which is ours
and not ours ("se donne et se refuse"), rich with gifts yet as
distinct as a loved face.

"Heure" proposes then a consummate moment, when time
takes for the poet the form of a divine visitant. The use of
capitals on the four occasions the word "heure" occurs in
the piece suggests from the start the miraculous nature of
his vision. There is awe, but also grace and legendary power.

> L'HEURE me vient sourire et se faire sirène:
> Tout s'éclaire d'un jour que jamais je ne vis:
> Danseras-tu longtemps, Rayon, sur le parvis
> De l'âme sombre et souveraine? [11]

This is the experience the observer has lived for, the light he has never seen. He realizes he is not only witnessing a beautiful sunset but discovering an influence which transmutes the shape of things and gives it new sense. At the same time he knows full well his privilege is fugitive as he anxiously questions the goddess who dances in the domain of gratuitous action: "cet être qui enfante, qui émet du profond de soi-même cette belle suite de transformations de sa forme dans l'espace; qui tantôt se transporte, mais sans aller véritablement nulle part; tantôt se modifie sur place, s'expose sous tous les aspects; et qui, parfois, module savamment des apparences successives, comme par phases ménagées; parfois se change vivement en un tourbillon qui s'accélère, pour se fixer tout à coup, cristallisée en statue, ornée d'un sourire étranger." [12] Such delight the poet of "Heure" cannot accept unthinkingly and must seek to know its fragile duration. In the midst of solemn watchfulness, in the presence of time enshrined, he is both sovereign and somber, at one with supreme beauty and yet wholly distinct, and conscious that light is not omnipotent. "O mon étonnement, Tête charmante et triste," exclaims Valéry's Angel, "Il y a donc autre chose que la lumière?" [13]

> Voici l'HEURE, la soif, la source et la sirène.

By its isolation and its internal pattern the fifth line composes for us a perfect conjunction of details. The poet knows and embraces a Time that transcends time like that of the dance or the poem itself. The elements compose a complex

---

11 *Œuvres*, I, 157.
12 "Philosophie de la danse," *Œuvres*, I, 1398–1399.
13 "L'Ange," *Œuvres*, I, 206.

and satisfying whole: thirst, fountain, siren; desire, and the
energy to fulfil this desire without which the poem could
never be anything more than words; origin, center, and
mainspring of being, and the fresh waters that rise from the
earth as if their sole aim were to assuage our thirst; and
finally the sensuous form of a legendary woman, unexpected
and inexplicable, who renews our desire. No line, I suppose,
more adequately than this resumes Valéry's dream of an
"aesthetic infinite."

> Pour toi, le passé brûle, HEURE qui m'assouvis;
> Enfin, splendeur du seul, ô biens que j'ai ravis,
> J'aime ce que je suis: ma solitude est reine!

As the poet addresses Time once more in the second person singular, his words take on a different character. No
longer does he offer a description of light and beauty, but a
revelation of the self. Here the present destroys the past in
a joyous holocaust: nothing can exist beyond the experience
of the moment. The observer is identified with radiance and
calls nature his own, like a prize he has won. The universe
becomes the extension of the self he proudly appropriates,
proclaiming his pleasure, declaring his sway. By such exultant self-love he discovers a reciprocity between what he
feels and sees. Magically, despite his solitude, he is in fact
what he contemplates.

> Mes plus secrets démons, librement asservis
> Accomplissent dans l'or de l'air même où je vis
> Une sagesse pure aux lucides avis:
>   Ma présence est toute sereine.

A vast projection of the poet's desires and fears is reflected
in three insistent masculine rhymes. From being hidden in
the innermost recesses of the self, his familiar spirits are now
seen in a miraculous wedding of freedom and discipline
("librement asservis") that traces a composition of Apollonian wisdom in the golden sky. The verb "accomplissent"
provides the keynote for these lines: the scene offers the ful-

filment of the intellectual sensibility which seems to be written objectively, like an artifact, beyond the vagaries of the
moment. The poet's intimately personal contemplation is in
complete harmony with the world, after the manner of a
visionary such as Baudelaire ("Vois se pencher les défuntes
Années / Sur les balcons du ciel en robes surannées . . .").
Thus once more, as in the phrase "Ma solitude est reine," the
self can rejoice in the coincidence of the observer and the
observed and formulate by way of a lapidary octosyllable
its profound reconciliation with all things. One is perhaps
tempted to find an additional justification for the epithet of
the last line in that it seems to refer by etymological confusion to a noble calm of the mind that we typically associate
with evening.

> Voici l'HEURE, la soif, la source et la sirène.

Again the incantatory refrain refutes the passage of time.
The poet's will is to isolate the moment, to make transient
being into durable form. "Il s'agit," Valéry writes, "de se
donner l'idée d'un être qui soit toujours comme l'homme
vrai n'est que par instants."

> Danscras-tu longtemps, rayon, sur le parvis
> Du soir, devant l'œil noir de ma nuit souveraine?

The last lines echo lines 3 and 4 in a kind of supplemen-
tary refrain. Again they question the tenuousness of the
moment, reminding us that time is passing and that we have
reached the end of this balance of rhymes, the wondrous
suspension of the sensibility fascinated by itself like the self-
sufficient poem. The law of the intellectual sensibility is to
move between its all and its nothing, to ply its delight with
questions, to remain aware of the essential variability in the
self as in nature. "Rayon" is here no longer written with
a capital letter; the soul has become a solitary eye in the
darkness of evening; and although it is still sovereign, it
rules over a domain of night in which it holds—but for how

long?—death in check. Thus it is that the details of language discover at the end of the poem a new austereness as
day yields to night and the poet lucidly perceives the fringe
of mortality.

We may be tempted to compare "Heure" with certain of
Mallarmé's poems in which the theme of the setting sun is
centrally important. In Mallarmé, however, the image is
inseparable from a philosophical attitude, a myth of death
and rebirth, a mystical theory of language, whereas Valéry
erects his experience into an expression that is sufficient unto
itself. His love song presents the trembling duality of intellect and sensibility, the eye and what it sees, the self and
the world. Indeed, by its form, it already suggests the exceptional nature of this meeting at a privileged moment of
time—when two rhymes echo lengthily and lovingly, and
two refrains retard the progression, and key words per-
sistently recur to weave a fascinated meditation ("heure"
four times, "sirène" three, "rayon," "danger," "longtemps,"
"parvis," "souveraine," "soif," "source" twice each), even if,
we surely realize, the enchantment is soon destined to end.
Yet for one brief span a kind of grace has ruled and composed a miraculous sequence.

As for the semantic structure, there is no simple immediacy of words or sentiment in Valéry's "romance," but
rather a richly qualified pattern which was only gradually
perceived during the act of composition. Just as in "La
Ceinture," the four parts are ordered to suggest the vast
correspondence between advancing darkness and a parallel
apprehension of the self's mortality. But we also discover
another law that plays across the temporal development and
imposes the specific definition of the poem as the locus of a
series of paradoxes within a complex and, as it were, immobile ambiguity. Here is the unique point of contact between light and darkness, seductiveness and solemnity, thirst
and the answer to thirst. It is flushed beauty that moves in-
violate in the presence of death and establishes, at the

furthest remove from the platitude of prose, a moment's
necessity.

Although these three poems can only provide an inadequate
survey of the theme, they suggest the sensuous attention
Valéry paid to it and the diversity of its manifestations. We
might continue and trace it back to his early poems, and,
before them, to his Mediterranean childhood and Apollonian ambitions; we could afterwards follow it step by step
through the *Cahiers,* his "exercice matinal." Yet if there is
a single point I should wish to emphasize in conclusion it is
less the relationship to reason and Valéry's quest for measure
and clarity than the kind of frenzy that constantly underpins
it. The reader naturally associates light with control, the
overriding principle of formal discipline, "l'obstinée
rigueur," and these traits are sufficiently apparent in his
work. Quite as often, however, they are linked to a violence
of feeling that strikes us as extraordinary. One thinks of
Sémiramis singing to the rising sun, burning all things in
the furnace of a vaulting pride; one remembers the passion
of "Profusion du soir" that is sung in the rays of the sunset.
I recall also a page that as much as any other—perhaps by
its very fragmentariness—captures the pent-up forces of un-
reason. It is illustrated by a drawing of two suns, one on a
high pedestal, the other larger and more central with the
word "Oh!" inscribed on it, like the self reduced to the
status of an exclamation. The poem begins by evoking a
particular instant of time in its beauty and vastness, its
pride and nervous suffering: "Le beau moment / Tout
gorgé d'espace / Etouffant de grandeur, / Souffrant d'un gros
soleil au flanc, / Irrité de tant de gens qui grouillent, pas-
sent, tas de pieds, pieds pieds vivent!" This light is stable and
exultant ("Mais immense statue de la dixième heure, / Sur
la place de la nuit dressée / *La Lumière du Jour!*"), bearing
within it the image of life itself ("Victoire de l'équilibre in-
stantané . . . la Vie"). It is a balance of forces that is vari-

able in appearance but unchanging in essence; it is the dazzling face of our own completeness. Yet in a surprising finale the poet is led from this point to formulate his dream of self-knowledge, of the contained contemplation of a bicephalous monster who would call on an equally monstrous female partner ("Où est la femme à deux têtes? / Pour le monstre que l'on serait / SI L'ON SE VOYAIT"). Thus the scene ends on this flight of fancy, this cry towards an impossible sufficiency of the intellectual sensibility, with an equally impossible woman to attend it. Light in Valéry is the luminous wonder of the mind but also intoxicated being that carries intellect as far as pride will take it. Nothing indeed could be more typical of him than that he should develop it through the cycle of natural description, affective response, and illusory transcendence, as in "Neige," "A l'aurore," and "Heure," which spell out the impulses of an "Ange" and "Contre-Ange." [14]

14 Compare *Correspondance André Gide-Paul Valéry,* 515: "En vérité, l'*homo* me fait vomir. Je me sens *ange* (comme Degas, je ne sais pourquoi, m'appelait) et *contre-ange.* L'entre-deux me donne le mal de mer. L'Homme est *redite,* et je suis *constance;* l'homme est *surprises* et je suis . . . *ratures* . . . *Comprends* si tu peux. Peux pas être plus clair" (Letter to Gide, 20 September 1932).

8: "Je pense . . . , je sens . . ."

WE HAVE COME to realize that there are three major creative periods in Valéry's career: from 1890 to 1900 when he
wrote the *Album de vers anciens* and, twenty years after,
arranged his poems in an order that suggests his intellectual
development over these crucial years; from 1912 to 1922, the
time of *La Jeune Parque* and *Charmes;* and finally, from
1935 to 1945, his tardy flowering. Of these periods none
would contest that the last is the least known, the reason
for which can be attributed partly to the fact that some
pieces collected under the title *Corona* have not yet been
published, but also, I suppose, to prevailing uncertainty
with regard to the dates of composition of his *Pièces diverses.*[1]

Now, having consulted the manuscripts and contemporary
volumes of the *Cahiers,* I would not wish to give the impression that the writings which may clearly be dated from these
years are comparable in quality to those of 1912–1922; but
that they present more than ordinary interest, and that a
handful of them are quite admirable, I am convinced. Above
all perhaps they strike us by the presence of a polarity that
is constant throughout his work and here as it were writ
large. I refer to the twin strands of the witty and the man-
nered, the pointed and the exultant, the low-key and the

[1] As I noted in the first chapter, twelve poems appeared under this
title in the 1942 edition of *Poésies* (Paris: Gallimard).

high. "Je pense en rationaliste archi-pur, je sens en mystique," he once declared.[2] My object then is to study three of his finest short poems from this period which will allow us to probe a fundamental tension as he expressed it in the last decade of his life.

Like many writings from these years, "L'Oiseau cruel" treats one of the facets of love. The dominance of the theme cannot fail to surprise Valéry's readers, and he himself was no less amazed; thus, in one of his last notebooks, we find a remark that appears quite eloquent in itself: "Il est étrange que les vers que je puis faire maintenant ne soient plus que dédiés à l'Eros—Soleil couchant . . . Bien plus étrange que jamais l'idée de versifier *par amour, sur l'amour* ne me soit venue entre quinze et trente ans. Elle m'eût choqué— n'admettant pas de relation directe entre Art et le moi d'amour." [3] One would not deny that sexual metaphors are central in *La Jeune Parque* and *Charmes* but, as we know, they are directed towards the expression of a theatre of the mind: the rape of the Pythia by the god, for instance, is the means by which a new voice of "pure poetry" is heard, the allegorical discovery of human language in its most godlike utterance. However, his work from the last years of his life shows a closer relationship to actual experience. "Il faut finir par l'improvisation," he wrote;[4] and one sees from *Corona* and other works of this time that his improvisation turned above all on erotic desire. A study of "L'Oiseau cruel" will show the oblique way this theme entered his poem and gave it a deeply personal accent.

The first trace of the image of the bird seems to date from before the First World War, that is to say, twenty-five years before the original version of "L'Oiseau cruel," when we read in the third *Cahier* the following remark: "L'oiseau secret se fait un chemin de toute chose. Il voit, il croit voir,

quand la vue manque, il parle—Il trouve toujours de quoi
fuir, de quoi être—et dans quoi que ce soit il se meut, et se
fait un espace." [5] His secret bird is an obsessive presence that
recurs incessantly, just as it ceaselessly escapes definition.
Suggestive of a fugitive mystery, it does not seem to have
given rise at the time to any further development. It was
however adopted in a most beautiful way at the heart of
La Jeune Parque in which the lone singer expresses the
all-powerful appeal of the senses:

> Moi si pure, mes genoux
> Pressentent les terreurs de genoux sans défense . . .
> L'air me brise. L'oiseau perce de cris d'enfance
> Inouïs . . . l'ombre même où se serre mon cœur,
> Et roses! mon soupir vous soulève, vainqueur
> Hélas! des bras si doux qui ferment la corbeille . . .[6]

The piercing cry goes back through the layers of the self
to tenderness and childlike spontaneity, the unsoundable
and irrefutable presence of the bird of instinct which will
play a vital role in the Parque's drama of the sensibility.

Some five years later, another notebook took up the same
image yet again and showed that, if the notion of an obsession was echoed, it now called up quite specific associations
with the poet's military service in the 122nd Infantry Regi-
ment in Montpellier between November 1889 and November 1890. There is even, we shall see, a Proustian touch in
the sudden confrontation of two widely distant sense impressions. "Cet oiseau," he writes.

Cet oiseau pique la nuit finissante de cris faibles et aigus. Me
rappelle quelque chose. Cette chose se fait un certain bleu de
ciel avec deux ou trois étoiles qui vont disparaître. Je traduis ceci
par souvenir de mon temps militaire. Je pense à la mélancolie et
à la Sibylle que m'étaient ces *mêmes* cris et ces astres dans la cour
du quartier. Ils étaient chargés d'une signification indéchiffrable

[5] Ibid., III, 853
[6] Lines 244–249 (*Œuvres*, I, 103).

—et l'avenir . . . Cet avenir est devenu du passé. Je sais ce qu'il y avait dans ces impressions.[7]

The passage is practically unique in the *Cahiers* for the personal nature of the memory evoked. To the notion of obsession we found in the preceding quotation it brings concrete and pathetic detail: not an almost abstract bird, but two quite precisely located ones that are separated in time by thirty years, signify the meeting of past and present as it relives the past. The poet rediscovers the sight and sound of a buried moment which he looks at with the wisdom and disabusement of middle age. As in Proust the child is father to the man, past sensation to the very same sensation experienced in the present; but, unlike Proust, Valéry finds no reason to rejoice in the redemption of time and derives heightened soberness from a new perspective that resolves the enigma of the bird. It is clear that his remark is of particular interest to us for the light it throws on the intimate nature of a detail of his imagination, for the atmosphere of stellar loneliness it conjures up, for the oracular mystery and melancholy with which it is associated. The mood is both tender and painful, but as yet there is not attached to it any plain allusion to the passions of love.

It would seem that, as a direct sequel to these lines, Valéry composed a prose-poem which he published for the first and only time in the 1930 collection of his selected writings and to which I have already referred in an earlier chapter. Here the hymn to the last moments of night is totally alert. Powerful and submissive, affectionate and awe-struck, a sleeping woman and an angel of light, the self that experiences the extremes of being lives as exultantly as a bird. The elements of the scene recompose the décor of youthful ecstasy, his dream of purity, and bring the double vision of himself as he was and as he is.

---

[7] *Cahiers*, IX, 198; later collected under the title "Il y a cinquante ans . . ." in *Mélange* (*Œuvres*, I, 349).

Comme le temps est calme, et la jeune fin de la nuit délicate-
ment colorée! Les volets repoussés à droite et à gauche par un acte
vif de nageur, je pénètre dans l'extase de l'espace. Il fait pur, il
fait vierge, il fait doux et divin. Je vous salue, grandeur offerte à
tous les actes d'un regard, commencement de la parfaite transparence! Quel événement pour l'esprit qu'une telle étendue! Je
voudrais vous bénir, ô toutes choses, si je savais! . . . Sur le
balcon qui se propose au-dessus des feuilles, sur le seuil de la
première heure et de tout ce qui est possible, je dors et je veille,
je suis jour et nuit, j'offre longtemps une aurore infinie, une
crainte sans mesure. L'âme s'abreuve à la source du temps, boit un
peu de ténèbres, un peu d'aurore; se sent femme endormie, ange
fait de lumière, se recueille, s'attriste, et s'enfuit sous forme
d'oiseau jusqu'à la cime nocturne. Quelque oranger respire là dans
l'ombre. Il subsiste très haut peu de fines étoiles à l'extrême de
l'aigu. La lune est ce fragment de glace fondante. Je sais trop
(tout à coup) qu'un enfant aux cheveux gris contemple d'an-
ciennes tristesses à demi mortes, à demi divinisées, dans cet objet
céleste de substance étincelante et mourante, tendre et froide qui
va se dissoudre insensiblement.

Je le regarde comme si je n'étais point dans mon cœur. Ma
jeunesse jadis a langui et senti la montée des larmes, vers la même
heure, et sous le même enchantement de la lune évanouissante.
Ma jeunesse a vu ce même matin et je me vois à côté de ma
jeunesse.[8]

We could hardly hope for a page that so concentratedly, so
movingly, creates for us the essential aspiration towards a
kind of supreme existence, proposing the images of bird
and stars, sadness and enchantment, which occur, as we
shall see, in the poem we have in hand. It also recalls the
highly original plan of a poem Valéry wrote under the title
Sibylle or *Les Fées* on the theme of "intelligence à l'état
d'instinct, de fonction, presque de travail matériel et végé-
tal" in which we find the following statement concerning the
tone and form he will seek to follow: "La voix doit être
comme le fil conducteur ininterrompu, le fil produit,
sécrété, infini qui se dévide de l'écheveau vivant inconnu et
forme des ouvrages étonnants comme machinalement, issus

8 *Morceaux choisis*, 51.

d'un puits de distraction sans fond, d'entrailles planétaires ou *comme l'oiseau qui chante depuis l'éternité, inconscient, et étant conscience."* [9]

With these passages as a background we can turn to "L'Oiseau cruel" in which Valéry took up the theme of pleasurable pain—a theme that had of course been characteristically linked with the sonnet (thus Petrarch: ". . . Se buona, onde l'effecto aspro mortale? / Se nia, onde si dolce ogni tormento . . ."), and in paying his own incidental tribute to one of the most fertile topoi of the Petrarchan tradition he developed an image of personal significance into what for us is one of his most moving poems.

> L'oiseau cruel toute la nuit me tint
> Au point aigu du délice d'entendre
> Sa voix qu'adresse une fureur si tendre
> Au ciel brûlant d'astres jusqu'au matin.[10]

The poet first looks back on his sleepless night that was held in the sway of the bird. His words are the direct account of personal experience and have the immediacy of a confession, but his voice wells up across the lines with such force that it finally encompasses the whole of things, from a small song in the darkness to the distant stars and nightlong wakefulness. A protracted duration is emphasized by the phrase "jusqu'au matin" which repeats "toute la nuit." His tone is one of subdued shrillness as a tale of fascinated subjection is told and suffered anew in which we find the paradoxical alliance of cruelty and delight, frenzy, gentleness and unresolved desire ("oiseau cruel," "point aigu du délice," "fureur si tendre"): this it is which created an enchantment and, by its association with the burning immobility of the stars, placed the soul under a universal sign of necessity.

9 Previously unpublished (italics mine).
10 *Œuvres*, I, 158.

> Tu perces l'âme et fixes le destin
> De tel regard qui ne peut se reprendre;
> Tout ce qui fut tu le changes en cendre,
> O voix trop haute, extase de l'instinct . . .

Instead of an objective description, the bird is now addressed in the second person, and the "tu," found again in line 7, further develops the grating sonority of the poem. Like Zeno's arrow the song has pierced the poet's soul and rendered movement and thought impossible.[11] Aware of the irremediable cast of fate wrought by a glance, he knows that his past has turned to ashes and that the only reality is this voice he cannot still. But is the obsessive presence beyond himself or within? More exactly perhaps both beyond and within like a call to which his whole being responds, or a spontaneous yet unbearable joy. The eighth line, with its invocation and apposition, maintains the ambiguity of pleasure and pain, object and subject; nor does it yet relate the bird explicitly to the theme of love.

> L'aube dans l'ombre ébauche le visage
> D'un jour très beau qui déjà ne m'est rien:
> Un jour de plus n'est qu'un vain paysage.

Time has moved forward with its own necessity and shows the splendid promise of a new day. It is like a beautiful woman who emerges from the shadows of night by some supreme painter's artistry. Yet such aesthetic wonder is meaningless for him whose treasure is hidden in the dark he sees not feels the future spread before him. In the same way as the past in the second quatrain, it has lost all savor; its plenitude is empty, its pleasures as nothing. The two uses of "jour" raise the tone as the emotion becomes more urgent and the poet measures the extent of his solitude.

> Qu'est-ce qu'un jour sans le visage tien?
> Non! . . . Vers la nuit mon âme retournée
> Refuse l'aube et la jeune journée.

---

[11] "Zénon! cruel Zénon! Zénon d'Elée / M'as-tu percé de cette flèche ailée / Qui vibre, vole et qui ne vole pas!" ("Le Cimetière marin").

The third use of "jour" in three successive lines takes us to
the climax of the sonnet before its sudden and surprising
dénouement. On the one hand the poet perceives the countenance of day; on the other he places his inner necessity
which is opposed to the effluxion of time and consists of the
desire and pain that have made of his night a single body.
Day would cause this known countenance of love to disappear. With what subtlety the e mute of "visage" and the
preciously adjectival "tien" convey the tenderness of the
self. Once more the familiar second person is introduced,
but this time it is not so much the bird and its over-loud
voice and the ecstasy of instinct that are evoked as the
woman herself who is the source of all charm. The poem
turns then on the fulcrum of a question and the emphatic
negative that follows. The self will not look to the future,
will refuse the evidence of time. In a magnificent flourish, it
rejects the world and chooses to pursue the bird of its yearning.

In love there is a perverseness which is nature's scandal.
The self of "L'Oiseau cruel" rejects ordinary beauty and
calm, repudiates the gifts of time; and, whereas one of
Valéry's most frequent themes is the excitement of dawn, we
here find him turning his back on all its bounties. "Aimer
passionnément quelqu'un, c'est avoir cédé à son image puissance de toxique." [12] The disciplined sonnet with its rapid
meter, its decasyllables, its regular caesura after the fourth
foot, expresses an emotional extravagance that makes of
memory pain, and of pain vital pleasure. The central image
derives, as we have seen, from an early impression which
was recalled on a few rare occasions and became a kind of
private symbol. It sounds an insistent summons to the sensibility that can neither be silenced nor transcended by
reason. This is naked instinct which coincides in the last
tercet with the tender face of the woman, the origin and
object of desire.

12 "Le Mal d'amour," *Mélange, Œuvres*, I, 349.

Characteristic of Valéry's handling of fixed forms, the four sections are conceived with sensuous artistry. We remember that he stated quite clearly his ambition to modify the point of view contained within the sonnet, to provide as it were a "rotation autour d'un axe." [13] In "L'Oiseau cruel," this goal has, I believe, been admirably achieved, offering us a varied yet balanced poem, opening up a vision and establishing its force before enclosing the structure upon itself. Thus the first quatrain constitutes the confession of experience, the extremes of suffering and delight in the presence of the bird ("l'oiseau cruel"), the self ("point aigu du délice"), the song ("fureur si tendre"), the heavens ("ciel brûlant d'astres"): an immense correspondence marks all things within the poet and without. The mode of address changes to the second person singular in the next lines, the effect of the bird's song being designated now as the lover's fate; it is both his death ("Tu perces l'âme et fixes le destin," "tu le changes en cendre") and his ecstasy ("extase de l'instinct"). In the first tercet the focus is modified once more to describe the attractions of morning light: time extends the grace of a virgin landscape, but for the poet such joy is abstract and alien to his sensibility ("ombre," "vain paysage"). The final tercet reverts to direct speech as day and night are again opposed; but now the poet, this rebel who prefers the cruelty of love to a loveless dawn, wilfully proclaims in the face of reason that time is reversible. The conclusion looks back then to its beginning and offers the formal counterpart of a sentiment which, like the idea of Valéry's poetry itself, is the poignant enemy of the world.

Whereas "L'Oiseau cruel" is in our eyes the poem of self-enchantment and of imagination tenuously triumphant, "Chanson à part," which is almost exactly contemporaneous (the original manuscript is dated 3 July 1938), possesses an entirely different tone. It is composed of fifteen questions

[13] Letter to Albert Mockel (1917), *Lettres à Quelques-uns,* 124.

and answers, of as many *boutades*. We know that no technique could be more central to Valéry's method in his notebooks, from his first fundamental enquiry "Que peut un
homme?" to his well-known published responses (thus, when
asked: "Pourquoi écrivez-vous?" he replied: "Par faib-
lesse").[14] Here is the dialogue of the disabused intellect. The
language of "Chanson à part" is spare; it has no adjectives
or adverbs and offers only the general vocabulary of the
abstract mind. The four six-line pentasyllabic stanzas have
the rapidity and restlessness of "Le Sylphe": "Ni vu ni
connu. . . ." To reinforce this effect, all twenty-four rhymes
are masculine, so that there is no resolution into softness and
no wave of emotion, but a simple pattern constantly repeated, the monotonous syntax of the thinker hesitating between his All and his Nothing, between life and death.

Self-awareness, then, is this bout of wit, these words that
are impudently put to the heart and soul and mind in the
name of lucidity.

> Que fais-tu? De tout,
> Que vaux-tu? Ne sais,
> Présages, essais,
> Puissance et dégoût . . .
> Que vaux-tu? Ne sais . . .
> Que veux-tu? Rien, mais tout.[15]

At the beginning of Valéry's inner dialogue is the enigma
of human action which, as the poet well knows, may adopt
any shape or form—good or bad, abstract or concrete, trivial
or grave—and touch on all things. By our nature we are
doomed to diversity. In the case of Valéry himself we know
he once exclaimed in his notebooks: "J'ai beau faire, tout
m'intéresse." [16] But if we can appreciate with some degree of
objectivity the action of another, and if, like Valéry, we may
happen to be convinced of the value of certain of our find-

14 *Littérature*, no. 10, (December 1919); compare *Œuvres*, II, 1845.
15 *Œuvres*, I, 162.
16 *Cahiers*, I, 232.

ings ("Je crois que ce que j'ai trouvé est important— *je suis
sûr de cette valeur"*),[17] we are in no position to judge our
own true worth. After all, who can establish a scale of values
for this inner self once it has been wise enough to look beyond praise or opprobrium? "Chaque esprit qu'on trouve
puissant," as Monsieur Teste well knew, "commence par la
faute qui le fait connaître." [18] A man can only answer for
his own experience, which is a cycle that does not lead beyond itself but moves from project to experiment, from experiment to power, and from power to disgust with an object
that is essentially ephemeral in the eyes of him who made it:
"Une œuvre n'est jamais nécessairement *finie,* car celui qui
l'a faite ne s'est jamais accompli, et la puissance et l'agilité
qu'il en a tirées, lui confèrent précisément le don de
l'améliorer, et ainsi de suite. . . . *Il en retire de quoi
l'effacer et la refaire."* [19] At this point the cycle of action can
only begin again in the likeness of the self-devouring Serpent
who declares:

> Tu peux repousser l'infini
> Qui n'est fait que de ta croissance,
> Et de la tombe jusqu'au nid,
> Te sentir toute connaissance.
> Mais ce vieil amateur d'échecs,
> Dans l'or oisif des soleils secs,
> Sur ton branchage vient se tordre;
> Ses yeux font frémir ton trésor.
> Il en cherra des fruits de mort,
> De désespoir et de désordre! [20]

Thus Valéry must continue to place his work constantly in
the balance, to ask what is its value and to answer that he
does not know. As for the goal he sets himself ("Grande
question. Pour moi, la plus embarrassante de toutes. Qu'est-

17 Ibid., XXIX, 908.
18 *Œuvres,* II, 16.
19 Ibid., I, 1451.
20 "Ebauche d'un Serpent," *Œuvres,* I, 145.

ce que tu veux? Qu'est-ce que *Je* veut?"),[21] he is obliged to
describe it in terms that appear contradictory (and the meter
itself momentarily lapses): he seeks nothing in particular
such as fame or wealth or a single discovery or a personal
monument—not one instant of success but rather a lever
that is capable of moving the world. As he wrote in similarly
paradoxical language in one of his notebooks: "Je cherche
ce qui est visible et non vu, qui n'importe pas et qui est
essentiel, qui est toujours et qui n'est jamais. Rien de profond." [22] He will define with absolute clarity all images,
words, and sensations as mere phenomena within the system
of the self, so that, possessing Nothing, he will at last possess
All.

> Que sais-tu? L'ennui.
> Que peux-tu? Songer.
> Songer pour changer
> Chaque jour en nuit.
> Que sais-tu? Songer
> Pour changer d'ennui.

The first question of the second stanza leads us into a new
cycle centered on the notion of knowledge. To an imperti-
nent summons Valéry replies by way of a *boutade* that makes
us smile by its unexpectedness, as by the devious truth it
offers. In a sense all experience can be resumed under the
heading of boredom, which spells out our dashed hopes, our
failure to conquer the world—"Un Ennui, désolé par les
cruels espoirs," as Mallarmé wrote; it also signifies our
civilized indifference to events like that of Baudelaire's
"monstre délicat" ("Les événements sont l'écume des
choses," said Valéry);[23] it is, characteristically in Valéry, the
disengagement that analysis brings—so that the more one
knows, the less one is duped, and the more one is prone to
boredom, or the Serpent's "tristesse"; it is similarly the fruit

21 *Cahiers,* XXI, 868.
22 Ibid., XXIV, 876.
23 "Propos me concernant," *Œuvres,* I, 205.

of self-knowledge that is sung by Narcissus when he discovers the finite form of his body in the calm waters of
meditation ("Pour l'inquiet Narcisse, il n'est ici qu'ennui")[24]
or the Angel of Valéry's last prose poem written in May
1945 ("O mon Mal, disait-il, que m'êtes vous?").[25] Boredom
is finally a word we associate with Valéry in another way as
the *taedium vitae* to which he referred so much in his correspondence and conversation from the earliest days, telling
Gide in 1891: "je ne suis pas un Poète, mais le Monsieur qui
s'ennuie," [26] and Albert Coste in 1915: "Ma nature est
extrémiste, changeante; je ne puis même compter sur la
constance de mes désespoirs. Mais parfois, maintenant, une
sorte d'intime froid irrésistible me gagne et je voudrais,
fût-ce au milieu du jour, me cacher la tête et dormir, dormir,
dormir." [27] We must then consider the word "ennui" as a
peculiarly apposite answer on several levels to the question
"Que sais-tu?" The second question, in its simplicity, evokes
a similar semantic plurivalence, the most evident sense of
which is an echo of the motto of the adolescent Valéry: "Que
peut un homme?" Man appears preeminently himself when
he thinks— and the more he thinks, as Valéry observed, the
more he thinks ("Plus je pense, plus je pense"). The act of
thinking is a way of passing the time, of changing day into
night; but it also reveals the depths of night where we
thought there was day alone, mystery instead of superficial
clarity. Is this a progression? Having recovered from many
an illusion the disabused intellect knows that, however much
we seem to alter, consciousness is a self-contained system
which any one point will not transcend, so that we entertain thoughts rather than maintain them. That was his
discovery of 1892: "Je suis un système terriblement *simple,
trouvé,* ou formé en 1892—par irritation insupportable qui

24 "Fragments du Narcisse," *Œuvres,* I, 124.
25 "L'Ange," *Œuvres,* I, 205.
26 *Correspondance André Gide–Paul Valéry,* 138.
27 *Lettres à Quelques-uns,* 105.

a excité un *moi* no 2 à détacher de soi un *moi* premier—
comme une meule centrifugée, ou une *masse nébuleuse en
rotation.*" [28] For the thinker who occupies such a strategic
position any change can only, in the last analysis, be a
change in the form of boredom, not in its nature.

> Que veux-tu? Mon bien.
> Que dois-tu? Savoir,
> Prévoir et pouvoir
> Qui ne sert de rien.
> Que crains-tu? Vouloir.
> Qui es-tu? Mais rien!

The self must now answer the same central question that
was put in the first stanza; and it replies with a word that,
while echoing "rien," is so to speak its contrary, but equally
justified. The expression "mon bien" is, of course, ambiguous: for Narcissus it indicates the godlike image he finds
in the water ("O mon bien souverain, cher corps, je n'ai
que toi! / Le plus beau des mortels ne peut chérir que soi
. . .");[29] for Semiramis it is the limitless dream of infinite
power ("Que je m'évanouisse en mes vastes pensées, / Sage
Sémiramis, enchanteresse et roi!");[30] for the Valéry of one
notebook it is the idea of a diamond point of consciousness
("J'aurais voulu te vouer à former le cristal de chaque chose,
ma Tête . . .").[31] Nevertheless, whatever form it takes from
year to year or from moment to moment, "mon bien" is the
unemphatic answer to which each one of us can subscribe.
The second question provokes a more distinctly personal
response when the issue of moral obligation is raised. Valéry
was called on many times in his career to address himself
publicly to this subject (as in his delightfully witty "Rap-
port sur les prix de vertu"),[32] and he could not but reflect in

---

28 *Cahiers*, XVI, 45.
29 "Fragments du Narcisse," *Œuvres*, I, 128.
30 "Air de Sémiramis," *Œuvres*, I, 94.
31 *Cahiers*, XXIV, 3.
32 *Œuvres*, I, 936–958.

what he said his intimate experience and the decision of his twenty-first year to be master in his own household. No borrowed code of behavior could suit him after he had determined to refuse the world and taken as his line of action the study of his own mental functions. This kind of knowledge—not an accumulation of facts but rigorous self-conscious thought—was the method his notebooks cultivated: "Je me suis éduqué dans le mépris continuel de ma pensée," he wrote.[33] In no sense was he attempting a diary that would shore up the past, but a scheme of analysis to construct the future, to define and discipline the magma of the mind. He could say with exactness: "Je travaille pour l'avenir de ma pensée"; and again *"Voir,* c'est *prévoir.* . . . Notre esprit, qui est vie, développe devant nous selon toutes ses ressources de savoir, de logique et d'analogie, l'image toujours changeante du possible."[34] It does not however follow that such knowledge will necessarily find its expression in any concrete action since it has its real end within itself, and all its products, even the finest poems, pale in importance before it: "Je ne suis poète que par raccroc." The power Valéry seeks is less of an effective kind than a potential one—"pouvoir / Qui ne sert de rien." He will be the Robinson of the intellect, or a Monsieur Teste. In a letter of 1894 stating the position from which he was never to veer in its essentials he said: "J'ai agi toujours pour me rendre un individu potentiel. . . . Avoir à ma disposition sans disposer."[35] But having adopted this attitude, the evil he feared most was, as he says, "vouloir," that is, the wiles of ambition, the desire to obtain particular effects, the temptation to exchange immanence ("étrange / Oisiveté, mais pleine de

[33] *Cahiers,* II, 866; compare "Je sais ce que l'on souffre de n'être que soi. Un jour que je n'en pouvais plus, j'ai pris la décision de m'accepter *tel quel.* J'ai résolu et tenu de mesurer mes pouvoirs dans le silence et de me borner à cet exercice secret" (*Cahiers,* XII, 392).

[34] *Œuvres,* I, 1427–1428.

[35] *Correspondance André Gide–Paul Valéry,* 217–218.

pouvoir") for practical results. He had to resist velleities of
the sort which were wholly inimical to his designs. The last
question of the stanza indicates the point to which all the
previous questions implicitly lead when an effort is made
to force the self to utter its name. On another occasion
Valéry put the same question to himself and answered thus:
"Qui es-tu? *Je suis ce que je puis,* me dis-je." [36] Here the
answer could be identical, as we have had occasion to see in
lines 14–16; but Valéry is now intent on escaping definition,
on showing the essential anonymity of the pure self which
he likens to the zero of mathematics and describes as "le
refus indéfini d'être quoi que ce soit." "Entre mon nom et
moi, je fais une distinction abyssale." [37] Valéry's I is not a
person but a point of view which establishes his freedom
from any local event or phenomenon, so that he can quite
properly answer the probing of the voice of self-consciousness by declaring that he is indeed—*nothing,* no defined
and circumscribed human being with the foibles that flesh
is heir to. But at the same time he is also ironically,
ambiguously, a reed, the nothing that is man.

> Où vas-tu? A mort.
> Qu'y faire? Finir,
> Ne plus revenir
> Au coquin de sort.
> Où vas-tu? Finir.
> Que faire? Le mort.

After his first three stanzas modulating on the theme of
Everything, Boredom, Nothing and tracing out the curve of
consciousness, Valéry takes us finally to the limits of thought
with the word "mort." He was not in the habit of writing a
great deal on death, or ascribing metaphysical significance to
it; as he remarked: "La mort nous parle d'une voix profonde pour ne rien dire." [38] His reply to the question "Où

[36] *Œuvres,* II, 1511.
[37] *Correspondance André Gide–Paul Valéry,* 509.
[38] *Œuvres,* II, 842.

vas-tu?" has then a medieval flavor, a kind of literary stylization by the omission of the definite article which adds to the lightness of tone. By this humor that is almost flippant he keeps at bay the flood of conventional emotion. "La mort, en littérature," he noted, "est un son grave. Il n'y a rien à en dire. Ceux qui en usent sont des faiseurs." [39] The next answer has likewise a dosage of familiarity that deflates any tendency to dramatize: death is an end to it all, and flatly Valéry states that he will not want to be coming back. "Coquin," colloquial as it is and unexpected in this bare poem, gives the necessary emphasis which dismisses any show of solemnity. In the same vein the poem concludes with two lines that constitute a veritable pirouette since they take up again the questions and answers of lines 19–20, repeating the same words but reversing the order, and taking "faire" in the extended sense of "to affect" or "to pretend," as if death itself were totally devoid of pathos and only a spectacle to be acted out. "Si tu veux vivre," he wrote with characteristic bluntness, "tu veux aussi mourir; ou bien tu ne conçois pas ce qu'est la vie";[40] and again: "Chaque pensée est une exception à une règle générale qui est de ne pas penser." [41]

Less ironic than "Chanson à part," "Le Philosophe et la 'Jeune Parque' " is likewise at the other extreme from the mood of "L'Oiseau cruel." Although it has been called by one of its exégètes "une paraphrase en vers," [42] the term can hardly be applied to a composition that has a zest of its own and in no way constitutes a running commentary or résumé. What Valéry offers is a fable in the style of La Fontaine, a poem whose tone and diction, direct and urbanely didactic, conform to the tradition of the genre. "Il cause et il chante," he once wrote of La Fontaine, and he himself gives us a

---

39 Ibid., 872.   40 Ibid., 907.   41 Ibid., 786.
42 J. Duchesne-Guillemin, *Essai sur "La Jeune Parque" de Paul Valéry* (Brussels: L'Ecran du Monde, 1947), 13.

witty statement about poetry and the human condition. Its
eighty-five lines are an admirable sequence of propositions
that, as it were, say everything about the *Parque* yet detract
not one jot from its true artistic virtue. As such they form a
rare expression indeed: a poem that is a critical observation
on another poem, and in which—even more unusually—the
original author and his apologist are one.

Published for the first time in 1936, it stood as a kind of
preface ("en guise de prologue") to Alain's famous critical
reading. Six years before, in his letter of thanks to the
philosopher who had just published his *Commentaires de
"Charmes,"* Valéry had observed that the hidden presence
of the Parque gave Alain's book an unexpected unity which
was thoroughly justified, since *"Charmes* naquit ou naqui-
rent de la *Parque."* He went on: "Si la *Parque* vous tentait,
vous en feriez quelque belle réflexion." [43] Thus Alain was
merely following up the invitation of his author when five
years later he wrote an essay and submitted it to Valéry.
"Mais que répondre à un compliment?" Would the poet
compose a detached note such as one finds in his preface to
Alain's previous criticism in which he affirmed the poet's
right to *mean* what he *means* to his reader, and not to have
a single personal connotation? "Mes vers ont le sens qu'on
leur prête," he observed;[44] for none could be further removed than he from the so-called intentional fallacy. Yet
instead of a discourse of this sort he chose to provide a poem
in which the Parque answers the Philosopher and her
readers, and at last, as he put it, "mange le morceau": spills
the beans! [45] We should note that its genesis undoubtedly
benefited from the meditations Valéry pursued in 1935 on
the *Parque* which resulted in the publication of his masterly
article in the *Revue de Paris* at the end of 1937 under the
title "Fragments des mémoires d'un poème." Here the rela-

43 *Lettres à Quelques-uns,* 184.
44 Preface to *Commentaires de "Charmes,"* Œuvres, I, 1509.
45 *Correspondance André Gide–Paul Valéry,* 447.

tionship he explored was that of the author and his poem, whereas "Le Philosophe et la 'Jeune Parque'" concentrates on the Reader's experience; but in both, as one might expect, we trace an illuminating convergence of views. Indeed it appears clear, when we study the eighteenth *Cahier* dated 1935, that article and poem had a common origin in his jottings. We observe first of all some isolated remarks (for instance, "*Jeune Parque*: J'ai essayé là de faire de la 'poésie' avec l'être vivant");[46] and this important statement that defines pure poetry as an elixir of styles: "Rien de plus opposé à la poésie raisonnable, à la narrative, à la fable de La Fontaine, à l'oratoire de Hugo et même au sentimental et lyrique 'humain' de Musset etc. dans lequel je retrouvais le parler direct. (Il suffisait d'un *choix* dans ces œuvres pour concevoir la poésie pure)."[47] But these remarks are preceded by a note written in Zurich on 19 November 1935 wherein, alongside further self-observations concerning his experience as an author—the "poème du travail de la J P"[48]—and the way in which it became for him, as he says, a vice like tobacco, he foreshadows the subject and manner of his fable:

> Parque raconte au Phil. son histoire naïve
> Mais le P. pense en prose.

We may note that in one of the above quotations Valéry sharply distinguished his poetic ideal from that of La Fontaine. It is evident, from the essays on "Adonis" and "Daphnis et Alcimadure," that he knew with the sure touch of long intimacy the less frequented élégies as well as the range of fables, and could speak of them magisterially ("la nonchalance, ici, est savante; la mollesse, étudiée; la facilité, le comble de l'art").[49] But if he could in a general way feel deep affinity with such a poet, he was particularly attracted by the formal possibilities of the *vers variés* on which La Fontaine had placed the most personal of imprints. On two

46 *Cahiers*, XVIII, 530.   47 Ibid., 281.
48 Ibid., 336.   49 *Œuvres*, I, 475.

or three occasions he used a prosodic scheme of this kind at
the time of the writing of *Charmes* (in "La Fausse Morte,"
and sporadically in "Fragments du Narcisse") and achieved
outstanding success. Later we discover him in the notebooks
weighing the function to be given to *vers variés* and asking
himself if he might not use them to personal ends: "Vers
variés," he writes in the ninth *Cahier*. "Essayer d'en faire le
moyen de mettre en vers mes personnages familiers—
états." [50] He thus had recourse to it in 1931 for his "mélodrame" *Amphion* and, even more strikingly, for the libretto
of his *Cantate du Narcisse* of 1938. In the meanwhile he had
also used it in the poem we are to examine in which the
requirements of a monologue are fulfilled after the manner
of La Fontaine, with lightness of tone. He even carried his
stylistic exercise so far as to write the two short passages at
the start and close of "Le Philosophe et la 'Jeune Parque'"
in the original edition in metrical prose that heralds and
later echoes in the author's name the prosody of his poem.
He begins on an alexandrine: "C'est une Fable ici que je
devrais écrire . . . / Ce titre le voudrait. / Ne fait-il point
songer / à quelqu'un de ces poèmes d'air négligé, / parfois
lyriques et parfois trop sagaces, / dont la voix variable nous
tient / dans La Fontaine un langage ambigu? / Mais oserai-
je en vers parler devant Alain? . . ." and so on. One could
not wish for lines that more pertinently set the rhythms of
the Parque's fable.

La Jeune Parque, un jour, trouva son Philosophe:

«Ah, dit-elle, de quelle étoffe
Je saurai donc mon être fait . . .[51]

In a sense the speaker is not looking for the answer to the
question she implicitly utters in the first lines of her monologue since, as we shall realize, she is well aware of her own
true nature. She is nothing but a poem, and the Philosopher
cannot penetrate more deeply into her being than by nam-

[50] *Cahiers*, IX, 225.   [51] *Œuvres*, I, 163.

ing the operatic genre to which she belongs with her succession of recitatives (not *epic*, as Alain quaintly observed), and describing the leitmotifs, the modulations, the diction, the prosody. He could also talk, as the Parque later will, of her sense as dependent on the reader's point of view, as *réflexion* rather than *transparence*.[52] We must then admit that her opening words are above all a way of gaining the attention of the reader, a lucid feigning of ignorance so that the directions of poetry may be used for her own ends. (It is also, of course, her courteous device for channeling an unspoken criticism of Alain.)

> A plus d'un je produis l'effet
> D'une personne tout obscure;
> Chaque mortel qui n'a point cure
> De songer ni d'approfondir,
> Au seul nom que je porte a tôt fait de bondir,
> Quand ce n'est la pitié, j'excite la colère,
> Et parmi les meilleurs esprits,
> S'il est quelqu'un qui me tolère,
> Le reste tient qu'il s'est mépris.
> Ces gens disent qu'il faut qu'une muse ne cause
> Non plus de peines qu'une rose!
> Qui la respire a purement plaisir.
> Mais les amours sont les plus précieuses
> Qu'un long labeur de l'âme et du désir
> Mène à leurs fins délicieuses.
> Aux cœurs profonds ne suffit point
> D'un regard, qu'un baiser rejoint,
> Pour qu'on vole au plus vif d'une brève aventure . . .
> Non! . . . L'objet vraiment cher s'orne de vos tourments,
> Vos yeux en pleurs lui voient des diamants,
> L'amère nuit en fait la plus tendre peinture.
> C'est pourquoi je me garde et mes secrets charmants.
> Mon cœur veut qu'on me force, et vous refuse, Amants
> Que rebutent les nœuds de ma belle ceinture.
> Mon Père l'a prescrit: j'appartiens à l'effort.
> Mes ténèbres me font maîtresse de mon sort,

---

[52] Compare "La musique belle par *transparence*, et la poésie par *réflexion*" ("Rhumbs," *Tel Quel II, Œuvres*, II, 639).

Et ne livrent enfin qu'à l'heureux petit nombre
Cette innocente MOI que fait frémir son ombre
Cependant que l'Amour ébranle ses genoux.

The thirty-two lines that go to make up the first section recall the Parque's apparent obscurity and the irrational effects of pity and anger she has on her readers. To a difficult and demanding love such as hers some prefer the rose of pure delight. In an extension of the same contrast which we may take to be likewise latent in the image, Claudel distinguished Valéry's poetic ideal from his own: "Contre la beauté et contre l'amour," he said, "cherchons donc un refuge dans le cœur de la rose." [53] The Parque, however, insists on the importance of the effort the reader must make to attain his goal, because the most precious beauty of all is not the proffered rose but the mistress, the wholly meaningful center of his search that can be won only by him who goes to the utmost pains, when the intensity of his own desire gauges the treasure discovered. He becomes a creator at a second level who finds in a semblance of meaninglessness a satisfying order and purpose. In this regard it is obvious that obscurity may be said to constitute one of the essential conditions of the highest art, and that Valéry wrote it into his work with the care of an exquisite technician: "Mon Père l'a prescrit. . . ." Literature is thereby raised above the state of prose or naïve verse which can be enjoyed and discarded without concern. To violate obscurity becomes a privilege reserved for the happy few like Stendhal's readers, who find at last in the Parque a virgin form, trembling, responsive, rendered dear by the closeness of silence, or death.

CERTES, d'un grand désir je fus l'œuvre anxieuse . . .
Mais je ne suis en moi pas plus mystérieuse
    Que le plus simple d'entre vous . . .
Mortels, vous êtes chair, souvenance, présage;

[53] "Le Poète et le Shamisen," *Œuvres en prose,* 835.

Vous fûtes; vous serez; vous portez tel visage:
　　Vous êtes tout; vous n'êtes rien,
　Supports du monde et roseaux que l'air brise,
　　Vous VIVEZ . . . Quelle surprise! . . .
　　Un mystère est tout votre bien,
Et cet arcane en vous s'étonnerait du mien?
　Que seriez-vous, si vous n'étiez mystère?
　　Un peu de songe sur la terre,
Un peu d'amour, de faim, de soif, qui font des pas
　　Dont aucun ne fuit le trépas,
Et vous partageriez le pur destin des bêtes
Si les Dieux n'eussent mis, comme un puissant ressort,
　　Au plus intime de vos têtes,
Le grand don de ne rien comprendre à votre sort.
«Qui suis-je?» dit au jour le vivant qui s'éveille
　　Et que redresse le soleil,
«Où vais-je?» fait l'esprit qu'immole le sommeil,
Quand la nuit le recueille en sa propre merveille.
　　Le plus habile est piqué de l'abeille,
Dans l'âme du moindre homme un serpent se remord;
Un sot même est orné d'énigmes par la mort
Qui le pare et le drape en personnage grave,
Glacé d'un tel secret qu'il en demeure esclave.

Of similar length, the second section (1.33–59) points to a structural balance within the poem ("Mais je ne suis en moi pas plus mystérieuse / Que le plus simple d'entre vous . . . ," ". . . Et cet arcane en vous s'étonnerait du mien"). It turns from the inevitable obscurity of the refined poem to the corresponding mystery within men. What are they but a collection of heterogeneous elements? What is consciousness but this mixture, or equation, of past, present and future, of flesh, memory, dreams; both universe and reed? "Un esprit n'est que ce mélange / Duquel à chaque instant, se démêle le MOI."[54] A Pascalian duality is underlined, not to be resolved in some mystical oxymoron, but as the very definition of life. This fate is in fact, says the Parque, our characteristic privilege: "Le grand don de ne rien comprendre à notre sort." While the animal is not a mystery to itself, man experiences the limits of his understanding: the more conscious he is, when he wakes, the more vainly he seeks his identity; he turns to sleep—or death—and cannot guide his voyage to the unforeseeable within him. No metaphysics, however scant, is needed to remind us of the fragility of consciousness, the mysteries of body and mind. The bee, the quivering image of desire—beauty that is also pain, life that is also death—is one such component of thought with which the Parque is well acquainted.

> Oh! parmi mes cheveux pèse d'un poids d'abeille,
> Plongeant toujours plus ivre au baiser plus aigu,
> Le point délicieux de mon jour ambigu . . .
> Lumière! . . . Ou toi, la Mort! . . . Mais le plus prompt me
>   prenne! . . .[55]

Nor is there any need to seek a precise literary influence to explain the Serpent. As old as Eden, it accompanies our sensibility with the same necessity and the same appetite as self-knowledge turning upon its prey.

> Quel repli de trésors, sa traîne! . . . Quel désordre
> De trésors s'arrachant à mon avidité,
> Et quelle sombre soif de la limpidité! [56]

What escape can there be within the mind from a will like that of the Serpent of lucidity? The Parque similarly expresses the condition of all men in that she is aware she must die and conveys in these extraordinary lines the mortality that breathes on her skin and moves along her veins and in the very rhythm of her words:

> . . . Et le vent semble au travers d'un linceul
> Ourdir de bruits marins une confuse trame,
> Mélange de la lame en ruine, et de rame . . .
> Tant de hoquets longtemps, et de râles heurtés,

---

[55] *La Jeune Parque, Œuvres*, I, 103.
[56] Ibid., 97.

> Brisés, repris au large . . . et tous les sorts jetés
> Eperdument divers roulant l'oubli vorace . . .[57]

But in this fable which places rapidity of movement above
sensuous suggestion, lines 58 and 59 also have a fine solemnity of their own in evoking the sculptured image of a corpse
who coldly meditates on his lot.

ALLEZ! . . . Que tout fût clair, tout vous semblerait vain!
Votre ennui peuplerait un univers sans ombre
D'une impassible vie aux âmes sans levain.
Mais quelque inquiétude est un présent divin.
L'espoir qui dans vos yeux brille sur un seuil sombre
Ne se repose pas sur un monde trop sûr;
De toutes vos grandeurs le principe est obscur.
Les plus profonds humains, incompris de soi-mêmes,
D'une certaine nuit tirent des biens suprêmes
Et les très purs objets de leurs nobles amours.
Un trésor ténébreux fait l'éclat de vos jours:
Un silence est la source étrange des poèmes.
Connaissez donc en vous le fond de mon discours!
C'est de vous que j'ai pris l'ombre qui vous éprouve.
Qui s'égare en soi-même aussitôt me retrouve.
Dans l'obscur de la vie où se perd le regard,
    Le temps travaille, la mort couve,
    Une Parque y songe à l'écart.
C'est MOI . . . Tentez d'aimer cette jeune rebelle:
    «*Je suis noire, mais je suis belle*»
Comme chante l'Amante, au Cantique du Roi,
    Et si j'inspire quelque effroi,
Poème que je suis, à qui ne peut me suivre,
    Quoi de plus prompt que de fermer un livre?

    C'est ainsi que l'on se délivre
De ces écrits si clairs qu'on n'y trouve que soi.»

The last lines draw together the two preceding sections
in a final resolution. The Parque refers once more to the
mystery of man and praises it for making hope, greatness,
genius—these deviations from the norm—precious and ir-
replaceable. It is only in the context of night that brightness

---

[57] Ibid., 105.

is truly meaningful, and the wealth of the mind, and the wondrous object of desire that is unidentifiable with any single person or thing. But this chiaroscuro which expresses the inner self when it utters only the simplest and most personal words, is also that of *La Jeune Parque*. Her secret is made in the image of man: not one person celebrating the memory of Lucy or Elvire but a self conceived from the start in universal terms, according to the rhythms and zones of consciousness attentive to its own sensibility. "J'ai (. . .) essayé de fabriquer des vivants de synthèse," [58] Valéry said of Monsieur and Madame Teste and the Parque; and he elsewhere explained his ambition in these terms:

Ce tropisme intellectuel voulait que je cherchasse à *construire* des poèmes, ou à en composer après une analyse des conditions que je trouvais dans l'action possible du langage (exploité selon les modes de la poésie) sur quelqu'un, ce qui exigeait une idée de ce quelqu'un et de son fonctionnement probable.

From this point of view there can be no surprise for us that Valéry chose as the title of his poem *La Jeune Parque,* which some critics have not found easy to justify. The voice that speaks is man's Fate—his body and mind—at a time when it possesses the nervousness and needs of youth. Facing the sky that is ever different and ever the same, she traverses a parallel galaxy of hidden movements in the heart and soul. She follows a fatal thread, which is her song of self-aware-ness, her discovery of time, death, the strangeness within the self, as well as the energies of new birth ("Doux et puis-sant retour du délice de naître"). Hers is the cycle of thought, the transformation of Life into Death and Death into Life, the Eternal Return. So it is that she can use to describe herself the Bride's words from the Song of Solomon: "I am black, but comely." If she seems to animate a par-

[58] *Cahiers*, XXVIII, 139.   [59] Ibid., XXVII, 166.

ticular destiny we recognize it as our own in a precise way
when we go to the limits of her opera of the mind.

Nevertheless the alliance of death and beauty cannot be
contemplated without concern, and the reader may well
object on such a score: obscurity is not alone the Muse's
girdle which needs to be untied, but the dark side of our
sensibility itself. The revelation the reader finds about himself, the equivalence between the fate he listens to and the
fate within him, can conceivably be too strong a dose to
stand, so that he refuses to pursue his reading as far as the
extreme point language will open up to him by way of a
mystery as clear as a mirror. In that case no harm is done;
after all, the Parque is but a poem, and her tragic contralto
overheard on the shores of destiny is nothing but a sequence
of alexandrines. The fable finds anew its beginning, having
answered its own question regarding its inner truth and
closing the book of poetry on itself, like the sudden breath
of spontaneous movement in "Le Cimetière marin" that
brings the monologue to a close.

"Le Philosophe et la 'Jeune Parque' " strikes us then first
and foremost as a triumph of tone which combines grace
and strength, elegance and reasonableness, lyricism and di-
dacticism. Certainly it cannot rank in our eyes with Valéry's
finest pieces, although in a sense it presupposes such compositions, for it presents a poet who is a felicitous master of
style, wholly sure of his ends in mingling alexandrines,
decasyllables, and octosyllables—a virtuoso not unworthy of
comparison with the persuasive presto of La Fontaine. Yet
on another level one must add that Valéry is at the furthest
remove from La Fontaine's *Fables* in that his poem so
obviously lacks the central ingredient of "fabulousness."
Here is no linear development of a narrative, no comic or
tragic plot. The interest is not in the least dramatic, but
rather, I would suggest, balletic in that it eschews fiction in
favor of refined variation. We have observed from our read-

ing how this is accomplished: each of the three parts takes
up the same theme, but treats it differently, the poem offering as it were three separate equations that possess an
identical value. In the first section the Parque speaks of the
obscurity for which others criticize and castigate her, but
with sensuous imagery she declares that effort creates the
price of beauty, and she is worth the effort. If the second
section points to the obscurity within the Parque's readers,
we learn that this very obscurity, like her own, is precious
and personal, and makes the least exalted of us a labyrin-
thine secret. In the same way the last section is composed of
a diptych that brings together the signal importance to
man of his own obscurity and the exact congruence of the
Parque's being, which is the reflected image of a universal
pattern. The moral, by a last pirouette, sums up these lines
and the rest of the poem as it postulates an obscurity that is
luminous: the Parque contains nothing but the reader and
what he finds in her substance of his hidden treasure of
desire and regret, fear and hope. Thus, within the tone and
rhythms of a fable, Valéry's poem constitutes a dance of
propositions around a single point, and flirts with sensuousness if it is too witty to espouse it. It stands on its own
through the voice of the Parque, but also through the form
she creates where none is intrinsic to the fable, achieving a
composition of contrasts, balances, and equivalences which
delights us in the final instance, less for what it asserts, than
for its intrinsic design.

Our reading of these poems will have served to indicate, I
believe, that the work of Valéry's last years, when he was
approaching the age of seventy, retains a vitality that requires no defense and is the admirably controlled expression of an original poet. But I should also wish to underline
once more another point: the importance within his work
of the tones that his notebooks contain quite as patently as
his poems, and which "Chanson à part" and "Le Philosophe

et la 'Jeune Parque' " on the one hand, and "L'Oiseau cruel"
on the other, capture in striking ways. Here is the primacy
of the intellect, there, that of the emotions, now analysis,
now, so to speak, a grandly illogical passion. For me it is
precisely this ambivalence which gives his work its constantly renewed interest, and is the measure of the range of
a poetry that contains incantation, magic, miracle, the "corps
incorruptible," and ironic statement. Between these opposite
yet complementary positions Valéry forged the language of
intellectual activity itself, not of ideas so much as the visions
—organized, precise, intense—of a marvelously agile mind.

9: "Il faut être un saint . . ."

THE MYTH of Narcissus as Valéry interpreted it corresponds in a suggestive way to his intellectual biography. In the beginning is the feeling of the mind's limitless power which a mirrored image delimits and disturbs. One cannot but recall in this respect a moving prose-poem dated May 1945 that finds again, for the last time, the essential note of his work: "Une manière d'ange était assis sur le bord d'une fontaine. Il s'y mirait, et se voyait Homme, et en larmes, et il s'étonnait à l'extrême de s'apparaître dans l'onde nue cette proie d'une tristesse infinie." The self contemplates a mortal whose disquieting charm is to define him; but what is this mask that is not the self? Who bears the name Narcissus? Now if it is true that he tried most often to couch his drama in general terms, we know that on occasion he also adopted a familiar mode. He took a singular interest in his own name, reflecting on his Italian origins, his aristocratic lineage; moreover, he did not fail to observe the wholly verbal appositeness of "Paul Valéry": small but strong. These cases strike us, but there were in fact countless other times when he turned to the question of his name; and he even went so far as to transcribe its Arabic equivalent in one of his *Cahiers* in the manner of a talisman.

It is, however, worthy of note that in 1890, and for several years following, Ambroise Paul Toussaint Jules Valéry signed his name in his correspondence and published works,

Paul-Ambroise. The Christian name Ambroise came to him
from his paternal grandfather, and the young Symbolist
found it much to his liking and that of his friends. Pierre
Louÿs thought it "merveilleusement rougeâtre et ecclésias-
tique," while Gide, as late as in *Les Faux-Monnayeurs,* used
it to designate his friend. Towards the time of *Monsieur
Teste* Valéry seems to have discarded it, using it thereafter
only on rare occasions, above all humorous ones, as in a
hasty note to Gide which he signed "Paolo Ambrogio Cur-
rente Calamo." Was this merely a passing fondness for a
name with *fin-de-siècle* overtones? On the contrary, it is curious that Valéry never quite lost "Ambroise" from sight but
continued all his life to find in it a special significance.
Thus, from the time of *Charmes,* a poem develops at length
the metaphor of ambrosia as a transparent source, the object of elevated desire, an absolute mathematics, an ideal
honey. The self sings of the intellectual purity from which
ideas and forms are born, celebrating with abstract fervor
"le libre amour du bel entendement":

> O dieu démon démiurge ou destin
> Mon appétit comme une abeille vive
> Scintille et sonne environ le festin
> Duquel ta grâce a permis que je vive.

Here once again is the drama of Narcissus, of an ambiguous
self that aspires passionately to the divine as the bee to
honey. The name of the thinker-poet is Ambroise, which
means in Greek "immortal"; the ambrosia of which he
speaks is the food the bee tastes as it seeks to become, however briefly, a god. The play on words at the center of this
poem dating from Valéry's maturity suggests the lasting
value of a particular name in his intimate language. Why
should he not find in the name Paul-Ambroise the reflected
image of the small but strong man who would be immortal,
of the self that would be an island, of the Man who sadly
sees himself to be a man and dreams of being an Angel?

La Jeune Parque, "Le Cimetière marin," and so many other compositions obtain their vitality from an inner tension of this kind; and if one day, towards the end of his life, the poet's aspiration reached such a degree of urgency as to seek to wipe out an unbearable reality, he would again sign his work, not Paul Valéry, but Monsieur de Saint-Ambroyse. A sonnet written by this strange signatory and bearing the date 1644 appeared for the first time in *Mélange* in 1942. One may feel that no poem is less oblique. The self that speaks bows to the requirements of the *sonnet galant,* addressing the woman, reasoning with her, boasting of its love. The language echoes the diction of the age of Louis XIII— an abstract tone that distances feelings and ennobles them; metaphors that one might expect in poetry composed under the sign of Malherbe; an intellectual preciousness that finds pleasure in repeating the same key-words: "désir," "cœur," "plaire," "vivre," "aimer," "souffrir"; a certain stiffness that the use of "combien que" and the inversion after "vainement" serve to underline. Yet, despite these obvious traits which indicate a clearly defined period in French poetry, the reader cannot neglect other features that show Valéry's own mark: the formal virtuosity; the theme of the wilful self, Caesar of its own sensibility; above all, the mask of impersonality emphasized by the chosen name of the signatory, this triumphant figure and face. "Mon masque," writes Valéry, "est ce que je voudrais être." [1] I wish, then, to examine what I shall call the legend of Saint Ambrose as portrayed in Valéry's writings—a legend, its author might have said, "aussi étrangère et aussi importante que l'est à un homme son nom." [2]

We may ask what weight can be given to the epithet "saint" in Valéry's vocabulary. Does it, as one might think at first, serve ironical ends? Or else, when he speaks of Saint Am-

---

[1] *Cahiers,* VI, 11.   [2] Compare *Œuvres,* II, 548.

broise, is he simply parodying the baroque seventeenth century poet Saint-Amant? We are perhaps all the more surprised by this use inasmuch as we remember a comment by one of the more recent commentators of his work: "Si le langage de la morale a été pour Valéry un langage étranger, celui de la religion l'a été encore plus." That is certainly not true of a writer who, far from eliminating from his vocabulary all vague words, handles terms like "divin," "mystique," "miracle," with so much liberality. He does not suppress the language of tradition but redefines it in his own way. As for "saintliness," the *Cahiers* show that it represents Valéry's reply to a question he had put to himself at an early date: *Que peut un homme?* What is a man capable of doing? "Il faut être un saint," announces Valéry in his fifteenth *Cahier*, "c'est-à-dire, rien qui ne soit (ou ne puisse être) orienté vers . . . mieux que soi—ou mieux que la veille." [3] His rule of conduct becomes an exercise in moral rigorousness, the touchstone of which is the rejection of the all-too-human: "L'*homo* me fait vomir." [4] He refuses to accept vague language, religions, events—all that he subsumes by the expression "écume des choses." The saint must rebel in order to assert his power: "Se faire plus grand que soi"; [5] "Tout ce qui relève l'homme est inhumain ou surhumain." [6]

It is perfectly clear in this regard that his 1892 crisis only brought to the point of highest lucidity a potential attitude. Before that night, he had spoken of "une belle vision cristalline du monde" that reduces thought and emotion to the abstract elegance of a theorem. The sonnets of his first "Chorus mysticus" are the sure testimony of this; however varied their themes, one finds the constant will to capture a moment of ecstasy, an ideal dream.

[3] *Cahiers,* XV, 853.
[4] *Correspondance André Gide–Paul Valéry,* 515.
[5] *Cahiers,* IX, 493.
[6] *Œuvres,* 1485.

Moi dont le rêve peut fuir dans l'immensité
Plus haut que les vautours, les astres et les anges . . .

The adolescent poet created his own domain which denied
the banal, having learnt that words could compose and perfect his mystical yearnings. Another Narcissus, his friend
Gide, had stated in one of his letters his kindred ambition
as a convinced Symbolist: "Quand le monde n'est pas tel
qu'on le rêve, il faut le rêver tel qu'on le veut." This point
of view is certainly not antagonistic to that which is developed throughout the *Cahiers*. Although the analyst tried
to pose as a "rationaliste archi-pur," he recognized that he
felt "en mystique," that is to say, according to his prime
intuition of transcendence. And when he passed the age of
fifty and produced the works that made him famous, he
again emphasized the primacy he had always given to imagination, to dream: "Quand je croyais de vous comprendre,
ô choses, je ne faisais que vous inventer." [7]

Valéryan saintliness is then an essential aspiration towards a closed, complete world, in which intellect is sovereign, "vers un point de souveraineté et simplicité de notre
puissance d'existence";[8] it is also, as we know from "Sinistre" and elsewhere, a technique of defense against an over
sensitive self. In one of the precious passages of self-analysis
that are to be found in the *Cahiers*, he speaks of his "volonté
d'épuiser, de—passer à la limite," and observes how strange
it seems to him that "cette fureur glacée d'extermination,
d'exécution par la rigueur soit liée étroitement en [lui] avec
le sentiment douloureux du cœur serré, de la tendresse à
un point infiniment tendre." [9] Passing from one pole to the
other, translating his intimate sensibility on an impersonal
plane, he changed, as he notes himself, "d'intuitif concret
en intuitif abstrait"—from concretely intuitive to abstractly
so.

7 *Cahiers*, VIII, 502.   8 Ibid., XXVIII, 534.
9 Ibid., XII, 352

"Etre un saint . . .": this injunction recalls a celebrated passage from Baudelaire's *Mon Cœur mis à nu*. Baudelaire wrote: "Etre un grand homme et un saint *pour soi-même,* voilà l'unique chose importante." Do Valéry's words denote a direct influence? That may well be; yet it appears to me more likely that both texts had a common source which Valéry, for his part, mentioned explicitly in his nineteenth *Cahier*: "Et enfin, observe-t-il, être un saint—disait Gracián." [10] He was, of course, referring to Baltasar Gracián, the Spanish baroque rationalist of the seventeenth century and author of the *Oráculo manual,* which dates from 1647. It is not so surprising to discover Valéry's interest in the work of Gracián who gave himself the task of scrutinizing the human condition and, from a morally neutral point of view, prescribing the way of becoming an "hombre en su punto"—a complete man. In three hundred maxims he exposed his art of *prudence,* the last of which resumes the two hundred and ninety-nine others in a single sentence: "Saint, in one word, which is to put everything in a nutshell." Like Valéry, Gracián established himself in a solitary egotism which is "the State reason of a person"; like him, his saint struggled against himself so as to be superior to the world. Indeed, he would have subscribed to many a statement of Valéry's own. He also could have written: "Pouvoir m'applaudir—le reste m'est étranger— le reste m'est froid." [11]

Thus, having depicted himself at twenty as a young priest —"le jeune prêtre"— Valéry deepened his intentions by seeking to be a "saint"; but whereas Catholicism had exalted his religious fervor, he had now to draw everything from himself. He cherished a hidden idol: "Chacun doit avoir sa Mystique, qu'il garde en soi jalousement." [12] Before all, he recognized that he must not act in haphazard fashion but reduce consciousness, that is to say, body, mind and

[10] Ibid., XIX, 59.   [11] Ibid., III, 533.   [12] Ibid., VIII, 611.

world, to clearly delimited elements which he could order
and arrange. "Mon idée fut de considérer *fini* ce qu l'on tient
pour *infini.* . . .[13] He named his method "Analyse" and
gave it a hallmark of "pureté." Thus he achieved a point of
view that embraced the infinity of particular moments of
the self, but was not to be identified with them; he postulated another self, "indépendant de mes états où il se sent
Moi, *un Moi insensible à lui-même*—et à ses variations
propres—à sa mémoire brute, à tout ce qui introduit ses
sensations corporelles (affectives ou somatiques)," [14] So it
was that Narcissus made himself master of his domain. He
convinced himself he possessed a glance "de la plus entière
généralité," which could encompass all mental phenomena
without being circumscribed by them. To be a saint is then
for Valéry to use this superior, ironic point of view in order
to "dominer, dominer, dominer les choses." [15]

He gave himself over to weighing words, to making his
dictionary. But if first of all he had to decompose so as to
purify, that was not the final end: "pour moi l'instinct
destructif n'est légitime que comme indication de quelque
naissance ou construction qui veut sa place à son heure." [16]
This ambition, named "musique," was properly speaking his
desire to make an inviolable world. Analysis of the mind
leads to music, that is to say, wholly coherent linguistic
structures, accomplished verse. Thereby he would triumph
over mortality.

For Valéry literature is the instrument before all others
which the saint has recourse to, for it allows him to surpass
himself: "un des moyens," he writes, "créés ou découverts
par l'homme pour se faire autre qu'il n'est." [17] It is, first of
all, the domain of form: a miraculous symmetry, a balance
of sonorous and semantic elements, a development from
which chance seems excluded. He takes as his model, not an

[13] Ibid., XXIII, 236.   [14] Ibid., XXVIII, 12
[15] Ibid., II, 125.   [16] Ibid., XXII, 203.
[17] Ibid., XIX, 570.

immobile perfection, but fullness of action, which he traces
out in the privileged images of the tree (which suggests
the idea of an intrinsic geometry: *"une géométrie intrinsèque* d'un seul tenant où dimensions, temps, masses, forces,
sont liées et s'expriment l'un par l'autre"),[18] the serpent
("O courbes, méandre, / Secret du menteur"—"formes dont
les mutations les unes dans les autres sont sa forme.
Spires, hélices, ondes, cercles"),[19] and the cristal, whose
beauty lies in its own refractivity. We know with what
poignant fervor he proclaimed his desire to reduce the
world to the perfection of a form that would be like the
ideal sonnet: "J'aurais voulu te vouer à former le cristal de
chaque chose, ma Tête, et que tu divises le désordre que
présente l'espace et que développe le temps, pour en tirer
les puretés qui te fassent ton monde propre, de manière
que ta lumière dans cette structure réfringente revienne et
se ferme sur elle-même dans l'instant, substituant à l'espace
l'ordre et au temps une éternité." [20]

Yet if literature contained the demon of such finished
forms, it also could allow him to treat themes in which the
glorious dream of the saint was incorporated with a precise
force. In the *Cahiers* we see Valéry baptizing the exultant
power under the names "Tiberius" and "Gladiator" and
"Caligula." We also think of Orpheus who composes by the
magic of his hymn a temple supreme, and "se sent toute-
puissante Cause"; of Sémiramis, the symbol of the formidable elevation of the Valéryan saint; of the Serpent also
who ruses, defines himself, makes himself into a master of
letters: ridiculous by his sophistry, by his parodic disguises,
he nevertheless captures the attention of Eve and the reader,
and triumphs by form. Like Orpheus, Caesar, and Sémiramis, he illustrates the sovereign self.

But literature is perhaps for Valéry, before all else, a
certain tone, an almost divine voice; it is no longer a man

18 Ibid., XI, 604.   19 Ibid., XI, 367.   20 Ibid., XXIV, 3.

speaking but a desirable mask, or soul, resolving an internal
drama that tames the human, the abyss of a sensibility. Such
is the subject of "La Pythie," the virgin self violated by a
foreign mind until at last, from her suffering, a "voix
nouvelle et blanche" emerges whose "saint langage" is the
honor of a poet as of all men.

> Honneur des Hommes, Saint LANGAGE,
> Discours prophétique et paré,
> Belles chaînes en qui s'engage
> Le dieu dans la chair égaré,
> Illumination, largesse!
> Voici parler une Sagesse
> Et sonner cette auguste Voix
> Qui se connaît quand elle sonne
> N'être plus la voix de personne
> Tant que des ondes et des bois!

We have seen in the course of this book many an example
of this will to transcend, but I find a piquant and touching
instance in the "Sonnet d'Irène" which takes as its model
preclassical poetry, and uses an archaic spelling and even
the date 1644. Valéry was of course an accomplished pasti-
cheur who made of *Charmes* a marvelously varied collection
in tone and form. He had a special predilection for French
literature of the first half of the seventeenth century: in
prose it offers, he once observed, "ce que la France a produit dans les lettres de plus rare et de plus consistant"; while
in poetry it reaches one of its high points when Father
Cyprien translates the hymns of St. John of the Cross.
We cannot doubt that Valéry also knew intimately the
works of the baroque poets which certain of his poems echo.

Such models do not prevent the authentic poet that he was
from expressing himself, quite the contrary; for as we delve
into the meaning of the "Sonnet d'Irène" it becomes clear
that it represents a central aspect of his art, and is so much
the more moving in that it undoubtedly springs from an
experience that affected him intimately. As a background to

our reading one may quote a few lines found on the back of the original manuscript, which no doubt preceded the first draft:

Chère amie,
    La cigarette fileuse développe son ouvrage de fil du feu perdu; déduit le rien. Nulle voix ne la rompt. Le néant est meublé. Le vide somptueux. L'absence est habitée. Des formes admirables et fraîches s'y complaisent. On ne sait si ce sont des figures humaines ou des couches et des colonnes. L'homme se contente de si peu qu'il a. L'espace vrai attend. Le temps réel se regarde et pleure sur soi-même. Mais la lumière n'éclaire que des mots . . .[21]

It is clear that these words are as it were the literary definition of a state of mind, above all the profound solitude which he would later exalt in his poem. They are the prelude to a self-contained lyricism that, exorcising the emptiness of space and time by way of words, imposes the reign of poetry on wayward love. The woman he addresses in this letter ("Chère amie") is not fickle but true, and submits to him alone, as the mathematical rigor of the poetic form requires. The first lines of the manuscript are likewise a declaration of the poet's mastery, his all-powerful isolation.

As regards the published version, the rich use of alliteration and assonance, the continuity of nasal a, and the repetition of rhymes at the caesura inform a substance that from the beginning has a marked originality, a clear raison d'être. We recognize the composition of a poet who is dedicated to increasing the auditory qualities of poetic language. On the other hand, just as in his other sonnets which were written at the time of his maturity, and with equal success, he pursues here the ambition of making full use of the four parts of this traditional form. The poem turns around an axis that is the loved woman: the two quatrains contrast the apparent multiplicity of her desires and of her lovers with the singleness the poet proclaims, whilst the tercets take up

[21] Previously unpublished.

again the same subject and develop the opposition between pleasure and suffering. We may note, however, that the relationship between the self and the woman is transformed by a substitution of the pronoun "elle" by "vous," then by "toi." There is, then, a progression of the line of the poem, which results less from the use of new elements than from a willed and conscious evolution that is imposed by the artist, a circular interplay of points of view. "Pour moi," Valéry once wrote, "grande œuvre signifie œuvre qui contient une révolution entière de l'être—(eût-elle deux lignes) une évolution. . . ."

The convention of the baroque sonnet is suggested to us from the start by the spelling, the capitals, and the quaintly dated use of "combien que" and "dire."

> De ses divers désirs combien qu'Elle se vante,
> Pour mon cœur enchanté Son dire est un détour;
> Elle n'ayme qu'un seul, Elle ayme dans l'Amour
> Une personne rare, et supresme et sçavante.[22]

Matching the form, the attitude of the lover is a pastiche: he is a supreme self-deceiver who places his whole confidence in words, refuses to accept the evidence of fickleness, and affirms that his mistress is only striving to hide from him the fact that she loves him alone. To the diversity she speaks of he responds by postulating a single affection; to her boasting (the verb "vante" carries with it the pained emphasis of the jealous lover), he boastfully replies in praise of his own supremacy and knowledge. This rhetoric, which is the speaker's defense against jealousy, traces out for us the enduring impulse to write in order to gain a fictional control.

> Vainement se plaist-Elle à Se feindre mouvante
> Et de trop de regards le divin quarrefour;
> Cette beauté n'est point pour les galants d'un jour
> Qui porte un corps si pur d'éternelle vivante!

---

22 *Mélange, Œuvres,* I, 289.

Another aspect of the poet's pain is assuaged, a demon exorcised. The woman thinks of herself as the moving center of multiple homage and accepts the host of adoring glances like a proud goddess, turning now to one, now to another; but the poet will not allow this thought, for she is in his eyes a true divinity whose body is incorruptible. He replaces impurity by purity, apparent wantonness by an unsullied idol. The antithetical structure of the quatrain thus echoes the opening lines, of which it provides the complementary image in the figure of the mistress seemingly beloved by all and sundry yet, in truth, worthy of one alone.

> Vous m'avez beau parler d'une trouppe d'amants
> Vous parer de désirs comme de diamants,
> Et me vouloir au cœur placer plus d'une flèche,

The lover returns once more to the heart of his flame as he addresses the woman directly, urgently, and recapitulates the matter of the octave. He repeats first of all the claim of the second quatrain, and gives it the additional poignancy of the phrase "trouppe d'amants" which can only envenom his wounded pride; he also recalls the opening boast, but now couches it in an image that is wonderfully perverse: the woman's infidelity becomes an adornment glittering with the fires of provocation like so many diamonds. For her attitude he provides a meaning and an end not previously stated, which line 11 resumes: her only wish is to make her lover suffer and to stir him more profoundly, as the precious image and phrasing indicate. (It matters little that the finalism he ascribes to her is typical of the jealous man who interprets words and events in a single sense: Monsieur de Saint-Ambroyse is solely concerned to assert his authority, however wild his fancies.) Just as in the second quatrain, the woman's actions are here all prefaced by words of exorcism ("Vous m'avez beau . . ."), the speaker being confident in his possession of higher powers.

J'en souffre, Irène d'or, mais j'en souffre sans foy,
Instruit qu'en chaque aurore, ô Rose toute fraîche,
Tu ne vis qu'en moy seul et ne Te plays qu'en moy.

The final tercet brings the lines that provide the traditional "chute" of the classical sonnet. Declaring the tension
of suffering, they transcend it in verbal self-assurance. The
name of the poet's mistress is Irene, or "peace," and Monsieur de Saint-Ambroyse affirms the evidence of consolation
in the midst of apparent turmoil. He cannot ignore the
shafts of pain which are at the very source of his poem and
of which his language contains, as we have seen, the plaintive echo; but in the wake of Petrarch and Ronsard he conjures them away by recourse to the most patently conventional of analogies. Irene is a rose in the light of dawn, who
brings with her the perfume of the literary past. Having
invoked her presence, he "thous" her for the first time, the
changed mode of address suggesting the growth in his realization of her love and of his own control. On her seeming
waywardness he has imposed his will; and the poem ends
with the vision, not of the woman transcended, but of the
poet as the single sun that bestows all life and happiness and
bloom on the rose.

If, as we have seen, the "Sonnet d'Irène" possesses the
characteristic traits of Valéry's formal imagination and his
remarkable sense of structure, the theme seems to me above
all suggestive of the particular kind of "saintliness" that
Valéry practiced. His poetry is opposed to the world, lives
on its struggle with appearances. Should the woman not
love, and yield in her attractiveness and perversity to other
temptations; should she adorn herself with fickle desires,
Orpheus will yet triumph, for the ritual word controls nature. A poet such as he necessarily places his confidence in
a sort of magic, writes in order to fix and create the elected
moment of his greatest power. Certainly we must not forget that the tone is playful, that the self smiles as it describes itself as "une personne rare, et supresme et sçavante";

and yet, despite this self-irony, the poet's objective is a
serious one. It cannot seem to us surprising that Valéry compared the voice of his poetry to that of the Serpent: like the
protagonist of the "Ebauche" the lover of Irene is a masked
enchanter who is amused at his artistry, his own pastiche,
but whispers to himself that he is more than mortal and
truly all-powerful. Such is the dream and the will of the
refined but tense voice of Monsieur de Saint-Ambroyse.

Valéry experienced the world as a trap, and his extreme
attention was devoted to freeing himself from it. He described himself as "furieux, au fond, d'être un homme, d'être
pris dans cette affaire d'Etre—sans l'avoir voulu" and believed that "tout est permis pour se défendre de la vie, des
choses et des événements—pour les atteindre, les déprécier,
les déjouer." [23] He, therefore, made an impregnable citadel
of his writings, continuing the dream of his Symbolist youth
under the sign of a universal mathematics. For if phenomena
could be purified by analysis, they might also serve to form
a construction as necessary as the temple of Eupalinos, or a
music that would prove one is master of one's own household. Thus his saintliness dwelt "entre le vide et l'événement
pur," between immanence and the poem, between the self
and its name; and how could there be an end to this activity other than the complete extinction of consciousness?
Valéry chose to inhabit a fragile position which was under
constant threat of its own lights; yet the suppleness and
control he brought to it, the exploitation of his disorder
and order, constituted for him his very domain, and for us
an area of unique admiration but also of pathos. As the
self plaintively sings to the image that it names Narcissus:

> Formons, toi sur ma lèvre, et moi dans mon silence,
> Une prière aux dieux qu'émus de tant d'amour
> Sur sa pente de pourpre ils arrêtent le jour! [24]

23 *Cahiers,* VIII, 378.
24 "Fragments du Narcisse," *Œuvres,* I, 129.

10: "Après tout, j'ai fait ce que j'ai pu . . ."

VALÉRY'S LAST eight notebooks are devoted to one of the most interesting periods in his life. We already knew works dating from the years 1935 to 1945 which show that there had been no slackening in his faculties but rather, as I have suggested, a renewed activity and a rich harvest. It was clear that these difficult years had induced a pressing need to write comparable to the time of composition of *La Jeune Parque*. Yet in other respects our image of him was vague; we did not know if he had pursued his research to the end along the same lines, whether he believed he had made important discoveries, what had been his final attitude towards the "chose littéraire." Above all, we wanted to examine the portrait he had drawn of himself during those last years. He had written to Gide at the age of twenty-three that he had been living "depuis longtemps dans la morale de la mort," but fifty years later such a limit had of necessity to be spelled out in a wholly different context.

Nevertheless, it would be wrong to seek here the precise register of his days: "Il m'ennuierait trop d'écrire *ce* que je vis d'oublier. . . ."[1] If the twenty-nine volumes of the *Cahiers* have one single intent and goal it may be said to lie in their refusal of facile satisfaction. Valéry believed,

[1] *Cahiers,* XXIII, 8.

like his rower in *Charmes,* that truth could come only from
struggling against the current; and his work demonstrates
an uncompromising will to go beyond events to the essential, which the *Cahiers* would seek to build stone by stone.
In a page that contrasts the majority of his writings with
what he himself takes to be his true work, he states that
"cette œuvre toute mienne se réduit à des poèmes, à des
fragments—et puis—mais surtout—à mes idées plus ou
moins notées, aux observations, aux vues, au système de
vues, et à la volonté et à la sensibilité que ces produits
supposent." [2] At the end of his life, then, the *Cahiers* occupy a privileged place in his writings since they represent
his enduring ambitions and inner demands. They are also a
personal resource, a kind of occult virtue: he could not but
keep to himself what he considered most important, the
thoughts he dearly cherished. "Il me semblait que ç'eût été
renoncer à ma raison d'être—que je plaçais non seulement
dans la valeur que je leur donnais, mais dans le secret de
cette valeur." [3] This secret god is present through the *Cahiers;* indeed, one cannot but be sensitive to the remarkable
unity of Valéry's preoccupations. On his deathbed he was to
say to J. P. Monod: "Les principaux thèmes autour desquels
j'ai ordonné ma pensée depuis cinquante ans demeurent
pour moi i-né-bran-lables." His notes are in a sense so many
successive tracings, his constant effort to "redessiner ce
qu'[il] avai[t] pensé de première intention." [4]

As in the previous volumes, we find here touching hymns
to the hour of awakening, which is also par excellence that
of the *Cahiers.* This is the pathetic moment when Narcissus
casts a solitary glance on things of the mind, when contrast
and shock move the sensibility, when the world forces him
to rediscover body and mind. "Il n'est pas de phénomène
plus excitant pour moi que le réveil. Rien ne tend à donner
une idée plus extraordinaire de . . . *tout,* que cette auto-

<hr/>

2 Ibid., XXVI, 500.   3 Ibid., XXIX, 479.   4 Ibid., XXII, 156.

genèse." [5] The observations and commentaries of the *Cahiers* likewise strike us by their images of nascent activity.

Yet could Valéry draw a line which would allow him to sum up the work of half a century? He was as incapable of so doing as Marcel Proust, who never ceased to nourish and overnourish a novel that had become one with his own life. Such a rule of conduct could not be brought to an end —that is, to a form—since it would mean falsifying endless beginnings:

> Peut-on composer un UN de tous ces moments et mouvements?
> Cet UN ne peut être qu'un minimum, un simulacre d'être, puisque ce qui se conserve est ce qui n'est pas détruit, annulé par des états contradictoires, etc.[6]

He did, it is true, entertain the idea of writing a philosophical dictionary which would set forth the matter of the *Cahiers* while sparing him "le mal, les défauts et le ridicule intime . . . d'un système . . . ," [7] but we know that this project was not pursued. We also find plans to order his notes in a less arbitrary way. And yet, although he left no methodical presentation, death, whether he wished it or not, was to impose on his life and work a final shape which the *Cahiers* have clarified.

Each group of notebooks is characterized by a particular tone, "l'écume des choses." These eight last volumes comprise references to occasional visits abroad in Brussels, Oxford, Geneva; a stay at Marrault in Burgundy on the eve of the war; a period in Dinard in 1940, during the difficult months before and after the armistice. Valéry notes the death of his friend Fourment, the funeral of Bergson in the sad cold winter of 1941: "En temps normal ç'eût été le Panthéon." [8] He mentions the publication of some of his works, and a reading of *Mon Faust,* in August 1944, in front of a distinguished gathering. How could he not also speak of the

[5] Ibid., XXVIII, 625.   [6] Ibid., XXIX, 85.
[7] Ibid., XXIV, 743.   [8] Ibid., XXIV, 149.

war, and its repercussions on him? Yet, as a matter of fact, he touches on it very little, and at long intervals, as much from the sense of the uselessness of such remarks ("Les grands événements excitent, mais ne méritent pas la réflexion"),[9] as out of prudence. The declaration of war, the armistice, the liberation are noted with pessimism and bitterness. "Je me demande si tout ceci—l'Europe—ne finira pas par une démence ou un ramollissement général", he wrote on the 3rd of September 1939; and in April–May 1945: "L'Allemagne expire. Et avec elle l'Europe puisqu'il n'y a plus de grande puissance que non-européenne (. . .). Je l'avais facilement prévu, sur la carte, dès 1900. . . ." [10] After the Liberation, he describes minutely a dinner followed by an audience with General de Gaulle, comments on the new political scene, indicates the important role national events played in the speech he made on Voltaire at the Sorbonne in December 1944: "Ce n'est là ce que je pense de (Voltaire) mais ce que j'ai pensé qu'il fallait que j'en dise, vu les circonstances." [11]

But of course it is internal time—sea and not foam—to which he continues to devote all the strength of his attention. The seventy-year-old man scrutinizes the memories of his intellectual adventure and his youth. He remembers the tenderness of festivities of the past;[12] alludes discreetly to his mother who taught him "l'importance des relations personnelles et des agréments de la société, de celle qu'elle avait connue enfant et dont les rites lui semblaient inviolables";[13] evokes, by way of association, the family house in Sète when he comes upon an edition of *Jane Eyre*,[14] his unsatisfactory schooling in college and at high school: "Ceci m'a contraint plus tard à faire comme Robinson." [15] He returns on several occasions to the "event of 1892" which he decomposes into two parts: the night in Genoa

[9] Ibid., XXVIII, 571.   [10] Ibid., XXIX, 798.
[11] Ibid., 315.   [12] Ibid., 366.   [13] Ibid., 630.
[14] Ibid., XXIII, 471.   [15] Ibid., XXIV, 510.

in October, Paris in November;[16] and finally he discovers in himself one day the same intellectual excitement that characterized him during the first years after he came to Paris and lived in the rue Gay-Lussac.[17] He analyzes also without indulgence the impatience that tortures him, and his continual disquietude. In spite of what he calls his "étrange paresse du corps," [18] he does not fail to insist on his violent will to consume, to destroy, to exhaust the moment: a feeling of haste, nervous and psychological tension, proud energy, that he calls "caligulisme." But destruction never satisfies him, for it must lead to a new construction. His words can be those of a nihilist, but also those of an architect, a musician, a poet: "pour moi, l'instinct destructif n'est légitime que comme indication de quelque naissance ou construction qui veut sa place à son heure." [19]

To struggle against the gulf his intelligence never ceases to find, against the *law of loss,* there are only two real activities possible, however desperate they be: "Amour, Esprit." [20] The word *Esprit* resumes a method and an ideal, to which Valéry also gave the magical name of "pureté"; it serves as a measure by which to criticize religion, to judge conversions *in extremis,*[21] to draw from the idea of death "des forces—de la *gaieté,* de l'entrain à vivre, à agir, à créer —une certitude! un solide," [22] to make his own language. By *Amour,* on the other hand, he means a "cycle prodigieux," [23] a type of complete action in which the whole sensibility, and functions, and resources, participate: "une danse . . . sacrée certes—qui tend à exhausser *quelque chose vers* un certain point—analogue à un *cri,*" [24] "un sommet du haut duquel on ne voit plus rien, limite de la vie, note aiguë,—fin de la personne—éblouissement dans toute la masse sensible du corps, avec démission, offrande,

---

16 Ibid., XXIII, 760.   17 Ibid., XXIX, 159.
18 Ibid., 159.   19 Ibid., XXII, 203.
20 Ibid., XXVI, 715.   21 Ibid., XXIX, 327.
22 Ibid., 453.   23 Ibid., 705.   24 Ibid., 456.

abandon à l'absolu de l'instant. . . ."[25] Only, perhaps, in
the last volume of the *Cahiers* did Valéry write a description as detailed, as intense, not only of the act of love, but
of love as a drama of knowledge,[26] "domination du phénomène d'*Absence-Présence.*"[27] No pages in his work equal
these in their pathos; he feels with an acuteness like some
"gêne ou douleur *toute physique*"[28] that his vaulting dream
of a stable and superior Love, which would have brought
love to a point where it had never before been, is a failure.

After examining these passages, one must read the last
reflexions in the last notebook which constitute a testament
of rare value not only on "Esprit" and "Amour" (we note
the use of the English word *heart* to suggest an inexpressi-
ble tenderness), but also on the whole experience of Valéry.
These deeply moving lines were written on the 30th of May
1945, seven weeks before his death:

> J'ai la sensation que ma vie est achevée—c'est-à-dire que je ne
> vois rien à présent qui demande un lendemain. Ce qui me reste
> à vivre ne peut plus désormais être que du temps à perdre. Après
> tout, j'ai fait ce que j'ai pu. Je connais assez mon esprit.
>
> Je crois que ce que j'ai trouvé est important—*je suis sûr de
> cette valeur.* Ce ne sera pas facile à déchiffrer de mes notes. Peu
> importe. Je connais *my heart* aussi. *Il triomphe. Plus fort que
> tout*—que l'esprit, que l'organisme. Voilà le *fait;* le plus obscur
> des faits. Plus fort que le vouloir vivre et que le pouvoir
> comprendre est donc le sacré C . . . Cœur, c'est mal nommé. Je
> voudrais au moins trouver le nom de ce terrible résonateur. . . .[29]

The most precious contribution of the *Cahiers,* however,
is that they allow us to understand the research which preceded, and in a certain sense justified, his diverse publications. Valéry went far in the obstinate, infinite study of the
problems he planned to examine in 1892 and which were
destined to be a precise representation of the mind. Nothing is more exciting than to follow this analytical exercise

[25] Ibid., 705.   [26] Ibid., 575.   [27] Ibid., 809.
[28] Ibid., 810.   [29] Ibid., 908–909.

which became a vital habit. Hardly a day passed on which
one or several pages were not written; the last period is
characterized by an even more urgent effort to resume himself, to define his ambitions, to measure his success. Did he
go astray in undertaking a task for which his studies, his
readings, the persons he knew over his formative years, had
ill prepared him? What strikes us on the contrary in Valéry's last years is his confidence in the procedure he adopted
at an early age.

The aim was not to elaborate a "philosophy," for everything had to be related to a particular *self*, the beginning
and end of his research. "Je ne fais pas de système. Mon
système—c'est moi." [30] And yet he knew that his discoveries, by their nature, would necessarily have relevance to
all if they were relevant to one. In words that sum up both
his pride and the very uncertainty of his enterprise, he
declared: "Je cherche ce qui est visible et non vu, qui
n'importe pas et qui est essentiel, qui est toujours et qui
n'est jamais. Rien de profond." [31] The means he used are
well-known: first of all the glance, that "lieu vague, errant,
mobile, libre des regards, maintes fois plus rapide que le
corps et que la tête même . . . ," directed at forms, objects,
relations, being, at the very act of knowing: "Si tu ne comprends pas quelque chose, arrête-toi et regarde-toi ne pas
comprendre." [32] But the "pure" glance is hardly separable
from the language it is obliged to use. Valéry perceived the
paradoxical role of language as a tool to express his observations, since that presupposes, as he recognized, "le
propos chimérique d'une bien difficile *théorie de la relativité*, c'est-à-dire d'une notation qui soit indépendante de
ce qui est variable dans l'observation, mais variation sui-
vie." [33] Having applied himself for fifty years to dividing
words into two groups, the first "fiduciary," the others "con-

30 Ibid., XXVI, 438.   31 Ibid., XXIV, 876.
32 Ibid., XXIX, 247.   33 Ibid., XXVIII, 677.

vertible into non-language," he could formulate in 1944, in a characteristic metaphor drawn from the world of finance, a view of "real" language: "Ce que j'indique par ces recherches et exemples, c'est la possibilité d'un langage qui soit *vérifiable*—c'est-à-dire dont les mots aient un *sens* —obtenu par une expérience réelle à quoi ce sens se réduit —et *contre lequel* le terme s'échange comme le papier contre l'or." [34]

Yet the glance, and real language, are nourished in Valéry by a third capital resource: the methods of modern science and mathematics. We have only to consider certain expressions that return constantly in these pages: relativity, functions, transformations, relations, entropy, groups, phases (a word that he borrowed from the terminology of the American physicist Josiah Willard Gibbs), references to Cantor, Carnot, Clausius, Boltzmann. . . . We can no longer doubt the scientific value to be attributed to such words or references employed in his essays and his writings on poetry; they are not a simple stylistic affectation but a fundamental way of seeing. When he was twenty, Poe had initiated him into the secrets of the law of Newton, to the hypothesis of Laplace; later he read at length the writings of Poincaré and many other scientists and mathematicians whose diversity surprises us. In the twenty-eighth volume of the *Cahiers*, for example, he speaks of the importance he saw in the work of the physicist Guillaume Duchenne (1806–1875), the author of *L'Électrisation localisée* (1855) and the *Physiologie des mouvements* (1867):

Duchenne de Boulogne
Faire une leçon du Cours où je parlerai de lui.
Je me rappelle l'intérêt que j'ai pris à regarder son album. Encore un hasard!
Cette anatomie fonctionnelle par l'excit-électris, toute la vie exprimable dissociée en fonct. simples et les combinaisons ou synthèse de sentiments obtenues. Certaines tout inédites. [35]

[34] Ibid., XXVIII, 494.   [35] Ibid., 748.

One can see that, however inadequate may have been the
notions of science and mathematics that he learnt at the
lycée ("Mes études, sous mes ternes et tristes maîtres,
m'avaient fait croire que la science n'est pas amour . . ."),[36]
he supplemented them in a remarkably extensive way by
his readings, and by his conversations with Perrin, Langevin,
Borel and others in the last twenty-five years of his life. He
was not at all the sorcerer's apprentice who clumsily handles
difficult concepts. On the contrary, science and mathematics
furnished him with supple metaphors, elegant analogies.

He was trying to make for himself "une idée de la méca-
nique sensitive, psychique et active (ou agissante) de l'individu," [37] a "représentation totale (et non du tout "explica-
tion") du fonctionnement car tout aboutit à cette notion." [38]
The term "function" became for him an idol against all
other idols, which allowed him to reduce notions, images,
words, sensations to phenomena within a given system:
"Dès 1892 . . . , tandis que les philosophes et esthéticiens
pensaient à l'échelle des mots, je pensais au fonctionnement—c'est-à-dire que je ne croyais pas à leurs problèmes
et que j'en faisais lever bien d'autres, à chaque instant." [39]
Armed with his mechanical analogy which protected him
(so he thought) from false values, he wanted to seize less
the meaning of a word, or idea, than the system they modify. He was ready to agree that his method was on occasion
simplistic ("Intuition évidemment naïve, mais comment
concevoir l'esprit?");[40] however, he devoted himself to making it more precise. The last volumes of the *Cahiers,* which
resume his research, insist on the example of physics and,
in particular, thermodynamics, in enabling him to refine
his concept of mental functioning. He postulated "une
sorte d'énergétique de l'activité mentale, avec ses équations

36 "Au sujet d'Eurêka," *Œuvres,* I, 855.
37 *Cahiers,* XXVII, 550.   38 Ibid., XXIII, 308.
39 Ibid., XXV, 850.   40 Ibid., XXIX, 159.

de condition, ses restrictions insensibles," [41] its states and transformations, its variations and conservations. He used the Gibbsian term "phases" in order to designate states in which "telles choses nous sont possibles à *faire,* à imaginer, à développer de toute façon,—et telles autres interdites ou différées." [42] He spoke of the "cycles" of consciousness and sensation like those of thermodynamics and found inspiration for his notion of complete action in the remarks of Sir William Rowan Hamilton (1805–1865), the Irish mathematician (and poet) who invented vector calculus and was the author of *Theory of Systems of Rays, The Principle of Varying Action,* and *Elements of Quaternions.* This key to his thought was never proclaimed, but the last notebook suggests Valéry's real debt to him:

> Il faut avoir des modèles dans l'esprit—non des modèles—immobiles——des œuvres—mais des modèles d'*action* parfaite—en général. Et pour chaque œuvre, il serait bel et bien de s'en faire un . . . plus particulier.
>
> Ainsi me fut jadis—Hamilton. [43]

By choosing models of action as "a fundamental fact," he could analyze the whole heterogeneous cycle of thinking—feeling—making, from initial excitement to response and subsequent return to a state of disponibility. Thus, in 1945, a short time before his death, he affirmed that his point of view had allowed him to overcome the Cartesian dichotomy of the physical and the mental:

> La fameuse dissociation de Descartes entre le monde physique et l'autre peut être précisée et fortifiée comme elle l'a été par l'événement—c'est-à-dire par le succès prodigieux de l'analyse quantitative des phénomènes.
>
> C'est ce que je crois avoir fait en introduisant l'idée d'action et pouvoir d'action (aux dépens de la connaissance convergente). [44]

These words should be weighed in the light of his whole

[41] Ibid., 159.   [42] Ibid., 613.   [43] Ibid., 502.
[44] Ibid., 895.

work, but they allow us at the very least to appreciate a final proud confidence in his own research centered on the idea of action, of total function, and in its success.

I could not hope to resume in a few pages the diverse ways of this patient effort to isolate a series of abstract principles. We should note, however, that nowhere in the *Cahiers* does one find a summary as clear as that which is contained in the last eight volumes in which, whether by fear that his ideas might be lost or by a personal need to indicate his own achievement, he returned constantly to the terms of this language by which he sought to figure the relationships between all things of the mind. His "première vraie découverte," [45] he says, was "self-variance," which designates the continuous change, either spontaneous or provoked, which characterizes consciousness and allows us to define the living organism as "une machine à fabriquer l'instant suivant," [46] and consequently, to say that "l'esprit, à soi seul, est (et doit être) incapable de vérité." [47] Another principle formulated as early as 1892 is that of "finitude," or consciousness as a closed, almost physical system. "J'ai pensé *Fini* depuis 92," he declared;[48] and a few years before: "Mon idée fut de considérer *fini* ce que l'on tient pour *infini*—et pour combinatoire le *possible* de chaque esprit." [49] This changing system with two variables—the physical and mental—possesses a tri-dimensional space which Valéry named CEM: Corps-Esprit-Monde: "trois axes . . . obtenus par une observation des plus simples— qui consiste à remarquer que les sensibilités qui s'opposent au sommeil emportent attribution de *causes* de cet effet à trois chefs: *Mon-Corps* (douleur); *Mon-Monde* (bruit, p. ex); et *Mon-Esprit* (soucis, etc.) . . .";[50] "C'est leur déséquilibre qui est sensation, pensée . . . et, en somme, *ex-*

45 Ibid., XXVIII, 293.   46 Ibid., XXIX, 108.
47 Ibid., XXVII, 237.   48 Ibid., XXIX, 447.
49 Ibid., XXIII, 236.   50 Ibid., 718.

istence";[51] "CEM—c'est 'mon Tout.' "[52] This "whole" conforms to the multiplicity designated by his "three laws": the accidental, the functional or formal, the meaningful; it is transformed according to a principle of conservation ($\phi + \psi = c$); and, since it is composed of heterogeneous elements, it presents "un échange fonctionnel entre éléments sensibles, figurés, moteurs, et, en outre, entre états et éléments, phases et actes—souvenir, réflexes, idées, etc."[53] This principle he enunciated in 1892 by the symbols $N + S$ ("Nombres plus subtils") and, elsewhere, by a formula composed of two octosyllables which he was to incorporate much later in a discarded stanza of the "Serpent":

> Un mouvement peut émouvoir
> Un temps attendrir et dissoudre[54]

We may also mention the fundamental discovery of a "Moi à plusieurs degrés" which is described in a poignant way in the letters to Gustave Fourment. At the end of his life, he came back to that experience which created a sort of precarious freedom from a pain of love he had too keenly felt:

Si je *me reconnais* dans ce que je *connais* je me sens *dupe*—et je vois que ma croyance ou confiance est composée de non-exercice de ma faculté de former toutes les combinaisons de ma sensibilisation précipitée.

Il faut donc se flatter de posséder un Moi indépendant de mes états où il se sent Moi, un *Moi insensible à lui-même*—et à ses variations propres—à sa mémoire brute, à tout ce qui introduit ses sensations corporelles (affectives ou somatiques)[55]

Valéryan freedom is, as we know, the postulate of the Self which comprehends the infinity of possible selves, of par-

---

[51] Ibid., 502. [52] Ibid., XXIX, 603.
[53] Ibid., XXIV, 509.
[54] Compare my *Lecture de Valéry*, p. 156. The words were intended to capture what he took to be "l'équivalence des événements psychesthésiques ou réactions affectivo-mentales" (*Cahiers*, XVII, 728).
[55] *Cahiers*, XXVIII, 12.

ticular moments, but which is not confused with them.
Teste says: *"C'est en se réduisant à Zéro que le Moi domine
le Tout (le Reste)."* [56] He is here clearly inspired by mathematical symbols and considers his invention to be "aussi
utile peut-être" as that of zero.[57] For fifty years, his most
efficient defense was the notion of this "bourdon de l'absolu," this free but unstable moment that allowed him to
cast an objective glance on his own mental phenomena.

He frequently used the image of the serpent to designate
the multiple facets of the mind that stretches out to know,
then waits for its body to join it. But if this self-observing
I is a snake, the I that sees itself observing is a self-devouring serpent. As he writes at the beginning of a notebook
dated May 1944: ". . . S'accoutumer à penser en Serpent
qui s'avale par la queue. Car c'est toute la question: Je
'contiens' ce qui me 'contient'. Et je suis successivement
contenant et contenu." [58] This is "l'autophagie" [59] of which
certain notebooks of the time of *Charmes* speak and for
which Valéry adopted a Greek word from the magical
papyri: *ouroboros.* The serpent describes the cycle of
knowledge: "C'est encore un cycle de serpents qui se dé-
vorent en sens inverse. Chacun a dans la gueule l'autre qui
l'a dans la gueule";[60] and, in an even more striking way,
the same image shows the process that leads to a theory
of knowledge in which the serpent "reconnaît dans ce qu'il
dévore le goût de serpent. Il s'arrête alors . . . Mais, au
bout d'un autre temps, n'ayant rien d'autre à manger, il
s'y remet. Il arrive alors à avoir sa tête dans sa gueule." [61]
The metaphor of the serpent is, then, a fertile one in
Valéry's thought; but he never completely forgets the fable
of Eden, on which theme he wrote his very personal
"Ebauche d'un Serpent"; and when the author of the *Cahiers* observes that things he has done are not those he

56 Ibid., XXVIII, 884.   57 Ibid., XXVIII, 87.
58 Ibid., XXVIII, 417.   59 Ibid., XXVI, 474.
60 Ibid., XXIX, 250.   61 Ibid., XXVIII, 24.

thought he had done, he echoes the terms of his burlesque Lucifer of *Charmes:* "Je me dis, avec mon serpent, que l'être est un défaut dans la pureté du Non-être." [62]

The last notebooks allow us to see Valéry's disabusement with respect to the future of literature. Although poetry has lost in his eyes none of its value as an exercise, it cannot claim, he believes, to maintain itself in a society wherein more urgent cares predominate, and pleasures more intense. "Il ne restera plus des Lettres que ce qui reste du culte de la Lune." [63] And yet, not unparadoxically, he continues with a constant determination to elaborate the analysis of literature he undertook fifty years before. He asks himself if his will to analyze, and the theories that came from it, do not emerge from an idiosyncratic distrust of facility ("... quand je produis par première intention je ne me sens pas assez 'créer' ...,"),[64] but he knows that he is as it were fatally devoted to considering the action of the creative mind as a problem. A precise definition of his "poïetics" is formulated in the twenty-fourth volume:

La Poïetique est une étude générale du *Faire*—qui a pour application et dérivation celle de faire des *œuvres de l'esprit*. Inutile et arbitraire traité en utile et nécessaire. Sensibilité intellectuelle ou *créatrice absolue* (c'est-à-dire créant aussi le *besoin* comme la *chose* qui la satisfait,—et subsidiairement les moyens de faire la chose).[65]

In the notes written around his course on poetics at the Collège de France, he scrutinizes this making, and seeks to find whether an extensive analysis of the producer can entail consequences for all kinds of production. Sometimes we appear to be reading a lesson in economics;[66] elsewhere he refers to a model of energy, or else to a cycle that unfolds

62 Ibid., 89.   63 Ibid., XXIII, 737.
64 Ibid., 271.   65 Ibid., XXIV, 801.
66 Ibid., 730.

according to the dynamics, rhythms, and the mental and physical alertness, of the sexual act.

Literature is a particular act of making which evolves "sur la frontière de la sensibilité générale et de la connaissance—comme la poésie entre son et sens." [67] The poet's work must engage him wholly—sensibility, affectivity, abstract reasoning; and he aims to produce a corresponding action in the reader. He utilizes and composes "harmonics," "implexes of the sensibility," [68] or what he names "des propriétés intrinsèques d'excitation réciproque des productions d'un domaine de sensibilité (cf. les complémentaires, effets de contraste, symétrie, etc)," [69] "des propriétés intrinsèques de la sensibilité fonctionnelle pure—*sans application à la connaissance 'extérieure,'* mais conditions énergétiques, sans doute, du fonctionnement local." [70] We see that symmetry, contrast, complementarity, far from being envisaged as aesthetic laws, are for Valéry basic needs of the sensibility which the artist uses, consciously or unconsciously. There exists, he says, a harmonic order for words in a sentence,[71] others for syntactic forms, for sounds, for images, which stir us before any precise representation: "Le 'monde' est composé *plus tard*. Nous ne percevons plus alors que le *son* est tout autre chose que la *couleur*." [72] This theory, although developing ideas that were previously expressed in the *Cahiers,* is exposed most explicitly in the last period of Valéry's life. To describe his conception, he has recourse to a musical expression (whereas when he speaks of the "universe of the sensibility" which makes a closed system of internal relations from these harmonics, he finds an analogy with set theory in mathematics). Harmonics allow us then to *musicalize,* to *compose,* as he believes he himself did consciously in his dialogues,[73] in

67 Ibid., XXIII, 723.   68 Ibid., XXIX, 305.
69 Ibid., XXVI, 59.   70 Ibid., XXVIII, 388.
71 Ibid., XXIX, 337.   72 Ibid., 305.
73 Ibid., XXVIII, 586.

his poems and, more recently, in *Le Solitaire*.[71] But he observes that this creative process can be produced in a natural way in fables and legends which come down to us through successive versions; he sees there a decorative, "harmonic" treatment of narrative prose:

On peut très souvent observer dans les formations de légendes ou quasi-histoires, l'adaptation de propriétés que j'ai baptisécs *harmoniques* à des récits—c'est-à-dire à des productions significatives—qui semblent donc des similitudes de choses *arrivées et ne dépendre que d'observations*.[75]

One would need to speak of many other aspects of Valéry's poetics which are formulated in striking terms in these pages, often for the first time, such as occasional remarks on style: "L'écrivain se rend quasi étrangère sa langue maternelle . . .";[76] a criticism of Heredia and other poets who were unable to "trouver l'être qui chante";[77] final words in praise of prosodic conventions—"volonté d'écart, de distinction, de non-imitation et de non-imitabilité"[78]—which bring princely rewards ("tu seras plus que toi, tu seras celui dont la durée domine l'instant, dont la Loi et la raison d'Etat maîtrisent les instincts divers et désordonnés").[79] The poetic maneuver consists in placing oneself "dans les mots,"[80] bowing to the physical nature of language,[81] limiting oneself to the consequences and combinations of the intrinsic as in mathematics.[82] Valéry considers the distinction between verse and rhythmical prose as a différence in the degree of prevision, for verse is capable of more variety than rhythmical prose, which is most frequently descriptive,[83] and characterized by the fact that it seems to possess "une sorte de causalité propre."[84] As far

74 Ibid., XXIV, 360.
76 Ibid., XXIX, 381.
78 Ibid., XXVI, 105.
80 Ibid., XXVI, 669.
82 Ibid., XXVIII, 656.
84 Ibid., XXVI, 404.

75 Ibid., XXVIII, 481.
77 Ibid., XXVII, 811.
79 Ibid., XXVIII, 605.
81 Ibid., XXVI, 606.
83 Ibid., XXVIII, 424.

as the art of verse is concerned, precision is brought to the use of a term that had appeared obscure in some texts already published: *travail second* ("J'appelais ainsi le travail sensible de l'esprit *créant* de la durée—de la sensation spécifique de *durée*").[85] Finally, a most important remark concerns the "imprégnation psychique d'une image"—an image the poet communicates without expressing it explicitly, by formal treatment alone.[86] The phrase is suggestive: is not his "Narcisse," we may ask, a pool calm and deep, "Au Platane" a knotted body, "La Pythie" a painful birth?

Thus the theorist of poetry developed more than he modified his ideas during this last period. Some readers may, however, be surprised to hear him enunciate in almost Proustian terms the following principle: "Sauver l'angle que fait cette arête de meuble avec le plan de la vitre . . . et tu seras récompensé au centuple";[87] likewise, when he observes: "Tout vrai poème n'est précisément qu'une espèce de *consécration*—liturgique!—de certains mots." [88] Yet we need to remember that Valéry saw intimate relations between poetry and mysticism,[89] and that the poet who planned an adolescent collection of poems under the title *Chorus mysticus* was also he who wrote beside his manuscript title "Charmes" the word *Liturgia*.

These years were marked by several publications, but Valéry formed the project of writing many other works, and indeed was already laboring on several of them. For an essay that would have summarized his intellectual position he dreamed of utilizing "toutes les formes," such as dialogues, prose and, doubtless, poetry in order to offer a "théorie du Monde et de l'esprit." [90] He was also led to call into question his own early writing such as *La Jeune Parque* and later works. He still considered his literary

---

85 Ibid., XXVIII, 689.
87 Ibid., XXIII, 480.
89 Ibid., XXVIII, 519.

86 Ibid., XXIV, 803.
88 Ibid., XXV, 589.
90 Ibid., XXVI, 13.

activity without vainglory, but recognized that it had revealed things he would not have seen otherwise; in particular, it had allowed him to "exprimer parfois certains
résultats de [son] autre activité." [91] It was this last aspect
to which he often returned and which one needs to realize
for any study of his poetry. "En résumé, mon vice littéraire
a été de vouloir (de ne pouvoir faire autrement que de)
toujours mettre dans l'ouvrage de type et de figure nor-
maux, une manière de voir les choses singulière—et des
connexions ou définitions issues de mes recherches—sur la
vie, les fonctions ψ, etc." [92] Although he said that he had
never succeeded other than fragmentarily, this ambition
served him as a model. His poetic obscurity, as we know,
results not only from the requirements of song but also
from the idea he held of the "transformations" to be imposed on a given image, which can be as revealing, and
as personal, as those we found in "Sinistre," "Sémiramis,"
"Profusion du soir," and the other poems we have read.

However, he does not forget that writing is first of all
the discovery of a voice, a personal song. He leaves us a
precise view on certain sounds that seem to characterize his
own verse: "En tant que poète, je suis spécialiste des sons:
é,è,ê. C'est assez curieux." And he goes on to make a most
important remark concerning the poetic act as he experiences it. "Je sens, dit-il, assez nettement se former ou se
chercher mes vers dans une région de l'appareil vocal-
auditif et moyennant une certaine attitude de cet appareil
(en tant qu'il est capable de modifications musculaires)." [93]
For Valéry it will naturally be a question of trying to pro-
voke this physical state, a propitious attitude of his vocal
cords, the "voice" of poetry.

He does not linger over his first works except to note the
exclusive cult he had for poetry at the time ("Poésie, 90—

91 Ibid., XXVIII, 613.   92 Ibid., XXIV, 117.
93 Ibid., XXVII, 444.

91—me fut culte et sport. Seule 'mystique' et seul 'exer-cice' ").[94] Then came the radical change of 1892 in which the virtual within him became essential, and brought about the rejection of literature as a cult. If he did not, properly speaking, abandon poetry, his approach was wholly changed. "Il faut, pour vraiment bien écrire, se retirer du langage et y revenir—au lieu de le subir comme réflexe (réfléchi au sens optique) le faire réfracté." [95] But how can the abstract mind find in poetry the means of satisfying itself? Such was the problem he grappled with in *La Jeune Parque*.

One may say that he continued in another genre what he had already attempted in *Monsieur Teste*. "J'ai . . . , le peu de fois que j'ai personnalisé—comme dans M. et Mme. Teste, et la Parque, essayé de fabriquer des vivants de synthèse. . . ." [96] It is not the individual, casual case that occupies him, but an idea of the general function of the living—feeling—thinking—human being. The mono-logue of his Parque is held together according to the re-quirements of this fictitious psycho-physiology of his re-search.

Tout un système de représentation des choses pré-inventé et donnant une homogénéité nouvelle,—un quasi-calcul symbolique —avec substitution de définitions personnelles aux sens ordinaires des mots,—ce qui permet des transformations plus vraies, plus surprenantes. Associer à chaque terme son rôle dans un être vivant.[97]

Elsewhere Valéry insists on his desire to compose a song "aussi uni et continu que possible," [98] having recourse to "tout ce qu'il y eut de chantant dans la poésie française— entre Racine et Mallarmé." [99] He was conscious of con-tinuing and crowning a poetic tradition; he felt responsible for Racine, Chénier, Baudelaire, Mallarmé, Rimbaud at a

94 Ibid., XXIII, 84.   95 Ibid., XXVIII, 489.
96 Ibid., 159.   97 Ibid., XXVII, 143.
98 Ibid., XXV, 706.   99 Ibid., 706.

time when the values these poets represented were in peril.

But studying *La Jeune Parque,* Valéry points to models that were other than abstract or literary. He says he was indebted to painting for his mode of formal composition;[100] however, quite naturally, he also renders a brilliant homage to music. More than to any one particular composition—some recitative of Gluck, for example, which deeply influenced him[101]—he felt that he had been inspired above all (and was not this also Mallarmé's position?) by the notion he conceived of a *possible* music. As he writes in 1944:

L'idée vague (chez moi, ignorant de cet art) et la magie du mot *Modulation* ont joué un rôle important—dans mes poèmes. *La Jeune Parque* fut obsédée par le désir de ce *continuum*—doublement demandé. D'abord, dans la suite musicale des syllabes et des vers,—et puis dans le glissement et la substitution des idées-images—suivant elles-mêmes les états de la conscience et sensibilité de la *Personne-qui-parle.*[102]

In the formation of this dream the work of Wagner played an important part. At seventy he was still incapable of speaking of it without enthusiasm. "Rien ne m'a plus désespéré que la musique de Wagner (et je suis loin d'être le seul). N'est-ce pas le but suprême de l'artiste—*Désespérer!*" [103] With Poe, Mallarmé and Rimbaud, and more than Nietzsche and even Leonardo, Wagner was a major demon of the Valéryan temple—"L'homme qu'[il a] le plus envié en somme (. . .) un genius extraordinaire." [104] In Valéry's reflexions, apart from his appreciation of the *Walkyrie* and *Lohengrin,*[105] we observe the meaning that he gave Wagner's work: its capacity to "éveiller l'inachevé plein de terreur qui dort si mal en nous, de son mauvais sommeil." [106] Yet this aspect fascinated Valéry less than Wagner's whole

---

100 Ibid., XXIX, 92.
101 Ibid., XXII, 33.
102 Ibid., XXIX, 92.
103 Ibid., XXIV, 564.
104 Ibid., XXVII, 136.
105 Ibid., XXVII, 220; XXVIII, 217.
106 Ibid., XXII, 608.

language addressed to the sensibility: "Un système . . .
qui est capable de construire de la *vie synthétique illusion-
niste nerveusement vraie*. . . ." [107] By his attention to this
music and the observations that he drew from it he received
his "idée ou découverte des 'phases' dont aucun psychologue
ni physiologue n'a eu conscience. . . ." [108] This conception, and the temptation to build a complete cycle of the
sensibility in the manner of the German master, took hold
of him when he came to compose *La Jeune Parque*.[109]

Although most of the notes concerning his poetic works
deal with *La Jeune Parque*, the galaxy of poems that sur-
rounds it is likewise named from time to time. Valéry returns to the genesis of "Le Cimetière marin" which began
without a subject, merely a preoccupation with formal
contrasts, tones, emotions to bring forth,[110] in the manner
of a painter: "Les parties successives devaient se modifier
réciproquement dans une simultanéité résolutoire." [111] The
themes he chose because they had to appear in it, "pour
satisfaire à des conditions de *plénitude* qu'[il] pensai[t]
alors (et pense encore) exigées par l'équilibre intrinsèque
d'une œuvre de quelque importance. . . ." [112] In this light
he attacks what he calls exegetic or semantic criticism. After
reprimanding those who divide sound from sense, he pursues in these terms:

> Quant à la "critique sémantique," c'est un tissu d'hypothèses, et
> d'explications imaginaires. Je le vois par mon expérience sur mes
> poèmes!
> Par exemple, sur "Les Pas," petit poème purement *sentimental*
> auquel on prête un sens intellectuel, un symbole de "l'inspira-
> tion"!
> Le vice des explicateurs est celui-ci: ils partent du poème *fait*
> —et ils supposent une fabrication qui *partirait* de l'idée ou résumé
> qu'il se sont faits de l'œuvre après la chose. L'œuvre se traduit en

107 Ibid., XXVII, 139.   108 Ibid., 139.
109 Ibid., XXXI, 706.   110 Ibid., XXVII, 73.
111 Ibid., XXIX, 91.   112 Ibid., 600.

un schéma intellectuel qu'ils prêtent au poète—lequel est supposé
le traduire en vers, en le *conservant de son mieux*—comme s'il
faisait une composition scolaire—avec le plan ou une volonté
d'expression fixe—tandis qu'en réalité il ne cherche et ne doit
chercher que ce qui lui semble efficace et possible poétiquement à
chaque instant.[113]

But, in this, Valéry is speaking less of semantic criticism, I
believe, which takes as the object of its study the complete
work, and the interrelationship of a system of words, than
genetic criticism. Doubtless he was closer to poetic truth
when he wrote that his verse has the meaning it is given
by a reader; for if "Les Pas" is indeed a sentimental poem,
one may say that it composes preeminently an attitude of
quasi-religious expectancy which accords as much with that
of the poet as that of the lover. Of course, the use of the
term "sentimental" is vague, and may refer to events of the
mind as well as those of love ("il existe une sensibilité des
choses intellectuelles," he wrote in 1941); moreover, we cannot fail to be struck by what appears to be a considerable
gap between the intentions as indicated in the draft of the
poem and this judgment of his intentions written twenty
years later: indeed, we read in the first manuscript of "Les
Pas": "Psyché de tes lèvres avancées / Tu présentes sans
l'apaiser / A la soif des pures pensées / . . . de ton baiser."
The words "Psyché" et "soif des pures pensées" are far from
nullifying the idea of a poem of adoration addressed to a
source of inspiration who is both goddess and voluptuous
woman. What matters most in the final instance is the poetic
state that is created—a mixture of warmth and measure,
voluptuousness and reserve, and it would be erroneous to
assert that "Les Pas" concerns inspiration and nothing more;
on the other hand, the fullness of tone, the abstract handling
of emotion, the language itself, make us think of Valéry's
words on the theme of "signification seconde" written in
1941 apropos of the hymns of St. John of the Cross, in which

113 Ibid., XXVIII, 427.

he justifies the coexistence of "un chant très tendre, qui suggère quelque ordinaire amour" alongside the deeper thought, the passion and mystery that are implied.

The references to the remaining poems of *Charmes* are rare: Valéry returns to the composition of "L'Abeille" to say that this octosyllabic sonnet with its original structure arose from a detail of language (no doubt the rhyme *abeille —corbeille*) to reach a "subject" by way of the form;[114] he thinks again of the finale of his "Narcisse" which might have ended on the frenzy of the self against its own image, and not on a mortal reconciliation.[115] We think of the "Ebauche d'un serpent" also when Valéry writes: "Je ne vois pas d'œuvre littéraire consacrée par son auteur à se moquer réellement de soi-même, à tourner en ridicule soi-même et son esprit." [116] Valéry recalls the details of composition of certain writings which came after 1920, such as his emotional state at the time of *Eupalinos* and *L'Ame et la Danse*;[117] or else the theories he used: in *Eupalinos* and "L'Homme et la Coquille" for example, that of "degrees of symmetry" ("les fabrications humaines se distinguent des productions de la nature par la non-cohérence, non-indépendance de la matière et de la forme; l'action humaine est extérieure à ce qu'elle meut").[118] He notes also his scenic conception for *Sémiramis*;[119] the almost embarrassing facility with which he wrote *La Cantate du Narcisse*;[120] the wholly formal composition of the prose poem "L'Ange" which was sketched out as early as 1922 (". . . une manière de s'avancer étant le *but* vrai; peu important à quel lieu il conduisît, puisqu'aussi bien il était convenu qu'elle dût en reconduire").[121]

If these pages offer important reflexions on his past work, we do not lose sight of the fact that the years 1939–1945

114 Ibid., XXIX, 910.
116 Ibid., 196.
118 Ibid., XXVI, 530.
120 Ibid., XXII, 697.

115 Ibid., XXIII, 196.
117 Ibid., XXIII, 590.
119 Ibid., XXIV, 12.
121 Ibid., 716.

were richly creative, one of his most dazzling works being *Mon Faust*. He had been considering this theme for many years: from 1925 his notes for a "Troisième Faust" envisage a hero of the European intellect in the present-day world passing consciously from knowledge to power. But the play was written only in 1940, after the armistice, in the Villa des Charmettes at Dinard, where it was undertaken as a means of relaxation. The twenty-third volume of the *Cahiers* is a precious document for the study of its genesis. In the following volumes also Valéry often returns to the themes of *Lust* and *Le Solitaire,* considering ways of developing his play through a sequence of poetic interludes.[122] Three pages written in September 1942 propose to treat several aspects of the Faustian theme, in particular, the questions: can one form a new idea of man? Can one create a new goal, a new desire? [123] In 1945 he was still working on his *Lust IV,* the subject of which would have been "amour comme je le conçois—et l'ai vu périr deux fois." [124]

Nevertheless, his *Faust* constituted only a small part of his creative activities at the time. There were projects, themes to be developed, an agenda that comprises a dozen titles of works already written or ready to be undertaken. Valéry preferred to elaborate several compositions at the same time, but such a number as we find here cannot fail to surprise us. Many reflexions, for example, concern an *Apocalypte Teste,* which, if brought to fruition, would certainly have been stimulating; we would have seen Monsieur Teste in the act of writing a Holy Book,[125] chanting a psalm.[126]

Yet can we say that Valéry's attitude to writing was different at this time? He was, of course, no longer the monk who devotes himself to the endless work of his *La Jeune*

122 Ibid., XXIV, 790.
124 Ibid., XXIX, 706.
126 Ibid., XXIX, 735.

123 Ibid., XXVI, 440–442.
125 Ibid., XXVII, 121.

Parque for, as he writes: "Il faut finir par l'improvisation." [127] He finds, when he reads the *Dieu* of Victor Hugo,
that "ces vers insensés du courant de la plume [l']excitent."
He says to himself that "tout lâchant, [il] pourrai[t] s'amu-
ser ainsi." [128] From that period date his own *Histoires
brisées* which were published after his death: and it was
also as a sequel to his readings of *Dieu* that he composed
"Calypso," the fragment placed at the beginning of *Histoires
brisées.* (But there was no question of improvisation pre-
venting the work of revision: once "Calypso" was finished,
Valéry considered his aims, the tone, the vocabulary, the
probable effect of his story on a reader).[129] Another fragment collected in the same volume, Assem, written "Acem"
(Valéry no doubt made up this proper name from the ab-
breviation CEM—"Corps," "Esprit," "Monde") was a free
development around a few initial words ("dans l'esprit, à
l'état le plus vague, un mélange de Teste, de 1001 nuits,
de souvenir de Schwob dans son fauteuil, couleur de cire
et gras").[130] Likewise, he began to improvise other "broken"
stories: *Xiphos* ("ou le lieu des Mauvaises choses pensées"),[131] *Robinson,* and the like.

Poetry itself was not neglected. One may presume that
"L'Oiseau cruel," collected in *Pièces diverses,* was elaborated at the beginning of this period as Valéry suggests by
a note in which he proposes to continue this same poem
by a phrase beginning with *"si . . . ,"* and to finish in the
air on this word *si.*[132] We see him trying, after "La Pythie,"
"Ebauche d'un Serpent," "Ode secrète," to develop the use
of octosyllabic verse; he speaks of a poem on which he was
working: "Tenté une fois de plus, mais avec plus de précision d'écrire *avant toute idée,* un module de VIII strophes

127 Ibid., XXII, 312.   128 Ibid., XXIX, 845.
129 Ibid., 893.   130 Ibid., XXVI, 563.
131 Ibid., 900.   132 Ibid., XXIII, 1135.

dont chaque vers ait son type rythmique et sonore (je veux
dire: diversifié par muettes et sonores." [133]

Although the previous volumes of the *Cahiers* offer little
apparent sign of his poetic compositions, the ones we are
examining contain several drafts of verse, as if poetry had
become more spontaneously associated with his morning
habit. Valéry turns to the pentasyllable which he had already used in "Le Sylphe" and "L'Insinuant":

> Mystère, mystère,
> Qu'es-tu devenu? . . .[134]

sketches out in the same meter a long development which
he entitles *Ou*:

> Je suis Pierre ou Paule
> Ou Jeanne ou Castor
> Mes mains n'ont encor
> Touché qui je sois . . .[135]

In octosyllables he sings of "Homo":

> Le plus méchant le plus mauvais
> Des animaux, vipère ou loup
> C'est moi l'Homo qui viens et vais
> Du singe à l'ange par le fou . . .[136]

Elsewhere he favors the decasyllable, but sings in a very
different tone from that of "Sinistre" and "Le Cimetière
marin." Thus one draft entitled "Malheur d'aimer son mal"
announces a new "Aurore":

> D'un doigt divin le dieu de feu désigne
> Les premiers dons que me fasse le jour
> Une suprême étoile meurt d'amour
> Vers le plus haut de l'éternelle vigne . . .[137]

---

[133] Ibid., XXIV, 267.
[135] Ibid., XXIII, 493.
[137] Ibid., XXIV, 823.

[134] Ibid., XXIII, 269.
[136] Ibid., XXVII, 253.

Another page, likewise in decasyllables, evokes the eternal awakening of an idea:

> Belle sans forme, ô naissante pensée,
> Aurore intime au teint de (à mon sort) fiancée . . .[138]

while his "Hymne au vrai Dieu" drafted in 1943 employs the decasyllable to compose an ironical prayer with characteristic paradoxes:

> Justice étrange, Inexistence auguste,
> Sublime Absence, Abîme d'ombre, ô Pur,
> Tout ce qu'on sait de Vous vous fait Injuste,
> Lumière immense et quoi de plus obscur? [139]

Finally, one recalls the prose-poems or poems in the rough ("poésie brute") found under the title *"Psaume"* ("A la fenêtre tout à coup . . .")[140] and "Fable" ("Etonné d'être, un arbre s'agitait . . .").[141] They recall that the poet's many unpublished papers contain works written in modes quite different from those of *Pièces diverses.*

Many writers are mentioned in these last volumes, for Valéry gave himself over to reading more than in any other period of his life. Like some literary historian he even went one day looking for the sources of Stevenson's *Treasure Island* in which he discovered borrowings from Poe and Jules Verne: "Jamais piraterie plus évidente que cette histoire de pirates." [142] However, this kind of interest is not in the least typical. What he sought before all things was to gain a clear idea of the qualities of craftsmanship, the rigor, of each author. Thus, when he judges Virgil, he holds him to be a great "primitive" poet whose work, like that of Dante, is not sufficient unto itself and has value also as a tale or story.[143] Since Virgil's true song (and that of all

---

138 Ibid., XXV, 409.   139 Ibid., XXVI, 52.
140 Ibid., XXIV, 691.   141 Ibid., XXVI, 870.
142 Ibid., XXIV, 861.   143 Ibid., XXIX, 376.

Greek and Roman poets) is unknown to us, he is not a poet "except by convention—and as it were by courtesy." [144]

He never seems to have spoken at length of Ronsard (except in 1934 in a letter to Gustave Cohen), but he recognized in him one of the great musicians of the French language, who in this regard may be placed alongside Mallarmé: "Le 'motif' en poésie. C'est tout! Le chanté. Ronsard-Mallarmé." [145] Everything has not perhaps yet been said about the influence of Ronsard's *Odes* on *Charmes* as well as that of the elegy "La Mort de Narcisse" on Valéry's treatment of the same theme. It is, however, of great interest, I feel, to see Valéry in his last years stating the importance of Ronsard and choosing as an inscription for a 1942 notebook three lines from "Elégie II," found among the posthumous verse, which he could happily underwrite:[146]

> Mais au contemplement l'heur de l'homme ne gist.
> Il gist à l'œuvre seul, impossible à la cendre
> De ceux que la Mort fait sous les ombres descendre.

The quotation could well serve as an alternative epigraph for "Le Cimetière Marin."

Pascal furnished Valéry with a target rather than a subject of serious meditation. How can we forget, in *Mon Faust*, for example, the series of parodic sentences like "L'absurde a ses raisons . . . que la raison soupçonne"? Just as a part of his notes is entitled "Zénonia" and contains remarks on thought and movement, so the last notebooks contain a "Pascaliana" which allows him to wield his pen with new vigor. Thus, in May 1945, he writes: "Pascal me paraît superficiel, comme tous ceux qui donnent valeur au langage sans s'assurer si ce qui est, ou semble signifié par le discours, peut être pensé ou observé *sans discours*, indépendamment de tout discours";[147] and a few months before: "Que de 'pensées' niaises et combien d'em-

144 Ibid., 361. 145 Ibid., XXIV, 862.
146 Ibid., 517. 147 Ibid., XXIX, 871.

pruntées. Infini, éternel, deux mots qui n'ont point de sens, car ils sont négation de toutes choses qui ont un sens." [148] It would therefore be vain to suppose that Valéry modified his original attitude to the author of the *Pensées* which he most notably expressed in his *Note et digression* of 1919.

Yet, so far as classical literature is concerned, he was conscious of a marked change in his position. After the bad memories his first schoolboy readings of Racine had left, the writing of *La Jeune Parque* forced his admiration for a poet who revealed "la continuité de la forme et les sacrifices qu'elle exige si on la place au-dessus de tout." [149] An important fragment written in 1945 refers to Racine and his contemporaries: "La tragédie française, *sommet de l'art*—voilà un jugement que je finis par *former*, et j'en apprécie tout le comique de cette formation en moi—tout ce qu'elle suppose de détachement des 'effets', des prétentions des poètes successifs . . . de mes 'idéaux' et des leurs." [150] This revised judgment is due in large part, he believes, to his distrust of contemporary literature which confuses art and mysticism.

Another modification of attitude that strikes us can be seen in the remarks devoted to Voltaire. He had begun to read his writings again, perhaps without enthusiasm, with a view to a formal lecture to be given at the Sorbonne in 1944 on the occasion of the 350th anniversary of Voltaire's birth. If he was unable to say at that moment—as we have already seen—all that he thought of Voltaire, a page written in April 1945 gives us a precise appreciation of the man he praised.

Je me saoule de Voltaire (lettres) depuis un mois.
C'est un personnage capital. Il a le front de ne croire à rien—ou de croire ne croire à rien, et il impose au public cette attitude. Il y a désormais un "grand public" pour la liberté de penser. Elle n'est plus chose réservée.

148 Ibid., 362.   149 Ibid., XXIII, 736.
150 Ibid., XXIX, 486.

Alors tous les grands hommes du siècle Louis XIV paraissent de petits garçons—Racine, etc.—des enfants de chœur embarrassés, des sornettes. Cf. ce que dit V. de Pascal.

En somme, V. divise le cours de la pensée européenne. Après lui, tout ce qui est pensée religieuse devient cas particulier, paradoxe, parti-pris.[151]

A few weeks later, Valéry goes through the correspondence again and savors it: "Cher Voltaire! . . . Je trouve souvent dans ces lettres des choses très miennes. Mais quel entrain à mon même âge! et il dit qu'il rit." [152]

He discovers, then, at the end of his life affinities with Voltaire; and likewise with Goethe: ". . . le nombre et l'énergie des traits communs sont remarquables." [153] "Je ne sais pas du tout," he continues, "comment je présente ces ressemblances remarquables d'égoesthésies avec G." [154] In order to explain this phenomenon he even supposes some "résonances *chrononomiques*. Je me sens de plus en plus 17. . . ." It is true that the composition of his *Faust* made him look at the second *Faust* in a new light; but what he saw above all was less the arbitrary and artificial [155] aspects of Goethe's work than the man himself and his "comedy." [156]

As usual, the French romantics are not his favorites.[157] Stendhal always occupied in his eyes a privileged position with respect to his peers, and although he classed him among the comedians and criticized his apparent naivetics, he admired the vivacity and excellence of the comedy: "Réussit à merveille ses trois ou quatre personnages. Son jeune premier, ses raisonneurs, ses "traîtres"—un peu toujours les mêmes, et de plus en plus d'*époque*, mais parfaitement établis." [158] As for Balzac, we know that he interested Valéry greatly; he never wrote an article on him, but placed him at the age of twenty-two beside Rimbaud, Poe and

---

151 Ibid., 722.   152 Ibid., 846.   153 Ibid., 721.
154 Ibid., 721.   155 Ibid., XXVI, 265.
156 Ibid., 776.   157 Ibid., XXIX, 347, 370.
158 Ibid., 882.

Stendhal as one of the few "engineers" of the nineteenth century. At Montrozier in 1942 he reread with great pleasure part of *La Comédie Humaine,* that "atroce, absurde et puissant mélange," [159] and lauded Balzac's "art de voir ses bonshommes." [160] The third great writer of the period who had always attracted Valéry just as he caused him great embarrassment was of course Victor Hugo. Here again he notes, when he takes up *Dieu,* the abundant monotony of the verse,[161] protests against the enormous quantity of words that Hugo introduced into poetry,[162] but does not hesitate to recognize the unique nature of the Hugolian universe. He speaks admiringly of the genius who created "un étrange monde à base de possibilités verbales, combinaisons quasi monstrueuses qu'enfantent l'accouplement de la rime avec ce qu'elle suggère d'images. Et ceci donne une sorte d'ébouissement mental qui interdit (ou doit interdire) la *station de l'esprit sur le sens,* et la force de la forme du vers le défend contre la connaissance de sa stabilité." [163] There is also an admirable page in which he states that he has "spent the night with the finest possible verse," a line from Hugo which he analyzes.[164]

In the *Cahiers* which date from the First World War and the following years several detailed discussions are to be found of the work of Baudelaire in preparation for his celebrated essay "Situation de Baudelaire" of 1924. Fifteen and twenty years later he is severe on Baudelaire's prose,[165] as well as the use of heptasyllables instead of octosyllables in "L'Invitation au voyage." [166] On one occasion, however, he praises Baudelaire for having written a few words on Poe ("Ce merveilleux cerveau toujours en éveil . . ."), in which he himself found "valeur d'un trésor de 1001 nuits entr'ouvert ou de ce simple mot *trésor* lu avec des yeux d'enfant

159 Ibid., XXIV, 838.   160 Ibid., XXV, 105.
161 Ibid., XXIX, 849.   162 Ibid., 535.
163 Ibid., XXVI, 9.   164 Ibid., XXV, 571.
165 Ibid., XXVIII, 220.   166 Ibid., XXVII, 441.

dans le conte arabe." [167] Curiously enough, one may observe that this expression is not properly speaking Baudelaire's own but that of Mrs. Frances Osgood who, in a letter to the biographer Griswold, said of Poe that he created "avec son admirable écriture les brillantes fantaisies qui traversaient son étonnant cerveau toujours en éveil."

As for Poe himself, Valéry does not tire of repeating all he owes to the reading of his work. He refers in particular to a story that struck him most forcefully. At nineteen he read *The Domain of Arnheim* in which he noted a sentence on the possibilities of perfection: "L'idée de perfection m'a possédé." [168] If we turn back to Poe's text we find that Valéry was doubtless referring to lines which are situated at the end of the first quarter of the narrative, on page 168 of the edition Conard: "Je crois que le monde n'a jamais vu et que, sauf le cas où une série d'accidents aiguillonnerait le génie du rang le plus noble et le contraindrait aux efforts répugnants de l'application pratique, le monde ne verra jamais la perfection triomphante d'exécution dont la nature humaine est positivement capable dans les domaines les plus riches de l'art." Colorless words, one may think; but this remark, he says, had the greatest influence on him.[169] Poe's sentence was not remembered precisely (as one might perhaps have expected it would be in the case of a formula with almost magical effects on the sensibility) but only its general meaning, for Valéry's memory seems to have been only rarely verbal.

It is a matter for regret that he never devoted a long study to Rimbaud. But we can henceforth, with the aid of the *Cahiers*, constitute an anthology of observations of the highest interest concerning the "prodige de nouveauté et de pouvoir excitant" that this work became for him. In 1943, on the occasion of the publication of Jean-Marie Carré's

[167] Ibid., 234.   [168] Ibid., XXIII, 188.
[169] Ibid., XXII, 489.

La Vie aventureuse d'Arthur Rimbaud, he made some penetrating comments in a letter, to which a note written at
the same time adds further details. Two other pages would
deserve a critical examination:[170] thus he employs the term
explexe to characterize Rimbaud's "modification du langage
courant qui n'introduit aucune forme particulière, mais
qui altère, soit par substitutions, soit par juxtaposition (des
propositions) la *complémentarité réciproque des mots,* laquelle est une attente virtuelle"; elsewhere, in another suggestive passage,[171] he compares *Une Saison en Enfer* ("Ce
ne sont qu'expressions directes, jaculations, intensité") with
what he takes to be the much superior originality of the
Illuminations ("Le don [très cultivé] de Rimbaud est de
saisir dans *l'à peu près* initial des produits verbaux d'une
impression—ou du souvenir d'impressions—les termes qui
forment un accord dissonant de 'sens' et une bonne con-
sonance musicale").

Amongst his contemporaries, Gide is quite clearly the
most often named. The publication of the *Journal* could
not fail to interest him keenly and many of his reflections
are inspired by his reading of it. He is sensitive to the way
Gide distorts facts,[172] to the "comedy of sincerity" Gide
played out: "G. est une cocotte. Son diary veut donner du
prix à ses moindres mouvements." [173] "Seul avec son papier,
il ne peut songer qu'à l'effet à produire";[174] "Gide a autant
voulu *personnaliser* sa vie productive que moi déperson-
naliser la mienne." [175] We read above all with interest a
page written in 1940 in which he attempts to define Gide
and points to the voluptuousness of his imagination. It is
nonetheless true that, in spite of their extreme differences,
the friendship established at twenty lasted for more than
fifty years; in this regard we possess a moving account of a

170 Ibid., XXV, 528.   171 Ibid., XXVI, 871.
172 Ibid., XXII, 201.   173 Ibid., XXVI, 69.
174 Ibid., 261.   175 Ibid., XXVII, 274.

conversation of May 1940[176] in which Valéry, after analyzing their relationship, concludes in these terms: "Pas du tout les mêmes dieux (. . .). Mais il n'y a plus de malentendu. Reste un grand faible mutuel, et quand nous nous rencontrons une joie particulière indépendante de tout, et douce entre ces vieux messieurs."

It is important to make particular mention of another writer to whom Valéry refers more than ever during this period. We know that the only article he wrote on Mallarmé during the war appeared in *Le Point* in 1944; but the *Cahiers* show that he was also preparing a long essay which would have been part of a kind of spiritual autobiography of himself ("SM—cette étude serait un chapitre de mes mémoires").[177] Indeed, he questions himself insistently on this influence: "C'était un étrange poison que versait à toute autre poésie celle de Mallarmé dans mon esprit." [178] But what were the exact constituents of this poison? "C'est une révolution que considérer l'espace de la parole—ou univers du langage *avant* tout dessin ou problème particulier . . .";[179] "il a vu, sans doute, le problème général de la littérature 'harmonique' (et donc, non représentative)." [180] Valéry quite clearly cannot prevent himself from regretting, as he had done already about 1895, the impure mixture of poetry with a system of aesthetics that was also a philosophy; however, in 1942, he is not far from seeing its explanation, if not its justification: "Peut-être faut-il ces ingrédients étrangers avant qu'on puisse réduire au nécessaire et suffisant—lequel manque des attraits et excitants." [181]

Henri Mondor's book *Vie de Mallarmé* had the effect of stirring personal memories and obliging him to put to himself with greater precision what he calls the essential prob-

176 Ibid., XXVI, 199–201.
178 Ibid., XXIII, 411.
180 Ibid., XXIV, 371.

177 Ibid., XXVI, 488.
179 Ibid., XXV, 239.
181 Ibid., XXV, 529.

lem of Mallarmé: "Comment et d'où naquit cette étrange et inébranlable *certitude* sur laquelle Mallarmé a pu fonder toute sa vie, ses renoncements, ses témérités inouïes, son entreprise si heureusement réussie de se recréer, de se faire, en un mot, l'homme même d'une œuvre qu'il n'a pas accomplie et qu'il savait ne pas pouvoir l'être?" He could not, we know, be content to name an influence of any kind, be it Plato, Hegel or the occultists. We must turn to volume XXV of the *Cahiers* in which Valéry proposes the probable reasoning which, in his eyes, is at the heart of this poetics:

S.M. Origine—la constatation, réflexion, anxiété devant le phénomène Production du vers. D'où les deux thèmes: *Mystère-Hasard*. Ces deux aspects de la transformation du rien (mental) en *objet* (vers). Ceci est le devoir. Mais le rien revient sur le tout, etc., et rien n'a eu lieu . . . Les mots absolu, mystère, hasard ont ici puissance magique—plus que sens.[182]

Previously Valéry had given little explicit importance to the idea of chance in Mallarmé's thought; but, doubtless in reading the *Coup de dés* (as the last quotation indicates), he came to adopt it as the very designation of Mallarmé's field of metaphors. In penetrating fashion, he compares this method, "à même le *hasard* mental," to that of the painter who finds in each object "un domaine de *possibilités harmoniques*—à plusieurs dimensions." [183] Is not this a fundamental aspect of Mallarmé's glissando?

Yet if Mallarmé profits consciously from mental chance, he knows also that form introduces order, makes a system of formlessness. This is the meaning Valéry discovered in the *Coup de dés* as volume XXV enunciates: "C'est dire, selon moi, qu'à l'infinité des perceptions et idées possibles ne correspond qu'un nombre restreint de types d'actes verbaux—possibles; et, en pratique, un nombre bien moindre de ces actes utilisés." [184] The Mallarméan poem offers

182 Ibid., 707.   183 Ibid., XXIX, 350.
184 Ibid., XXV, 527.

then a relationship between the infinite and the final. Concerning the same poem, Valéry observes in passing the particular color Mallarmé gave the word "abolir" and infers its capital importance at the time of composition;[185] he relates, moreover, one most interesting detail when he observes that "Mallarmé [lui] a dit en [lui] communiquant le *Coup de dés* qu'il pensait, sur ce type, faire, *chaque année,* un ouvrage *plus intellectuel* que l'expression poétique ordinaire ne l'admettait. . . ." [186]

Valéry reacted violently to certain of Mallarmé's critics who seek the poetic meaning elsewhere than in the words.[187] No, Mallarmé's is not an art of expression but of creation. The subject of a Mallarméan piece is less important than its "programme": "Une sorte de *programme* consisterait dans un recueil de mots (parmi lesquels des *conjonctions aussi importantes que les substantifs*) et des types de *moments syntaxiques,* et surtout une table de tonalités verbales, etc." [188] This abstract arrangement, the effect of obscurity or deferred understanding that comes from some sonnets, is for Valéry modeled on music—"Wagneris causa" —and he finds this confirmed by Mallarmé himself in *Le Mystère et les lettres.*[189]

We are struck above all by the pages in which he compares Mallarmé with himself, and tries to circumscribe the point of divergence. He formulates their likeness in these terms: "En somme, Mallarmé et moi, ceci de commun— poème est problème. Et ceci, très important." [190] As for their differences, he says briefly: "Pour lui, l'œuvre. Pour moi, le moi." [191] But we note in particular two passages: in the first[192] Valéry returns to determining the role that his conception of Mallarmé's system had on his own formation: "Je m'avisai que le système supposé par l'art de Mal-

[185] Ibid., XXIII, 554.
[186] Ibid., 152.
[187] Ibid., 147, 172; XXV, 668.
[188] Ibid., XXV, 557.
[189] Ibid., XXIV, 150.
[190] Ibid., XXIII, 149.
[191] Ibid., 147.
[192] Ibid., XXIX, 536–537.

larmé était plus *profond* qu'une théorie de littérature et consistait en un secret d'attitude 'universelle' (. . .) La *liberté* que supposait la versification et l'obscurité de M. . . ." He concluded that Mallarmé must have a hidden god, that he venerated the ideal of a perfect self which gives "au moins l'illusion de la plus entière généralité." Yet, with his reading of Poe to help him, he felt that he was going beyond Mallarmé, "au point de [se] sentir bientôt bien plus brutal encore que Mallarmé (qui, lui, conservait la Poésie, au moins . . .)." In the second passage, Valéry considers the differences between *Hérodiade* and *L'Après-midi d'un Faune* on one hand, and *La Jeune Parque* on the other. While recognizing his own great debt to Mallarmé's work, he emphasizes the wholly different conditions that he imposed on himself which have their origin in his abstract research on total functioning ("Il ne suffit pas d'expliquer le *texte*, il faut aussi expliquer la *thèse*.") [193] If it is true that Mallarmé allowed him to grow, he makes a point of insisting on the continuity of his own attitude which put purity, and not poetry, at the end of the world.

It is therefore clear that the last *Cahiers* are some of the most important documents Valéry has left us. The thought, the method are as incisive as before, his will to analyze just as dominant. Whether it is a question of examining literature, or more general themes that include literature, his reflexions contain the unique light produced by his "impossible goal" that for fifty years was the bearing of the pure self. The poet of "Le Cimetière marin" sings of proud reason, "Tête complète et parfait diadème"; likewise, the late Valéry reaffirms his constant quest for a crystalline universe. He does not waver in seeing his god in the form of a limitless refusal of silliness,[194] in speaking of his dream of transcendence.[195] His ambition to bestride all things, this

193 Ibid., XXIV, 117.   194 Ibid., XXVIII, 127.
195 Ibid., 290.

"saintliness," had of necessity to be brought to the point where it was transformed, and transformed the world, into a kind of eternity. Where his poems create for us the imaginative sense and dramatic substance of just such a world, the *Cahiers* are his grandiose attempt, obsessively pursued, to elucidate hte idea that dwelt within him.[196]

[196] Since the original appearance of this essay, much research has been devoted to aspects of the *Cahiers*, the results of which have been given almost exclusively in synchronic rather than diachronic terms. I refer in particular to Judith Robinson's *L'Analyse de l'esprit dans les Cahiers de Valéry* (Paris: José Corti, 1963); Pierre Laurette's *Le Thème de l'arbre chez Paul Valéry* (Paris: C. Klincksieck, 1967); and Christine M. Crow's *Paul Valéry: Consciousness and Nature* (Cambridge: Cambridge University Press, 1972). The selections from the *Cahiers* which Judith Robinson has chosen and presented with admirable care (Paul Valéry, *Cahiers* [Paris: Gallimard, Pleiade, 1973]), are likewise arranged thematically.

Epilogue: Two Confrontations

VALÉRY has been well served outside France: one thinks of Rilke's translation of *Charmes*, of C. Day Lewis's version of "Le Cimetière marin," of the sumptuous American edition of the major writings to which Jackson Mathews has devoted twenty years of his life. Among the many foreign interpreters, one also calls to mind several illustrious names, including that of E. M. Cioran to whose recent appraisal I shall return. But none showed himself to be more attentive to Valéry's work over a period of forty years than T. S. Eliot. From 1918 when, it seems, he first read *La Jeune Parque*, Eliot studied Valéry's poetry and prose with vigilance and care; and the esteem in which he came to hold him was certainly as great as that which he felt for any other of his major contemporaries.

Eliot's readings in French literature were of course vast. His essays on Pascal and Baudelaire, for instance, are landmarks in modern English criticism; he meditated on the work of Mallarmé; while his comments on Laforgue and Corbière, and the poems that were directly inspired by his study of these two poets, offer an outstanding example of literary assimilation and recreation. The contact with Valéry, however, if it had no clearly definable influence on his poetry or prose, seems to me to possess a unique character because of the length of its duration and the numerous essays it provoked from a writer who disliked repeating himself. Perhaps we might be justified in calling the relationship a kind of "fascination." Indeed, is it not significant that as late as 1958 Eliot described Valéry as "a singularly fascinating mind," and spoke of the "perennial fascination" of his work?

The two men appear to have met for the first time in the early twenties—in October 1923, I believe, when Valéry came to London to lecture on Baudelaire and Victor Hugo. (They had already had occasion to exchange letters in August 1922 concerning a proposed translation of "Le Serpent").[1] Both men were just reaching the height of fame in their respective countries. Although Eliot was seventeen years Valéry's junior their careers had up to that time presented a curious parallelism: university studies had been followed by a sojourn in Paris (Eliot arrived in 1910, was tutored by Alain Fournier, attended Bergson's lectures, and stayed a year), then by perfunctory work (Valéry was rédacteur at the War Ministry prior to becoming private secretary to Edouard Lebey; Eliot was a schoolmaster at Highgate and, as he tells us in one of his French poems, "un peu banquier"). Finally, in 1917, at a few weeks' interval, *La Jeune Parque* and *Prufrock and Other Observations* appeared. These poems, and several important critical statements by both writers,[2] were followed by the publication in 1922 of the volumes that won each of them sudden and lasting notoriety: *Charmes* and *The Waste Land*.

Over the next twenty-odd years there ensued several meetings between the two poets (but "only as many . . . , I think," said Eliot, "as could be counted on the fingers"), the

---

[1] Piece no. 515, Catalogue of the Exhibition Paul Valéry at the Bibliothèque Nationale, 1956. According to the catalogue (p. 74), Eliot "remercie Valéry de lui avoir envoyé la traduction anglaise du *Serpent*. . . . Il se propose de la comparer minutieusement à l'original."

[2] Between 1917 and 1922, Eliot published "Tradition and the Individual Talent" (1919), "The Metaphysical Poets," "Andrew Marvell," "John Dryden" (1921); Valéry published several works including a new edition of his "Introduction à la méthode de Léonard de Vinci" and his "Avant-Propos" to the *Connaissance de la Déesse* by Lucien Fabre.

last taking place in May 1945. Eliot had just returned to
Paris where he was to lecture and attend a performance of
Murder in the Cathedral. On the ninth of that month he
dined at Pierre Brisson's with Valéry and Gide, who had not
seen each other since 1942. Ten days later Valéry had his
last outing when he went to the first communion of his
granddaughter Martine. He died on July 20 in his apart-
ment in the rue de Villejust (now rue Paul-Valéry).

In their conversations Eliot was greatly impressed by the
French poet's personality, especially of course by his restless
intelligence which could not find consolation in any faith.
Here was "the perfection, the culmination of a type of
civilized mind." [3] Eliot's own views were frequently echoed
and, as he said, clarified by those of Valéry; but, despite the
similarity of their opinions on many subjects, a gulf separated them: Eliot's spiritual itinerary and ultimate convictions were foreign to the "skepticism" he found in his friend.
Both writers might think of themselves as classicists in literature, and conservatives in politics; but nothing in Valéry
corresponded to the other's pastoral concern.

The object of this study is to examine the five essays in
which Eliot spoke in some detail of Valéry. The last appeared in 1958, the first thirty-eight years before. We shall,
therefore, have occasion to examine the variations of approach that an English writer—perhaps the greatest of his
age—adopted in discussing his French counterpart; to show
a remarkable case, not of literary influence, but of the admiration and the misgivings that Valéry inspired in a distinguished reader and friend.

In April 1920 Eliot published in *The Athenaeum* a review
of Henry Dwight Sidgwick's book on Dante, which he en-

---

[3] Preface to *Contemporary French Poetry* by Joseph Chiari (Man-
chester University Press, 1952), 4.

titlcd "Dantc as a 'Spiritual Leader.' " Gathering together several of his essays later that same year to form the collection *The Sacred Wood,* he revised his review and reentitled it simply "Dante." [4] It is in this second version that we find his first detailed reference to Valéry. He makes no allusion to *La Jeune Parque* or to any of the other poems that Valéry had published since 1917, but instead takes up a point of criticism that the French writer had made in his foreword to the *Connaissance de la Déesse* of Lucien Fabre published early in 1920. The revised article now begins: "M. Paul Valéry, a writer for whom I have considerable respect, has placed in his most recent statement upon poetry a paragraph which seems to me of very doubtful validity."

It is important to note—and the young critic himself recognizes the fact—that Eliot had not read Valéry's preface in its entirety: he was making his attack, albeit a mild one, on the strength of an extract that appeared in the July 23rd number of *The Athenaeum.* This is of course not a normal or advisable practice, and Eliot adds: "It may be that I do M. Valéry an injustice which I must endeavor to repair when I have the pleasure of reading his article entire"; but he presumably saw no reason to change his stand in a later edition, for the essay was not altered. Here, then, is the paragraph to which Eliot objected: "La philosophie et même la morale tendirent à fuir les œuvres pour se placer dans les réflexions qui les précèdent (. . .) Parler aujourd'hui de poésie philosophique (fût-ce en invoquant Alfred de Vigny, Leconte de Lisle, et quelques autres), c'est naïvement confondre des conditions et des applications de l'esprit incompatibles entre elles. N'est-ce pas oublier que le but de celui qui spécule est de fixer ou de créer une notion—c'est-à-dire un *pouvoir* et un *instrument* de pouvoir, cependant que

---

[4] *The Sacred Wood: Essays on Poetry and Criticism* (London: Methuen, 1920; second edition, 1928), 159–171.

le poète moderne essaie de produire en nous un *état* et de porter cet état exceptionnel au point d'une jouissance parfaite?" [5]

From these lines Eliot proceeds in rather dogmatic fashion —different from that of his more mature essays—to develop his position, which is centered around two main points. The first is his defense of philosophical poetry against what he deems to be Valéry's attack. He interprets the paragraph as suggesting "that conditions have changed, that 'philosophical' poetry may once have been permissible, but that (perhaps owing to the greater specialization of the modern world) it is now intolerable." If this is the sense of what Valéry is saying, Eliot has no hesitation in affirming that the poet can deal with philosophical ideas, not as matter for argument, but as matter for inspection. "The original form of a philosophy cannot be poetic. But poetry can be penetrated with this idea when it has reached the point of immediate acceptance, when it has become almost a physical modification."

Looking back on this essay, one cannot help thinking that this aspect of the debate was without much basis. Sufficient proof that the attitude ascribed by Eliot to Valéry was not in fact his might have been found in striking form in "Le Cimetière marin," which the *Nouvelle Revue Française* had published in its June 1920 number. What work could better conform to the remarks concerning Dante's "philosophical" poetry that Eliot makes in the course of his study: "Dante (. . .) does not analyze the emotion so much as he exhibits its relation to other emotions (. . .). We are not here studying the philosophy, we *see* it, as part of the ordered world (. . .) the significance of any single passage, of any of the passages that are selected as 'poetry,' is incomplete unless we ourselves apprehend the whole." But by referring to "Le Cimetière marin" I do not mean to sug-

5 "Avant-Propos" à la *Connaissance de la Déesse, Œuvres* I, 1273–1274.

gest that Valéry's position as evidenced in his essay is not
defensible. The misunderstanding between the two critics
arises from the fact that Eliot has not observed the particular
use that Valéry is giving to the word "philosophy." For
Eliot a philosophy is, as he says in his article, "a vision of
life," "an articulate formulation of the world." Valéry, on
the other hand, takes the analyst's attitude that philosophy
today is not meditation on God and nature, life and death,
time and justice; it is not a preoccupation with ends; philosophy has become aware of itself as form, as instrument,
and its concern is to refine the subtlety of its own logic, its
form. "Notre philosophie est définie par son appareil, et
non par son objet. Elle ne peut se séparer de ses difficultés
propres, qui constituent sa forme." Now, says Valéry, philosophical activity thus conceived cannot coincide with that
of the poet, that is to say, the author of a poetic form. An
analytic philosopher may write verse; but if this verse is to
be poetry and not rhymed ideas, the laws of poetry must
prevail. Valéry would agree with Eliot in placing Dante's
poetry among the greatest,[6] but the term philosophical poetry is for him a logical monstrosity. Analysis may inform
the poem as it constantly informs his own work in the most
striking and necessary way; it should never dictate it.

So much, then, for the first point of Eliot's criticism. The
second is expressed in the opening lines of the review and
taken up again in the conclusion: "if M. Valéry," Eliot
writes, "is in error in his complete exorcism of 'philosophy,'
perhaps the basis of his error is his apparently com-
mendatory interpretation of the effort of the modern poet,
namely, that the latter endeavors 'to produce in us a
state?'" No, he replies, "the aim of the poet is to state a
vision . . ."; and again: "the poet does not aim to excite—

6 Valéry acknowledged the link between the verse he used in "Le
Cimetière marin" and that of the *Divine Comedy*. Furthermore, he
spoke in his ninth notebook of the "ton de soi à soi," the "vers *savant*,"
and the "vers *vivant*" which for him characterized Dante's work and
which reminded him of "Le Cimetière marin."

that is not even a test of his success—but to set something
down, the state of the reader is merely that reader's mode of
perceiving what the poet has caught in words." For Eliot
the vision preexists the poem and the author must express it.
Valéry, however, is saying that poetry since Baudelaire has
become more and more self-conscious in the same way as
philosophy, and that the poet does not write to say but to
create. Against the quasi-Romantic concept Eliot is formulating, Valéry places the idea of the poet who discovers his
vision word by word. And the desirable form must be, as
he says, an object of delight for the reader. Valéry himself
found it impossible not to write with some ideal reader in
mind (no doubt most poets do the same thing, but Valéry
was always acutely conscious of this need); he sought, however, not to impose his emotions by the all-too-human
themes of traditional lyricism, but to provide the means
whereby the reader could create a rare state such as the
poet's moment of inspiration.

I shall conclude my remarks about this short essay by
noting that the differences between the two poets seem
considerable at this stage. Yet we must recognize that Eliot
had not fully grasped Valéry's argument so that his essay
remains interesting to us, not so much for his criticism of
Valéry, as for the affirmation of his own views. That the
observations of the French writer are "of very doubtful
validity" is certainly not proven. But it is also true to say
that Eliot has implicitly pointed to an apparent lacuna in
Valéry's critical position. The question is: even if we grant
the approach to poetry as "an exceptional state brought to
the point of perfect delight," how do we evaluate the seriousness of a poem, the significance of the vision it composes?
Eliot will return to this point in a later essay.

Four years later, in 1924, Eliot wrote an important study
which served to introduce an English translation of
"Ebauche d'un Serpent." The title of his essay, inspired by

Valéry's meditation on Leonardo, was: "A Brief Introduction to the Method of Paul Valéry." For the previous two years Eliot had been editing *The Criterion,* and the plaquette was one of the journal's early ventures in book production.

The essay provides us with the first and only occasion on which Eliot turned his attention specifically to Valéry's poetry. The original edition of *Charmes* had appeared in 1922, a short time after the separate publication of "Le Serpent," to which Valéry dedicated so much time and care; and these poems, perhaps more than *La Jeune Parque,* arrested Eliot's attention. He ends his essay with the hope that Valéry's work may become better known in England: "his influence, so great in France, might be great and valuable here."

It is not Eliot's object to discuss the poem in detail. Only incidentally does he describe the theme as being "as old as the Upanishads and perpetually new: the Red Slayer and *La plaie et le couteau.*" "But," he continues, "this theme has never before, and will never again, have this expression; the magnificence of the ending—the first version (. . .) I prefer to the second—will never be repeated.

> . . . éternellement
> Eternellement le bout mordre."

These remarks are, we feel, highly pertinent. One might enlarge on them, emphasizing the parodic element in the poem, the burlesque yet menacing tone, the extraordinary form, the place the poem occupies in the architecture of *Charmes,* the relationship of the theme to the rest of Valéry's thought; but in any case Eliot's poetic instinct did not lead him astray. He had discerned the universal drama that lies at the heart of Valéry's poem.

The argument of the essay is, however, centered less on "Le Serpent" than on three main points concerning the French poet himself. Eliot finds in Valéry an admirable example of a writer who rediscovers the main tradition of his country's poetry. Instead of being an isolated experimenter, he absorbs the experiments of the preceding generation and, not by imitation but by his own genius, gives them full and final expression: "what Valéry represents and for which he is honored and admired by even the youngest in France, is the reintegration of the Symbolist movement into the great tradition"; "Valéry is the heir, so to speak, of the experimental work of the last generation: he is its completion and its explanation." This preoccupation with a writer's sense of the past will be familiar to all who have read Eliot's poetry or criticism. It underlies on one plane the language and theme of *The Waste Land;* on another it constitutes the subject of his key-essay of 1919, "Tradition and the Individual Talent." Although we cannot, therefore, consider it surprising that he should introduce this preoccupation into his study of Valéry, it is noteworthy that he should do it with such appropriateness when discussing a French poet. It is well to remember that, around 1920, there were critics in France who could not see the wood for the trees when it came to evaluating *La Jeune Parque* and *Charmes.* Eliot, guided in part by Albert Thibaudet whose book on Valéry appeared in 1923, had the merit of recognizing with promptness the historical importance of Valéry's poetic achievement and expressing it in personal terms. Nor was he content to leave us with a general observation: comparing Nerval's "Les Cydalises" and Rimbaud's "O Saisons! O châteaux! . . ." with the hexasyllables of the "Cantique des colonnes," he commented in these terms:

The indefinable difference is the difference between the fluid and the static: between that which is moving toward an end and that which knows its end and has reached it; which can afford to stand, changeless, like a statue. There are two considerations about *order.* One is the amount of material organized, and the degree of difficulty of that material; the other is the completeness of the organization. Rimbaud, for instance, may have had the vision of a larger organization than Valéry's but it is not so achieved. And in comparison with such poets as Stuart Merrill, there is no question: Valéry is their justification.

Thus Valéry, Eliot believes, amply illustrates the genuine artist's solution to the dilemma of tradition and the individual talent. He justifies the endeavors of the masters and epigoni of Symbolism; in so doing, he writes verse that echoes back across the centuries of French poetry—reminding us, in "Le Cimetière marin" for instance, of certain lines of Malherbe. In this way a classicism is realized that has little in common with the neo-classicism of the turn of the century. "More substantially than Moréas—that gallant and uneasy metic—Valéry has come naturally and by his proper impulse toward classicism: toward an individual and *new* organization of many poetic elements. And at the same time he is a continuation of the experiment, the enquiry of Mallarmé."

It is piquant to speculate whether Eliot may not have been influenced in this section of his essay by certain remarks of Valéry himself, especially in "Situation de Baudelaire," an early version of which was given as a lecture in London in October 1923. Having no doubt been present at the lecture, Eliot wrote Valéry immediately afterwards requesting permission to publish it in *The Criterion,* and praising him in particular for what he had to say on the question of an author's originality. The tenor of Valéry's argument was that Baudelaire had sought to be a great poet, but not another Lamartine, Hugo, or Musset; he was predetermined by the great Romantics, and yet in a sense was their opposite; his originality lies in the critical eye with which he examined the works of his elders before undertaking to write: this attitude Valéry describes as classicist. *"Tout classicisme suppose un romantisme antérieur . . . ,"* Valéry had written. *"L'essence du classicisme est de venir après. L'ordre suppose un certain désordre qu'il vient réduire."* It is easy to imagine how Eliot, applying these remarks on Baudelaire to Valéry himself, was able to see in him the classicist of Symbolism.

Turning from Valéry's relationship to the French literary tradition, Eliot went on to discuss another aspect of his poetry: its "impersonality." This is a theme which recurs throughout his critical essays, and is in fact a cornerstone of Eliot's whole attitude. Time and again he depicts "the struggle—which alone constitutes life for the poet—to transmute his personal and private agonies into something rich and strange, something universal and impersonal." He recognizes that "Le Serpent" may not appeal to English readers because of their tendency to look above all for the personal note, the self-revelation: they "peer lasciviously between the lines for biographical confession." But such is not the way of art, for the artist takes his emotions and experiences as a material, not an end. Yet, if Valéry's poems are far from crude emotion, Eliot knows also that they are no simple game of words: "Valéry's interest in 'technique' is something much more than an interest in the skilful disposition of words for their own sake: it is a recognition of the truth that not our feelings, but the pattern which we make of our feelings, is the center of value." This statement underlines a vital trait of Valéry's work: in each of his poems, he seeks, not to deny his personality, but to extend it, to give it structure and significance. Did not he say of "Le Cimetière marin" that he had aimed to write "as personal, but as universal a monologue as he could compose"? (We also think of Eliot observing in 1942, in "A Note on War Poetry," that "private experience at its greatest intensity, becoming universal, is 'poetry.' ")

The last pages of the introduction characterize Valéry's poetry in another way. Interestingly enough, Eliot takes up a point he had made in the paper on "Dante" and expresses it here in terms that closely approximate Valéry's own in the "Avant-Propos" which Eliot first criticized. No longer defending the concept of philosophical poetry, he now attacks those who, like Thibaudet, emphasize the philosophical or metaphysical aspect of Valéry's work. "A poet who is also a metaphysician, and unites the two activities, is conceivable as an unicorn or a wyvern is conceivable (. . .). Such a poet would be two men. It is more convenient to use, if necessary, the philosophy of other men, than to burden oneself with the philosophy of a monstrous brother in one's own bosom (. . .). As to Valéry, if he has a philosophy, that is to say a metaphysical system over and above his poetical system of organization, then I do not know what that system is." We must assume that Eliot had occasion between 1920 and 1924 to become better acquainted with Valéry's critical approach, which enabled him to see the relationship between philosophy and poetry in rather changed terms. He adopts the essential attitude that Valéry developed in his 1920 essay: for Eliot, as for Valéry, the philosopher and the poet pursue two distinct activities, creating separate forms, or "systems of organization."

A long period of twenty-two years followed during which Eliot and Valéry met on a few occasions while, in their respective ways, they played strangely parallel roles in literature. Both exercised enormous influence as poets despite the comparative smallness of their output: both found—though differently—new fields of expression on the stage; both were the outstanding critics and theorists writing at that time in their two countries.

A year after Valéry's death (the *achevé d'imprimer* is dated 30 July 1946), the *Cahiers du Sud* published a remarkable commemorative number entitled *Paul Valéry vivant*. Among the many famous writers invited to contribute was T. S. Eliot, who wrote a homage under the title "Leçon de Valéry." Eliot's style was never better, nor his sense of composition. He begins with a portrait of the man as he had come to know him through their occasional meetings over the previous years. The traits of personality are finely observed: "the social qualities and the charm—such an un-affected modesty of manner more impressive than any grandeur, and the kind of impish wit that indicates a man who needs no assumed dignity." But this was no surface patina, a mere *gentillesse*, but part of his total and coherent outlook. "His modesty and his informality were the qualities of a man without illusions, who maintained no pretence about himself to himself, and found it idle to pretend to others"; again, more incisively: "His was, I think, a pro-foundly destructive mind, even nihilistic." In the light of this observation our judgment of his poems does not alter, but admiration for the man must grow since creation was only possible for him, Eliot says, by way of a "desperate heroism which is a triumph of character."

He recalls that, when he saw him in May 1945 Valéry had said: "L'Europe est finie." Eliot questions the rightness of the observation, and says that it is true at least in the sense that "my language is finished, for me (and for a poet, his language represents his country, and Europe too) when I have come to the end of my resources in endeavoring to extend and develop that language." These words could only have been written by a poet with similar maturity of ex-perience to Valéry's own: a poet who described himself in *Four Quartets* as having spent twenty years trying to learn to use words. Yet it was Valéry who had, more than any other of his contemporaries, the right to say "L'Europe est finie" in his generation; "it is he who will remain for posterity the representative poet, the symbol of the poet, of the first half of the twentieth century." Eliot concludes with the hope that Valéry's example and achievement will be a new point of departure and not an end. He was the poet (and here Eliot recalls his 1924 essay) who brought to its classical completion a long line of Romanticism; now a new Ro-manticism must appear which will somehow reinvigorate the language. Europe, to survive, must be ready for new ventures, willing to quit the known for the unknown and to go beyond.

A short time later, in November 1948, Eliot crossed the Atlantic to deliver a lecture in the Library of Congress under the title, "From Poe to Valéry." Just as in his "Brief Introduction," he discussed a poetic tradition; yet here, instead of references to many writers, he chose to study the influence of Poe on Baudelaire, Mallarmé, and Valéry, who "represent the beginning, the middle, and the end of a particular tradition in poetry." In contrast to the approach adopted in the early essay where he spoke in detail of poetic diction, Eliot was now concerned with a "peculiar attitude towards poetry, by the poets themselves," "the most interesting development of poetic consciousness anywhere" over the last century.

After delimiting his subject, Eliot proceeds to an analysis of the work of Poe as he appears today to English and American readers. Essentially, Poe remains for them "the author of a few poems and a few tales one read when one was a boy"; but we do not reread his tales, and his poetry, despite its incantatory elements, is too often crudely musical, sacrificing sense to sound. As for his poetics, it is not taken seriously, and even his proscription of the long poem we relate to what we deem to be his inability to write anything but a short one. We try him, and he is found wanting, both in theory and in practice. Eliot suggests that Poe had "the intellect of a highly gifted young man before puberty (. . .). There is just that lacking which gives dignity to the mature man: a consistent view of life."

Now it is more than probable that Eliot has not completely explained for us the attitude of Poe and the interest his life and work still afford: perhaps he was, as Allan Tate has maintained, an important transitional figure who recognized the disintegration, the spiritual disunity brought about by scientism, and vainly attempted to transcend it by hyperbolic claims for the "poetic intellect," an "angelism" of his imagination; but that hardly affects the literary judgment that Eliot made. Poe remains for the English and American reader a minor writer, a minor theorist. Yet how are we to explain the tremendous impact he had in France? Was it because Baudelaire, Mallarmé, and Valéry had an imperfect knowledge of English? Such an answer, that many English and American readers would be ready to support, is surely unsatisfactory: if it may possibly help to explain the overrating of Poe's poetry, it does not explain the vitality of his thought.

Eliot is mainly concerned with the relationship of Poe to Valéry, and treats cursorily the role of Poe in the formation of Baudelaire and Mallarmé. It is no doubt true, by and large, that the author of *Les Fleurs du Mal* found in Poe first and foremost the prototype of *le poète maudit,* and the aesthetician of the *poème-objet;* but Eliot is certainly wrong when he says that "the interest of Mallarmé is rather in the technique of verse." His remarks on Valéry, on the other hand, go further and into greater depth. Eliot sees Poe as affecting Valéry's poetic theory, which gives the culminating expression to two notions found originally in the American writer: the ideal of *poésie pure;* and the supreme value attached to the conscious act of composition. Concerning the first of these notions, Eliot's use of the term *poésie pure* coincides neither with the exact way Valéry conceived it ("Je n'avais entendu faire allusion qu'à la poésie qui résulterait, par une sorte d'exhaustion, de la suppression progressive des éléments prosaïques d'un poème"), nor with that of the Abbé Brémond, to whom he refers. What Eliot designates by this term is the poem in which "the subject is little, the treatment is everything: the subject exists for the poem, not the poem for the subject." (It is, of course, a central detail of Valéry's poetics, but let us note that it was precisely this point, expressed in the form of a dichotomy between poetry and philosophy, with which Eliot took issue in his "Dante" article, and which he modified in his longer essay of 1924.) Valéry, then, was guided by this notion and strove for purity in his work; but Poe, say Eliot, "did not have to achieve purity by a process of purification, for his material was already tenuous."

The second notion was found by Valéry in "The Philosophy of Composition," which may have been "a hoax, or a piece of self-deception, or a more or less accurate record of Poe's calculations in writing the poem"; yet whatever its relation to actual fact, "it suggested to Valéry a method and an occupation—that of observing himself write." The French poet became the most self-conscious of all poets, preoccupied with processes.

Eliot observes that the conception of the creative act as being more interesting than the poem does not coincide with the theory of the pure poem, which should have nothing in view but itself; in fact, the two notions, are, he says, paradoxically inconsistent. If this is so, Valéry is guilty of a serious hiatus in his analysis. One may suggest, however, that Eliot has perhaps not seen the coherence of Valéry's argument and that the notions are in fact "paradoxically consistent." Valéry is saying that the mind of the poet advances from the vague to the determinate by means of the poem, in which it enjoys the exercise of its powers and discovers itself; his poem can be abandoned when it has reached the state of complete coherence, harmony, "the body incorruptible"; on the other hand, the mind is infinite and must forever begin again its desperate search for self-knowledge. In Valéry we feel the two notions to be subtly, necessarily wedded. Eliot may not have agreed on this point; but it seems to be a further illustration of the maturity of Valéry and the comparative immaturity of Poe, even when they seem to be saying similar things. As Eliot says: "With Poe and Valéry, extremes meet, the immature mind playing with ideas because it has not developed to the point of

convictions, and the very adult mind playing with ideas because it was too skeptical to hold convictions." To convince
the reader fully of this last remark, it would be necessary to
discuss the importance "Eureka" had for Valéry when he
read it in March 1892. Quite apart from Poe's poetics, here
was a work that fascinated him by its scientific theories, by
its poetic subject ("l'expression d'une volonté de relativité
généralisée") and, significantly, by the form adopted, which
coincides, one may say, with Valéry's own literary practice
in *La Jeune Parque* and *Charmes* ("exemple et mise en
œuvre de la réciprocité d'appropriation (. . .) L'univers est
construit sur un plan dont la symétrie profonde est en
quelque sorte présente dans l'intime structure de notre
esprit").

The conclusion of Eliot's essay is couched in terms similar
to those of the 1946 homage. Valéry's death has brought to
an end the tradition that stems from Poe, and "I do not believe that this aesthetic can be of any help to later poets."
The future of poetry, Eliot acknowledges, is impossible to
forecast; yet he leaves us with a suggestion of the new direction that may be followed: "it is a tenable hypothesis that
this advance of self-consciousness, the extreme awareness of
and concern for language which we find in Valéry, is something which must ultimately break down, owing to an increasing strain against which the human mind and nerves
will rebel. . . ."

The sixteen finely written pages that introduce *The Art of
Poetry* (1958) constitute Eliot's definitive analysis of Valéry.[7]
Here he chose to concentrate on the critical essays, the aspect
of the work which he found constantly stimulating. No one
has followed Valéry's propositions with greater awareness
of the questions involved; and, while remaining objective,

---

[7] *The Art of Poetry*, translated by Denise Folliot, with an introduction
by T. S. Eliot, *The Collected Works of Paul Valéry*, Bollingen Series
XLV, 15 vols. (New York: Pantheon Books, 1958), 7, vii–xxiv.

and adopting his usual dialectical method of inquiry, Eliot yet shows his instinctive sympathy and admiration ("If the best of his poems are among the masterpieces, the best of his critical essays are among the most remarkable curiosities of French literature").

The plan, a clear and elegant one, is developed in five sections. The writer begins by acknowledging the occasional nature of Valéry's criticism which owes its existence to "molestations of fortune"; nevertheless, it is never perfunctory and reveals, alongside apparent inconsistencies and repetitions, a constant return to topics that are peculiarly Valéry's own. Second, he defines the trait which distinguishes Valéry from all other poets writing about poetry, with the single exception of Poe: "he is perpetually engaged in solving an insoluble puzzle—the puzzle of how poetry gets written; and the material upon which he works is his own poetry." Third, he analyzes at length certain good, and less good, aspects of Valéry's work: he approves the emphasis on conscious labor as against inspiration, the value attached to difficult and complicated rhyming schemes and the "exercise" they afford the poet, the importance given to structure, the insistence that poetry must be enjoyed, and enjoyed as poetry; on the other hand, he warns against dangers that are inherent in Valéry's sharp distinction between poetry and prose, with its corollary separation of the vocabulary and idiom of poetry from that of ordinary speech. Fourth, he turns to the essential problem of the essays, Valéry's idea of the poet as a scientist which the young student of Montpellier was already formulating in 1889 and which he later developed and, says Eliot, imposed on his age: "the satanist, the Dandy, the *poète maudit* have had their day: eleven years before the end of the nineteenth century Valéry invents the role which is to make him representative of the twentieth. . . ." This role, which penetrates both his theory and practice, is found expressed in the essays, and the account given of his own experience cannot fail to arouse the response of other poets, whether to agree or disagree. The introduction ends on a tribute to Valéry, "a singularly interesting, enigmatic, and disturbing author, a poet who has realized in his life and work one conception of the role of the poet so amply as to have acquired also a kind of mythological status." Eliot finds, however, that this poetics is deficient in one respect, and he returns to an argument that we felt was at least implicit in the 1920 article on Dante: the essays offer no criterion of seriousness, show no concern with the question of how the poem "is related to the rest of life in such a way as to give the reader the shock of feeling that the poem has been to him, not merely an experience, but a serious experience." By experience is not meant merely the fleeting enjoyment of the poem, a moment that enhances life and then is rapidly forgotten, but experience that "has entered into and been fused with a multitude of other experiences in the formation of the person that the reader is developing into." And yet, as Eliot observes, if this important critical question does not seem to be broached by Valéry, we can certainly impute no lack of seriousness to the poetry that he himself wrote.

It will be seen that the article is well balanced and that, given the limits of a short introduction, Eliot has managed to combine an exposition of the salient points of Valéry's poetics, praise for the fruitful originality of his approach, and some criticism. The main observations are penetrating, and economically expressed. I should like, however, to return to a few statements that seem to me of special interest, and to examine them in greater detail.

Eliot's first major reproach concerns the distinction Valéry makes between poetry and prose, which he compares, after Malherbe, to the difference between dancing and walking. This analogy Eliot castigates in his own figurative terms: "it illuminates," he writes, "like the flash of an empty cigarette lighter in the dark: if there is no fuel in the lighter, the momentary flash leaves a sense of darkness more im-

penetrable than before." Why is this so? Because Valéry has
gone too far, he has forgotten that poetry can possess practical value, and prose bring the delight of the dance. Instead
of really helping us to distinguish between two modes of
communication, Eliot believes that Valéry only manages to
confuse us further. Yet surely his criticism is too harsh.
Valéry would not deny that there are many kinds of poetry
and many kinds of prose. All that he is attempting to do is,
as usual, to define his terms in their "purest" sense (just as
he did, for example, when discussing the philosopher and
the poet in his foreword to the *Connaissance de la Déesse*).
Prose and poetry use a common language, syntax, system of
sounds, but the end-term to which poetry aspires is not a
precise object as in prose, but "un ravissement, un fantôme
de fleur, un extrême de vie, un sourire . . . ," the dance of
the sensibility. When we realize that Valéry is concerned
with pure poetry and pure prose, which in practice are
rarely obtained, when we admit that he has sought to indicate directions and not formulate watertight categories,
Eliot's argument loses its force. It suggests, nevertheless, that
he himself is acutely aware of poetry's role as a social instrument—a point he makes, as we shall see, in his conclusion.

He offers another criticism that is closely linked to the
preceding one: Valéry, he affirms, too closely identifies poetic language with music, separates it too strictly from the
language that we readers ourselves speak. He is here revert-
ing to one principle that had commanded his own poetic
practice, above all since the time he received, through
Arthur Symonds's book,[8] the revelation of the works of
Laforgue and Corbière. In his own theory the same principle is found expressed in categorical terms: "it is the poet's
business," he writes in 1942 in "The Music of Poetry," "to
use the speech which he finds about him, that with which
he is most familiar. . . . The music of poetry . . . must be

[8] *The Symbolist Movement in Literature* (London: Heinemann,
1899).

a music latent in the common speech of its time." Now it is
obvious that the attitudes of the two poets are divergent,
that Eliot's view would be echoed by Apollinaire for instance, but not by the author of *Charmes*. Whereas *The
Waste Land* and *Four Quartets* and *Alcools* speak with the
voices of men of our time, yet voices heightened and controlled, the poems of Valéry seem to stand outside the twentieth century by their diction, if not by their themes. And
yet who would deny that they conform profoundly to the
genius of the French language? Valéry certainly did consider the possibility of creating a language that would es-
chew all concessions to everyday speech; but "je ne crois pas
possible de bâtir des arts sur des considérations trop éloi-
gnées des vues moyennes. Langage ordinaire, perspective,
etc . . ."; such an art would be "trop *instructif* pour être
enivrant." [9] He chose instead a palette of words which have
an extremely rich range of secondary meanings, and which
avoid the immediacy and the familiarity that Baudelaire,
Laforgue, Apollinaire, Cendrars, and others had brought
into French poetry ("J'ai passé dix ans à chercher une
langue 'absolue' ").[10] Few readers, least of all Eliot, would
deny that Valéry succeeded magnificently in his task. The
fact remains, however, that Valéry's example, as well as his
theory, have inherent dangers. To seek above all a pattern
freed from the norms of contemporary speech is to reject
the sources that renew and refresh the poet's diction. In
this respect, Eliot is attacking an attitude which for him and
for his fellow poets would have been stifling; Valéry, on the
other hand, is as usual engaged in the realization of a personal ideal of pure poetry, which may perhaps be best left
alone by his immediate successors.

Another reflexion in Eliot's preface that must draw our

[9] *Cahiers*, VI, 537.
[10] Ibid., IX, 23. What is for Valéry the keystone of poetic language?
"La plus belle poésie a la voix d'une femme idéale, Mlle. Ame. Pour
moi la voix intérieure me sert de repère. Je rejette tout ce qu'elle refuse
comme exagéré" (ibid., VI, 170).

attention concerns the image he deduced of Valéry as poet:
"very much like that of the austere, bespectacled man in a
white coat, whose portrait appears in advertisements, weighing out or testing the drugs of which is compounded some
medicine with an impressive name." Many quotations from
Valéry could be supplied which would support this image;
but it is patent oversimplification. It recalls Jules Romains's
parodical poet in *Les Créateurs* rather than the real author
of "Sinistre" or "Sémiramis" or "Profusion du soir," the
true poet who was constantly surprised by what he created
("ce que j'ai voulu m'impose de vouloir aussi ce que j'étais
à mille lieues de songer à vouloir").[11] Eliot errs even more
when he tries to illustrate how the identification of the poet
and the scientist can become mere "eyewash." He is referring
to the lines in "Poésie et pensée abstraite" in which Valéry
states: "J'ai coutume de procéder à la mode des chirurgiens
qui purifient d'abord leurs mains et préparent leur champ
opératoire. C'est ce que j'appelle le *nettoyage de la situation
verbale*."[12] Eliot takes this to refer to steps preliminary to
the writing of a poem; if this were so it would indeed be
eyewash; but the context makes it clear that Valéry is speaking of problems of a speculative nature such as the one he
has in hand: what is "poetry," what is "abstract thought"?

The most telling criticism, however, is to be found in
Eliot's conclusion to the introduction; his remark goes to
the heart of Valéry's poetics. There is, Eliot observes, no
detailed discussion, let alone solution, of the question of the
relative seriousness of different poems, their value as experiences affecting the reader. On this point Eliot's own attitude has apparently developed: where originally he traces
"greatness" to "the intensity of the artistic process, the pressure so to speak, under which the fusion takes place,"[13] he

11 Ibid., VI, 106.
12 "Poésie et pensée abstraite," *Œuvres*, I, 1316.
13 "Tradition and the Individual Talent" (1919), *The Sacred Wood*,
55.

later places emphasis on an open moral—even moralistic—concern: "Literary criticism should be completed by criticism from a definite ethical and theological standpoint. . . . The 'greatness' of literature cannot be determined solely by literary standards." [14] Nothing could be further from Valéry's own attitude; the only aspect of literature to which he would apply the word "morality" is to the act of creation itself. When he discusses the moment of execution, his prose shows the wonder that it stirs in him: "Est-il tourment plus pur, division de soi-même plus profonde que ce combat du Même avec le Même, quand l'âme tour à tour épouse ce qu'elle veut contre ce qu'elle peut, ce qu'elle peut contre ce qu'elle veut, et tantôt du parti de sa puissance, tantôt du parti de son désir, passe et repasse du tout au rien?" [15] But if we are sure that the creative act was for him the most exciting aspect of a topic to which he constantly returned, is it right to assume that no criterion of seriousness can be deduced from his writings? Would he condone for instance Jacques Rivière's preference for "La Fausse Morte," with its eleven lines, as the high point of *Charmes*? I think not; his own ideal is that "la poésie doit donner l'idée d'une parfaite pensée," [16] and the thought which engages our sensibility most "perfectly" is, in his own eyes, the supreme poem—a work which invites from the reader the total play of feelings, emotions, intellect. Once again, however, he would warn that, although such a poem is itself the criterion of seriousness that Eliot seeks, Valéry would not prescribe it for any but himself. There are other poets, other attitudes, other readers. To those who do not like this ideal, Valéry can reply in the words of the Jeune Parque to the Philosopher: "Quoi de plus prompt que de fermer un livre?"

---

14 "Religion and Literature" (1935), reprinted in *Essays Ancient and Modern* (London: Faber and Faber, 1936).
15 "Je disais quelquefois à Stéphane Mallarmé . . . ," *Œuvres*, I, 659.
16 *Cahiers*, V, 871.

It used to be customary to say that Eliot's critical position changed in some vital fashion after his conversion to Anglo-Catholicism in the late twenties. He himself seemed to give support to this opinion by declaring in 1928 "that he had passed from a preoccupation with the problem of the integrity of poetry" to "that of the relation of poetry to the spiritual and social life of its time and other times." Scholars have come to see, however, that there was a deepening of his views, a different focus, rather than any fundamental volte-face. What strikes us in the five articles we have examined is the constancy of his interest, the lasting concern for the questions and answers proposed by Valéry. His permanent object was to discern the concrete lesson the French poet left us, and this he sought to do with what I felt obliged to call fascination.

I do not mean, of course, that there was no diversity in his tone or approach. After beginning with a rather categorical rebuttal, he changed quickly to admiration, even enthusiasm, hardly crossed by a reproach. He studied many different aspects of Valéry: the man as he appeared to a personal acquaintance; the poetry; the poetics, its virtues and dangers. This diversity of approach brings to our notice an important teaching implicit in Eliot's criticism: the reader should study all of Valéry's work for only thus can he truly understand any part of it. A great artist, a major poet like Valéry is one whose every expression helps us to appreciate the whole, and the whole the parts.

Another valuable contribution concerns Eliot's analysis of the debt to Poe, which brings out Valéry's essential originality in transforming an intuition and an idea into a mature method. His critical writings are the most exciting testimony we have with respect to the act of writing a poem. But Eliot realizes that they fall short if we do not accept Valéry's proposition that "le seul vrai de l'art c'est l'art." [17]

[17] "La Tentation de (saint) Flaubert," *Œuvres,* I, 613.

The comparison of the two men makes us aware that it is around this last point that their attitudes differ most significantly. Eliot was a Christian, and a teacher, whose poetry leads us from "fear in a handful of dust" to the virtues of humility and love; whose critical essays revolve around the conviction that literature should not be written or studied in isolation, but in relation to "the language, the sensibility, and the literary tradition of a people"; furthermore, "that literary criticism should be completed by criticism from a definite ethical and theological standpoint." Valéry, on the other hand, confesses his own "inhumanity," his "purity": poetry must be for the reader a "charm": not something which turns the reader back on himself or towards other men, but conveys to him a sense of *ravissement sans référence*. In a solemn speech given at a time of national crisis in September 1939, he affirmed no less strongly the uselessness of poetry, its "monde des formes idéales et des résonances infinies." How urbane, then, is Eliot's approach beside this unceasing rage for transcendence, the relentless will to go beyond the limits of personality, society, Christianity.

And yet, if we are aware of radical differences between them, we cannot but feel on another plane a real and close affinity. Both represent in their separate ways a moment of commitment to a high idea of language, and to a poetic tradition, amid a modern disorder of which they are acutely conscious. Eliot's long attempt to gauge Valéry's achievement forms in a sense a mirror in which one finds the complementary image of the author himself.

Eliot's last essay on Valéry—no doubt the most perceptive of all—appeared in 1958. But recent years have brought new views to bear on a work that is eminently capable of engendering diverse appraisals. Thus, in 1970, on the eve of the centenary of Valéry's birth, an essay strikingly different from any Eliot offers us sought to dispel some of the chimeras with which the French writer's name is associated. It was published by the small but lively publishing house "L'Herne" and written by the Rumanian-born author E. M. Cioran whose works have shown long familiarity with his present subject. Indeed, his polemic adopts a procedure, and many a phrase, that are taken straight from the Valéryan mould. Yet it has the virtue of putting some criticisms with a vigor that suggests the personal encounter from which they spring; it also serves more generally to express some reactions of a new generation, twenty-five years after Valéry's death, to the influence of Monsieur Teste.

It was composed in response to an invitation from the general editor of the Bollingen "Valéry in English" to preface a volume given over to the essays on Leonardo, Poe, and Mallarmé. If one sympathizes with the editor who subsequently rejected the essay as inappropriate, it is, I think, good that it should have appeared as a plaquette which carries the full responsibility of its author. The approach is stylish and highly controlled and this, together with Cioran's iconoclasm, has attracted widespread attention. It captures our interest by lapidary formulas, lucid exposition, and the quite evident pleasure Cioran finds in judging one of his masters. "Quand on aborde un esprit aussi délié que le sien," he writes, "on éprouve une rare volupté à déceler ses illusions et ses failles, qui, pour n'être pas évidentes, n'en sont pas moins réelles. . . ." [18] There is, we might even say, something of the masochist in the deliberateness with which he aims his blows at a figure of past veneration.

As for the substance of his criticism, he postulates a Valéry who was the victim of a rigid method. "Contaminé par le positivisme, il souscrit sans réserves au scientisme, cette grande illusion des temps modernes . . .";[19] so much so that method became his way of escape from a basic absence

18 E. M. Cioran, *Valéry face à ses idoles* (Paris: L'Herne, 1970), 23.
19 Ibid., 31.

of spontaneity. "En bon technicien, il a essayé de réhabiliter le procédé et le métier aux dépens du *don*." [20] With such premises it is not surprising that Cioran can do nothing but damn with faint praise when he comes to sum up Valéry's career, branding his poetry bloodless, his poetics bankrupt, separating from the chaff only the peripheral Valéry who commented from time to time on history and politics. Having donned the mantle of spokesman for his time, Cioran flourishes a final paradox: "On doute de ses poèmes, on repousse sa poétique mais on se réclame de plus en plus du moraliste et de l'analyste attentif aux événements." [21] Such remarks are well in the tone of the essay as a whole, which deals with three of Valéry's "idols" of the spiritual life.

They are treated in inverse chronological order. Firstly, Mallarmé who for more than fifty years, as we have had ample opportunity to discover in this book, was scrutinized by Valéry in some of the best studies that have yet appeared. In his estimate no poem was greater than *L'Après-midi d'un Faune,* no lifetime's effort more nobly dedicated to the idea of beauty: "Son œuvre me fut dès le premier regard, et pour toujours," he wrote, "un sujet de merveille." [22] But Mallarmé's poetry turns on the conception of a book—a composition which would be the expression of an age-old ideal, the fulfilment of man's dream of transcendence. Although the work was never written Valéry found in this ambition —bringing together as it does in a unique synthesis a disaffected Catholicism, Hegel, Wagner—cause for high praise. Cioran, on the other hand, treats Mallarmé harshly as "un écrivain qu'on est parfois enclin à appeler naïf ou imposteur et qui ne fut en réalité qu'un halluciné," and isolates what he calls "un rien de mise en scène, un désir de se tromper, de vivre intellectuellement au-dessus de ses moy-

20 Ibid., 22.   21 Ibid., 44.
22 "Lettre sur Mallarmé," *Œuvres,* I, 634.

ens, une volonté de légende, et d'échec. . . ." [23] There is
not a little question-begging in these words: one would be
hard put to square them with the facts; but they are used
to cast a shadow upon Valéry's career since Cioran holds
that the *Cahiers* were his abortive attempt to write a Mallarméan book of his own. Thus, says Cioran, he followed
his master and was similarly deluded: "Il alla plus avant
que Mallarmé mais, pas plus que ce dernier, il ne put
mener à bien un dessein qui exige de l'obstination et une
grande invulnérabilité à l'ennui, à cette plaie qui, de son
propre aveu, ne cessait de le tourmenter." [24]

With regard to Poe we know Valéry's commitment to one
of the "supreme engineers" of the nineteenth century, and,
in particular, to the author who represented for him the
power to orientate thought and metaphor to a precise end,
the heady union of science and imagination. It was Poe
who inspired the first of the public lectures Valéry gave in
Montpellier at the age of eighteen which Cioran, like Eliot,
singles out for its provocative opening: "La littérature est
l'art de se jouer de l'âme des autres." And even if Valéry
might have agreed that Poe's short stories and verse were of
limited intrinsic worth, he could still respect their author
who for the first time defined literature as a problem of effi-
ciency. "Cet opium vertigineux et comme Mathématique:
Poe, Poe!" [25] There can be no doubt that the pages of "The
Philosophy of Composition" gave him much he would develop with extreme subtlety. But Cioran considers Poe's
treatise on the fabrication of a poem to be nothing but a
joke—although it fooled some illustrious authors like Baudelaire and Mallarmé. In the case of Valéry, the reason
for his adoption of the text was "un enthousiasme naïf":
he swallowed Poe hook, line and sinker because it answered

23 Cioran, *Valéry face à ses idoles*, 14.
24 Ibid., 16.
25 *Correspondance André Gide-Paul Valéry*, 86.

a need, allowing him to escape from an incapacity to write
naturally; he would henceforth dwell in the general, weigh
poetics rather than individual poems, emphasize the demands of classical prosody to the exclusion of matter. "Il
a prôné le difficile par impuissance: toutes ses exigences
sont celles d'un artiste et non d'un poète." [26] This was the
analytical attitude Valéry brought to poetry and enunciated
when he described the steps he followed in writing "Le
Cimetière marin." He made no secret of it, and Cioran does
not doubt the veracity of Valéry's account. What he condemns in Valéry is the fact that he was not a "true" poet,
which in his eyes is tantamount to accomplishing a fatal
act ("the ineluctable," "destiny"), whereas Valéry's play of
detachment, his irony, the importance he gave to form, can
only annoy him.

Poe, then, conveyed the idea of an absolute craft, just as
Mallarmé evoked the absolute work. What of Leonardo?
Valéry owed much of his early fame to the brilliant essay
which appeared in the *Nouvelle Revue* when he was not
yet twenty-four under the title "Introduction a la méthode
de Léonard de Vinci," to be followed by his "Note et digression" of 1919, "Léonard et les philosophes" (1929), a
marginal commentary on his previous writings (1931), and
finally, a short article on Leonardo's notebooks (1942). Certainly this point of admiration remained firm, giving
him ample pretext for meditation, suggesting an exemplary
aloofness—"une indifférence royale"—to petty details of
life, run-of-the-mill incidents, "les débris extérieurs d'une
personnalité." Leonardo's concern was with the "Comedy of
the Intellect," which he dissected with unflagging rigor. Or
was this Leonardo a mere figment of Valéry's imagination?
"En réalité," he observed in 1931, looking back on his first
essay, "j'ai nommé *homme* et *Léonard* ce qui m'apparais-
sait alors comme le pouvoir de l'esprit." Nevertheless, it was

26 Cioran, *Valéry face à ses idoles*, 22.

the historical Leonardo who, in the beginning, fired his desire and suggested a spiritual freedom with respect to the world. Everything became a problem to be considered, analyzed, reconstructed by the span of a man's thought. "Que peut un homme?" was, we recall, his Vincian motto. In its name he attacked traditional philosophy as a misuse of language; but, in so doing, he had to cultivate an approach of his own for which Cioran calls him to order, since "il vivait d'une manière quasi absolue dans son langage à lui." [27] This of course is not true, as any reader of Valéry will agree: words were used judiciously by him, but in no sense hermetically: there is indeed very little Valéryan jargon. Cioran also makes a brief show of defending Pascal, whom Valéry condemned for abandoning science in favor of metaphysics; and here again his defense begs at least as many questions as Valéry's attack: "cet abandon fut le résultat d'un *éveil* spirituel autrement important que les découvertes scientifiques qu'il aurait pu faire par la suite." [28] Valéry preferred the early Pascal, says Cioran, because of an ingenuous passion for science, the embarrassing enthusiasm of a rank amateur, which makes us think of "ces femmes du siècle des Lumières dont il a parlé dans sa préface aux *Lettres persanes,* et qui couraient les laboratoires, se passionnaient pour l'anatomie ou pour l'astronomie." [29] This too is a fallacy clear to anyone who has taken the pains to look, as we did in our last chapter, at Valéry's notebooks. That Valéry's knowledge of mathematics and science grew, that he made use of it constantly, that it afforded him illuminating insights, can no longer be denied. Cioran, however, must hold it to be superficial for such is the image of Valéry he wants us to share: that of a man who dreamed wild dreams of intellectual power, developed a method, but finally deceived himself no less than he deceives his readers.

It can, therefore, be no surprise that he concludes by re-

---

[27] Ibid., 31.   [28] Ibid., 33.   [29] Ibid., 37.

ducing Valéry to the condition of a formalist hemmed in
with words. Leonardo, Poe, and Mallarmé were means of
closing this circle, supports for eliminating the real world
in favor of the only reality—a verbal one—he could accept:
"Les mots seuls nous préservent du néant, tel paraît être
le *fond* de sa pensée, bien que *fond* soit un terme dont il
a refusé et l'acception esthétique et métaphysique." [30] He
was obsessed by language, nuances, refractions in the same
way as Mallarmé and, by and large, the whole French tradition. One may well ask whether Cioran, writing in his
adopted French, meticulous to a fault in his observance of
classical vocabulary, syntax, and tone, realizes the implicit
rebuke he administers himself when he wags a moral finger
at France. "Depuis longtemps, depuis toujours, serait-on
tenté de soutenir, la littérature française semble avoir suc-
combé à l'envoûtement, et au despotisme du Mot. De là
sa ténuité, sa fragilité, son extrême délicatesse, et aussi son
maniérisme." [31] He finds Valéry carrying to its peak this
French concern for language, this self-awareness that is the
enemy of life, "peut-être sa ruine." At the center of a crystalline system of words is the pure self, always separate from
any one emotion or thought or act, "somme de refus, quin-
tessence de rien, néant conscient." [32]

> Amère, sombre et sonore citerne
> Sonnant dans l'âme un creux toujours futur! . . .

Thus Cioran completes the portrait of a man who could
well have authored his own *Syllogismes de l'amertume* and
La Tentation d'exister: a stateless observer, an implacable
decadent, a moralist of crepuscular Europe. In rounding
out the definition and the lesson to be drawn, his last words
have recourse—disingenuously I think—to a solemn text:
"Dans je ne sais plus quelle Upanishad, il est dit que 'l'es-

[30] Ibid., 39.   [31] Ibid., 41.   [32] Ibid., 44.

scnce de l'homme est la parole, l'essence de la parole est l'hymne.' C'est dans ce consentement et dans ce refus qu'il faut chercher la clef de ses accomplissements et de ses limites." [33]

Nevertheless, the value of these reflections is clear. On the basis of what we might call a love-hate relationship with Valéry's work, Cioran attempts to strip it of some myths, to force us to consider it afresh; and although he writes with acerbity, he may be said to resume many views, published or spoken, that have been current of late. Yet the Valéry that is offered for conviction is grossly caricatured as I should like briefly to indicate.

In the first place, the *Cahiers* are not given their due. We saw that they are as far removed from intimate journals as they are from Mallarmé's ideal work with which Cioran connects them. Valéry was pursuing what he referred to as a personal goal, learning the notes, practicing the scales of a language he could think with. His intention, his central concerns do not change. As he put it in 1943: "Ma seule 'constante', mon seul instinct permanent fut, sans doute, de me représenter de plus en plus nettement mon 'fonctionnement mental', et de garder ou de reprendre aussi souvent que possible ma liberté contre les illusions et les 'parasites' que nous impose l'emploi inévitable du langage." [34] Even this does not adequately describe his project since precise definition is not felt as being in any sense contrary to construction. Analysis is the hygiene of the mind, the care to see and know—to see what one knows— whereby knowledge comes to converge with the act of making. In this way the lesson learnt from, or read into, Leonardo's notebooks is applied in order to develop the method of "becoming universal" (*farsi universale*). Valéry

---

[33] Ibid., 44–45.   [34] *Lettres à Quelques-uns,* 244.

oscillates between the small and the great, the detail and the whole: "J'ai l'esprit unitaire—en mille morceaux," [35] he observes. He takes up time and again the same questions such as dreams and attention, memory and sensation, probing the how and not the why, the representation and not the cause. The models of consciousness he borrows from mechanics or thermodynamics; however naive he himself considers them on occasion to be, they are Vincian ways of translating "functions," like nonmechanical models or analogies he also uses, or mathematical equations. Great variety is to be found in these languages, and varied are the tones in which they are put, ranging from scorn and something aproaching violence, to abstract neutrality and even vibrant lyricism—all within the space of a few pages. Because of the very intrication of his notes he had the idea of classifying them, and to this end drew up a table of headings as for an anthology or, perhaps better, a chrestomathy ("a collection of choice passages, especially one intended to be used in the acquirement of a language"). Yet such a selection must needs fail to reflect one of the most remarkable traits of the *Cahiers:* their discontinuity underlines a prevailing liveliness, their disorder ceaselessly rearranges central themes; in sum, they trace out the pattern, the unique rhythms of a sensibility, a passion.

Cioran's summary of Valéry's poetics is similarly unfortunate, for he again takes a small part in order to portray the whole. If Poe was indeed fundamental in weaning Valéry from his early romanticism and inspiring a radical bent for artistic self-awareness, "The Philosophy of Composition" gives no idea of the brilliant criticism contained in the five volumes of *Variété*, in *Pièces sur l'art*, in *Eupalinos*. Nor does Cioran allow his readers to surmise the subtlety of the lectures given at the Collège de France between 1937 and 1945. These were not written up, but we

35 *Cahiers*, II, 137.

have a fair knowledge of what was said from the steno-
graphic record of the first twenty-nine lectures, summaries
by assiduous listeners like Georges Le Breton and Maurice
Blanchot, occasional notes by Valéry himself in the *Cahiers,*
and two or three articles. We know that his theme was not,
properly speaking, the art of poetry but a broader one
which embraced it: rather, it was the mind's act of making,
this alliance of conscious and unconscious processes in the
most complete human act possible. "Le faire, le *poïein,*
dont je veux m'occuper, est celui qui s'achève en quelque
œuvre et que je viendrai à restreindre bientôt à ce genre
d'œuvres qu'on est convenu d'appeler œuvres de l'esprit.
Ce sont celles que l'esprit veut se faire pour son propre
usage en employant à cette fin tous les moyens physiques
qui lui peuvent servir." [36] He began with an analysis of the
sensibility which for him was the foundation of being, the
most general notion of life itself, and distinguished the state
of non-attention, which is natural to it, from the making of
order, which is the task of the mind. From disorder to sensation and back again, the sensibility fluctuates: this is our
"self-variance." But we produce many more sensations than
we functionally need, just as we can perform many more
acts than those that are required for us to go on living.
These sensations and acts constitute the domain of the arts,
in which the creative mind endows useless sensations with
utility, arbitrary acts with necessity. Always the point of
reference is Valéry himself, his attempt to pursue his own
analysis, to make his own notations (or "analects"), to compose a "system" (or table of relations, or mode of transformations). His project is vast, his conceptions refined. To
call them, as Cioran does, the elucubrations of an "impo-
tent" poet is a blatant travesty.

Yet, despite his elaborate research in the name of precision, Valéry recognized that the creative act bathes in mys-

---

[36] "Première leçon du cours de poétique," *Œuvres,* I, 1342.

tery. "Tout se réduit à la conscience," he writes, "mais la conscience ne répond pas de son contenu." [37] The very disorder of the sensibility is our chance of discovering the treasure we did not know. A path can suddenly be cleared by a rhythm, a rhyme, a combination of words, something unexpected, magical. "Le commencement vrai d'un poème (qui n'est pas du tout nécessairement le premier vers) doit venir à l'auteur comme une formule magique dont il ignore encore tout ce qu'elle lui ouvrira. Car elle ouvre en effet— une demeure, une cave et un labyrinthe qui lui était intime et inconnu." [38] The decasyllabic meter he one day found himself humming led him "where he had not thought to go"—to the composition of a philosophical meditation on mortality in the framework of sea, sky and sun ("Le Cimetière marin"); an apparently meaningless octosyllable was the spur to write a few lines above it and many beneath, for reasons syntactic, phonetic, and, in the last resort of course, personal to the poet alone; and this culminated in the long monologue that expresses the discovery of poetic language in the image of a woman's travail, or the coming of a tear from the depths of being ("La Pythie"). Such poems are the direct continuation, the alternate face, of the *Cahiers* and the poetics. The shades of Leonardo, Poe, and Mallarmé are all present in Valéry's attempt to express the life of the intellect, its morning, noon, and evening, and the lonely night in which the Jeune Parque wakens to a weeping presence beside her which is her own self-awareness. But the movement of ideas is conveyed with all the concrete ambiguity of "la belle endormie"—inwardly aware, her senses vibrant, her beauty alert. In this way the play of the intellect is projected with a fierce sensuality that is at the opposite extreme from Mallarmé's characteristic evanescence, and reminiscent of the baroque poets and Rimbaud.

It would be wrong, however, to suggest that his verse is

---

[37] *L'Idée fixe, Œuvres*, II, 110.   [38] *Cahiers*, XV, 301.

today an object of widespread emulation. The very reach of its themes, the creative tension it presupposes, its loftiness of language and form make it difficult, if not impossible, to imitate. But that it "sings," that it reaches beyond ideas and words to express a complex sensibility, is sufficiently clear. Its range is admirable, from burlesque verse to elegy and pastoral, from irony to exultation. One note that recurs regularly is the shrillness of the bird—the piercing cry of instinct, the poignant reminder of the passage of time and love, the "cruel" bird that "makes a path in all things." Still another familiar tone achieves at times a musical richness that is worthy of comparison with the greatest in French poetry—Ronsard in his elegies, Racine, Chénier, Hugo, Baudelaire, Mallarmé: the "contralto" of emotion, a harmonious continuity dear to Valéry throughout his life. "A un certain âge tendre," he writes in a notebook of the time just before *La Jeune Parque,* "j'ai peut-être entendu une voix, un contralto profondément émouvant. Ce chant me dut mettre dans un état dont nul objet ne m'avait donné l'idée. Il a imprimé en moi la tension, l'attitude suprême qu'il demandait, sans donner un objet, une idée, une cause (comme fait la musique). Et je l'ai pris pour mesure des états et j'ai tendu, toute ma vie, à faire, chercher, penser ce qui eût pu nécessiter de moi—c'était correspondant à ce chant de hasard—la chose réelle, introduite, absolue dont le creux était, depuis l'enfance, préparé par ce chant oublié." [39] Of all he wrote, *La Jeune Parque* no doubt most closely approximates this melodic ideal, but all his verse tends toward it.

His *Cahiers,* poetics and poetry are, then, implicitly his self-portrait; for if he refused the facility of anecdotes and confessions, he gave time without counting to the preservation of the best moments of his thought. In his quest for a definition of the self, an epitaph as it were to place upon

[39] Ibid., IV, 587.

his grave, he found a not inappropriate one when he noted
the following words: "Je suis le lieu géométrique de toutes
les contradictions"; again: "Se connaître—n'est-ce pas sentir
qu'on pourrait être tout autre?" He underwrote seemingly
contrary maneuvers—adherence to the world and detachment from it, fragmentation and construction, voluptuousness and scorn; his attitudes to life, literature, even God,
were subject to continual restatement since they mirrored
the all-or-nothing of an intellect ready to consume or be
consumed.

Thus, at far remove from Eliot's readings, Cioran has
chosen to praise only the aphoristic observer of a disabused
civilization. Yet we know, from the studies in this book,
that here was no "esprit sans pente," as Claudel said of
Gide—a mind without inclination—but a sensibility whose
drama was constantly reenacted. He was shipwreck, regal
scepter, sunset, tomb, but also sentiment, ambiguous
splendor, will, sacrifice. Although anguish ("Angoisse, mon
véritable métier," he wrote) was in him and served to found
his determination, it also gave rise to exceptional verse:
bitter revolt, as in "Sinistre"; intense angelism, as in "Sémiramis" and "Profusion du soir"; deep affection, as well as
the "tears" of self-awareness; a persistent impulse to apprehend and hold the beloved form; the conscious folly of his
cult of the sun; both involvement and irony. He was the
poet of the equivocal relationship between body and mind,
reason and feeling, who studied their connections with the
vast resourcefulness of his *Cahiers*. His analysis, like some
proud extension of the Symbolist myth of purity, turns on
a need to rarefy and refine, the consummation of which
would be a point of solemn acceptance and lucid self-pos-
session:

40 *La Jeune Parque, Œuvres*, I, 110.

Feu vers qui se soulève une vierge de sang
Sous les espèces d'or d'un sein reconnaissant.[40]

The *Cahiers* show his search for this world of pure substance, while his poems, composed with endless care for
words and a severe sense of form, give the abundant measure of his overriding desires. We are not surprised to find
that he once observed: "Grandeur des poètes—de saisir avec
leurs mots, ce qu'ils n'ont fait qu'entrevoir dans leur esprit." [41] None more than he looked doubtingly at literature;
none tried more keenly to divest it of certain pretensions;
but it is in the last instance above all as a visionary poet—
perhaps the most scrupulously committed of any—that we
now recognize him. A few Latin words, another projected
epitaph written just two years before his death, help to resume the integrity of spirit with which his work speaks to
us: "Poeta fui, nunc poemata factus sum" [42]—"I was a poet,
and am become poetry."

41 *Cahiers*, X, 205.   42 Ibid., XXVIII, 354.

Appendix

SINISTRE

Quelle heure cogne aux membres de la coque
Ce grand coup d'ombre où craque notre sort?
Quelle puissance impalpable entre-choque
Dans nos agrès des ossements de mort?

Sur l'avant nu, l'écroulement des trombes
Lave l'odeur de la vie et du vin:
La mer élève et recreuse des tombes,
La même eau creuse et comble le ravin.

Homme hideux, en qui le cœur chavire,
Ivrogne étrange égaré sur la mer
Dont la nausée attachée au navire
Arrache à l'âme un désir de l'enfer,

Homme total, je tremble et je calcule,
Cerveau trop clair, capable du moment
Où, dans un phénomène minuscule,
Le temps se brise ainsi qu'un instrument . . .

Maudit soit-il le porc qui t'a gréée,
Arche pourrie en qui grouille le lest!

Dans tes fonds noirs, toute chose créée
Bat ton bois mort en dérive vers l'Est . . .

L'abîme et moi formons une machine
Qui jongle avec des souvenirs épars:
Je vois ma mère et mes tasses de Chine,
La putain grasse au seuil fauve des bars;

Je vois le Christ amarré sur la vergue! . . .
Il danse à mort, sombrant avec les siens;
Son œil sanglant m'éclaire cet exergue:
UN GRAND NAVIRE A PÉRI CORPS ET BIENS! . . .

AIR DE SÉMIRAMIS

Dès l'aube, chers Rayons, mon front songe à vous ceindre!
A peine il se redresse, il voit d'un œil qui dort
Sur le marbre absolu, le temps pâle se peindre,
L'heure sur moi descendre et croître jusqu'à l'or . . .

*

. . . «Existe! . . . Sois enfin toi-même! dit l'Aurore,
O grande âme, il est temps que tu formes un corps!
Hâte-toi de choisir un jour digne d'éclore,
Parmi tant d'autres feux, tes immortels trésors!

Déjà, contre la nuit, lutte l'âpre trompette!
Une lèvre vivante attaque l'air glacé;
L'or pur, de tour en tour, éclate et se répète,
Rappelant tout l'espace aux splendeurs du passé!

Remonte aux vrais regards! Tire-toi de tes ombres
Et comme du nageur, dans le plein de la mer,
Le talon tout-puissant l'expulse des eaux sombres,
Toi, frappe au fond de l'être! Interpelle ta chair,

Traverse sans retard ses invincibles trames,
Épuise l'infini de l'effort impuissant,
Et débarrasse-toi d'un désordre de drames
Qu'engendrent sur ton lit les monstres de ton sang!

J'accours de l'Orient suffire à ton caprice!
Et je te viens offrir mes plus purs aliments;
Que d'espace et de vent ta flamme se nourrisse!
Viens te joindre à l'éclat de mes pressentiments!»

*

————Je réponds! . . . Je surgis de ma profonde absence!
Mon cœur m'arrache aux morts que frôlait mon sommeil,
Et vers mon but, grand aigle éclatant de puissance,
Il m'emporte! . . . Je vole au-devant du soleil!

Je ne prends qu'une rose et fuis . . . La belle flèche
Au flanc! . . . Ma tête enfante une foule de pas . . .
Ils courent vers ma tour favorite, où la fraîche
Altitude m'appelle, et je lui tends les bras!

Monte, ô Sémiramis, maîtresse d'une spire
Qui d'un cœur sans amour s'élance au seul honneur!
Ton œil impérial a soif du grand empire
A qui ton spectre dur fait sentir le bonheur . . .

Ose l'abîme! . . . Passe un dernier pont de roses!
Je t'approche, péril! Orgueil plus irrité!
Ces fourmis sont à moi! Ces villes sont mes choses,
Ces chemins sont les traits de mon autorité!

C'est une vaste peau fauve que mon royaume!
J'ai tué le lion qui portait cette peau;
Mais encor le fumet du féroce fantôme
Flotte chargé de mort, et garde mon troupeau.

Enfin, j'offre au soleil le secret de mes charmes!
Jamais il n'a doré de seuil si gracieux!
De ma fragilité je goûte les alarmes
Entre le double appel de la terre et des cieux.

Repas de ma puissance, intelligible orgie,
Quel parvis vaporeux de toits et de forêts
Place aux pieds de la pure et divine vigie,
Ce calme éloignement d'événements secrets!

L'âme enfin sur ce faîte a trouvé ses demeures!
O de quelle grandeur, elle tient sa grandeur
Quand mon cœur soulevé d'ailes intérieures
Ouvre au ciel en moi-même une autre profondeur!

Anxieuse d'azur, de gloire consumée,
Poitrine, gouffre d'ombre aux narines de chair,
Aspire cet encens d'âmes et de fumée
Qui monte d'une ville analogue à la mer!

Soleil, soleil, regarde en toi rire mes ruches!
L'intense et sans repos Babylone bruit,
Toute rumeurs de chars, clairons, chaînes de cruches
Et plaintes de la pierre au mortel qui construit.

Qu'ils flattent mon désir de temples implacables,
Les sons aigus de scie et les cris des ciseaux,
Et ces gémissements de marbres et de câbles
Qui peuplent l'air vivant de structure et d'oiseaux!

Je vois mon temple neuf naître parmi les mondes,
Et mon vœu prendre place au séjour des destins;

Il semble de soi-même au ciel monter par ondes
Sous le bouillonnement des actes indistincts.

Peuple stupide, à qui ma puissance m'enchaîne,
Hélas! mon orgueil même a besoin de tes bras!
Et que ferait mon cœur s'il n'aimait cette haine
Dont l'innombrable tête est si douce à mes pas?

Plate, elle me murmure une musique telle
Que le calme de l'onde en fait de sa fureur,
Quand elle se rapaise aux pieds d'une mortelle
Mais qu'elle se réserve un retour de terreur.

En vain j'entends monter contre ma face auguste
Ce murmure de crainte et de férocité:
A l'image des dieux la grande âme est injuste
Tant elle s'appareille à la nécessité!

Des douceurs de l'amour quoique parfois touchée,
Pourtant nulle tendresse et nuls renoncements
Ne me laissent captive et victime couchée
Dans les puissants liens du sommeil des amants!

Baisers, baves d'amour, basses béatitudes,
O mouvements marins des amants confondus,
Mon cœur m'a conseillé de telles solitudes,
Et j'ai placé si haut mes jardins suspendus

Que mes suprêmes fleurs n'attendent que la foudre
Et qu'en dépit des pleurs des amants les plus beaux,
A mes roses, la main qui touche tombe en poudre;
Mes plus doux souvenirs bâtissent des tombeaux!

Qu'ils sont doux à mon cœur les temples qu'il enfante,
Quand tiré lentement du songe de mes seins,
Je vois un monument de masse triomphante
Joindre dans mes regards l'ombre de mes desseins!

Battez, cymbales d'or, mamelles cadencées,
Et roses palpitant sur ma pure paroi!
Que je m'évanouisse en mes vastes pensées,
Sage Sémiramis, enchanteresse et roi!

PROFUSION DU SOIR,
POÈME ABANDONNÉ . . .

Du Soleil soutenant la puissante paresse
Qui plane et s'abandonne à l'œil contemplateur,
Regard! . . . Je bois le vin céleste, et je caresse
Le grain mystérieux de l'extrême hauteur.

Je porte au sein brûlant ma lucide tendresse,
Je joue avec les feux de l'antique inventeur;
Mais le dieu par degrés qui se désintéresse
Dans la pourpre de l'air s'altère avec lenteur.

Laissant dans le champ pur battre toute l'idée,
Les travaux du couchant dans la sphère vidée
Connaissent sans oiseaux leur entière grandeur.

L'Ange frais de l'œil nu pressent dans sa pudeur,
Haute nativité d'étoile élucidée,
Un diamant agir qui berce la splendeur . . .

*

O soir, tu viens épandre un délice tranquille,
Horizon des sommeils, stupeur des cœurs pieux,
Persuasive approche, insidieux reptile,

Et rose que respire un mortel immobile
Dont l'œil doré s'engage aux promesses des cieux!

*

Sur tes ardents autels son regard favorable
Brûle, l'âme distraite, un passé précieux.
Il adore dans l'or qui se rend adorable
Bâtir d'une vapeur un temple mémorable,
Suspendre au sombre éther son risque et son récif,
Et vole, ivre des feux d'un triomphe passif,
Sur l'abîme aux ponts d'or rejoindre la Fortune;
————Tandis qu'aux bords lointains du Théâtre pensif,
Sous un masque léger glisse la mince lune . . .

*

. . . Ce vin bu, l'homme bâille, et brise le flacon.
Aux merveilles du vide il garde une rancune;
Mais le charme du soir fume sur le balcon
Une confusion de femme et de flocon . . .

*

O Conseil! . . . Station solennelle! . . . Balance
D'un doigt doré pesant les motifs du silence!
O sagesse sensible entre les dieux ardents!
————De l'espace trop beau, préserve-moi, balustre!
Là, m'appelle la mer! . . . Là, se penche l'illustre
Vénus Vertigineuse avec ses bras fondants!

*

Mon œil, quoiqu'il s'attache au sort souple des ondes,
Et boive comme en songe à l'éternel verseau,
Garde une chambre fixe et capable des mondes;

Et ma cupidité des surprises profondes
Voit à peine au travers du transparent berceau
Cette femme d'écume et d'algue et d'or que roule
Sur le sable et le sel la meule de la houle.

*

Pourtant je place aux cieux les ébats d'un esprit;
Je vois dans leurs vapeurs des terres inconnues,
Des déesses de fleurs feindre d'être des nues,
Des puissances d'orage errer à demi nues,
Et sur les roches d'air du soir qui s'assombrit,
Telle divinité s'accoude. Un ange nage.
Il restaure l'espace à chaque tour de rein.
Moi, qui jette ici-bas l'ombre d'un personnage,
Toutefois délié dane le plein souverain
Je me sens qui me trempe, et pur qui me dédaigne!
Vivant au sein futur le souvenir marin,
Tout le corps de mon choix dans mes regards se baigne!

*

Une crête écumeuse, énorme et colorée
Barre, puissamment pure, et plisse le parvis.
Roule jusqu'à mon cœur la distance dorée,
Vague! . . . Croulants soleils aux horizons ravis,
Tu n'iras pas plus loin que la ligne ignorée
Qui divise les dieux des ombres où je vis.

*

Une volute lente et longue d'une lieue
Semant les charmes lourds de sa blanche torpeur
Où se joue une joie, une soif d'être bleue,
Tire le noir navire épuisé de vapeur . . .

*

Mais pesants et neigeux les monts du crépuscule,
Les nuages trop pleins et leurs seins copieux,
Toute la majesté de l'Olympe recule,
Car voici le signal, voici l'or des adieux,
Et l'espace a humé la barque minuscule . . .

*

Lourds frontons du sommeil toujours inachevés,
Rideaux bizarrement d'un rubis relevés
Pour le mauvais regard d'une sombre planète,
Les temps sont accomplis, les désirs se sont tus,
Et dans la bouche d'or, bâillements combattus,
S'écartèlent les mots que charmait le poète . . .
Les temps sont accomplis, les désirs se sont tus.

*

Adieu, Adieu! . . . Vers vous, ô mes belles images,
Mes bras tendent toujours l'insatiable port!
Venez, effarouchés, hérissant vos plumages,
Voiliers aventureux que talonne la mort!
Hâtez-vous, hâtez-vous! . . . La nuit presse! . . . Tantale
Va périr! Et la joie éphémère des cieux!
Une rose naguère aux ténèbres fatale,
Une toute dernière rose occidentale
Pâlit affreusement sur le soir spacieux . . .
Je ne vois plus frémir au mât du belvédère,
Ivre de brise un sylphe aux couleurs de drapeau,
Et ce grand port n'est plus qu'un noir débarcadère
Couru du vent glacé que sent venir ma peau!

Fermez-vous! Fermez-vous! Fenêtres offensées!
Grands yeux qui redoutez la véritable nuit!
Et toi, de ces hauteurs d'astres ensemencées,

Accepte, fécondé de mystère et d'ennui,
Une maternité muette de pensées . . .

VALVINS

Si tu veux dénouer la forêt qui t'aère
Heureuse, tu te fonds aux feuilles, si tu es
Dans la fluide yole à jamais littéraire,
Traînant quelques soleils ardemment situés

Aux blancheurs de son flanc que la Seine caresse
Emue, ou pressentant l'après-midi chanté,
Selon que le grand bois trempe une longue tresse
Et mélange ta voile au meilleur de l'été.

Mais toujours près de toi que le silence livre
Aux cris multipliés de tout le brut azur,
L'ombre de quelque page éparse d'aucun livre

Tremble, reflet de voile vagabonde sur
La poudreuse peau de la rivière verte
Parmi le long regard de la Seine entr'ouverte.

PSAUME SUR UNE VOIX

A demi-voix,
D'une voix douce et faible disant de grandes choses;
D'importantes, d'étonnantes, de profondes et justes choses,

D'une voix douce et faible.
La menace du tonnerre, la présence d'absolus
Dans une voix de rouge-gorge,
Dans le détail fin d'une flûte, et la délicatesse du son pur.
Tout le soleil suggéré
Au moyen d'un demi-sourire.
(O demi-voix),
Et d'une sorte de murmure
En français infiniment pur.
Qui n'eût saisi les mots, qui l'eût ouï à quelque distance,
Aurait cru qu'il disait des riens.
Et c'étaient des riens pour l'oreille
Rassurée.
Mais ce contraste et cette musique,
Cette voix ridant l'air à peine,
Cette puissance chuchotée,
Ces perspectives, ces découvertes,
Ces abîmes et ces manœuvres devinés,

Ce sourire congédiant l'univers! . . .

Je songe aussi pour finir
Au bruit de soie seul et discret
D'un feu qui se consume en créant toute la chambre,
Et qui se parle.
Ou qui me parle
Presque pour soi.

LA JEUNE PARQUE

Je n'implorerai plus que tes faibles clartés,
Longtemps sur mon visage envieuse de fondre,

Très imminente larme, et seule à me répondre,
Larme qui fais trembler à mes regards humains
Une variété de funèbres chemins;
Tu procèdes de l'âme, orgueil du labyrinthe.
Tu me portes du cœur cette goutte contrainte,
Cette distraction de mon suc précieux
Qui vient sacrifier mes ombres sur mes yeux,
Tendre libation de l'arrière-pensée!
D'une grotte de crainte au fond de moi creusée
Le sel mystérieux suinte muette l'eau.
D'où nais-tu? Quel travail toujours triste et nouveau
Te tire avec retard, larme, de l'ombre amère?
Tu gravis mes degrés de mortelle et de mère,
Et déchirant ta route, opiniâtre faix,
Dans le temps que je vis, les lenteurs que tu fais
M'étouffent . . . Je me tais, buvant ta marche sûre . . .
————Qui t'appelle au secours de ma jeune blessure?

                                          (Lines 280–298)

LA PYTHIE

Noirs témoins de tant de lumières
Ne cherchez plus . . . Pleurez, mes yeux! . . .
O pleurs dont les sources premières
Sont trop profondes dans les cieux! . . .
Jamais plus amère demande! . . .
Mais la prunelle la plus grande
De ténèbres se doit nourrir! . . .
Tenant notre race atterrée,
La distance désespérée
Nous laisse le temps de mourir!

Entends, mon âme, entends ces fleuves!
Quelles cavernes sont ici?
Est-ce mon sang? . . . Sont-ce les neuves
Rumeurs des ondes sans merci?
Mes secrets sonnent leurs aurores!
Tristes airains, tempes sonores,
Que dites-vous de l'avenir!
Frappez, frappez, dans une roche,
Abattez l'heure la plus proche . . .
Mes deux natures vont s'unir!

O formidablement gravie,
Et sur d'effrayants échelons,
Je sens dans l'arbre de ma vie
La mort monter de mes talons!
Le long de ma ligne frileuse,
Le doigt mouillé de la fileuse
Trace une atroce volonté!
Et par sanglots grimpe la crise
Jusque dans ma nuque où se brise
Une cime de volupté!

(Lines 171–200)

LA FILEUSE

Lilia . . . , neque nent.

Assise, la fileuse au bleu de la croisée
Où le jardin mélodieux se dodeline;
Le rouet ancien qui ronfle l'a grisée.

Lasse, ayant bu l'azur, de filer la câline

Chevelure, à ses doigts si faibles évasive,
Elle songe, et sa tête petite s'incline.

Un arbuste et l'air pur font une source vive
Qui, suspendue au jour, délicieuse arrose
De ses pertes de fleurs le jardin de l'oisive.

Une tige, où le vent vagabond se repose,
Courbe le salut vain de sa grâce étoilée,
Dédiant magnifique, au vieux rouet, sa rose.

Mais la dormeuse file une laine isolée;
Mystérieusement l'ombre frêle se tresse
Au fil de ses doigts longs et qui dorment, filée.

Le songe se dévide avec une paresse
Angélique, et sans cesse, au doux fuseau crédule,
La chevelure ondule au gré de la caresse . . .

Derrière tant de fleurs, l'azur se dissimule,
Fileuse de feuillage et de lumière ceinte:
Tout le ciel vert se meurt. Le dernier arbre brûle.

Ta sœur, la grande rose où sourit une sainte,
Parfume ton front vague au vent de son haleine
Innocente, et tu crois languir . . . Tu es éteinte

Au bleu de la croisée où tu filais la laine.

AU BOIS DORMANT

La princesse, dans un palais de rose pure,
Sous les murmures, sous la mobile ombre dort;

Et de corail ébauche une parole obscure
Quand les oiseaux perdus mordent ses bagues d'or.

Elle n'écoute ni les gouttes, dans leurs chutes,
Tinter d'un siècle vide au lointain le trésor,
Ni, sur la forêt vague, un vent fondu de flûtes
Déchirer la rumeur d'une phrase de cor.

Laisse, longue, l'écho rendormir la diane,
O toujours plus égale à la molle liane
Qui se balance et bat tes yeux ensevelis.

Si proche de ta joue et si lente la rose
Ne va pas dissiper ce délice de plis
Secrètement sensible au rayon qui s'y pose.

BALLET

Sur tes lèvres, sommeil d'or où l'ombreuse bouche
Bâille (pour mieux se taire à tout le bête azur),
Sens-tu, tel un vil astre indifférent, la mouche
Transparente tourner autour du mot très pur

Que tu ne diras pas—fleur, diamant ou pierre
Ou rose jeune encor dans un vierge jardin
Une nudité fraîche sous une paupière
Balancée, amusée hors du chaos mondain.

Cette minute ailée éparpille un sonore
Vol d'étincelles au vent solaire pour briller
Sur tes dents, sur tes hauts fruits de chair, sur l'aurore

Des cheveux où j'eus peur à la voir scintiller
Petit feu naturel d'un sidéral insecte
Né sous le souffle d'or qui tes songes humecte.

ANNE

Anne qui se mélange au drap pâle et délaisse
Des cheveux endormis sur ses yeux mal ouverts
Mire ses bras lointains tournés avec mollesse
Sur la peau sans couleur du ventre découvert.

Elle vide, elle enfle d'ombre sa gorge lente,
Et comme un souvenir pressant ses propres chairs,
Une bouche brisée et pleine d'eau brûlante
Roule le goût immense et le reflet des mers.

Enfin désemparée et libre d'être fraîche,
La dormeuse déserte aux touffes de couleur
Flotte sur son lit blême, et d'une lèvre sèche,
Tette dans la ténèbre un souffle amer de fleur.

Et sur le linge où l'aube insensible se plisse,
Tombe, d'un bras de glace effleuré de carmin,
Toute une main défaite et perdant le délice
A travers ses doigts nus dénoués de l'humain.

Au hasard! A jamais, dans le sommeil sans hommes,
Pur des tristes éclairs de leurs embrassements,
Elle laisse rouler les grappes et les pommes
Puissantes, qui pendaient aux treilles d'ossement,

Qui riaient, dans leur ambre appelant les vendanges,
Et dont le nombre d'or de riches mouvements

Invoquait la vigueur et les gestes étranges
Que pour tuer l'amour inventent les amants . . .

*

Sur toi, quand le regard de leurs âmes s'égare,
Leur cœur bouleversé change comme leurs voix,
Car les tendres apprêts de leur festin barbare
Hâtent les chiens ardents qui tremblent dans ces rois.

A peine effleurent-ils de doigts errants ta vie,
Tout leur sang les accable aussi lourd que la mer
Et quelque violence aux abîmes ravie
Jette ces blancs nageurs sur tes roches de chair.

Récifs délicieux, Ile toute prochaine,
Terre tendre, promise aux démons apaisés,
L'amour t'aborde, armé des regards de la haine,
Pour combattre dans l'ombre une hydre de baisers!

*

Ah, plus nue et qu'imprègne une prochaine aurore,
Si l'or triste interroge un tiède contour,
Rentre au plus pur de l'ombre où le Même s'ignore,
Et te fais un vain marbre ébauché par le jour!

Laisse au pâle rayon ta lèvre violée
Mordre dans un sourire un long germe de pleur,
Masque d'âme au sommeil à jamais immolée
Sur qui la paix soudaine a surpris la douleur!

Plus jamais redorant tes ombres satinées,
La vieille aux doigts de feu qui fendent les volets
Ne viendra t'arracher aux grasses matinées
Et rendre au doux soleil tes joyeux bracelets . . .

Mais suave, de l'arbre extérieur, la palme
Vaporeuse remue au delà du remords,
Et dans le feu, parmi trois feuilles, l'oiseau calme
Commence le chant seul qui réprime les morts.

MA NUIT, LE TOUR DORMANT . . .

Ma nuit, le tour dormant de ton flanc pur amène
Un tiède fragment d'épaule pleine, peu
Sur ma bouche, et buvant cette vivante, dieu
Je me tais sur ma rive opposée à l'humaine.

Toute d'ombre et d'instinct amassée à ma peine,
Chère cendre insensible aux fantômes du feu,
Tu me tiens à demi dans le pli de ton vœu
O toujours plus absente et toujours plus prochaine.

Et ce bras mollement à tes songes m'enchaîne
Dont je sens m'effleurer le fluide dessin
De fraîcheur descendue au velours d'une haleine

Jusqu'à la masse d'ambre et d'âme de ton sein
Où perdu que je suis comme dans une mère
Tu respires l'enfant de ma seule chimère.

LA DORMEUSE

A Lucien Fabre.

Quels secrets dans son cœur brûle ma jeune amie,
Ame par le doux masque aspirant une fleur?
De quels vains aliments sa naïve chaleur
Fait ce rayonnement d'une femme endormie?

Souffle, songes, silence, invincible accalmie,
Tu triomphes, ô paix plus puissante qu'un pleur,
Quand de ce plein sommeil l'onde grave et l'ampleur
Conspirent sur le sein d'une telle ennemie.

Dormeuse, amas doré d'ombres et d'abandons,
Ton repos redoutable est chargé de tels dons,
O biche avec langueur longue auprès d'une grappe,

Que malgré l'âme absente, occupée aux enfers,
Ta forme au ventre pur qu'un bras fluide drape,
Veille; ta forme veille, et mes yeux sont ouverts.

LA FAUSSE MORTE

Humblement, tendrement, sur le tombeau charmant,
Sur l'insensible monument,

Que d'ombres, d'abandons, et d'amour prodiguée,
    Forme ta grâce fatiguée,
Je meurs, je meurs sur toi, je tombe et je m'abats,   .

Mais à peine abattu sur le sépulcre bas,
Dont la close étendue aux cendres me convie,
Cette morte apparente, en qui revient la vie,
Frémit, rouvre les yeux, m'illumine et me mord,
Et m'arrache toujours une nouvelle mort
    Plus précieuse que la vie.

NEIGE

Quel silence, battu d'un simple bruit de bêche! . . .

Je m'éveille, attendu par cette neige fraîche
Qui me saisit au creux de ma chère chaleur.
Mes yeux trouvent un jour d'une dure pâleur
Et ma chair langoureuse a peur de l'innocence.
Oh! combien de flocons, pendant ma douce absence,
Durent les sombres cieux perdre toute la nuit!
Quel pur désert tombé des ténèbres sans bruit
Vint effacer les traits de la terre enchantée
Sous cette ample candeur sourdement augmentée
Et la fondre en un lieu sans visage et sans voix,
Où le regard perdu relève quelques toits
Qui cachent leur trésor de vie accoutumée
A peine offrant le vœu d'une vague fumée.

A L'AURORE . . .

A l'aurore, avant la chaleur,
La tendresse de la couleur
A peine éparse sur le monde,
Étonne et blesse la douleur.

O Nuit, que j'ai toute soufferte,
Souffrez ce sourire des cieux
Et cette immense fleur offerte
Sur le front d'un jour gracieux.

Grande offrande de tant de roses,
Le mal vous peut-il soutenir
Et voir rougissantes les choses
A leurs promesses revenir?

J'ai vu se feindre tant de songes
Sur mes ténèbres sans sommeil
Que je range entre les mensonges
Même la force du soleil,

Et que je doute si j'accueille
Par le dégoût, par le désir,
Ce jour très jeune sur la feuille
Dont l'or vierge se peut saisir.

HEURE

L'HEURE me vient sourire et se faire sirène:
Tout s'éclaire d'un jour que jamais je ne vis:
Danseras-tu longtemps, Rayon, sur le parvis
    De l'âme sombre et souveraine?

Voici l'HEURE, la soif, la source et la sirène.

Pour toi, le passé brûle, HEURE qui m'assouvis;
Enfin, splendeur du seul, ô biens que j'ai ravis,
J'aime ce que je suis: ma solitude est reine!
Mes plus secrets démons, librement asservis
Accomplissent dans l'or de l'air même où je vis
Une sagesse pure aux lucides avis:
    Ma présence est toute sereine.

Voici l'HEURE, la soif, la source et la sirène,

Danseras-tu longtemps, rayon, sur le parvis
Du soir, devant l'œil noir de ma nuit souveraine?

L'OISEAU CRUEL . . .

L'oiseau cruel toute la nuit me tint
Au point aigu du délice d'entendre
Sa voix qu'adresse une fureur si tendre
Au ciel brûlant d'astres jusqu'au matin.

Tu perces l'âme et fixes le destin
De tel regard qui ne peut se reprendre;
Tout ce qui fut tu le changes en cendre,
O voix trop haute, extase de l'instinct . . .

L'aube dans l'ombre ébauche le visage
D'un jour très beau qui déjà ne m'est rien:
Un jour de plus n'est qu'un vain paysage.

Qu'est-ce qu'un jour sans le visage tien?
Non! . . . Vers la nuit mon âme retournée
Refuse l'aube et la jeune journée.

CHANSON A PART

Que fais-tu? De tout.
Que vaux-tu? Ne sais,
Présages, essais,
Puissance et dégoût . . .
Que vaux-tu? Ne sais . . .
Que veux-tu? Rien, mais tout.

Que sais tu? L'ennui.
Que peux-tu? Songer.
Songer pour changer
Chaque jour en nuit.
Que sais-tu? Songer
Pour changer d'ennui.

Que veux-tu? Mon bien.
Que dois-tu? Savoir,
Prévoir et pouvoir

Qui ne sert de rien.
Que crains-tu? Vouloir.
Qui es-tu? Mais rien!

Où vas-tu? A mort.
Qu'y faire? Finir,
Ne plus revenir
Au coquin de sort.
Où vas-tu? Finir.
Que faire? Le mort.

LE PHILOSOPHE
ET LA "JEUNE PARQUE"

Cette sorte de Fable fut écrite en guise de Préface au Com-
mentaire de la «Jeune Parque», par Alain.

La Jeune Parque, un jour, trouva son Philosophe:

«Ah, dit-elle, de quelle étoffe
Je saurai donc mon être fait . . .
A plus d'un je produis l'effet
D'une personne tout obscure;
Chaque mortel qui n'a point cure
De songer ni d'approfondir,
Au seul nom que je porte a tôt fait de bondir.
Quand ce n'est la pitié, j'excite la colère,
Et parmi les meilleurs esprits,
S'il est quelqu'un qui me tolère,
Le reste tient qu'il s'est mépris.
Ces gens disent qu'il faut qu'une muse ne cause

Non plus de peines qu'une rose!
Qui la respire a purement plaisir.
Mais les amours sont les plus précieuses
Qu'un long labeur de l'âme et du désir
Mène à leurs fins délicieuses.
Aux cœurs profonds ne suffit point
D'un regard, qu'un baiser rejoint,
Pour qu'on vole au plus vif d'une brève aventure . . .
Non! . . . L'objet vraiment cher s'orne de vos tourments,
Vos yeux en pleurs lui voient des diamants,
L'amère nuit en fait la plus tendre peinture.
C'est pourquoi je me garde et mes secrets charmants.
Mon cœur veut qu'on me force, et vous refuse, Amants
Que rebutent les nœuds de ma belle ceinture.
Mon Père l'a prescrit: j'appartiens à l'effort.
Mes ténèbres me font maîtresse de mon sort,
Et ne livrent enfin qu'à l'heureux petit nombre
Cette innocente MOI que fait frémir son ombre
Cependant que l'Amour ébranle ses genoux.
CERTES, d'un grand désir je fus l'œuvre anxieuse . . .
Mais je ne suis en moi pas plus mystérieuse
Que le plus simple d'entre vous . . .
Mortels, vous êtes chair, souvenance, présage;
Vous fûtes; vous serez; vous portez tel visage:
Vous êtes tout; vous n'êtes rien,
Supports du monde et roseaux que l'air brise,
Vous VIVEZ . . . Quelle surprise! . . .
Un mystère est tout votre bien,
Et cet arcane en vous s'étonnerait du mien?
Que seriez-vous, si vous n'étiez mystère?
Un peu de songe sur la terre,
Un peu d'amour, de faim, de soif, qui font des pas
Dont aucun ne fuit le trépas,
Et vous partageriez le pur destin des bêtes
Si les Dieux n'eussent mis, comme un puissant ressort,
Au plus intime de vos têtes,

Le grand don de ne rien comprendre à votre sort.
«Qui suis-je?» dit au jour le vivant qui s'éveille
       Et que redresse le soleil.
«Où vais-je?» fait l'esprit qu'immole le sommeil,
Quand la nuit le recueille en sa propre merveille.
     Le plus habile est piqué de l'abeille,
Dans l'âme du moindre homme un serpent se remord;
Un sot même est orné d'énigmes par la mort
Qui le pare et le drape en personnage grave,
Glacé d'un tel secret qu'il en demeure esclave.
   ALLEZ! . . . Que tout fût clair, tout vous semblerait vain!
Votre ennui peuplerait un univers sans ombre
D'une impassible vie aux âmes sans levain.
Mais quelque inquiétude est un présent divin.
L'espoir qui dans vos yeux brille sur un seuil sombre
Ne se repose pas sur un monde trop sûr;
De toutes vos grandeurs le principe est obscur.
Les plus profonds humains, incompris de soi-mêmes,
D'une certaine nuit tirent des biens suprêmes
Et les très purs objets de leurs nobles amours.
Un trésor ténébreux fait l'éclat de vos jours:
Un silence est la source étrange des poèmes.
Connaissez donc en vous le fond de mon discours:
C'est de vous que j'ai pris l'ombre qui vous éprouve.
Qui s'égare en soi-même aussitôt me retrouve.
Dans l'obscur de la vie où se perd le regard,
      Le temps travaille, la mort couve,
      Une Parque y songe à l'écart.
C'est MOI . . . Tentez d'aimer cette jeune rebelle:
    «Je suis noire, mais je suis belle»
Comme chante l'Amante, au Cantique du Roi,
      Et si j'inspire quelque effroi,
Poème que je suis, à qui ne peut me suivre,
    Quoi de plus prompt que de fermer un livre?

 C'est ainsi que l'on se délivre
De ces écrits si clairs qu'on n'y trouve que soi.»

LE SONNET D'IRENE
par Monsieur de Saint Ambroyse
1644

De ses divers désirs combien qu'Elle se vante,
Pour mon cœur enchanté Son dire est un détour;
Elle n'ayme qu'un seul, Elle ayme dans l'Amour
Une personne rare, et supresme et sçavante.

Vainement se plaist-Elle à Se feindre mouvante
Et de trop de regards le divin quarrefour;
Cette beauté n'est point pour les galants d'un jour
Qui porte un corps si pur d'éternelle vivante!

Vous m'avez beau parler d'une trouppe d'amants,
Vous parer de désirs comme de diamants,
Et me vouloir au cœur placer plus d'une flèche,

J'en souffre, Irène d'or, mais j'en souffre sans foy,
Instruit qu'en chaque aurore, ô Rose toute fraîche,
Tu ne vis qu'en moy seul et ne Te plays qu'en moy.

Index

"Abeille(L')," 266
Agathe ou la sainte du sommeil,
  163–164
"Air de Sémiramis," viii, ix, 36–
  73, 128, 135, 167, 199, 214, 261,
  303, 318
Alain, 218, 220, 221; *Commentaires
  de "Charmes,"* 218
"A l'aurore," 166, 175–181, 200
Album de vers anciens, 7, 36–37,
  52, 74, 76, 79, 96, 102, 121, 122,
  143, 151, 152, 153, 155, 159, 201
"Ambroise," 231
Ame(L') et la Danse, 266
Amphion, 220
Analecta, 141
"Ange(L')," 72–73, 145, 195, 213,
  230, 266
"Anne," 52, 155–157, 160, 162
Apollinaire, Guillaume, 302; *Al-
  cools,* 302
"Au bois dormant," 152–154, 157,
  162
Auden, W. H., 6; *The Enchafèd
  Flood,* 6
"Au-dessous d'un portrait," ix
"Au Platane," 91, 144, 163, 174,
  260
"Aurore," 4, 47, 167, 269
Austin, Lloyd James, 120
"Au sujet du Cimetière marin," 22
Autres Rhumbs, 127
"Avant propos à la Connaissance
  de la Déesse," 283, 285, 292, 301
"Avis au lecteur," 4

"Baignée," 155
Baldensperger, Fernand, 14
"Ballet," 154–155, 157, 162
Balzac, Honoré de, 273–274; *La
  Comédie humaine,* 274
Banville, Théodore de, 40, 42;
  Œuvres, 41; *Les Princesses,* 40
Baudelaire, Charles, ix, 5, 28, 29,
  139, 151, 163, 186, 197, 212, 235,
  262, 274, 275, 282, 283, 291, 292,
  295, 296, 302, 317; *Les Fleurs du
  mal,* 296; *Mon Cœur mis à nu,*
  235
"Belle (La) au bois dormant," 152–
  153
Bergson, Henri, 246, 283
Blanchot, Maurice, 117, 315
"Bois(Le) amical," 143
Boltzmann, Ludwig, 251
Borel, Emile, 252
Bréal, Michel, 133
Brémond, Henri, 296
Brisson, Pierre, 283
Brontë, Charlotte, *Jane Eyre,* 247
Byron, Lord, 5

Cahiers, vii, xii, xlii, 2, 3, 10, 26,
  27, 28, 32, 34, 36, 43, 72, 78, 79,
  84, 86, 87, 107, 114, 117, 126, 127,
  138, 142, 147, 150, 151, 161, 163,
  165, 167, 199, 201, 202, 203, 204,
  210, 211, 212, 214, 215, 219, 220,
  226, 230, 232, 233, 234, 235, 236,
  237, 243, 244–281, 302, 304, 309,
  313, 314, 315, 316, 317, 318, 319

349

Cain, Lucienne Julien, 74, 80, 84;
    Trois Essais sur Paul Valéry, 80,
    84
"Calepin d'un poète," 162
"Calypso," 268
Cantate(La) du Narcisse, xi, 220,
    266
"Cantique des colonnes," 290
"Cantiques spirituels," 48
Cantor, Georg, 251
"Caresse(La)," 4
Carnot, Sadi, 251
Carré, Jean-Marie, *La Vie aven-
    tureuse d'Arthur Rimbaud*, 275
"Ceinture(La)," 181, 198
Cendrars, Blaise, 302
"César," 7, 37
"Chanson à part," 209–217, 228
Chapon, François, ed. *Paul Valéry,
    Pré-Teste*, 76, 85
Charmes, 1, 2, 3, 4, 7, 9, 22, 31,
    37, 43, 47, 48, 49, 50, 52, 76, 79,
    88, 91, 141, 142, 147, 157, 159,
    160, 163, 168, 182, 184, 201, 202,
    220, 238, 257, 271, 283, 289, 290,
    298, 304
Chénier, André, 262, 317
Chiari, Joseph, *Contemporary
    French Poetry*, 284
"Cimetière(Le) marin," 2, 4, 15, 17,
    19, 22, 23, 34, 61, 65, 69–70, 76,
    77, 79, 90, 115, 143, 174, 188,
    207, 227, 232, 264, 268, 271, 280,
    282, 286, 287, 291, 292, 312, 316
Cioran, E. M., xii, xiii, 282, 307–
    318; *Valéry face à ses idoles*,
    307; *La Tentation d'exister*,
    312; *Syllogismes de l'amertume*,
    312
Claudel, Paul, 8, 23, 57, 70, 74,
    115, 121, 129, 134, 149, 157, 222,
    318; *La Cantate à trois voix*,
    146–147; *Journal*, 70, 115;
    Œuvres en prose, 23, 129, 157,
    222
Clausius, Rudolf Julius Emanuel,
    251
Coleridge, Samuel Taylor, 5
"Colloque dans un être," 5
"Comme au bord de la mer," 25
"Comme le temps est calme . . . ,"
    137

Corbière, Tristan, 282, 301
Corona, 201, 202
Coste, Albert, 213
Courbet, Gustave, 152
Crébillon, 41
Crow, Christine M., *Paul Valéry:
    Consciousness and Nature*, 281

Dante, 270, 284–287, 300; *Divine
    Comedy*, 300
Degas, Edgar, ix, 8, 38, 39, 40, 42,
    43, 69, 149, 200
Degas Danse Dessin, 40
de Gaulle, Charles, 247
"De l'éminente dignité des arts
    du feu," 169
"Dernière visite à Mallarmé," 126
Descartes, René, 253
Dimier, Louis, 38, 43
"Discours sur Emile Verhaeren,"
    32
"Dormeuse(La)," 144, 160–161, 162
Dubu, Jean, 152
Duchenne, Guillaume, 251
Duchesne-Guillemin,   Jacques,
    Etudes pour un Paul Valéry, 4,
    217, 200

"Ebauche d'un Serpent," 2, 9, 66,
    90, 211, 243, 255, 256, 266, 268,
    283, 288, 289, 292
Ecrits divers sur Paul Valéry, 120
Eliot, T. S., xii, 81, 282–306, 309;
    Essays Ancient and Modern,
    304; *Four Quartets*, 81, 294, 302;
    Murder in the Cathedral, 285;
    *Prufrock and Other Observa-
    tions*, 283; *The Sacred Wood*,
    285; *The Waste Land*, 283, 290,
    302
Entretiens sur Paul Valéry, 120
Eunapius, *Lives of the Philoso-
    phers*, 11
Eupalinos, 266, 314

Faivre, J. L., 166
Fasano, Giancarlo, 76–77
"Fausse Morte (La)," 161–162, 220,
    304
"Fileuse(La)," 96, 151–153, 157, 162
"Final," 5
Folliot, Denise, 298

Fourment, Gustave, 32, 255
Fournier, Alain, 283
"Fragments des mémoires d'un poème," x
"Fragments du Narcisse," 99, 143, 145, 161, 166, 188, 213, 214, 220, 243, 260, 266

Galpérine, Charles, ed. (with Jacques Petit) Paul Claudel, *Œuvres en prose,* 23, 129, 157, 222
Gautier, Théophile, 5, 174
Gibbs, Josiah Willard, 251, 253
Gide, André, 6, 8, 24, 32, 118, 119, 130, 131, 153, 155, 174, 200, 213, 230, 234, 244, 276–277, 284, 318; *Les Faux-Monnayeurs,* 230; *Journal,* 130
Gillet, Reverend, 33
Gluck, Christoph Willibald, 263
Goethe, Johann Wolfgang von, 130, 273
Gracián, Baltasar, *Oráculo manual,* 235
"Grenades(Les)," 4, 174

Hamilton, William Rowan, 141, 253
Hardy, Thomas, 21
Hegel, Friedrich, 278, 308
"Hélène," 143, 145
Heredia, José María de, 259
"Heure," 4, 87, 88, 166, 181–200
Histoires brisées, 268
"Homme(L') et la coquille," 14, 266
Honnegger, Arthur, 69
Hopkins, Gerard Manley, 5
Hugo, Victor, 41, 47, 78, 99, 143, 219, 268, 274, 283, 291, 317; *Les Contemplations,* 78; *Dieu,* 268; *La Légende des siècles,* 41
Huysmans, Joris-Karl, 133
Hytier, Jean, 40; ed. Paul Valéry, *Œuvres,* ix, x, 4, 22, 48, 52, 54, 67, 75, 86, 96, 122, 140, 141, 145, 151, 159, 160, 161, 162, 163, 164, 166, 171, 178, 181, 195, 203, 206, 208, 210, 211, 212, 213, 214, 215, 216, 217, 218, 219, 220, 221, 223, 224, 232, 233, 243, 252, 303, 304,

305, 308, 316, 318; *Questions de littérature,* 40

Idée(L') fixe, 316
"Il y a cinquante ans . . . ," 204
"Insinuant(L')," 4, 269
"Inspirations méditerranéennes," 54
"Intérieur," 184, 186, 192, 193
"Introduction à la méthode de Léonard de Vinci," 36, 133, 283

Jean-Aubry, G., ed. (with Henri Mondor) Stéphane Mallarmé, *Œuvres complètes,* 101, 114, 119, 123
"Je disais quelquefois à Stéphane Mallarmé . . . ," 304
Jeune Parque (La), x, 9, 43, 72, 73, 76, 77, 79, 91, 99, 105, 115, 116, 117, 130, 139–140, 144–148, 150, 151, 152, 160, 164, 166, 167, 174, 201, 202, 203, 218, 219, 224, 226, 232, 244, 260, 262, 263, 264, 267–268, 272, 280, 282, 283, 285, 289, 290, 298, 316, 317, 318
John of the Cross, St., 238, 265

Kahn, Gustave, 129
Keats, John, 152

La Fontaine, Jean de, 217, 219, 220; "Adonis," 219; "Daphnis et Alcimadure," 219; *Fables,* 227
Laforgue, Jules, 282, 301, 302
Lamartine, Alphonse de, 78, 291
Langevin, Paul, 252
Laplace, Pierre Simon, 251
Laurette, Pierre, *Le Thème de l'arbre chez Paul Valéry,* 281
Léautaud, Paul, 117
Lebey, Edouard, 283
Le Breton, Georges, 315
Leconte de Lisle, Charles-Marie-René, 285
Le Dantec, Y.-G., ed. Paul Verlaine, *Œuvres poétiques complètes,* 175
Lefèvre, Frédéric, 145
Lemoisne, Paul A., *Degas et son œuvre,* 39

Leonardo da Vinci, 39, 42, 263, 307, 310, 311, 312, 314, 316
"Le Philosophe et la 'Jeune Parque'," 217–229
Lettres à Quelques-uns, 33, 34, 120, 209, 213, 218, 313
"Lettre sur Mallarmé," 308
Levaillant, Jean, 166
Lewis, Cecil Day, 282
"Littérature," 127
Louÿs, Pierre, 7, 230
Lust, 267

"Mal(Le) d'amour," 208
Malherbe, François de, 232, 291, 300
Mallarmé, Mademoiselle Geneviève, 124, 131
Mallarmé, Madame Stéphane, 124
Mallarmé, Stéphane, vii, viii, ix, x, 6, 28, 32, 34, 36, 43, 50, 66, 73, 80, 99, 101, 114, 117–136, 138–140, 145, 151, 154, 155, 158, 164, 185, 198, 212, 262, 263, 277–280, 282, 291, 295, 296, 307, 308, 309, 312, 313, 316, 317; *L'Après-midi d'un faune,* 123, 130, 280, 308; *Divagations,* 128; *Hérodiade,* 130, 131, 132, 280; *Igitur,* 164; *Les Mots anglais,* 134; *Propos sur la poésie,* 135; *Vers de circonstance,* 130
Mallet, Robert, ed. André Gide et Paul Valéry, *Correspondance,* 2, 6, 8, 25, 87, 118, 131, 153, 200, 213, 215, 216, 218, 233, 309
"Ma nuit . . . ," 157–160, 162
Mathews, Jackson, 282
Mauvaises Pensées et autres, 140
Mélange, ix, 4, 24, 25, 67, 140, 141, 171, 181, 204, 208, 232
Merrill, Stuart, 291
"Messe(La) angélique," 143
Mockel, Albert, 209
Mondor, Henri, 279, ed. Stéphane Mallarmé, *Œuvres complètes,* 101, 114, 119, 123; *Vie de Mallarmé,* 279
Mon Faust, x, 74, 75, 181, 246, 267, 271, 273
Monod, Julien P., 4, 74, 75, 120, 124, 125, 126, 154, 245; *Regard sur Paul Valéry,* 4, 6, 74, 84, 120, 124*
Monsieur Teste,* 36, 52, 171, 211, 226, 262, 307
Montesquieu, Charles de Secondat, *Lettres persanes,* 311
Morceaux choisis, 25, 205
Moréas, Jean, 291
"Mort(La) du juste," 142
Musset, Alfred de, 219, 291

Nadal, Octave, 8; ed. Paul Valéry et Gustave Fourment, *Correspondance,* 33
"Naissance de Vénus," 37
"Narcisse parle," 69, 143
"Neige," 166–175, 200
Nerval, Gérard de, 5, 290
Newton, Isaac, 25
Nietzsche, Friedrich, 263

"Ode secrète," 4, 268
"Oiseau(L') cruelle," 176, 180, 202–209, 217, 229, 268
"Orphée," 37
Osgood, Mrs. Frances, 275

"Palme," 4, 47
"Pas (Les)," 49, 264–266
Pascal, Blaise, 85, 223, 271–272, 273, 282, 311; *Pensées,* 272
Paulhan, Jean, 160
Paul Valéry vivant, 293
Péladan, Joséphin, 41
Perrin, Jean, 252
Petit, Jacques, ed. (with Charles Galpérine) Paul Claudel, *Œuvres en prose,* 23, 129, 157, 122; ed. (with François Varillon) Paul Claudel, *Journal,* 70
Petrarch, 206
"Philosophie de la danse," 195
Pièces diverses, 1, 41, 182, 201, 268, 270
Pièces sur l'art, 314
Plato, 278
Plotinus, 11
Poe, Edgar Allan, ix, 6, 7, 9, 15, 16, 29, 85, 125, 139, 251, 263, 273, 275, 295, 296, 297, 298, 299, 305, 307, 309, 310, 312, 314, 316;

The Adventures of Arthur Gordon Pym, 7, 16, 18, 27, 29, 30
"Poésie brute," 166
"Poésie et pensée abstraite," 303
Poésies, 201
Poincaré, Henri, 251
Pompignan, Lefranc de, 41
Porphyry, 11
"Pour votre Hêtre 'Suprême,' " 91
"Profusion du soir," viii, ix, 43, 45, 73, 74–116, 135, 181, 199, 261, 303, 318
"Propos me concernant," 212
Proust, Marcel, 204, 246
Prudentius, *Apotheosis*, 9
"Psaume sur une voix," 127–129, 135
"Purs drames," 86, 87, 143
"Pythie (La)," x, 2, 4, 9, 46, 49, 50, 90, 144, 147, 202, 238, 260, 268, 314

Quelques Vers anciens, 102
Quillard, Pierre, 124

Racine, Jean, 40, 99, 262, 272, 273, 317
"Rameur (Le)," 2, 49
Rhumbs, 14, 221
Rimbaud, Arthur, ix, 6–9, 13, 14, 28, 29, 33, 37, 70, 80, 124, 262, 273, 275–276, 290, 316
Rivière, Jacques, 304
Robinson, Judith, *L'Analyse de l'esprit dans les Cahiers de Valéry*, 281; ed. Paul Valéry, *Cahiers*, 281
Romains, Jules, 142, 303; *Les Hommes de bonne volonté*, 142
Ronsard, Pierre de, 271, 317, *Odes*, 271
Rossini, Gioacchino, 41
Rouart-Valéry, Agathe, 4, 130

Saint-Amant (Marc-Antoine Girard), 233
Sartre, Jean-Paul, 6
Scarfe, Francis, *The Art of Paul Valéry*, 41
Sémiramis, 69, 266
Sidgwick, Henry Dwight, 284

"Sinistre," viii, 1–35, 135, 261, 269, 303, 318
"Situation de Baudelaire," 291
Solitaire(Le), 181, 259, 267
"Sonnet(Le) d'Irène," 232, 238–243
Stendhal, 222, 273, 274
"Stéphane Mallarmé," 126
Stevenson, Robert Louis, *Treasure Island*, 270
"Suave Agonie (La)," 96
"Sylphe (Le)," 210, 269
Symonds, Arthur, *The Symbolist Movement in Literature*, 301

Tate, Allan, 295
Tel Quel, 127, 221
"Tentation (La) de (saint) Flaubert," 305
Thibaudet, Albert, 119, 125, 131, 290, 293
Thorel, Jean, 124
Titian, 149

Valéry, Jules, 119, 138
Valéry, Madame Paul, 158
"Valvins," 121–124, 135, 138
Variété, 314
Varillon, François, ed. (with Jacques Petit) Paul Claudel; *Journal*, 70
Verlaine, Paul, 15, 175, 176, 181; *Fêtes galantes*, 15; *Les Poèmes saturniens*, 175–176; *Romances sans paroles*, 176
"Vierge incertaine," 143
Vigny, Alfred de, 5, 14, 285
Villiers de l'Isle-Adam, Auguste, 124
Villon, François, 23
Virgil, 119, 270; *Éneid*, 109
Voilier, Madame Jean, 2
Voltaire, François Marie Arouet, 40, 247, 272, 273; *Sémiramis*, 40

Wagner, Richard, 263, 308; *Siegfried*, 85; *Walkyrie*, 263; *Lohengrin*, 263
Whiting, Charles, 75; *Valéry jeune poète*, 41, 76
Williams, Charles, 5